Women in Israel

Pennsylvania Studies in Human Rights

Bert B. Lockwood, Jr., Series Editor

A complete list of books in the series is available from the publisher.

Women in Israel

A State of Their Own

Ruth Halperin-Kaddari

PENN

University of Pennsylvania Press

Philadelphia

Printed in the United States of America on acid-free paper

10 9 8 7 6 5 4 3 2 1

Published by
University of Pennsylvania Press
Philadelphia, Pennsylvania 19104–4011

Library of Congress Cataloging-in-Publication Data

Halperin-Kaddari, Ruth
Women in Israel : a state of their own / Ruth Halperin-Kaddari.
p. cm. (Pennsylvania studies in human rights)
ISBN: 0-8122-3752-8 (cloth. : alk. paper)
Includes bibliographical references and index.
1. Women—Israel—Social conditions. 2. Women—Legal status, laws, etc.—Israel. 3. Sex discrimination against women—Israel. 4. Equality—Israel. I. Title. II. Series
HQ1728.5 .H35 2004
305.42/095694—dc22 003061077

Contents

Part I
The Legal Stage

Chapter 1
Introduction

Some Background

When Israel made its Declaration of Independence in May 1948, it vowed to guarantee equality to all its citizens, regardless of religion, race, or gender. Reality, however, shows that Israel has failed to keep this promise to its women citizens. Women in Israel have a state of their own, not necessarily in the sense of liberating refuge found in Virginia Woolf's *A Room of One's Own*, but rather in the sense of different, and generally worse, conditions than those of men in Israel. This book tells the story of women in Israel in the 1990s. It does so from a sociolegal perspective, analyzed from the viewpoint of feminist legal theories.

In telling the story of women in Israel, the book covers all aspects of women's lives, starting from legal issues such as affirmative action and accommodation of motherhood in the workplace and mechanisms for the advancement of women, moving on to more sociological and descriptive issues such as representation in public life, education, employment, health, social benefits, media, family, violence against women, and prostitution and trafficking in women. Underlying this narrative is a secondary story: about information and the process of controlling and obtaining information, as these are revealed in the work that was the basis for the book—the official Report of the State of Israel Concerning the Implementation of the United Nations Convention on the Elimination of All Forms of Discrimination Against Women (CEDAW), which I wrote in 1997.[1] Yet another theoretical theme underlying this book is the limits of law to create social change, the story of women in Israel being a case study in this respect.

The book has three major parts organized around themes of progress versus the limits of law as a tool for social change, and the movement and progression of feminist legal theories.

Part I, "The Legal Setting," introduces the subject matter and the theoretical thesis, expands on the legal framework, and describes the development of awareness to gender discrimination and general initiatives to eliminate it on the government level as well as by nongovernmental organizations (NGOs).

Part II, "Progress and the Limits of Law," outlines and analyzes women's situation in a range of areas: health, education, and welfare needs, employment, and representation in political and public life. This sequence of topics moves from the basic conditions of women's lives toward more complex goals and from progress to stalemate. Each chapter contains legal analyses followed by sociological discussion. From the perspective of feminist legal theories, each of these areas can be accommodated within the framework of liberal legal feminism, and any developments that may have taken place in them conform with developments within liberal feminist legal theory.

Part III, "Power Politics, Body Politics, and Radical Feminism," represents the areas where liberal legal feminism remains powerless to offer means for analysis or generate change. These are the areas where radical feminism is most pertinent: women's sexuality and violence against women. Also included here is a chapter on family, not only in light of familiar critiques of the Western patriarchal family, but particularly because of the unique legal situation of the family in Israel, which is simultaneously governed by the religious and civil legal systems with certain areas under the exclusive jurisdiction of the religious system. Chapter 12, "Multiple Voices," represents to a certain extent the third generation of feminist legal theories, including standpoint feminism, and seeks to expose the intersection of gender with other categories such as race, ethnicity, and nationality.

This work, like the original report, is written from the perspective of an Ashkenazi woman,[2] and clearly addresses her as a point of reference to the whole discussion. The original report did not address Mizrachi women, women immigrants from Ethiopia, Druze women, and others, partly due to its monolithic hegemonic perspective, but also because of the absence of studies and materials regarding many of these understudied groups. This absence of information causes absence of representation and leads to what may be termed double-marginality. In this book I take a different approach. Chapter 12 focuses on groups of women who, in one sense or another, challenge the hegemonic perspective and offer some divergence from the monolithic point of view, without purporting to to be exhaustive coverage of any topic, but points out where research is severely lacking.

Since the book originated from Israel's CEDAW Report, some background on CEDAW and its reporting process are in place. While the recent trend in feminist critique of international human rights law has been to find ways human rights law can become "less male and more truly human" (Charlesworth 1999, xix), and the current struggle is to convince that "women's rights are human rights," the women-specific international instruments remain pivotal for the advancement of women on the international arena (Cook 1993). First and foremost among them is the CEDAW convention, which placed women's rights, for the first time in history, at the center of international legal discourse. In a broad-based comprehensive document, CEDAW emerged as the major source of governmental human rights obligations toward women, encompassing all rights—civil, political, economic, social, and cultural. Although it has lately been criticized as outdated because of its reliance on the male standard for conferring "equal rights" (Hernandez-Truyol 1999, 4), its valuable challenge of the traditional gendered public/private dichotomy that permeated human rights law cannot be underestimated. CEDAW enjoys worldwide acceptance and by May 2001 was ratified by 168 states (more than two-thirds of the members of the UN).[3] By giving member states a yardstick to measure their performance with regard to gender equality, CEDAW reporting provides an international mechanism for monitoring women's position worldwide. By ratifying CEDAW, member states commit themselves to actively eradicate all forms of discrimination against women, whether in law or in practice, as well as to prevent such discrimination and to protect women against abuses of their rights by other individuals (Cook 1994).

These are quite far-reaching commitments, which nonetheless states take upon themselves almost globally, as prohibition of gender discrimination has become one of the hallmarks of enlightened nations. By ratifying CEDAW, states are accountable to their own population, not only to the international community. A strong case can be made that discrimination against women is now prohibited worldwide by all three main sources of international law: treaties, customary law, and general principles of international law (Cassel and Guzman 1999). This is not to say that in reality gender discrimination has actually been eliminated. In fact, as put by Cassel and Guzman (1999, 287), "Never has the global gap between noble laws and ignoble realities of discrimination against women been wider." Still, the ratification of CEDAW, with the prime obligation of reporting, makes states accountable by international standards and subjects them to international scrutiny. This makes the CEDAW convention and its reporting process a potent tool not only in the international arena but also in the domestic struggle for the advancement of women. The reporting process provides the opportunity to assess the conformity of domestic guarantees for equal rights for women with the international framework, to develop baseline data concerning the factual position of women, and to identify obstacles to the implementation of CEDAW. All this has great potential for use by women on the domestic front in making claims against the government. These claims can gain support from the CEDAW committee's "concluding observations" evaluating the reporting state's compliance to CEDAW, prepared after the report is presented to the committee.[4]

A prerequisite for making use of CEDAW and its reporting mechanism is, of course, knowing about it. The Israeli experience in this respect has not been successful. For a start, the Report has not been translated into Hebrew or Arabic, Israel's two official languages. Similarly, although the Report itself was widely distributed among all government agencies and NGOs, the CEDAW committee's concluding observations were neither published nor distributed, despite the Committee's clear request to do so.[5] In fact, no use whatsoever was made of these comments. While some of the concerns and the suggestions expressed in the comments had clear political innuendos relating to the Arab-Israeli conflict (Baker and Schonmann 1998), many of them could serve as a basis for an agenda for the promotion of women. The opportunity presented by reporting to CEDAW, then, was totally missed. This missed opportunity is also a poignant case of the politics of information, in the sense here of holding back available and useful information, which leads us to what I call the "information story."

The (In)Formation of Information

The materials used in this book and the Report on which it is based are a combination of government materials, including official reports or responses to inquiries, data collected and produced by the Central Bureau of Statistics (CBS) and the National Insurance Institute, academic and other independent research, and information obtained by NGOs. This combination of sources contributes to the uniqueness of this work but also to its limitations, in the sense of having to rely on existing materials supplied by other sources. Thus, in areas where information and research is lacking, this work reflects this lack. Significantly, this is mostly felt in the context of specifically disadvantaged groups of women, such as Bedouin or Druze women, or Jewish Ethiopian women. All too often, efforts to obtain information for this work and for further analysis were unsuccessful. Only scant sociological and anthropological research is available regarding these women, who are more vulnerable to begin with, and neglecting their study only reinforces their marginality and their absence from the central scene. These circular relationships further silence many women and create an impression that they do not exist. In this sense, the missing parts of the picture tell us more than what the existing information does.

Access to information and the lack of sufficient research should be of major concern to anyone interested in the advancement of women in Israel. The lack of information and research reflects a more basic problem faced by women in Israel, that of indifference toward women and discrimination. The information problem clearly stands as one of the primary factors that adversely affect women's advancement in Israel, yet it is one that should not be too difficult to overcome, if only there were enough awareness and will to do so. There should not have been so many parts missing from the puzzle of women's status in Israel. The crucial importance of knowledge—of data and information—cannot be overstressed. The concept of "naming, blaming, claiming" has by now become classic in sociology of law studies, describing the stages in the process before a dispute is recognized as such (Felstiner, Abel, and Sarat 1980). Unless something is named as an injury, it cannot lead to dispute. Unless the injured person knows that her experience is recognized as an injury, she cannot proceed with "blaming" and "claiming." The first stage in the process, naming, requires information, which is essential to mobilize the process of demanding rectification and amelioration. The problem is that much of this precondition for mobilization is controlled by the entity that would be the target of the resulting demands, the government.

On the governmental and semigovernmental level, not only is little research done concerning women's status or women's issues, but there is a repeated pattern of neglect toward these matters. Perhaps the clearest illustration of this is the lack of a policy directive that would order a systematic collection of data that is of special concern for women, or that would provide for a routine breakdown of any regularly acquired data along gender lines. A particularly poignant example of an outcome of this deficiency is the striking omission of women as a category, just like the elderly or children, in the Annual Report on Poverty produced by the research division of the National Insurance Institute.[6] Similarly, within the important work of the CBS, the main government authority in charge of the collection and dissemination of statistical data, all too often women's perspectives and experiences are totally ignored. This can happen either through failing to analyze data along gender lines or through omission of particular questions and inquiries that could yield information that would be particularly revealing of women's perspectives and concerns. Needless to say, gender perspectives are not included in the CBS areas of research.[7] For example, in the regular publication of data related to the educational system, until 2000 school drop-out rates were not divided along gender lines.[8] Apparently, the data were actually available and could be provided upon special inquiry, but no one thought them important enough to include in the regular publication.[9]

Similarly, the data concerning women's participation in the labor market do not reflect the different experiences of men and women. For example, although information related to the employment of household help is gathered and the relationship between that and women's participation in the workforce is examined, it is impossible to infer whether "household help" refers to such work as cleaning or cooking or to child care.[10] The difference is important, and so is the effect the two types of help have on women's participation in the work force, on forming day care policy, and the like.

The production, processing, and dissemination of information are much more crucial than is ordinarily thought. The questions that are asked and the variables that are examined control the outcome and construct its inferences. In more than one sense, they construct the reality itself. For example, when the number of children a worker has is examined only when the worker is a mother, and not a father, as in CBS labor force surveys, it presupposes a very specific parenting model, where the mother is the primary caretaker of the children. Another sense in which the political use of information constructs reality can be demonstrated in the following example: the periodic CBS analysis of households in Israel considers personal characteristics of the head of the household but never reveals the gender of the head of the household.[11] Gender is not seen as a relevant variable in this type of publication or in the CBS annual publication. The message is that it makes no difference to a family's economy whether a woman or man heads the household. This not only results in the impression that there are no households headed by women,[12] but also dismisses, or disguises the growing impoverishment of family units headed by single mothers.

Significantly, the CEDAW committee addressed the requirement of gender-disaggregated data and information in its 1989 general recommendation.[13] Researchers note that the lack of sex-disaggregated data has been a constant theme in the committee's examinations of government reports and remains the biggest obstacle to monitoring (Tomasevski 1998, 12). In Israel, as far as one can tell, this does not seem to have changed since the reporting. A casual glance at a recent CBS quarterly publication titled *New Statistical Projects and Publications in Israel* reveals that the government agency is not alone in this omission (State of Israel 1996b). This publication purportedly surveys and summarizes all new statistical and other empirical research projects published or underway in Israel. Not only is there no separate classification on women, but hardly any of the projects summarized use gender variables, nor does "Women" appear as a category in the subject index.

In addition, there are hardly any official efforts to empirically investigate the social effects of legal reforms such as the Prevention of Violence in the Family Law (1991) or the Single Parent Families Law (1992).[14] Needless to say, such empirical investigation is crucial for policy formation. Demands for legal, policy, or economic reforms cannot be made without an empirical basis. When the government neither initiates nor funds such follow-up studies, the seriousness of its commitment to social reform regarding women must be questioned. It also suggests that the Israeli myth of equality and the "no problem" problem still reign (Rhode 1991). In other words, it's not that "the State" does not care, it's that there is nothing to care about, since, as is often claimed, there is no real problem concerning women's rights. Such attitudes reflect and reinforce indifference, lack of awareness, and denial of women's discrimination and subordination.

The Story of Women in Israel

A Sociolegal Approach

In relating the story of women in Israel, this book focuses on the 1990s, using statistical data and sociological materials in combination with legal description and analysis. The scope of the work, in terms of time frame, is rather narrow. However, the integration of a sociological perspective with legal analysis allows for a much broader view, for a survey of legal developments helps extend and deepen a sociological examination of women's issues. Within the various social-studies methodologies, legal analysis, by its nature, provides a potent yet concise tool for observing social processes and developments. Law is perhaps the most powerful social institution, certainly a central one in constructing social conventions and social reality (Bourdieu 1987). As scholars of law and society maintain, law both embodies and reflects social ideologies and developments (Vago 2000, 318–20). Some even go so far as to claim that "the law in any social system is, in fact, a fundamental framework (a skeleton, if you like) of the nature of *all* its forms of association and institutions. If we know the law of any society, we have an excellent outline of the nature of the social system as a whole" (Fletcher 1981, 33). We must of course bear in mind the obvious fact that social behavior never exactly corresponds to the set of official norms. Thus, to get a true outline, the legal survey must be supplemented with some description of social reality, as suggested in this book. Mary Ann Glendon's *Transformation of Family Law* (1989) can serve as a good example. In this work, the changing legal arrangements of family law in four states, collated with observations of social behavior, serve as body of knowledge from which to ascertain social ideas, beliefs, trends, and policy. Furthermore, the use of legal survey and analysis as a baseline for telling a social story has a special advantage, since law maintains a unique quality that makes it easily accessible and susceptible to developmental narration. The legal norm, in whatever form it is embedded (rules, regulations, formal legal decisions, and so on), is a special type of social text. Due to its social role as a tool for regulating behavior, which ought to be done in the most precise and concentrated manner, a legal text contains all the elements of a social story in a consolidated fashion. In this sense the legal text condenses social concerns.

Interestingly, most research conducted on women in Israel has emerged out of a sociological perspective alone.[15] The only comprehensive and definite attempt thus far to integrate sociological research with legal analysis resulted in a work that was almost entirely legal, with only some sociological observations, which covered diverse topics separately, thus making it rather difficult to achieve a comprehensive overview (Raday, Shalev, and Liban-Kooby 1995). Some truly integrative work on particular issues of women's citizenship in Israel has shown the significance of legal analysis to feminist research (Berkovitch 1997, 607–8); nevertheless, the present volume is the first attempt at a comprehensive integrative overview.[16] My own training as a legal scholar gives me an obvious bias toward seeing the legal analysis as central. Indeed, I do think that even within an integrative work the legal level should be the threshold and guideline for an integrated analysis. The legal perspective, which also utilizes legal theories such as feminist critique, is essential as a prime discourse that makes sense of social processes. In line with these methodological propositions, this chapter offers a sociological description of the situation of women in Israel, as well as a legal account, both leading to a theoretical analysis using feminist theories of law.

The Situation of Women in Israel—An Overview

There are various ways to present the situation of women in any given society or state. Different sociological variables and types of data account for different factors and tell different stories. For the formal presentation of the CEDAW report at the UN in 1997, a strategic decision was made to identify two parameters that inform women's status. The first parameter reflects the basic quality of women's lives: life expectancy, maternal and infant mortality, levels of literacy, marital age, and so on. The second parameter is somewhat more complex and can be understood by evaluating such issues as participation of women in public life and in the workplace, wage equity, educational opportunities, and so on. Usually, the latter level is looked at when women's situation is examined broadly, and the former is often taken for granted. However, especially in the international comparative arena, it is the basic parameter that delineates the quality of women's lives and distinguishes women's situations in different places (Charlesworth 1999, xix).

Much progress has been made in Israel, but it is primarily at the basic level of the quality of women's lives. The same cannot be said about the more sophisticated, advanced level. The two-tiered analysis was strategically developed for purposes of international comparison, since it emphasized the positive aspects of women's status in Israel on the most basic level. One of the most exciting moments in work on the book was when I realized that this strategic methodological decision, which serves my overall thesis, is in fact fully compatible with an analytical tool developed by the United Nations Development Program (UNDP) for its annual Human Development Report (HDR). The HDRs, published since 1990, serve as a comprehensive guide to global human development. The reports are prepared by the HDR office team in consultation with economists and development professionals. They contain analyses of major issues, updated Human Development Indicators that compare the relative levels of human development of over 175 countries, and agendas to help transform development priorities.[17] One of their most significant contributions is the presentation of simple methods for the analysis of human development at the international, national, and subnational levels as means for assessing human development situations, trends, and gaps and as analytical tools for policy choice.[18] They have introduced the Human Development Index (HDI), which measures the overall achievements in a country in three basic dimensions of human development—longevity, knowledge, and standard of living. It is measured by life expectancy, educational attainment (adult literacy and combined primary, secondary, and tertiary school enrollment), and adjusted income.[19]

The 1995 HDR, titled "Gender and Human Development," analyzed worldwide progress in reducing gender disparities in 1975–95.[20] The report offered an unprecedented opportunity to grasp and analyze gender inequality in relation to human development in a comprehensive, comparative manner. It introduced two new composite indices—the Gender-Related Development Index (GDI) and the Gender Empowerment Measure (GEM)—both of which rank countries on a global scale by their performance in gender equality. According to the 1995 HDR, the GDI "captures gender inequality in human capabilities," while the GEM "reflects inequality in key areas of political and economic participation and decision-making" (Human Development Report 1995).[21] The fit between these definitions and my own methodological distinction is further seen through the variables of the two measurements. The

GDI measures achievements in the same dimensions and variables as the HDI, but captures inequalities in achievement between women and men. It is simply the HDI adjusted for gender inequality. The GEM, on the other hand, focuses on participation, measuring gender inequality in key areas of economic and political participation and decision-making. It tracks the percentages of women in parliament, among administrators and managers, and among professional and technical workers, and looks at women's earned income share as a percentage of men's. Differing from the GDI, it exposes inequality in opportunities rather than capabilities (Human Development Report 1995). These two measures clearly correspond with the two-tiered analysis I suggest.

Israel's performance on these two measures supports my conclusion as to Israel's achievements on gender equality and supplies an international comparative perspective. The first thing that stands out upon initial inspection of the Human Development Indicators is the gap between Israel's GDI and GEM ranks. While the 1999 report ranks Israel's GDI at 23 (after reaching 22 in 1997), its GEM is ranked only 37 (a dramatic drop down from 30 in 1997).

How to Make Sense of Paradoxes and Disparities

I argue that the improvement in women's situation and status in Israel has not been due to broad-based egalitarian consciousness or feminist awareness, but is rather a side effect of Israel's impressive progress as a welfare state for all its citizens.[22] In other words, most of the progress in women's status for the first forty years of the state's existence is incidental to Israel's overall socioeconomic advancement. This contention is unmistakably supported by the findings of the HDRs. If we reexamine the three indicators delineated above,[23] they can be clearly seen as corresponding respectively to Israel's overall socioeconomic situation, the elementary level of women's lives, and the more sophisticated level of women's situation. And indeed, perhaps the most striking fact is that Israel's GDI rank exactly parallels its HDI rank: Israel was consistently ranked 23rd out of 175 countries throughout the 1990s.[24] This clearly supports my contention that the advancement on the basic parameter of women's lives merely reflects the general progress on the overall socioeconomic front, the basic dimensions of human development.

A simplistic sequence of legal developments would cause great confusion. The legal realm offers a completely contrasting picture, especially in the 1990s. An impressive amount of new reform-minded legislation promoting women's rights and well-being has emerged, including the 1991 Prevention of Violence in the Family Law, the 1996 Equal Pay (Male and Female Employees) Law, the 1992 Single Parent Families

Law, the 1993 amendment to the 1975 Government Corporation Law, the 1995 amendment to the 1959 State Service (Appointments) Law (both amendments direct the use of affirmative action), and more.[25] This recent wave of legislation is indeed impressive. Moreover, the emerging alliance of diverse governmental actions concerning women's status with numerous legislative achievements in this area during the past decade indicates the beginning of a heightened awareness of women's plight and the need to address and redress it.

Nevertheless, despite these significant developments, the disparity between men and women still remains substantially unchanged. Why? As I explain below, part of the reason is the gap between progressive legislation and its implementation. The almost impulsive nature of some of this legislation and its failure to account for practical impediments are partly responsible for this gap.[26] But what causes this intensive legislation in the first place? And what causes the gap, not only between the legislative level and its specific implementation, but also between the progressive normative level and the regressive overall situation? I attempt to answer these questions in the following discussion.

Feminist Legal Theories, Social Change, and the Advancement of Women in Israel

Law as a Tool for Social Change

Let us pause for a moment and take a metaphoric step back. It then becomes clear that what we have here is a case study of law and social change. In other words, it is the age-old question of the relationship between the legal norm and the social reality: why doesn't the law—the progressive, advanced law—translate into improved and progressive social reality? This question has been preoccupying the literature on law and society for decades (Pound 1917; Cotterrell 1992; Vago 2000). While there is a general agreement as to the power of law to influence social change, there is also a growing recognition of the limits of law's capacity to mold society. Many studies of "the limits of effective legal action" propose explanations for the failure of the law in many areas; some—such as racial discrimination—resemble our subject of women's status and gender discrimination. Among the most often cited works in this area is that of the sociologist William M. Evan, who listed seven conditions under which law can effectively influence behavior and perhaps even attitudes (Evan 1965).

Several of these conditions that seem particularly relevant to our context concentrate on the question of implementation and enforcement. For example, if a new law is to be enforced, it must have pragmatic models for compliance (people must be able to understand what the new norm is, who it is directed to, etc.) and not appear utopian in its aims. Furthermore, enforcement agents must be committed to the behavior required; any evidence of hypocrisy or corruption is likely to undermine the law. Moreover, there must be positive incentives for compliance with the law and not just negative sanctions. In addition to these aspects of law enforcement and implementation, it is often stressed that any new legal norm that aims at creating social change must be compatible with established cultural and legal principles. As shown throughout this book, these factors pertain to the attempt to advance women's situation in Israel through the law. New legal norms are often created with no particular model for enforcement, as in the case of the wage equity legislation, or the introduction of affirmative action into the civil service. Law enforcement agents can usually be characterized by insufficient awareness and lack of commitment to or internalization of egalitarian and feminist ideas. This is evident in such areas as police handling of gender-based violence against women, sentencing in areas of sexual violence and violence within the family, official approaches toward prostitution and trafficking in women, and more.

While all this seems particularly pertinent to the case of women's situation in Israel, the truth is that many of these factors are typical of women's situation worldwide. Other factors include severe lack of government resources allocated to women's needs and concerns or toward implementation of legislative reforms; lack of an organizational apparatus to coordinate all the work that is being done; deeply held beliefs that create cultural barriers to the advancement of women; and more. There are, nonetheless, at least two factors that are unique to Israel and are accordingly given a broader discussion further on. These are the formal and informal effects of religion and the importance of security concerns on the national agenda and in public life in general.[27]

All these factors, however, still lack a deeper rationalization. Something is still missing. In other words, saying that the law fails because not enough resources are allocated for its implementation and enforcement still leaves us wondering *why* not enough resources are allocated. In pointing to law enforcement agencies' lack of commitment to the cause we still seek the *reasons* for this deficiency. These questions are even more striking in light of the abundance of liberal legislation. Indeed, nothing in the above observations explains the legislation in the first place.

The Use of Feminist Legal Theories

I turn to feminist theories in an attempt to shed some light on these issues. Social theories in general have explanatory qualities that aim at creating a consistent matrix through which to decipher social phenomena. In this sense, they have a reflective function. They also have forward-looking qualities that can be used to offer prospective guidelines. Accordingly, I turn to feminist theories of law to seek an explanation of the past (in our case, explaining the gaps, for example), but also as a tool in forming guidelines for the future. Feminist legal theories, like other theories of law, have some attributes unshared by other social theories. They relate not only to social and human behavior per se, but also to the conscious and calculated arrangement of such conduct. Like other theories of law, their field of examination is also the normative instrument for regulating human behavior. They sometimes serve not just as an explanatory tool to analyze and reflect upon social phenomena, but also as means to construct in advance that very same field of analysis. This process may take place either consciously or unconsciously. In other words, specific theoretic perceptions shape and influence the construction of the normative sphere. Therefore, just as legal theorists often ask what theory of justice is incorporated in a specific piece of legislation, it is helpful to ask what, if any, specific perception of legal feminism can be seen as reflected in the legislative and judicial developments in Israel. In other words, I take feminist legal theories as lenses through which the legal developments surveyed here can be reviewed, in an attempt to explain, among other things, their complex nature and their irregularity.

Liberal legal feminism is often referred to as the "first phase" or "first generation" in legal feminism, chronologically spreading from the late 1960s to the early 1980s. Its vision has been described as "informed largely by instrumental liberal legalism, the pursuit of legal equality, and little challenge to the nature of legal knowledge and traditional public/private dichotomy" (Villmoare 1999, 445–46). Its basic assumption, rooted in liberalism, was that law and rights could be better fashioned to meet the needs of women (Finley 1993), and that courts, through constitutional adjudication, would aid in equalizing the "rights, responsibilities, and opportunities of women and men" (Ginsburg 1985, 376). Reliance on liberalism as the dominant political ethos in Western democratic society and in law in particular is a meaningful characterization of liberal legal feminism. Liberal legal feminism works within the system, without necessarily questioning the system itself (Barnett 1998, 5), and its goals are limited to promoting women and getting them into areas from which they have previously been excluded. By no means does it undermine basic principles of the hegemonic legal discourse or social order. On the contrary, it employs the very basic tools of rights, and could even be termed "equal-rights feminism," acknowledging its reluctance to go beyond the formal level of the law (West 1988; Bartlett 1991; Ross 1993).

This is, of course, the major critique of liberal legal feminism by cultural legal feminism and radical feminism, each coming from a different discursive background and direction. Cultural or difference feminism, coming from psychoanalytic and psychological analysis, emphasizes and celebrates women's difference from men (epitomized in Carol Gilligan's notion of women's "different voice"), unveils and challenges law's inherent maleness, and seeks ways to restructure the institution of law in a manner that will give space to women's voices (Gilligan 1982; Barnett 1998, 6). Radical feminism, on the other hand, uses political science tools and analyzes gender relations in terms of power. Radical feminists move beyond the legal sphere and focus on the societal structure which forms the foundation for law (Barnett 1998, 6). When gender relations are reconceptualized in terms of the distribution of power or of male supremacy and female subordination, many issues that have not been traditionally regarded by law as sex discrimination, such as rape, battery, prostitution, and pornography, become subjects for feminist legal analysis and critique (MacKinnon 1989). Cultural legal feminism and radical feminism are often described as belonging to a second generation or phase of legal feminism (Barnett 1998; Villmoare 1999). In a sense, they both depart from the plain structure of the legal system in order to understand the societal structure that warrants the masculinity of law and legal systems. Notwithstanding their departure from law, their eventual visions seek to be incorporated into the law, as they define and envision this social field. As put by Adelaide Villmoare, the critiques of second-generation feminists "have been more expansive than those of the first generation, and they suggest wide-ranging political visions that move well beyond public, formal legal arenas into the most private and personal spheres of life. . . . They sought to build a woman-informed, experiential knowledge that would end disabling legal distinctions between public and private and that would lead to much greater equality in law and society" (Villmoare 1999, 456).

There are obviously some parallels between the developments within legal feminism and feminist theories in general, although feminist legal scholarship is often said to have been "lagging behind the general movement" (Barnett 1998, 4). The third generation or phase in legal feminism is more compatible with general feminist theory in calling for a multiplicity of voices and espousing "standpoint epistemology" as a jurisprudential method (Matsuda 1989). However, this phase is often criticized as lacking the possibility of concretization into policy terms and particularly in legal tools (Villmoare 1999, 458–59). My analysis of the legal developments with respect to women's situation in Israel relates mostly to the first and second phases of legal feminism.

Stages of Women's Advancement from a Feminist Legal Perspective

The formative years of "women's legislation" in Israel can be seen as compatible with the perception of liberal legal feminism.[28] This is not to claim that the driving force behind that legislation was liberal feminist ideology alone. Of course there were much more powerful forces promoting that legislation, primarily the emergence of the Israeli welfare state. Nevertheless, as explained above, even proving a complete lack of feminist consciousness does not invalidate this argument, and it can still be analyzed in feminist terms. Such an examination, I think, reveals that the prime legislation, the Women's Equal Rights Law (1951),[29] certainly reflects a typical liberal approach in its central declaration that "A man and a woman shall have equal status with regard to any legal action." Both the identity approach ("equal status") and the focal point of the law ("to any legal action") are pertinent to this observation (Lahav 1993).[30] Other early pieces of "women's legislation," such as the 1949 Compulsory Education Law, the 1964 Equal Pay (Male and Female Employees) Law,[31] and others, continued this trend. They all reflect the typical liberal perception that once equal rights in such basic areas as employment and education are formally guaranteed, nothing else is needed. Special treatment of women or the formation of specific mechanisms for the advancement of women were deemed unnecessary, as could be expected in light of what has been described as the "myth of equality" during Israel's formative years (Hazelton 1977; Azmon and Izraeli 1993; Lahav 1993).[32]

These beliefs of the first stage lasted a quarter of a century, until the equality myth, together with many other formative myths central to the founding ideology of the State, was shattered during the 1973 Yom Kippur War (Azmon and Izraeli 1993). Following the 1975 International Year for Women, a National Commission on the Status of Women was appointed.[33] However, most of the proposals contained in its 1978 report, though impressive and ambitious, were allocated few or no resources for their realization. Significantly, this transitive stage of myth-shattering and bureaucratization of women's equality contained very little legislative development with respect to women's status.

It is only in the third stage, which started in the late 1980s and is still going on to some extent, that a gradual change has been taking place with respect to the position of women in Israeli society, most notably on the legal front. In a sense, the 1990s were the decade of women's legal reform in both the judicial and the legislative arenas. I consider the legislative work, which is structurally more independent in its initiatives and more representative of the state and the government, more important in trying to assess what change has taken place in the area (Shachar 1998; Mautner 1999). Interestingly, though, legal scholarship in Israel has traditionally turned to case law analysis, concentrating in particular on the Supreme Court. Law and society scholarship, on the other hand, mostly turns to legislation when studying law and social change. Thus, for example, the chapter on "Law as an Instrument of Social Change" in Roger Cotterrell's classic *The Sociology of Law* focuses entirely on legislation (Cotterrell 1992).

If the overall legal developments of the last decade can be described as intensive, the legislative initiatives can be described as impulsive. I choose this term to hint at the extraordinary pace at which legislation has progressed, not always with enough premeditation, planning, or reliance on hard facts and core research. The list of new and quite often innovative laws is very long.[34] The extent of the phenomenon has been attributed to the introduction in the early 1990s of primaries as a means for selecting parliamentary candidates, as "catering to women's interests . . . appears promising from the electoral perspective, at least as viewed by prospective candidates" (Yishai 1997, 21). Until then, candidates were appointed by a party Central Committee with no direct accountability established between candidates and party members. This explanation implies policy-makers' recognition and appreciation of women as a distinct interest group, perhaps for the first time on such a scale: of women's interests and needs, women's adversity, and their political power. Legislation presents a relatively easy form of political achievement with immediate gratification and certification. But after investigating the legislative process that preceded many of the new laws and examining their initiation through various stages of enactment, I believe the phenomenon truly indicates a new phase in appreciating the position of women in Israeli society, not just a cynical use of another newly discovered political power group.

Feminist Ideology, Legal Evolution, and Social Reform

Using feminist legal analysis and taking on the retrospective qualities of the theories, a deep change can be traced. The clearest development is the informed acceptance of the idea of substantive equality, that is, the recognition that treating likes alike cannot ameliorate past discriminations, nor can it handle situations in which concrete and "real" gender differences exist. This acceptance is manifested by expressions of affirmative action[35] and by other areas where the legislature condones purposeful disparate treatment of women (for example, as victims of sexual violence who are now protected from testifying in the presence of the accused; or as employees, who have the option of retiring at 60 or 65[36]). It is also seen by the beginning of a deeper understanding of the phenomenon of gender wage gap and women's subordinate position in the workforce in general, as manifested in the enactment of the 1996 Equal Pay (Male and Female Employees) Law,[37] thus giving statutory approval to the concept of wage equity and equitable worth. An even more significant indication is the move from maternal employment rights to parental employment rights, thus recognizing the need to accommodate workplace and career requirements not just to motherhood but to parenthood and to the family unit as a whole.[38]

This move goes beyond mere replacement of a formal perception of equality by adherence to substantive equality. It also indicates an entry into a more mature era of feminist understanding and awareness, an era of feminist consciousness that strives not only beyond formal equality, but beyond legal liberal feminism altogether. Disillusionment with first-phase legal feminism is a familiar development, and the realization that the attainment of rights—even in their substantive form—cannot bring forth any real change without a systemic structural transformation has characterized the evolution of feminist theories in general, and of feminist legal theories in particular (Lorber 1998; Weisberg 1993). While general feminist theories have been concerned with such questions as inclusion and exclusion, reflections of women's experiences, thoughts, qualities, and realities, the questions confronted by legal feminist theories have had an added component, that of law as a discourse of social change, and the theories' applicability to that discourse. Feminist legal theories, more than general feminist theories, are concerned with turning abstract theories into concrete social change through law. Law invites concretization. All this has been a major factor in the development of mainly the second phase of legal feminism, representing more sophisticated and richer challenges to law and society.

This process can be seen in the Israeli context as well and can easily be interpreted as calling for a radically different conception of social structure. When the move to substantive equality is accompanied by a broader ideology and vision of changing gender relations, it can be a step toward the next phase of legal feminism. Adoption of affirmative action demonstrates the recognition that special measures are needed to truly advance women and get over past discrimination so that women's full and equal potential is realized; pay equity legislation indicates the realization that assurance of equal pay for equal work is not sufficient, and only interoccupational matching can overcome occupational segregation, which is the major cause for wage gaps; the move to parental rights reflects the understanding that guaranteeing women's workplace through periods of childbearing is an inadequate solution, and only a change in parental roles—or at least society's provision for such a change—would accomplish concrete advancement. All this reflects an aspiration for fundamental social change. In its fullest impetus, it is a call to alter gender power relations as a whole.

The sweeping amendment to the Women's Equal Rights Law (in fact, a complete revision of the 1951 law)[39] proves the validity of attributing such radical ideas to the normative layer. From this perspective, a line can be drawn from the 1951 law to its 2000 revision, epitomizing the whole evolutionary process and ultimately symbolizing the call for radical change described above. If the 1951 law was reflective of legal liberalism's formal equality, its revision half a century later is exactly its antithesis. The revision, in fact, reads almost like a radical feminist manifesto, except for one issue—the rule of religious laws in the area of family law—where it acquiesced to the existing norm so as not to hinder the passage of the law. Reading it gives a sense of educational legislation par excellence. It is all in there: starting from a declaration of the law's intention to ensure total gender equality and women's advancement in all areas of state, society, economy and family; going on to prohibit all forms of discrimination against women; proceeding with the guarantee of substantive equality, including affirmative action; explicitly relating to equality in human dignity, including delineation of social rights; expressly ensuring a woman's right over her body and providing for protection from violence, sexual harassment, sexual abuse, and trafficking; proceeding with a broad provision of adequate representation in public bodies; and concluding in a provision of equal service in the security forces. Some of the provisions, such as protection from violence and sexual harassment, are reiterations of existing legal norms. Some, such as the mandate for adequate representation or for affirmative action, are an expansion of existing norms. And some present completely novel rights, for example, the guarantee of a woman's right over her body, which clearly implies reproductive freedom.

Indeed, if it were not for the religious issue, the revised law would have the potential of creating a total revision of women's legal status in Israel and of the gender regime from the legal perspective. However, and there always seems to be a "however" in this area, leaving the religious sphere out of the scope of the revised law has a detrimental effect that is probably even stronger than in the situation that preceded the revision. I already mentioned the educational quality of this legislation. It is particularly because of this educational value that I see the acquiescence to political-religious considerations as detrimental, since it is a reaffirmation of existing normative discrimination, on the occasion of such an impressive reformation of women's status.[40] The religious exclusion has not been the only grounds for criticizing the amendment. Criticism was made of the amendment's reserved nature, evident not only in the amendment's heavily qualified language,[41] but also in the mere fact that no budget whatsoever was allocated to implement the allegedly strengthened equality norm.

While I support the critique regarding the religious constraint, I do not accept the other doubts expressed in relation to the amendment. Financial support is always a better option, but I believe that the significance of this law should not be underestimated, regardless of its budgetary deficiency. Its significance lies in its educational nature, which, as law and social change literature tells us, is particularly important in value-laden areas such as this. Following Roscoe Pound's work (1917), a distinction is often made between the "outside and the inside of people and things." According to Pound, law as a practical matter can deal only with the "outside," observable behavior, and not the "inside," attitudes and beliefs. However, changes in external behavior may often lead to changes in values and attitudes. As argued by Morroe Berger, "Law can influence 'external' acts which affect or constitute the conditions for the exercise of the private inclinations and tastes that are said to be beyond the realm of law" (1952, 172). The amended Women's Equal Rights Law can indeed be described as dealing with the "outside" and constructing an overall social framework based on the principle of equality. This construction does not necessarily require specific financial resources. What it requires is ardent commitment to the cause on the part of public policy implementers.

Berger's construction, as well as others, seems to be relevant for the formation of this commitment on the basis of the law. This is not the only sense in which such legislation influences ideas and attitudes. In fact, it has been claimed that "legislation and education are not incompatible, legislation is a powerful form of education" (Lester and Bindman 1972, 86). The area of women's status and gender relations is clearly rooted in traditions and values. In such areas any external change imposed by law might be resisted because it conflicts with traditional values, beliefs, and prevailing customs (Dror 1959; Vago 2000). It seems to me that the educational function of legislation has a special role in such an area. While indeed rooted in customs and tradition, women's status, women's roles, and gender relations in general are among the most mutable and unsettled social institutions in Western societies, as a direct result of the feminist revolution. By representing an unequivocal declaration of public policy against gender discrimination and for women's equality, legislation such as the Women's Equal Rights Law supplies a powerful expression of the desired social norm. Such an authoritative expression is especially valuable in times of uncertainty and changing reality.

These observations are supported by two other legislative measures—the Prevention of Sexual Harassment Law and the Authority for the Advancement of Women Law—which can be seen as counterparts and as forerunners of the revision of the Women's Equal Rights Law.[42] In fact, these three laws should be viewed as a whole, since they demonstrate a new approach to "women's legislation" quite distinct from what I termed the impulsive legislative initiatives of the 1990s. In this sense, these three laws may be labeled as the fourth stage of women's legislation in Israel. All three propose a broad vision of social change, envisioning a complete transformation of gender power and relationship.

There is a connection between the legal feminist theoretic evolution that I attribute to these laws, and their assessment from a law and social change perspective. In terms of feminist legal analysis, these are all reflections of the move to the second phase of feminist legal theories. In terms of law and social change, they represent a combination of methods that have the potential to bring change. Viewing these measures as a reflection of the emergence of second-phase legal feminism is quite clear. The ideology of radical feminism is obviously present in the Prevention of Sexual Harassment Law, and ideas of cultural feminism can be traced in all three laws, in the sense of accepting women's difference from men in certain areas while denying any possibility of discrimination on that basis. But the most prominent characteristic of these laws as expressing second-phase legal feminism is their comprehensive scope that reaches to underlying social and cultural attitudes, well beyond what traditionally has been thought of as the realm of law and what liberal legal feminism saw as its domain. From the perspective of law and social change, these measures reflect a potentially effective combination of educational legislation, indirect use of law to promote change, and construction of a supervising apparatus.

The significance of educational legislation in this specific area has already been mentioned, and the dialectic process of external legal obligations that may lead to changes in internal perceptions and attitudes discussed. These courses of operation are just as pertinent to the Prevention of Sexual Harassment Law as they are to the Women's Equal Rights Law. The notion of the indirect use of law to produce social change was first brought by the sociologist Yehezkel Dror (1959), who suggested that, while the direct imposition of legal duties to change behavior and attitudes is problematic, law can play an important indirect role in fostering social change in many ways. Law, then, is a facilitator of social change, through "setting up organs which directly try to further various social developments" (Dror 1959, 798). This seems to describe the operational method of the Authority for the Advancement of Women Law, in providing the institutional framework for the governmental agency that is specifically set up to exert influence for change and advancement in women's status. This law also relates to the third function mentioned above in terms of law as a tool for social change, namely the establishment of supervising apparatus. The need for an effective mechanism of enforcement has been a constant theme in law and social change studies (Pound 1917; Evan 1965). The lack of such a mechanism has been a constant obstacle with respect to the situation of women in Israel.

The establishment of the Authority may represent a turning point, but it is far cry from what is usually meant by this term. Legislation against racial discrimination is a case at point. In Roger Cotterrell's discussion of the British experience he contrasts the first Race Relations Act of 1965 and the second Act of 1976, the distinguishing factor being the existence of an extensive institutional framework for implementation and enforcement in the latter and its lack in the former (Cotterrell 1992, 53–58). The Authority for the Advancement of Women has no enforcement powers whatsoever. Further reservations regarding the Authority are presented later on. Nevertheless, it is a modest beginning toward change, if change is indeed sought.

The implementation of these theories is examined throughout the chapters of this book; it is only in the final chapter that we can attempt to reexamine the question of social change through legislation.

Chapter 2
Gender Equality in the Israeli Legal System

The Principle of Gender Equality in the Israeli Legal System

The Constitutional Level

Israel did not adopt a written constitution upon its establishment. Various attempts have been made over the years to enact a bill of rights, one of the main obstacles being the issue of gender equality and equal status for women under the law. Since Israel maintains the rule of religious law over the area of family law,[1] and since religious systems of law are generally traditional and patriarchal in nature, that is, prejudiced and discriminatory to women (Greenberg 1981; Ruether 1983; Adler 1998; Hauptman 1998; Plaskow 1990), no full equality for women can be guaranteed. The maintenance of the rule of religious law in family matters has thus become a major barrier to the adoption of a comprehensive constitution or bill of rights (Raday 1994, 254).

Instead, Israel enacted in 1992 two new "Basic Laws" that address two human rights guarantees: Basic Law: Human Dignity and Liberty and Basic Law: Freedom of Occupation.[2] Many jurists in Israel, Chief Justice Aharon Barak central among them, refer to these as a "semi-constitution," and identify them as the beginning of the judicial review process in Israeli law. In other words, courts now have the power to strike down any legislation that violates the basic rights guaranteed by the two Basic Laws, and which does not fulfill the requirements of the limitation clause in those laws.[3] This analysis was approved and was recently implemented (to a moderate extent) by the Supreme Court.[4] However, existing legislation is immune from any kind of review,[5] and subject only to interpretation that accommodates the Basic Laws, according to the Basic Laws themselves (Barak 1994, 560–64).

The right to equality is not mentioned specifically as a basic right in the Basic Laws. The source of this omission is the subject of debate. Some scholars attribute it to the problematic history of the right to full equality in Israeli law due to religious considerations (Sommer 1997). The more common opinion, however, is the one advanced by Chief Justice Barak: that the scope of the basic right to human dignity is very broad and encompasses various unenumerated human rights, such as the right to equality (Barak 1994, 423–26). This interpretation was approved in several Supreme Court cases.[6] If the broad interpretation is conclusively accepted by the Supreme Court, it would obviously carry great significance, implying that future legislation that violates the right to equality could theoretically be struck down, if it does not meet the requirements of the limitation clause. Nevertheless, the power of judicial review would still be limited to future legislation. This obviously excludes the rule of religious laws in the area of marriage and divorce. In other words, this rule cannot be subject to judicial review, as detailed in Chapter 11.

The constitutional level is merely one level of normative regulation. Other legal sources for the creation of human rights exist, and have special significance in Israel, particularly due to the lack of a written constitution. First and foremost is Israel's Declaration of Independence, which was one of the first of its kind to include sex as a group classification for the purpose of equal social and political rights. The document states: "The State of Israel will maintain equal social and political rights for all citizens, irrespective of religion, race or sex." The declaration, though lacking any constitutional force, has been interpreted by Israeli courts in such a way that often makes it close to a constitutional document with constitutional powers (Rubinstein 1996, 53–60). The 1992 Basic Law: Human Dignity and Liberty explicitly provides that the human rights set out in it shall be interpreted in the spirit of the principles of the Declaration of Independence.

The Legislative Level

Significantly, the submission to religious values has accompanied the most recent and significant legislation in this area, namely the recent amendment of the Women's Equal Rights Law, as discussed in Chapter 1. After Member of Knesset (MK) Yael Dayan tabled the proposal in May 1998, a joint committee to the Knesset Committee on the Status of Women and the Knesset legal committee was formed, charged with reforming the Women's Equal Rights Law. The original plan was to enact a new version of the Women's Equal Rights Law as a Basic Law. It soon became clear that due to political constraints no such law could pass without maintaining the power of religious law over marriage and divorce. It became just as clear that no feminist women's organization and no self-respecting feminist Knesset member would support a Basic Law that is supposed to advance women, while entrenching their inferiority in matters of marriage and divorce in a Basic Law. Therefore the law that was finally passed in March 2000[7] only amends the original Women's Equal Rights Law, while maintaining the exclusion of marriage and divorce from its application. Nevertheless, the amendments themselves are sweeping, and apart from maintaining that exclusionary rule, the content of the law has been substantially reformed, as noted in Chapter 1. For example, instead of guaranteeing "one law" to woman and man, the amendment specifically prohibits "discrimination against women as women," and explains that "It shall be immaterial whether or not there was an intention to discriminate at the basis of the act resulting in the discrimination." These changes are far from linguistic. Despite the critique offered before, the different wording embodies a renunciation of the liberal approach of formal equality and a major step toward embracing the substantive equality approach. Of course, even such extensive reform leaves the rule of religious laws over marriage and divorce intact.[8]

Although the Women's Equal Rights Law lacks constitutional force and can actually be revoked by subsequent legislation, it has been given great symbolic value in several Supreme Court cases. It was originally labeled "an ideological law, revolutionary, a change of social structure" and in some recent Supreme Court cases was termed "a majestic legislation."[9] In reality, its concrete effect was almost negligible. Apart from its significant impact in the area of family property that led to the de facto abolishing of a religious law,[10] no other existing laws were actually abolished because of it. The few cases that did make use of this law had dealt with custom or with internal by-laws of pension funds, not with actual legislation.[11] And where legislation was indeed in question, no laws were actually abolished.[12] The law has guaranteed equal rights mainly in the public sphere and has referred primarily to the government and its delegates, rather than to the private sector. This omission was partly repaired by two complementary initiatives, legislative and judicial. The legislative effort centered on the area of employment, in both the public and the private sectors. Judicial developments supplemented that and enhanced the notion of substantive equality.

Judicial Rejoinders

Lacking a statutory codification of the general right to equality, except for the Women's Equal Rights Law, the legal definition of equality and its inverse, discrimination, is found mainly in Israeli case law and in scattered legislative expressions of the right to equality. Although most of the early cases suggest the implementation of a formal Aristotelian theory of equality, some clearly adopt the concept of substantive equality. For example, the *Bavli v. The Rabbinical High Court* case[13] emphasizes that unintentional discrimination is just as prohibited as intentional discrimination and deduces the existence of discrimination from disparate outcomes. In *Alice Miller v. The Minister of Defense*,[14] at least two of the justices had explicitly maintained that the guarantee of equality may sometimes lead to burdening the budget and cause extra expenses. The principle of equality may thus mandate action and investment, putting the government under positive rather than negative obligation. Consequently, the military authorities in the Miller case were ordered to allow women to be trained as pilots, making the necessary adaptations to their special needs, even if that imposes budgetary and planning hardship. Last, in the *Israel Women's Network* (IWN) case, the court affirmed the policy of affirmative action, mandated by the 1993 amendment to the Government Corporations Law (Appointments),[15] and emphasized its role as a primary component in the broad area of the basic right to equality. More recently, *IWN v. The Minister of Labor and Welfare* has established an all-encompassing basic principle in the Israeli legal system, of adequate representation of men and women in public bodies, as part of the principle of equality.[16]

Remaining Questions

There are, however, problems with the concept of discrimination in Israeli case law. It is unclear whether discrimination by private institutions and individuals is included in the legal definition of this term. Answers need to be deduced from the overall legal framework, including legislation and case law that involve women's rights. The concern regarding the application of the principle of gender equality to private institutions and individuals is part of a larger legal framework known as "the privatization of constitutional norms." The central question here is whether constitutional rights and norms apply equally to relationships between individuals and to the relationships between the government and individuals. In the past few years there has been a growing judicial tendency to apply to the private sphere principles and norms that were developed and recognized in the public sphere. This is particularly true when the "private" sphere contains "hybrid" entities whose nature could be characterized as both public and private, or when it involves rendering services to the public at large (Rubinstein 1996, 967–69).

In 1988, the Equal Employment Opportunities Law[17] was enacted, prohibiting all forms of discrimination in the workplace. Its enactment resolved the question whether the principle of equality applies to the private sphere with respect to labor market relations. The broader question is still unsettled, although it could be suggested that private entities are prohibited from discriminating on the basis of sex or some other "group category" if they supply an important social service, or if their general character is more of a public nature and not private.[18] The occasional precedents in that direction should be viewed together with other cases that prohibited discrimination by private organizations on other grounds such as nationality, ethnicity, or sexual orientation. This could be viewed as a consistent trend toward broader application of the right to equality and nondiscrimination in the private sphere, while its protection depends on the specific balance between this right and the weight of the rights that may be understood to oppose it. A significant move in the direction of more substantial application of the principle of nondiscrimination in the private sphere can be attributed to the 1998 broad legislation against sexual harassment, detailed in Chapter 9.

The question remains whether gender-based violence in the family is included under the legal definition of discrimination. This is of particular concern in international human rights and women's rights law and is regularly emphasized in international instruments and in writings (Thomas 1990). Legislation that deals with aspects of violence against women suggests that this phenomenon is conceptualized as part of larger legislative concerns about discrimination on the basis of gender. This conclusion is supported, for instance, by themes expressed in the 1996 report issued by the Parliamentary Inquiry Commission on the Question of Murder of Women by Their Spouses, discussed later. The report specifically states that the murder of women, and all forms of violence against women, can be understood as expressions of more general discrimination against women in Israeli society. As to other forms of gender discrimination in the domestic sphere, this has been somewhat paradoxically subject to intense regulations that affect women's status. The 1973 Spouses (Property Relations) Law, the 1991 Prevention of Violence in the Family Law,[19] and, to some degree, the 1951 Women's Equal Rights Law are all attempts of the civil legal system to mitigate the discriminatory nature of the religious laws that govern the area of marriage and divorce, which also explain their relatively large scope.

Apart from internal measures of legislation, Israel has signed and ratified the Convention on the Elimination of All Forms of Discrimination Against Women (CEDAW) in 1991, which led to this current study. Unlike international customary law, which automatically becomes the law of the country, where international conventional law is concerned, it becomes part of the law of the country only insofar as it is incorporated into the local system. Otherwise, although it is binding upon the state at the international level, it cannot be enforced through the local judicial system. This is not to suggest that conventional law has no effect on the internal level: it serves as an interpretive tool, a guideline for monitoring state activities. Thus, there is a presumption that unless otherwise specifically indicated by the legislator, local law must conform to conventional law in force in Israel (Zilbershatz 1996). Consequently, while CEDAW has no formal status under internal Israeli law, its directives function as an interpretive guide. Indeed, the fact that the UN Convention was ratified in 1991 and the human rights Basic Laws were enacted in 1992 should be understood to be significantly related, for the convention clearly influenced the legislation of the Basic Laws. Yet only in recent years has the convention been invoked in Israeli academic circles and law review articles. Hopefully, these developments will soon reach the judiciary and the legislature. The stage is indeed set for a more consistent, admissible use of the convention itself in the legislature and judiciary.

Affirmative Action

The Legal Framework

The earliest expression of affirmative action in Israeli law was section 18A of the 1975 Government Corporations Law, added in a 1993 amendment to the statute,[20] dealing with the manner of appointing directors to government companies. Section 18A mandates "adequate representation" for both genders on every board of directors of a government company.[21] Until such representation is achieved, the responsible ministers are to appoint directors of the "less represented gender"—thereby explicitly affirming the temporary nature of the practice, that is, until the "appropriate" level of representation is reached. In the explanatory memorandum to the proposed amendment, the drafters acknowledged the minority of women in boards of directors (35 of 1,800 in March 1993) and emphasized the need to eradicate this distortion by any means possible.[22]

Presently, the most expansive formulation of affirmative action under Israeli law is found in two separate cases, both brought to the High Court of Justice by the IWN, objecting to appointments of men to positions where women's representation was far from adequate. While both cases developed a firm doctrine of affirmative action in Israeli law, their outcomes were somewhat different. The 1994 case *IWN v. The Government of Israel*[23] accepted the IWN's petition to void appointments of three men to the board of directors in two government corporations in which there were no women members. In the 1998 case *IWN v. The Minister of*

Labor and Welfare, the High Court of Justice ordered the minister to actively seek suitable women candidates for the office of deputy general director of the National Insurance Institute (NII) and recommended that the minister not proceed with appointing the male candidate already chosen for a trial period, but declined actually to void the appointment.[24]

Justice Mazza's opinion, writing for the majority in the first IWN case, is of particular significance because it contains rigorous statements and far-reaching suggestions about the practice of affirmative action, which served as the basis for the holding in the second IWN case. It is composed of four specific steps. The first a clarification that section 18A is not simply a statutory embodiment of the well-entrenched right to equality, but the constitution of a novel norm that positively imposes proper representation of both genders in boards of directors and administrative councils of governmental and statutory corporations. He then emphasizes the remedial purpose of the amendment, which aims at correcting the social distortion of women's minimal representation by means of positively imposing the norm of affirmative action. Next, Mazza describes the essential special legislative measures enacting gender equality, as opposed to the general acceptance of the principle of equality at large. Justice Mazza clearly concludes that the low representation of women in government corporations' boards of directors is just one manifestation of the discrimination women face in Israeli society; he notes that this discrimination is neither specifically intended nor ideologically mandated, but caused by internalized social norms and practices.

Justice Mazza clearly rejects the notion that the approval of affirmative action was meant only as a temporary or extraordinary measure to specifically correct past discrimination and not to maintain present and future social balance. In an elaborate "dictum," he calls for its acceptance as an integral part and a main guarantee of the principle of equality, similar to the Canadian approach. In an effort to solve this problem, he proposes to interpret section 18A in the context of the comprehensive social need to advance women's share in the labor market in general, and in managerial positions in particular. This statement, together with the adoption of the broad interpretation of Basic Law: Human Dignity and Freedom,[25] which incorporates the right to equality in the private sphere, initiates a movement towards legislative reform that would introduce affirmative action into every part of the labor market, public or private.

Concluding the practical part of his decision, while declining to give concrete guidelines for the implementation of section 18A, Justice Mazza also rejects the policy of implementation offered by one of the ministers, whereby a special effort to appoint a woman would only be made when the board is exclusively male and the appointments in question are for the last vacancies. In addition, he suggests that qualities and capabilities need not necessarily be identical in order for a woman candidate to be preferred over the man. Demand for identity of qualities could lead to perpetuation of the discriminatory situation, since many differences in qualities are the result of continuous discrimination. Justice Mazza concludes that the burden of proving that a woman's appointment was impossible under the circumstances lies on the appointing minister (turning to external organizations such as academia, professional unions, or women's organizations for suggestions as to suitable candidates) when the appointments are to be made from among the general public.

This elaborate decision prepared the ground for Justice Heshin's extremely broad proclamations in the second IWN case, in essence establishing an all-encompassing basic principle in the Israeli legal system of adequate representation of men and women in public bodies, as part of the principle of equality. Justice Heshin arrived at this conclusion after realizing that none of the specific rules of adequate representation applied to the case at hand. Refusing to accept a formalistic approach, he proceeded to examine current law on gender equality and adequate representation and reached the formulation of that basic principle. The absence of a specific direct rule under the circumstances of that particular case, together with the fact that the appointment at issue was only temporary for a trial period that was about to end, convinced Justice Heshin not to order the actual termination of that appointment. Unfortunately, this enabled the Minister eventually to ignore the unequivocal message of the decision.[26]

Examination of the Actual Situation

On the empirical level, according to the chair of the Public Committee established by the above amendment to monitor and advise ministers on their appointments, the number of women on boards of directors increased from about 60 in 1993 to 312 in November 1996. The full picture, however, may be seen in the results of academic research comparing the number of women on all government corporations' boards of directors in September 1993 and March 1996 (Izraeli 1996): although section 18A was indeed being implemented, its implementation was carried out at a much slower pace than one would have hoped for. Thus, for example, while in nearly half (48.6 percent) of the government corporations that had no women directors at all in 1993, in 1996 there was at least one woman on the board. However, in two-thirds of the corporations (66.9 percent) there was still no adequate representation, when the term was defined as women composing at least 30 percent of the boards' members. Interestingly, the research clearly shows that the major part of the increase in women's appointments to the boards came from the assignment of "public designated directors," and not from within the civil service.

These findings are clearly supported by the special 1998 State Comptroller Report on Government Corporations, which, among other issues, addressed the question of compliance with section 18A. After citing the Government Corporations Authority's data referring to a 30 percent rate of women in boards of directors in March 1998, it nevertheless concluded that the implementation of the law has not been fully satisfactory, and that much of the increase in women's representation is attributed to the operation of the Public Committee and not to the ministers' proposals (State Comptroller 1998, 25).

According to 2000 data, the rate of women on boards of directors has since increased, with women currently constituting 39 percent of directors. It must be noted, however, that according to these data only one woman (2 percent) serves as a head of a board of directors, only eight (10 percent) serve as CEOs of government corporations, and in 14 percent of all government corporations no women are on the board of directors. In addition, the rate of women among new appointees seems to have dropped (from 44 percent in 1998 and 43 percent in 1999 to only 32 percent in the first 8 months of 2000).[27] Leaving aside the sociological and critical explanations for this situation, the comparative data clearly show the effect and need for affirmative action as a crucial tool in the struggle for the advancement of women.

The amendment to the Government Corporations Law indeed turned out to be only the first expression of legislative affirmative action in Israel. The civil service was the next to follow in the July 1995 amendment to the 1959 State Service (Appointments) Law,[28] which may be regarded as an adoption of Justice Mazza's broad dictum. Section 15A, which was added to the law in that amendment, may be described as basically incorporating the practice of affirmative action into the civil service, in mandating appropriate representation of both sexes in the civil service, and in obligating the Civil Service Commissioner to act, as far as possible under the circumstances, toward the achievement of this goal, through the use of the mechanism of affirmative action among other possible means. Affirmative action is defined in the amendment as giving preference to the candidate who belongs to the gender that is not appropriately represented, where the two candidates' capabilities are comparable.[29]

The data presented later concerning women's representation in senior positions and ranks in the civil service prove far from encouraging. Obviously, the process of remedying past discrimination takes time, even with the temporary use of such means as affirmative action, which is nevertheless an imperative mechanism. Yet it seems there are certain aspects in which affirmative action in the civil service is lacking, and certainly its implementation is far from satisfactory. There are no formal means for supervision and the control of the tender committees. Furthermore, as the supervisor on the status of women in the civil service has pointed out, the supervisors in each government ministry and unit are not involved in the appointments processes or in the workings of the tender committees (Shaked 1997). In addition, the provision only provides for affirmative action in appointments through tenders, and can easily be circumvented through tender-exempt appointments and through appointments of temporary replacements and de facto appointments.[30]

The second IWN case, *Israel Women's Network v. The Minister of Labor and Welfare,*[31] is a particularly poignant illustration of this last point. The appointment in question concerned the ninth deputy general director, where only one out of the operating eight was a woman, and the Public Committee in charge of approving the minister's nominations had rejected that specific candidate both for lack of qualifications (lack of computer skills and training for a position of heading the Data and Information Department) and for breach of the adequate representation provision. Acting as if fulfilling the High Court's order, upon the conclusion of the trial period the ministry placed an advertisement in the national newspapers, specifically seeking a woman candidate for that office. Furthermore, regular and full proceedings were carried out to select the most suitable of the 22 women candidates. Eventually, however, the same male candidate was appointed to the office, thus "ridiculing the decision of the High Court of Justice," as put by Rachel Benziman, then manager of the IWN Legal Department,[32] and leaving no doubt as to the stand of the government officials in charge of implementing these laws.

Going back to the grim findings of Izraeli and Talmud's (1996) research concerning women's representation in public corporation boards, the most recent legislative intervention in the form of affirmative action has indeed been a 1998 amendment to the Corporate Ordinance.[33] Unlike the first two affirmative actions fiats, this amendment orders a much weaker form of affirmative action: it only refers to the two directors appointed as public representatives in every public corporation, and mandates that one of them should be a woman, but only where there are no women at all on the board of directors. Unlike the previous amendments, this time the law intrudes into the private sector, even when perceiving that the public corporations traded on the stock exchange have some public traits. Apart from these significant expressions of substantive equality, there have been at least five other cases in somewhat less prominent pieces of legislation in recent years where the norm of adequate representation has been enacted.[34] While this may not seem impressive, the 2000 Amendment to the Women's Equal Rights Law once again offers the most radical vision of substantive equality in legislation, in its sweeping provisions that enable, and in some cases even mandate, the use of affirmative action measures to reach gender equality. Thus, for example, section 1B contains a general provision legitimizing the use of measures that are aimed at correcting past discrimination against women, thus blocking any allegation of illegitimate "reverse discrimination." In addition, section 6C, "Adequate Representation," significantly expands the span of institutions in which the principle of affirmative action is to be adopted by mandating adequate representation in all governmental ministries, local authorities, municipal corporations, statutory corporations, and government corporations. Remarkably, after Justice Heshin's elaborate construction of the principle of adequate representation, these provisions almost seem superfluous.

In an attempt to remedy the previously noted shortcomings of the affirmative action legislation within the Civil Service, an amendment to section 15A of the 1959 Civil Service Law (Appointments) was passed in December 2000.[35] The amendment obligates the application of affirmative action in all methods of hiring for the Civil Service. This includes actual de facto appointments and nontendered appointments. This amendment also authorizes the safeguarding of certain positions for women only. While the amendment carries tremendous significance with regards to the implementation of the Law, its application might prove to be problematic given that these principles have been simultaneously employed for the advancement of other populations—minorities and people with disabilities. It is still not clear how the Civil Service will adapt to the application of this important amendment.

Several surveys have been made in order to determine public perceptions regarding affirmative action. One such survey, conducted in April 1996 to determine the public's perceptions of women's participation in politics (Bar-Tzuri, Fischer, and Hendeles 1996), revealed general support for the use of affirmative action, especially among women. Affirmative action was thus seen as a particularly important issue in national and local politics, as well as in the labor market.

Among those who support the use of a quota system in parties' lists of electorates, 90 percent think the rate of representation should be higher than it was at that time (only 10 percent of Knesset members were women), and close to half think that 40 percent of the places should be guaranteed to women. Many of the women who support affirmative action think it should be guaranteed in legislation. Interestingly, these women also tend to value the contribution of women to the Knesset and to the labor market more highly than do the rest of the population interviewed, and tend to explain the low representation of women in Israeli politics in terms of gender bias. Another interesting finding, contrary to conventional thinking, was that women with a higher level of education tend to support affirmative action in the Knesset less than do other women.

Accommodation of Parenthood as an Expression of Substantive Equality

Other expressions of substantive equality are the special measures taken to adapt the workplace and to grant women special privileges to enable them to combine maternal functions with work requirements. The dilemma surrounding the adoption of such measures from the perspective of women's advancement is well known; it is termed in the feminist literature the "equal-treatment/special-treatment" debate (Williams 1982; Littleton 1987). Through the adoption of the "special-treatment" concept of equality, this theory once again reflects the recognition that equality is not just about comparison, but rather about accommodating legal and social norms to gendered needs and interests, so that full participation of both genders can be achieved.

The Israeli legal system seems to have overcome this dilemma as early as the1950s, in according women many rights and privileges to accommodate maternity with workplace requirements. However, these measures actually stemmed from Israel's strong pronatalist policy, combined with the simple need for more workers (Raday 1995). In fact, the strong familial character of Israeli society and the deep patriarchal legacy of the founding generation, together with nationalistic-demographic concerns, had initially prompted the adoption of these special measures to such an extent that they had become a major hindrance to women's integration and advancement in the workforce. Absolute prohibitions of night work for women or against working overtime for pregnant women, originally contained in the 1954 Employment of Women Law,[36] supposedly aimed at protecting women from work hazards that might harm their reproductive capabilities, had the impact of preventing women from entering more profitable occupations or increasing their income by working overtime (Shalev 1995b). Likewise, provisions guaranteeing several rights in relation to the birth or raising of children were initially given only to mothers, thus targeting women as potentially unreliable workers due to child-rearing responsibilities that only they, by definition, could fulfill. No public debate over special rights for working women ever took place in Israel. The reason for this seeming endorsement of the "special rights" approach, I think, was not heightened feminist awareness but rather the fact that women's central role as bearers of children had always been strongly embedded in the public consciousness, in line with Israel's pronatalist demographic policy.

These legislative arrangements were strongly criticized, and a process of mitigation ensued even prior to the passage of the 1988 Equal Employment Opportunities Law.[37] The general policy of change has been to turn the original prohibitions into options that are available to women. Thus, in 1986 the absolute prohibition of night work for women was abolished.[38] The 1998 amendment to the 1954 Employment of Women Law gave pregnant women the option to decide whether to work overtime, subject to medical approval.[39] Similarly, the prohibition against employing a woman during maternity leave was criticized, although it should be noted that during these twelve weeks a woman receives the equivalent of her full salary from the NII and her social rights keep accumulating. This prohibition, therefore, could more easily be justified on the basis of the physical and emotional needs of adjustment surrounding the experience of giving birth. Nevertheless, even this provision was amended in 1997 to allow the couple (defined in this law as a married couple only) to decide who would take the second half of the maternity leave, namely the six to twelve weeks following the birth of a child.[40] This particular move is even more revolutionary than the previous ones, since it relates to deeply held convictions and perceptions of motherhood versus fatherhood. Indeed, data from the NII indicate that this time the law far surpassed public readiness. In the first year of its enactment, only 232 fathers used this option to take the six-week leave instead of the mothers—a mere third percent (0.34 percent) of the requests for postnatal leave. Even more disappointing is the rate in 2000: only 224 fathers out of 70,641 requests (0.31 percent).[41]

More progress came with the passage of the Equal Employment Opportunities Law in 1988. It prohibits discrimination in the workplace, whether based on gender, sexual orientation, marital status, parenthood, race, age, religion, nationality, country of birth, or political or other orientation. Neither government nor private employers may take the above classifications into account in determining employment, promotion, termination of employment, training, or work and retirement conditions of employees, except in special cases where the unique nature of the position makes these classifications relevant. Furthermore, protections offered to women employees that take into account their special needs as women or mothers are not considered discriminatory. Finally, in transforming maternal rights into parental rights, the law also specifies that any such rights offered to working mothers must be equally given to fathers who either have sole custody of their childre, or have partners (not only wives) who are employed and have chosen not to make use of these provisions.[42] This move gives parents the option to choose who will take advantage of these rights. Such arrangements as the right to a leave of absence of up to a year following a child's birth or the adoption of a child are all detailed in Chapter 7. There are also specific provisions in collective agreements that grant working mothers special benefits, such as a shorter workday, or the option of flexible working hours, as in the civil service, to fit their maternal obligations. These accommodations in collective agreements are generally granted to mothers alone.[43]

This overall legislative change, unfortunately, has not been consistent, but done through an incremental process, producing occasional incoherence regarding some paternal rights, and failing to provide a clear and permanent framework. Even where the rights have been extended from maternal to parental rights, the stereotypical perception of women as primary caretakers of children remains in the shape of requiring the father who elects to take advantage of such rights to prove his spouse's employment or his sole responsibility for the child, proofs that are not required of women. Another such reflection, changed in 1998, was the granting of right to the twelve weeks of paid maternity leave in the case of an adoption of a child only to women. Realizing the fact that in the case of adoption there are supposedly no physical or emotional grounds for distinction between the prospective mother and father, the Employment of Women Law was amended in 1998, and this right is now awarded to either of the adoptive parents according to their own choice.[44]

Overall, these changes signify the development of a much more mature perception of gender equality, one that takes into account gender differences, yet is totally aware of the dangers inherent in doing so, and is careful not to penalize women for these differences. A much less encouraging process is the wide gap between the law's provisions and the public's convictions: the legal changes described in this chapter are sometimes met with hesitancy and even resistance . Whether it is male ministers who find it difficult to put aside male loyalties and camaraderie, or new fathers who find it difficult to change gender roles and take their spouse's place by the baby's side, these societal reactions indicate that legal changes are far from enough.

Gender Bias in Israeli Courts

Empirical Study

During the late 1980s, studies in the United States tracing and documenting gender bias in the judiciary have proliferated (Resnik 1996). As insights from these studies permeated legal research and writings, women in Israel, as elsewhere in the world, began questioning the relevance of these findings to the Israeli context. At a meeting with the then Chief Justice of the Supreme Court, Justice Meir Shamgar, the IWN asked for the introduction of educational programs on gender bias into the judges' learning seminars. Justice Shamgar agreed to introduce such programs only if an independent study conducted within the Israeli judicial system demonstrated evidence of gender bias in Israel. At the initiative of the IWN, and with the financial support of the Ford Foundation and the academic backing of the Jerusalem Institute of Israel Research, a study was conducted from 1992 to 1996 to determine whether and how gender bias was manifested in Israeli courts (Bogoch and Don-Yechiya 1999, 3).

The two researchers, sociologist Bryna Bogoch and attorney Rochelle Don-Yechiya, specifically sought to discover whether there were gender-linked differences in judicial judgments and decisions in criminal cases, and whether there was evidence of gender bias in interaction and communication in the courtroom or in the texts of judicial decisions. Unlike most task force studies of gender bias in the courts, which mainly documented subjective experiences and perceptions of participants in the system (both lay and professional), this study sought to determine whether these perceptions about gender bias were manifested in actual behavior in the Israeli court system. This was accomplished by the systematic and empirical examination of large samples of judicial decisions and courtroom interactions and employed sociolinguistic methods, textual analyses, and innovative measures of sentencing. Overall, the study includes analysis of about 1,300 files and judicial decisions and observations of 565 segments of testimony (each 25 minutes long).

Some of the Findings

Gender and the defendant. Of the 868 defendants whose cases were examined in the Magistrate and District Court sample, a mere 28 were female offenders. It is for this reason that conclusions drawn from these results must be considered cautiously. Still, in general, it was found that, contrary to popular conceptions, women defendants were not treated more leniently than men, and in some cases they were treated more harshly.

For example, none of the women were acquitted on the basis of reasonable doubt, as compared with 6 percent of men in similar situations. This means that, despite the similarity in the overall rate of convictions, women were acquitted only when their innocence was unequivocally established, while men were acquitted also when their innocence was in doubt but the legal requirements of guilt had not been completely demonstrated. Furthermore, all nine women accused of offenses against life were convicted, while the conviction rate for men for these offenses was 84 percent. Women were much less likely than men to resolve their cases through plea bargaining; the researchers remark that this may reflect their lower social position and inexperience with the judicial system. The state appealed the leniency of the sentence given to women twice as frequently as that given men, and in all these cases the Court accepted the appeal and increased the sentence. The only area of examination in which no differences were found between men and women was with respect to prison sentences. The study found no statistically significant differences between the prison sentences for convicted women and men, in effect repudiating the notion of chivalry in sentencing.

Gender and the victim. In order to examine the perception in feminist circles that crimes against women are regarded as less serious than crimes against men, the rate of convictions and length of sentences imposed on those convicted of harming women were compared to those for harming men. It was found that conviction rates were lower when the defendant was accused of killing or attempting to kill a woman than when defendants were accused of similar crimes against men. Moreover, although there was no statistically significant difference in the length of sentences for those harming female or male victims, there was an indirect connection between the gender of the victim and sentencing. Lower sentences were imposed on those who harmed family members or friends than on those who harmed strangers. It was precisely in these family and acquaintance crimes that women were most likely to be the victim.

Gender and the judges. One of the predictions made by some feminist legal scholars is that women would bring a "different voice" to the judging process and that this would be reflected in a special sensitivity to crimes against women. In order to ascertain the relationship between the gender of the judges and the outcome of criminal cases, the researchers distinguished between women judging alone and those judging on a panel of three judges with men, versus men judging alone or in all-male panels. The study found that a judge's gender had a distinct effect on the sentencing of a defendant, with lower sentences given by lone female judges than by lone male judges, and higher sentences by panels that included women than those that did not. In virtually all offenses, the highest sentences were imposed by panels that included female judges. However, whether alone or in a panel, women judges were less punitive of sexual offenders than of other violent offenders. In contrast to male judges, female judges tended to impose lower sentences on defendants convicted of sexual offenses than those convicted of bodily harm, both in number of months and in the ratio of the imposed prison term to the maximum sentence. No relationship was found between the gender of the judges and the rate of convictions or sentences imposed in cases of domestic violence or in cases in which the victims were women or minors. The authors suggest two possible explanations for these findings. One is that women judges were as yet uncertain of their place in the professional community and thus were unwilling to make judgments that could be interpreted as favoring women. The other explanation, particularly for the findings about lower sentences for sexual offenders, is based on the psychological theory of defensive attribution, which maintains that people hold victims responsible for their predicament as protection against the stress of regarding themselves as vulnerable to a similar catastrophe. Thus, women judges, who perceive themselves are potential victims of sexual offenses, would try to distance themselves from such a possibility by attributing characteristics to the victim that would in effect blame her in some way for the offense. This would then be reflected in the lower sentences imposed on sexual offenders.

Gender and the lawyers. The public sector in Israel, especially the state attorney's office, has more female than male lawyers; while the private sector is male dominated.[45] The study found a distinct effect of the attorney's gender on his or her success in persuading judges. While there was no difference in the rate of convictions and the use of plea bargains between male and female lawyers, female attorneys have been significantly less successful than male ones in measures of both sentence length and the ratio between the imposed prison term and the maximum sentence. Lower sentences were imposed when women were the prosecutors and higher sentences were imposed when women were the defense attorneys. In addition, male prosecutors were most persuasive when the defense attorney was a woman, and women defense attorneys appeared to be least persuasive when the prosecutor was a man.

Gender stereotypes in judicial decisions. The study confirmed the long-held impression that little consideration is given the victim in judicial decisions. Moreover, while various social characteristics, such as service in the army (compulsory for all Jewish citizens, male and female), can act in the male defendant's favor, army service is never even mentioned regarding women defendants or victims. Paradoxically, if the victim and the defendant are married to each other or otherwise romantically involved, it is considered a mitigating rather than an aggravating factor in judges' decisions regarding conviction or sentencing. Women judges, alone or in panel, are more likely to cite negative characteristics of the victim, thus in essence blaming the victim in sexual offenses. With regard to strategies used by defense attorneys, the study found that different rationales were used for men and women defendants. An attorney defending a woman is likely to minimize her role in the offense and describe her as having been drawn into the act. According to the researchers, it is apparently considered an advantage in such cases to emphasize the passivity or helplessness of the woman defendant. In other words, Bogoch and Don-Yechiya conclude that the rationales used by male and female lawyers and judges reflect the gender stereotypes and patriarchal assumptions of Israeli society.

Courtroom interactions. The study revealed clear gender bias in courtroom interactions, whether women were judges, attorneys, or witnesses. The greatest number of interruptions were made by male judges when female defense attorneys were speaking. Women, who served as witnesses much less frequently than men, were disproportionately challenged for their infractions of the rules of courtroom discourse. All judges challenged the credibility of women witnesses much more frequently than that of men witnesses. Judges tended to give more instructions to women than to men on the witness stand, and male judges were especially more likely to give orders to women lawyers. Judges of either sex were much harsher in their comments to female than to male lawyers. While judges virtually never made overt sexist comments to women lawyers or witnesses, their general behavior was more supportive of the professional identity of men lawyers and more challenging to that of women lawyers. In terms of attitude toward women judges, all participants addressed women judges less deferentially than they did their male counterparts, and both men and women judges, in turn addressed women lawyers less deferentially than men lawyers.

Following the Study

As a result of this study, the researchers recommended that continuing educational programs for judges be instituted to raise the issue of gender bias (as well as other forms of bias in the courts). Experimental programs in that direction were initiated prior to the study by Judge Rotlevi of the Tel Aviv District Court, but according to her report, the seminars were not very successful, and attendance was low. On the initiative of Judge Rotlevi, the subject of domestic violence, divided into violence against children and violence against women, has been developed into a seminar for all family court judges and other interested judges. The subject of gender-based violence against women as a whole, however, has hardly been discussed. Most significantly, gender bias as an issue and the results of the empirical study have, until the completion of this book, only been discussed on one occasion in a judicial forum, and the judges as a community have never, to my knowledge, received a systematic report of this study.[46] Significantly, the CEDAW Committee specifically addressed the issue of gender bias in the courts in its concluding observations, calling upon the State of Israel to conduct special "programmes for gender sensitization of the judiciary."[47] In reply to my official request as part of the preparation of the Third Periodic Report of the State of Israel to CEDAW, I was told that the subject of gender bias was on the agenda of the Institute for Judges' Seminars, to be included in its upcoming annual program.[48] It has not appeared on the program so far.

Chapter 3
The Promotion of Gender Equality

State Feminism

This chapter tells the story of Israel's governments' efforts to establish mechanisms for the advancement of women. In this sense, it addresses and challenges state feminism in Israel. While the term "state feminism" does not necessarily have an agreed-upon definition, it generally refers to government or otherwise official initiatives to advance women and promote their status, which may include some sort of assistance and cooperation with women's organizations (Stetson 2001). State feminism may sometimes be related to another theoretic concept, that of "feminism from above," which may be taken as presenting a more skeptical perspective on this subject matter. Feminism from above usually refers to the raising of women's issues and concerns by the political establishment (B. Swirski 1989), hence the top-down direction of movements, in contrast to the feminist ideal of action from the bottom up. It seems that the Israeli experience indeed combines these two concepts, but not very successfully. With regard to state feminism, this chapter describes a continuing course of endeavors and undertakings that can be viewed as embodying all that is perplexing and confusing in the situation of women in Israel: much action, without many results. There have been many genuine efforts over the past two decades to address and redress the plight of Israeli women, probably more than one would have thought. I describe these efforts, with emphasis on information-gathering initiatives. Nevertheless, as I show throughout the book, the end results of most of these efforts are not very reassuring.

A major part of this chapter is devoted to the civil service, which in a sense serves as a case study for the official policy and government performance as a whole. The employer in the civil service is the state, and thus civil service is a field within which the state applies both its overall policies of gender equality and its approach as an employer to advance its women employees. Because of this unique nature of the civil service, all its aspects are discussed in this chapter, although data and information that specifically relate to positions of women and salary gaps within the civil service are discussed in Chapters 7 and 8. Following this discussion, the chapter turns from top-down state feminism to the bottom-up feminism of women's movements. Empirical research on state feminism is unsettled on such questions as the conditions required for its success, yet the emerging picture puts the presence of an active women's movement in a central position (Mazur 2001). The second part of this chapter, then, sketches in broad strokes some of the main efforts of mobilization taken by Israeli women's organizations.

Much of this chapter discusses government activities and state operation, and as readers may be unfamiliar with Israel's parliamentary system, I draw attention to differences distinguishing it from, for example, the U.S. "presidentialist system."[1] Generally, separation of powers between the executive and the legislature is not an absolute principle in Israel. In terms of the people, the process of appointments and their qualifications, the Basic Law: The Government provides that at least half of the ministers should also be MKs—members of parliament, the Knesset.[2] The law also subjects the prime minister's appointment power to parliamentary review; in practice this is limited by political considerations, and appointment of ministers who are not MKs is rare. Thus, the executive government is not an appointed body in the true sense of the term, but more of an elected body, a de facto part of the Knesset, or more accurately part of the Knesset's majority, with powers, for example, to pass or refrain from passing legislation (Rubinstein 1996, 361). Rather than being experienced professionals, ministers are more likely to be experienced politicians leading the coalition parties. Furthermore, while theoretically the ministers are accountable to the prime minister who appointed them, in fact their allegiance is to their own party. Their motivation is often political and their considerations are electoral. All this obviously has ramifications for issues, such as women's rights, which seldom enjoy political patronage and are not perceived to be electorally attractive.

Knowledge as Power and How to Obtain It

Knowledge and understanding are key factors for generating action and devising mechanisms for change. The nonexistence of official data, reports, or information on a specific phenomenon makes the social problem even more invisible and thus renders the raising of the problem illegitimate. A major impediment to work for the advancement of women in Israel is lack of information and data. During Israel's formative years and into the late 1970s, this deficiency led to a profound lack of awareness as to the situation of women in Israel. Attention was focused on the formal levels of the legal system, which, as already explained, contained explicit provisions guaranteeing complete equality for women in all areas of life except marriage and divorce, and thus in fact had reinforced the equality myth that dominated public opinion. Conventional perceptions did not seem to go beyond the formal layer, for lack of appreciation of the gap between formal regulations and daily life. There was and still is an urgent need to fill that gap. But first, information needed to be obtained. The 1975 International Year of Women was a trigger for the designation of an ad hoc Commission on the Status of Women, appointed by then Prime Minister Yitzhak Rabin and headed by Ora Namir, a member of Knesset (Labor Party), who later became minister of labor and social affairs (Yishai 1997, 20). The operation of this commission, two years after the 1973 Yom Kippur war, which painfully served as an initial collective awakening of Israeli women to the discriminatory reality (Herzog 1999, 339–42), played the important role of completely shattering the equality myth through the presentation of hard facts and straight information.

The Namir Commission's main function was to investigate the issue of the status of women in Israel. It acted mainly as a fact-finding body but was also asked to present the government with proposals on the social, cultural, educational, economic, and legal measures necessary to promote equality between men and women in Israel. Sure enough, after three years of work, the commission supplied the government with a list of 241 comprehensive recommendations and detailed proposals on how to improve the existing situation. These recommendations had the potential to serve as a blueprint for women's equality, yet few of them were adopted and implemented. In fact, an investigation conducted by the Israel Women's Network (Shdulat ha-Nashim, IWN) in 1988 revealed that of the 241 recommendations only 32 had been fully implemented, 39 had been partially implemented, and the remaining 170 had not been implemented at all (Israel Women's Network 1987). Nevertheless, the commission's central contribution to the introduction of women's concerns into the center of the public sphere and on the national agenda cannot be denied. Furthermore, the origins of many government initiatives for the advancement of women can be attributed to the work and recommendations of this commission.

Since the operation of the Namir Commission, there have been a few other commissions to investigate specific issues, such as domestic violence and murder of women by their spouses or the role and status of women in the civil service.[3] Unfortunately, no other major government study (as opposed to academic research) was commissioned to investigate the overall status of women in Israel, nor has there been a follow-up survey on the Namir Commission recommendations. Similarly, no use was made of external institutions operating in the international arena that reach sites of knowledge and information. Thus, until 1998, no machinery had been established to oversee the CEDAW convention's implementation. Even graver is Israel's lack of serious and professional address of the 1995 Fourth World Conference on Women in Beijing. The Beijing Conference was the fourth in a row of intergovernmental conferences convened by the United Nations, which aimed at broadening its methods of work from the slow process of negotiating conventions to the adoption of global plans of action (Tomasevski 1998, 8). The Beijing Conference had indeed generated a great deal of publicity, and its Platform for Action received much international attention and commitment. In Israel, however, the Beijing Conference received no official discussion in the government or Knesset. Consequently, no overall plan for the implementation of the platform was ever adopted.[4]

Special Machinery for the Advancement of Women

History

One of the main obstacles to full implementation of women's rights and the advancement of women's status in Israel was the lack of a central organization to connect governmental and nongovernmental actors in the area, to oversee their operation, compose overall plans and policies, and process complaints of women whose rights were violated or who suffered gender discrimination. The first recommendation in the Namir Commission's report was the statutory establishment of a National Authority for the Advancement of the Status of Women to fulfill these purposes. It took two decades for this recommendation to be finally implemented and for the 1998 Authority for the Advancement of Women Law to be enacted.[5]

The Namir Commission's report generated the establishment of two new government functions: the office of the Prime Minister's Advisor on the Status of Women, established in 1980, and the nonstatutory National Council for the Advancement of the Status of Women, set up in 1984. Although these two functions differed in scope and in operation, they had in common the personal enthusiasm of their personnel, on the one hand, negated by a total lack of resources on the other. The Prime Minister's Advisor on the Status of Women was charged with the task of advising the prime minister on all issues pertaining to women and coordinating the government's actions with relation to the status of women. The office, however, was not provided with special resources and its budget was to be drawn from the general budget of the prime minister's bureau. This recurring motif in government treatment of the subject of women's status was undoubtedly the main cause for the gradual decline in the powers and significance of this office since the end of the 1980s. Notwithstanding the lack of resources, the first two advisors who operated until 1992 had a significant impact in several areas, including the promotion of legislation, such as the 1998 Equal Employment Opportunities Law. Another substantial contribution was the regular publication of the periodical *Woman's Status*, which continued to appear until several years ago and was an important source of information as well as consciousness raising.

Unlike the Office of the Prime Minister's Advisor, the functions and prerogatives of the National Council were not clearly set, but like the Office of the Prime Minister's Advisor, no separate budget was allocated to it. The number of Council members gradually expanded, until it had reached close to 200 in 1992, thus making it a totally inoperative body.[6] In 1992, Prime Minister Rabin abolished the Office of Prime Minister's Advisors altogether, including the Office of the Advisor on the Status of Women. In its place, he formed a steering committee to reframe the structure of both the office of the advisor and the function of the National Authority. Its recommendations, presented in January 1993, included the establishment of a bureau in the prime minister's office for the implementation of the council's policies. The recommendations were not attended to, and the operation of the council was put to a halt, and in effect were not renewed, not even when a new advisor was appointed in 1993 and a narrower council established, consisting of only 35 members.

The Authority for the Advancement of Women

The bottom line of this history is that the National Council never really functioned, and the budget-deficient Office of the Prime Minister's Advisor was very dependent on the individual heading it. But, all along, the idea of the establishment of a statutory authority was not neglected, and a bill for the establishment of the authority was drafted in 1996 and was proposed by nine MKs as a private bill. The Authority for the Advancement of Women Law was passed on International Women's Day (March 8) 1998. It declares its goal to be the promotion of gender equality in the broadest sense and establishes a statutory Authority for the Advancement of Women.

Some evaluation of the law's significance can be formed by comparing it with the 1996 bill. Such a comparison shows regression in at least one important area. The 1996 bill had proposed the establishment of an office of Commissioner for Women's Affairs, whose role was to handle direct complaints from the public concerning violations of women's rights or discrimination on the basis of gender. The commissioner was to have investigative powers equal to those of the general Public Complaints Commissioner, including the power to demand any necessary documents and records. Most important, its jurisdiction was to encompass not just the public sphere but the private sphere as well, in the sense that any person or organization who dealt with women's rights could issue a complaint about discrimination against women against any other person or organization, public or private.[7] When the 1996 private bill turned into an officially published government bill, there was no mention of such an office.[8] Surprisingly, the law that eventually passed does include something reminiscent of this office, in the form of a provision that permits the authority to transfer complaints issued to the authority to the Public Complaints Commissioner, who is also to provide an annual report to the Knesset concerning all complaints of discrimination against women.[9] This, however, is a disappointingly pale version of the original office, making the Authority into nothing but a channel for the regular operation of the Public Complaints Commissioner.[10]

Another, more positive change is worth mentioning. This change relates to the authority's title (and hence to the law's title), and therefore seems to be merely linguistic, or symbolic at best. In my opinion, however, it is quite a significant change, and a positive one. The uthority's original title was Authority for the *Advancement of Women.* This gender-specific terminology caused some disapproval, and sure enough, the 1997 officially published government bill was titled Authority for the *Promotion of Gender Equality*, a gender-neutral term. The final law, though, went back to the original gender-specific title, thus expressing an appropriate rejection of the seemingly neutral language that only maintains the discriminatory status quo under the guise of neutrality. This rejection reflects mature understanding that sometimes insistence on gender-neutral language only serves to deny the existence of a problem of gender discrimination and thus in fact to reinforce it.

A major deficiency of the law, which almost caused some women's organizations such as the IWN to object to it, is the allocation of the authority's budget within the general budget of the prime minister's office. Drawing on the past experience of the authority's predecessors, that is, the Prime Minister's Advisor on the Status of Women and the National Council, it seemed that the current enterprise of the statutory authority would end up just like them, for lack of a guaranteed independent budget. Notwithstanding these hesitations, the law was eventually supported by most nongovernmental organizations (NGOs), with the hope that this is only the first step, and that, once statutorily established, the authority will be able to draw sufficient funding for its proper operation. However, soon after its establishment, some organizations expressed further reservations regarding the appearance of political involvement in the authority's operation, through questionable appointments of individuals and organizations to the authority's advisory and experts committee.[11]

An examination of the authority's performance so far reveals some incompatibility with the law's provision, along with what seems to be a lot of action. It seems that the authority has turned into a facilitator and catalyst of mostly existing programs; not much has been done of the more substantial tasks conferred on it. It has certainly not become the revolutionary, activist body that some had hoped for. First and foremost, the authority has not established a concrete, overall policy for the attainment of its goals to be approved by the government. Furthermore, it has not yet used its power to request ministries, local authorities, and other statutory organizations to consult with it on policy and other matters that concern women's advancement. Evidence of the authority's lack of action on a broad level can be seen from the 1999 Public Complaints Commissioner's report, stating that no complaints on discrimination against women were filed with the Commissioner in accordance with the authority's law that year (Public Complaints Commissioner 1999, 20). The Commissioner remarks that action is needed to raise the public's awareness of this possibility.

While not part of the Authority for the Advancement of Women, the most recent formal mechanism for women's advancement is the 2000 Local Authorities Law (Advisor on the Status of Women).[12] This law requires every municipality to appoint an advisor on women's status issues, whose role is to outline policy for the advancement of women within the purview of the local authority, while ensuring that necessary resources are provided to this end. The law provides for the advisor to be invited to all the meetings of the local authority and any of its committees, and to be given the opportunity to express her opinions in every subject that relates to the status of women. The advisor is expected to give an annual report to the Knesset Committee on the Status of Women as well as to the Authority for the Advancement of Women and to her local authority. Once again, this is a perfect example of state feminism, as well as feminism from above. The legislature designated an official role and filled it with substance but with absolutely no resources, thus guaranteeing the advisor's dependence on the goodwill of the head of the local authority. Furthermore, the law did not ensure the advisor's executionary powers or concrete veto power over plans that might impede women. Nevertheless, as seen before, this might lead to more powerful positions in the future.

The Knesset Committee on the Status of Women

Other attempts not in the general scheme of things have been made to assist women. Perhaps the most important of these initiatives is the unusual coalition of women members of Knesset from across the political map that established the Committee on the Status of Women in 1992. The committee has since been extremely instrumental in promoting important legislative measures and in raising awareness of women's concerns. The committee has made significant contributions to the efforts to improve women's status and to focus public attention on "women's issues." The chair usually rotates between two members, from the coalition and the opposition parties respectively. In January 1996, the committee was granted the status of a permanent Knesset Committee with the following tasks: advancement of women's equality in public representation, education, and personal status, prevention of discrimination on the basis of sex or sexual orientation in all areas; reduction of wage gaps in the economy and labor market; and elimination of violence against women.

Among the recent legislation facilitated by the committee's work are the Authority for the 1988 Advancement of Women Law, the 1988 Prevention of Sexual Harassment Law, the 1996 Equal Pay (Male and Female Employees) Law, the 1995 State Service (Appointments) Law (Adequate Representation) (Amendment no. 7), the 1996 Prevention of Violence in the Family Law (Amendment no. 2), and the 1995 Family Court Law.[13] All in all, well over 40 legislative measures relating to the advancement of women's status have been passed since the establishment of the Committee. During the 14th Knesset alone (1996–99) 16 laws pertaining to women's advancement were passed.[14] The committee has also utilized other parliamentary means, such as the establishment and operation of the parliamentary investigative Committee on Women's Murder by Their Spouses.

Looking at the whole picture, it does seem that this committee is the only ongoing governmental forum (that is, not in the sense of actually belonging to the government, but in the sense of officially belonging to the state administration) where women's issues and concerns are being seriously examined, discussed, and handled. Although its executive powers are limited, as the committee belongs to the legislative and not to the executive branch, it takes maximum advantage of the tools available within the Knesset, such as motions to convene parliamentary discussions, specific requests to government ministers, and so on. Perhaps in light of the overall lack of a government agency that would oversee all these matters, the committee steps in to fill this void. However, its limited power does take its toll. Thus, for example, while the committee often uses its authority to demand action from various organs and requests that they report back to it, it lacks the power to enforce these demands, and there is not even a mechanism to impose accountability. In other words, compliance with the committee's demands remains a matter of goodwill, as is the reporting back to it. One example of positive cooperation and compliance with this tool is the establishment of a regular semiannual report on sexual harassment in the army.[15] Still, not all agencies are equally cooperative. In terms of demands for information, the committee, like all other Knesset committees, can request information only through the minister in charge of the relevant matters.

Notwithstanding these weaknesses, it is important to note that the committee's contribution to the advancement of women extends far beyond the formal level of parliamentary performance to the more informal level of women's alliance building and coordination of activities for furthering the common goal of mobilization and social change. The committee maintains close contacts with women's NGOs, and representatives from various NGOs regularly attend its meetings. It also receives input from women in senior positions in business and academia, and thus serves as a forum where women's voices are officially heard and political mobilization around women's issues can be discussed. In fact, if it were not for the committee's meetings, women's issues would specifically be addressed at the Knesset only twice a year: on International Women's Day and on International Fight Against Violence Day (November 25). Except for these two routine occasions, the Knesset has not seen fit to put women's concerns on its agenda, though it occasionally responds to an external trigger in the sensational form of violence against women.

In some sense, the Knesset Committee on the Status of Women can also be taken as demonstrating the working of "feminism from above," as discussed previously. If feminism from above means raising feminist issues by the political establishment, sometimes through appropriating them from grassroots organizations (B. Swirski 1989), this is certainly reflected in the operation of the committee. For this purpose the committee is certainly part of the establishment. However, it is definitely also part of the feminist movement. Therefore, perhaps, the somewhat negative attitude toward the model of feminism from above should not be applied to the committee. On the contrary, since the committee manages to maintain a critical feminist approach, this is a case where feminism from above should be viewed as a positive development. This contention gains support from the "state feminism" literature, which often highlights the contributions that can be made to women's causes by women politicians, who—as Amy Mazur puts it—act as "policy entrepreneurs" (Mazur 2001).

Women in the Civil Service

The Israeli government is the largest employer in Israel, and more than 60 percent of civil servants are women. The civil service can be taken as a paradigm for examination of both women's participation and status in the labor market, and—of more interest to us at this point in the investigation—of the government's performance and the efforts it has made to promote women's status. The classic pyramid structure reflecting the glass-ceiling phenomenon has always characterized women's position in the civil service.[16] However, once this reality was raised by the Namir Commission Report, the government could no longer ignore it. Indeed, the civil service has become a central arena for government enterprises for the advancement of women. In a sense, it has even become a field for experimentation on this theme. When these observations are added to the depiction of the civil service as an ordinary employer within the labor market, yet one that is governmentally controlled and constantly supervised, making formal interventions more feasible, the significance of the civil service as a case study becomes clear. What follows is a chronicle of government performance for the advancement of women in the civil service. Of course, this description should be read bearing in mind the basic data of women's position in the civil service. And despite all the efforts described below, these data have hardly changed (see Chapter 8 and the general discussion of women's representation in the public sphere). Here, I examine what the government has been doing in general to improve women's situation and to advance women in the civil service. I focus on the plans and the means that the government has utilized for that purpose.

Government management of the civil service with respect to women began in April 1985, when it adopted an additional recommendation of the Namir Commission and decided to appoint a supervisor in each of the government ministries to oversee the status of female workers. The roles of these supervisors included six specific tasks: acting for the implementation of equal opportunities for women employees in all areas of the service, monitoring the obligation to include women in all professional and tender committees, developing special tracks for the promotion of women, acting for an increase in the percentage of women in top positions, handling women employees' complaints of gender discrimination including sexual harassment complaints, and preparing annual reports about progress made in this area (Public Professional Committee 1989, 2: 296).

In line with the pattern already observed, the decision did not allocate a special budget for its implementation, and despite appointments and facilitative efforts made in some ministries, a process of gradual decline in action and prestige has ensued. A similar fate met the two other parts of the 1985 government resolution, which were to ensure women's participation as members in every tender or professional committee and to establish a committee to monitor the implementation of the whole resolution. That committee was never established.

What salvaged these endeavors was the operation of another investigative commission, the Koberski Commission. Significantly, this commission's original goal had nothing specific to do with women but was to investigate and propose reforms to the civil service in general. The commission decided to include a special report on the status of women in the civil service. Its conclusions made it clear that discrimination against women is the major cause of women's low status in the service (Public Professional Committee 1989, 2: 262). As the Koberski Commission's main focus was not the status of women in the civic service, its recommendations in this respect remained somewhat generalized and blurry. This was the setting for the establishment of yet another commission, to implement recommendations for the improvement of the status of women (Ben-Israel 1998, 546).

The proposals of that commission were presented in December 1993. They consisted of specific directives for ensuring women's participation in tender committees, improving the function of the supervisors on the status of women in the various ministries, and securing firmer treatment for sexual harassment.[17] Most of these proposals, such as mandating the representation of both sexes in tender committees and voiding tenders in which this was not followed, were adopted and incorporated into the Civil Service Code.[18] In addition, a special post was designated for a General Supervisor for the Advancement of Women in the Civil Service, who was to be in charge of all matters concerning women and their advancement in the service and was to report directly to the Civil Service Commissioner. This post later became part of a new unit, established in 1997, responsible for hiring and promoting women in the civil service.[19]

A major change seemed to have occurred in 1995 with the introduction of an affirmative action policy to the civil service through the State Service (Appointments) Law (Adequate Representation) (Amendment no. 7). As explained in Chapter 2, the amendment states that both sexes should be adequately represented in the civil service and obligates the Civil Service Commissioner to use all necessary means, including affirmative action, to achieve appropriate representation. The amendment is routinely read to committee members at the beginning of every tender committee section, with an emphasis on the explicit provision that preference be given to the candidate of the less represented sex, when candidates' qualifications for the office are similar. As many critics have pointed out, these means are hardly satisfactory for implementation of the amendment's goal of adequate representation (Tirosh 1999, 217–18). Political scientist Moshe Maor has given all these developments the derogatory label "symbolic reform," referring to the vague nature of the goals, lack of budgetary backing and concrete powers for implementation, and intensive distribution of symbols (Maor 2001). Symbolic reform implies the lack of honest reformative intentions on the part of policymakers.

Indeed, the ultimate criterion for evaluating this long line of actions and ventures is the data concerning women's ranks, positions, and salaries. These data are detailed later, in the discussion of women's representation in the public sphere and women's employment as a whole. For now, a quick glance at the data is almost an anticlimax to the chronicle just described. In short, all the government efforts and struggles hardly seem to have produced any significant outcome. For instance, in 1995 the percentage of women among the top three ranks of the four main classifications in the civil service (the primary resource for managerial positions) was only 10.5 percent. In 1999, four years after the legislative change, this figure had improved only slightly: fewer than 12 percent of the employees in the top three ranks were women.[20] The figures relating to the highest ranks in the service and those that describe the tenders outcomes are even more disturbing. As for women's salaries, the earnings gap between women and men in the civil service decreased by 9 percent between 1987 and 1996. This gap is still substantial, however, as women's average salary in the administrative classification in 1996 was equivalent to 75 percent of that of men (Civil Service Commissioner 1998, 11), and in 2000 the salary gap throughout the civil service reached 28 percent.[21]

Perhaps in this sense too the story of women in the civil service is a paradigm for women's participation in the workforce and in leadership positions at large. A familiar pattern is discerned here, one that applies to many other contexts: no matter how extensive the official endeavors are, they are not enough. Furthermore, these endeavors tend to take the form of one committee after another, with little practical outcome in reality, and when a normative change is finally made, not only it is a far cry from what it should be, its implementation is also severely lacking. Four years after its introduction is not too early to evaluate the success of the legal reform in the form of the affirmative action mechanism. Legal reform is of course essential, but it cannot succeed without much deeper social and cultural reform, as demonstrated in Chapter 8 discussing tender data. Although women's success rates have risen impressively and are now equal to men's, their proportions in the appointments still fall short of men's, particularly when the tenders are external.[22] This is so for the simple reason of women's strikingly lower proportion of candidacy to external tenders. There is enough basis to suggest that the main reasons for this would be women's lack of confidence in the integrity of the process (Tirosh 1999). When this is the case, a simple equality in rate of success is not enough and is certainly not a fulfillment of an affirmative action policy. When the number of women candidates is significantly lower than that of men candidates, in addition to encouraging women to put forth their candidacy, a temporary preference for women candidates is also called for. Moreover, many have pointed to the inadequacy of the amendment itself, in referring only to appointments through tenders, while in reality tenders are very often bypassed through de facto appointments, or through a large number of tender-exempt positions (Tirosh 1999).[23] Indeed, as already mentioned in Chapter 2, the law was amended once again in December 2000, with the apparent goal of rectifying the shortcomings in the appointment process. As suggested there, and later in Chapter 8, there are reasons enough for skepticism about this amendment too.[24]

Another facet of the incompetence of all the reforms in the civil service is seen in the status of the General Supervisor on the Advancement of Women. Like a story that repeats itself over and over, this significant position and the unit that was later formed were given a task to do, but little power and very little budget and human resources with which to fulfill it.[25] As eloquently phrased by Rivka Shaked, the general supervisor, in yet another Knesset discussion of the grim data, "we were given responsibility, but no authority nor resources."[26] Symbolically, the general supervisor herself was not promoted to a position of senior director; she is therefore not part of the decision-making organ in the service and does not participate in policy and operative debates that affect the whole subject she is in charge of.[27] None of the supervisors are authorized to intervene in the workings of the tender committees, and no penalty can be imposed on officials who disregard the law of adequate representation. All these observations point out that the impediments to the advancement of women will not go away through such a narrow legal reform alone. The establishment of a special agency without affording it the means of operation raises doubts as to the sincerity of the step. Battling the impediments requires an even firmer legal reform that gives concrete means for inspecting its implementation and for redressing its violations, accompanied by a thorough educational campaign to remove gender biases and prejudice and to empower women.

Women as Agents of Change

In examining the extent of Israeli women's role as agents of social change, it is worthwhile to use sociologist Hanna Herzog's method of placing the operation of women's organizations within the context of politics, and analyzing them as political action, no less than women's activities within the traditional political establishment (Herzog 1999, 312–13). This methodology is especially significant in the Israeli context, where women's organizations have always played a fundamental role in society in general, and for the advancement of women in particular. It demonstrates the fact that women have always been doing politics, albeit not in the conventional sense. When juxtaposing women's doings through women's associations with the previous chronology of official government operation for the advancement of women, women's role as agents of social change is revealed in its full scope.

Women's Organizations in Israel

Women's organizations have been the subject of much academic interest and research (Izraeli 1988; Azmon 1993; B. Swirski 1993a; Wenzel 1996). The most comprehensive work in this area is that of sociologist Yael Yishai (1997), analyzing Israeli women's dilemma: whether to focus on women's rights and feminism or to show national allegiance and fulfill the desire to belong and integrate from within. Most researchers agree that despite the large number of women's associations in Israel, Israeli women do not appear to represent a decisive political force in society as a whole. This relative powerlessness, Yishai suggests, can be attributed largely to the priority traditionally given by all—including women—to building and strengthening the national-political entity—a priority coming at the expense of a particular feminist voice in Israeli society (Yishai 1997, 57). Perhaps another reason can be suggested. In recent years, the general evolution affecting Israeli society as a whole, moving from collectivism to particularism, and contemplating the identity of a multicultural society (Eisenstadt 1985; Mautner 1993, 122–41), seem to point in the direction of increased openness to new trends and ideas, allowing for more women's voices to be heard in the present socio-political debate. At the same time, however, this increasing pluralism also affects the women's movement as such. As suggested by Herzog, this may weaken the movement, in making it impossible to gather around shared causes and find common interests. This obviously impedes on its capacity to become an influential political power (Herzog 1999, 353–54). This pluralism is reflected in this chapter as well, which starts by covering the more inclusive women's movement (since the pre-state era), moves on to women's political (in the sense of national politics) activism, and concludes with a discussion of more particular groups of women, including minorities and other groups with distinct concerns.

When recognizing the significance of women's organizations in Israel, it is somewhat surprising, and certainly discouraging, to view the findings of a recent survey showing that only 7 percent of Israeli women belong to any organization and that most women are not aware of the organizations' activities and performance (Tzameret 1999). Yishai suggests that a partial explanation is the organizations' traditional image as service providers, catering to women's needs, mainly as mothers.[28] In other words, following up on Yishai's general thesis, Israeli women's organizations are still perceived mostly as part of the political establishment, concentrating on traditional familial women's needs, not as carrying the banner of feminism.

Jewish Women's Organizations in Pre-State Palestine and Their Evolution in the Israeli Context

Social historians agree that women militants seeking equal political participation for men and women in the Yishuv—the Jewish communities of pre-state Palestine—were not able to garner significant support for their demands (Bernstein 1992; Izraeli 1990). The battle over the ballot, which ended in 1925, was certainly an impressive achievement, but it did not serve as a turning point in gender politics in pre-Israel society. As early as the 1930s, liberal demands for equal political participation were overshadowed by the Zionist concept of the Socialist Labor Movement, which demanded that all workers, men and women alike, devote themselves utterly to building a Jewish political entity. The Yishuv's suffragettes thus increasingly withdrew from the political scene, eventually giving way to women's organizations concentrating primarily on domestic matters (Wenzel 1996, 8). Even within the workers' movement, women's voices were more often than not toned down. Not only did women militants within the labor movement never choose to consider themselves a separate political faction (Wenzel 1996, 13), in fact they even repeatedly declared their loyalty to future state institutions like the Histadrut—the labor movement's Labor Federation—rarely demanding influence or voicing demands specific to women. While lip service was frequently paid to the need to prevent socioeconomic discrimination of female workers, David Ben Gurion (the central political figure of the Zionist Labor Movement and Israel's first prime minister) and the labor movement's leadership increasingly stigmatized appeals for a separate women's movement as unrealistic, radical, and disruptive to the social consensus within the Yishuv.

To preclude their marginalization, the Israeli women's organizations generally avoided declaring that they represented the specific political interests of women. These organizations appeared as the direct heirs of the Zionist movement and thus reflected their traditional partisan divisions. To this day, the religious women's movement Emunah is associated with the National Religious Party; the National Labor Unions women's division Isha haLeumit with Herut, the Revisionist wing of the right-wing Likud; Tandi with the Communist Party (Hadash); and the largest movement, Na'amat (formerly Moetzet haPoalot), with the Labor Party. Only WIZO, the Women's International Zionist Organization of America, never had any affiliation to political parties in Israel (Yishai 1997, 61). Initially at least, these organizations effectively played the part of "women's sections" of the various political parties, and were also responsible for attracting women voters. As such, they were made accountable for the party's image in the area of women's political interests and the interests of the female party members, but did not usually help bring about any marked improvement in women's intraparty situation (Wenzel 1996, 21–22).

With time, instead of serving as a tool to restructure the division of political power and labor, these women's organizations made temporary respite to working mothers their primary commitment, by taking care of their children. Na'amat, the Movement of Working Women and Volunteers, today the largest women's movement in Israel (founded in 1976 through the merging of Moetzet haPoalot and the Association of Working Mothers), is a case in point of the role of traditional women's organizations in Israel. Inheriting the ethos of the socialist Zionist women's movement in the Yishuv, Na'amat's goal is defined by the desire to encourage women to engage in productive work. By attempting to offer every Israeli woman full-day nursery care for her children, they have effectively defined the care of young children as a role for women's organizations. With more than half of childcare in Israel under their wings, women's organizations in Israel have in essence allowed the state to renounce its role in financing and equipping child-care centers (Pope 1993, 228–29).

Thus Na'amat and similar organizations present a feminist agenda on the one hand, by promoting women's political participation and economic independence, while on the other hand stopping short of criticizing the sociopolitical consequences of the reproductive role to which women have to bow because of their work in the areas of childcare and running a household (Yishai 1997, 67).

The Women's Liberation Movement

Unlike the traditional women's welfare organizations, later feminist movements have sought not only to eliminate all discrimination against women, but also to promote a fundamental modification in social structures of power. Unlike the Woman's Liberation movements in the United States and Western Europe that found legitimacy in the context of flourishing protest movements, the first Israeli feminists were confronted from the start with widespread mistrust. In the early 1970s their call for sociopolitical changes ran the risk of being perceived as an attack on national security rather than as a proposal for reform. Indeed, to some extent the failure of the Israeli feminist movement to grow into a national movement can be ascribed to the attempt by certain sections in the movement to place its protest against the sociopolitical discrimination of women in the context of a struggle against all forms of oppression, demanding that women's liberation express solidarity with the Palestinian people (Wenzel 1996, 28–30). At a time when Israeli society had trouble addressing Palestinian identity and suffering, this became a major point of conflict between the forces that stressed their solidarity with the Palestinian liberation movement and a majority of the feminists who felt an obligation to women's liberation only (B. Swirski 1993a, 298). These gaps also harmed the legitimacy of the movement as a whole in the eyes of the wider public.

Despite this barrage of suspicion, the feminist movement was among the first to protest its dissatisfaction with the sociopolitical situation in Israel. Refusing to give the question of national security and uniformity priority, it instead declared self-development to be a sociopolitical goal. The advent of the first feminist consciousness-raising groups allowed a new understanding of women's political and social domination by men. Among other issues, it exposed the central place of the Israeli army in forming political leadership, through the creation of an "old boy network" in effect closed to women (Wenzel 1996, 20). Eventually, issues and problems such as illegal abortions, domestic abuse, gender wage gaps, and more—to which most Israelis had closed their eyes for years—were brought to light by the feminist movement. The feminist movement was also a primary contributor to establishing the first battered women's shelters (Wenzel 1996, 29–33; B. Swirski 1989).

The feminist movement became especially active in expanding women's political status in Israel. In this spirit, the IWN was founded in 1984 as an expression of the solidarity of women MKs of various political factions with the feminist demand for an improvement in the "status of women" (Yishai 1997, 71). This organization has come to function as a political lobby and, at the same time, as a network working toward improving the status of women in Israel. It has set up specialist committees on topics of health, law, municipal and parliamentary work, and violence in the family; held leadership training courses for women local politicians; and established a nonparty forum of women MKs. In the 1990s, the IWN also exerted substantial influence in matters relating to legal precedent and legislation, as seen throughout this book. In effect, the organization has achieved a monopoly in terms of promoting women's political participation, and some contend that this is to a certain extent at the expense of less powerful grassroots organizations (Wenzel 1996, 38). Moreover, some have claimed that Israeli feminism, epitomized by the IWN, has been reduced to a list of reforms, an enterprise concerned with adding "the women's component" to existing institutions but lacking a vision of society in which relations between women and men are basically different. Moreover, the feminist movement is increasingly perceived as being an elitist movement largely disconnected from the grass roots (Swirski 1993a, 300). The use of this term, which is conventionally reserved for the political establishment, is in itself an indication of discontent with the situation, designating such successful organizations as the IWN as being in fact part of the system. The growth of more specified groups discussed below should be viewed in this light.

Women's Extra-Parliamentary Political Activism and Women's Movements for Peace

The women's peace movements of the 1980s and 1990s represent an exception to this "feminism from above," having started from the grass roots to spread into wide sectors of Israeli society.

From the outset, women were actively involved in movements such as Shalom Achshav (Peace Now) whose aim was to pressure the Israeli government to consider constructive peace proposals, but separate women's organizations in favor of peace began making their mark especially with the advent of the war in Lebanon. As early as 1982, following the "Peace for Galilee" operation in Lebanon, women were at the forefront of two organizations—Parents Against Silence and Women Against the Invasion of Lebanon—demanding the immediate withdrawal of Israeli troops from Lebanon (Gillath 1993, 142–46). The Intifada (the Palestinian national uprising of the late 1980s and early 1990s) triggered the formation of several women's peace movements, most famous of them Women in Black, who gathered every Friday afternoon at a central square in Jerusalem. Their quiet protest often generated angry reactions from passersby, who viewed them as traitors (Helman and Rapoport 1997). Gradually, women's peace activism took on an added dimension. Inspired by the idea that women are genuinely more peace-loving and committed to a different drive to preserve human life (Wenzel 1996, 46), women's peace organizations began underlining the impact of the politico-military balance in Israel on the sociopolitical situation of women. In their eyes, the search for peace became linked to the larger goal of changing the structure and priorities of the societies in which

Israeli and Palestinian women were living. Thus, beyond protesting Israel's military policy in the occupied West Bank and Gaza Strip, Israeli women's organizations began showing solidarity with Palestinian efforts to achieve national self-determination and respect for their national dignity (Wenzel 1996, 44; Emmett 1996). In this context, organizations were founded such as the Women's Organization for Political Prisoners, which concentrated on the fate of individual Palestinian women and continually brought human rights violations in military jails to the attention of the Israeli public.

Many of the women's peace groups and activities were guided by the more general attempt to establish and institutionalize a Palestinian-Israeli dialogue. For this purpose in particular, women's organizations in Israel such as Reshet—the Israel Women's Peace Net—organized encounters of Israeli and Palestinian activists, joint conferences as well as visits to families, with personal conversations as a tool to eliminate the stereotyped prejudices (Hazan 1993, 155). The efforts of Israeli women to participate and influence the peace process continued after the Oslo Accords were signed in September 1993, and have been felt through the establishment of such organizations as the Jerusalem Link, a coordinating committee of two women's centers, one Jewish and the other Arab, protesting human rights violations and more generally concerned with promoting feminist ideas in the Israeli and Palestinian public.

Formed during a period of structural change within Israeli society, these women's peace movements were largely spared the stigma of anti-Zionism and hence sociopolitical insignificance. Indeed, movements such as Women in Black gradually became an embodiment of peaceful protest that was widely approved and imitated (Hazan 1993, 154). The Israeli women's peace movement managed, through various interlinked organizations, to establish a nationwide network and uniquely coordinate local activities transcending traditional partisan politics (Wenzel 1996, 48). This transcending of partisan politics and the mobilization of wider groups in society, both men and women, has also characterized Arba Imahot (the Four Mothers) the most recent incarnation of women's peace movement which led the struggle for Israel's withdrawal from Lebanon in May 2000.

Representation of Minorities and Subgroups in the Women's Movements in Israel

Up until the early 1980s, "improving the status of women" had been neutrally perceived as a slogan applying to all women regardless of cultural, ethnic, religious, sexual orientation or other social distinction. Hence, feminist activities in Israel frequently failed to address the specific circumstances of various population groups. During the 1980s, in parallel with growing criticism of the sociopolitical domination of Ashkenazi Jews (the Jews from Central and Eastern Europe) within Israeli society, some feminists began arguing that "improving the status of women" was all too often equated with the specific struggles of the hegemonic educated and affluent women of European American origin, who make up a minority within Israeli society (Shiran 1993, 308). There were growing calls for feminist organizations that would relate to the specific situation of non-Ashkenazi women and, moreover, to non-Jewish women in Israel. The discussion that follows parallels, to some extent, the discussion in Chapter 12, which addresses various groups of women in Israel, who in one sense or another, challenge the hegemonic perspective.[29]

The Palestinian Women's Movement

Arab women's organizations in pre-1948 Palestine such as the Arab Women's Committee and the Arab Executive Committee were set up as early as the British mandate period. They usually did not make demands specific to women but served mostly to provide political support for the male-led rebellion and foster the construction of a national Palestinian identity. After the foundation of Israel in 1948, these organizations disbanded and in their stead, organizations dominated by Jewish women—Na'amat and WIZO—set up women's leagues and day care centers in Arab villages. During this time only the Movement of Democratic Women in Israel—Tandi, founded in 1951 as the women's organization of the Communist Party—offered Palestinian women the possibility of political involvement. Like other political parties' women's divisions, Tandi often merely represented the female party members and ensured that the public knew of their welfare-oriented activities, while granting women little real influence within the party itself (Wenzel 1996, 40–41).

The 1967 Six Day War reunited the Palestinians in Israel with the most important segments of the Palestinian people, and a process of re-Palestinization ensued. In the 1970s, imitating general organizations of Palestinians in Israel, Palestinian women began to organize in order to counter deficiencies caused by Israeli government policy, primarily in the under-financed area of education, and with housing policy issues. In 1975, for example, a women's organization was founded in Acre, soon setting up an organization for the education of young children, Dar al-Tifle al-Arabi, which was to run vocational courses. These followed the idea that only the economic and intellectual freedom of Palestinian women could ensure any successful political and social involvement (Mar'i and Mar'i 1993, 219–20). During the 1980s, beyond offering important services for women in the area of educational work, these organizations also became catalysts for the growing self-awareness of Palestinian women in Israel. Parallel to that, the 1980s saw an increased involvement of Palestinian women in Israel in Jewish-Arab coeducation work. In the women's organization HaGesher (The Bridge), as well as the Project for the Advancement and Involvement of Women (Kidma)—affiliated with Haifa University—discussion groups for Jewish and Arab (Palestinian, Druze, Bedouin) women were set up (Hazan 1993, 154). Similarly, cooperation between Jewish and Arab women in different realms began to appear in the established women's organizations like Na'amat, WIZO and the IWN.

Increasingly, however, some Palestinian women began viewing these Jewish-led women's organizations as a form of tutelage. During the Intifada, the need to debate the specific Palestinian situation of gender iniquities grew constantly in response to escalating conservatism and Islamic fundamentalism and acts of violence against women in Palestinian society. The 1990-established Gafra, the Movement of Palestinian Women in Israel, stated its goal as improving women's situation politically, socially, economically, and culturally. Currently it is campaigning against the widespread convention of arranged marriages and offers a forum to women who are subjected to acts of violence in their own families (Wenzel 1996, 43). The more radical Movement of Palestinian Feminists—Al-Fanar (the Lighthouse), has gone as far as considering acts of violence against women to be an integral part of the patriarchal structure of Palestinian society (Yishai 1997, 85). Together, these organizations have struggled to inform Arab women of their right to control their own bodies and determine their own sexuality.

Yet today's Palestinian women's activism is largely tied in with political demands directed at the Israeli public as a whole. Indeed, current Palestinian feminists see the sociopolitical discrimination of the Palestinian population in Israel as being largely responsible for the forms of discrimination suffered specifically by Palestinian women. According to them, only a completely restructured Israeli society can ensure Arab women's emancipation from the male-dominated balance of power surrounding them. This position is well reflected in the important initiative that took place in relation to Israel reporting to the CEDAW committee, in the form of a national network of Palestinian NGO representatives and activists that established the Working Group on the Status of Palestinian Women in Israel, comprised of several organizations, including the Association of Women Against Violence (WAV), Al-Tufula Pedagogical Center, and the Haifa Rape Crisis Center. It was formed in 1996, following the submission of Israel's Report to the CEDAW committee, for the purpose of submitting an alternative (or "shadow") report. In that shadow report the Working Group had indeed presented the case of Palestinian women in Israel as suffering from a three-tiered discrimination: as women in Israel, as Palestinians in Israel, and as women in Palestinian society.[30] Some critiques of such an approach, however, warn that it also entails a risk: If the Palestinian women's movement appears to dedicate itself entirely to the national liberation movement, it might neglect the struggle for change within the male-dominated Israeli-Palestinian society (Wenzel 1996, 44).

The Emergence of Mizrachi Women's Organizations

Another expression of women's groups seeking to trace a link between gender and cultural, social and national identity was seen in 1989, with the establishment of a Mizrachi (Jews whose origins are in the orient) Jewish women's consciousness-raising group, Nashim Mizrachiot. Initially set up to analyze the status of the cultural identity of oriental women, it was on its initiative that, in 1992, affirmative action was granted to members of specific minority groups within the Annual Feminist Conference (Wenzel 1996, 54). The formation of such a group is in fact an expression of deep discontent within the larger feminist movement. Mizrachi feminists instituted their own First Mizrachi Feminist Conference in 1996 (Dahan-Kalev 1999, 251–55). Presently, an increasing number of women who identify first as Mizrachiot are voicing their doubts about cooperation with feminists of different national, cultural, and social population groups. The widespread idea that shared gender identity is sufficient to bridge cultural differences is being labeled as the unequivocal indication of the domination of Ashkenazi women in the feminist movement (Shiran 1993).

This development (discussed broadly again in Chapter 12) now imposes an urgent debate to define feminist awareness in Israel today. Beyond defining the point of cooperation of women from different national, cultural, and social affinities, this discussion—so it is claimed—must question some of the most basic feminist assumptions, including the very assumption that "male domination" is the sole source of discrimination suffered by women. The emergence of Mizrachi feminism is now taken as representing the shattering of the abstract illusion of "sisterhood." Moreover, in building upon Black feminist writings and theory, not only is oppression not perceived to be a sufficient connection between women who have nothing in common, it is also claimed to exist among women themselves: oppression of Mizrachi women by their Ashkenazi counterparts (Dahan-Kalev 1997).

The Emergence of a Religious Women's Movement

Another expression of the trend toward more particularism and away from collectivism can be seen in the 1998 formation of a religious women's movement. In choosing the name Kolech ("your voice" in the feminine form, a quote from Song of Songs 2:14 "let me hear thy voice; for sweet [is] thy voice"), this movement strives toward inclusion of women into all areas and spheres of religious life and religious community. Unlike Emunah, its former counterpart, Kolech openly identifies itself as conforming with feminist ideology and is distinctly bipartisan and politically unaffiliated. In what can be seen as epitomizing the development toward multidimensional feminism within Israeli feminism, Kolech is laboring for the advancement of women both in the Orthodox religious community itself and in Israeli society in general. This movement cannot be separated from the changes that have taken place in Orthodox women's education, which truly amount to a revolution in women's learning (see Chapter 5). Women's entry into the world of advanced Jewish studies, including study of Gemara (Jewish Oral Law), from which they have been historically excluded, has sharpened the discrepancy between women's position in general society and their position in religious life, and has generated energy and urgency in changing their position. Undoubtedly, the familiar process by which gaining knowledge leads to claims for power can be traced here, as well as influences from the United States, where the feminist revolution has already penetrated modern Orthodox circles. As this is indeed a fairly recent development, it is only beginning to produce academic research and writing (El-Or 1998; Shilo 2001), as well as provoking interest in popular media.[31]

Apart from this wide, all-encompassing movement, religious women have been advancing other, more specific, feminist initiatives. A case at point is the Jerusalem Crisis Center for Religious Women, established to provide emotional support and advice for Orthodox and ultra-Orthodox women, who usually would not turn to other existing help centers or welfare authorities. The center operates a twenty-four-hour hot line in addition to offering workshops to the religious community and engaging in activities to facilitate relations between the ultra-Orthodox community and the secular state institutions in the area of domestic and gender-based violence. During 1993–99 the center handled over 5,000 cases, with a sharp increase in 1999. Recently, the center has begun workshops for rabbis who serve as informal religious community leaders and whose influence on the ultra-Orthodox community is quite vast.[32] Even if such specific initiatives are not self-identified with feminism, their emergence cannot be separated from the growing feminist awareness among religious women and the overall process Israeli feminism is undergoing that leads to realizing the need for independent action by nondominant groups with particular needs and concerns.

Part II
Progress and the Limits of the Law

Chapter 4
Women and Health Care

Health services in Israel are provided to all residents. The level of care ranks favorably with that of Western countries, with high life expectancy and low infant mortality. There is no formal discrimination against women regarding health care, nor are treatments for Israeli women, including birth control, contingent upon the approval or permission of their partners or parents. However, factors ranging from male bias in medical research and treatment to the lack of female decision-makers in the field have put women at a disadvantage in some areas. After the 1995 UN/NGO Fourth World Conference on Women in Beijing, women's health was placed on Israel's national agenda; women's health centers now exist in every major hospital, the ministry of health established a steering committee on women's health needs and appointed a counselor to the minister on women's issues, and the National Center for Disease Control appointed a special researcher to collect data on women's health. The steering committee was made into a National Council on Woman's Health in early 2000. The post of the minister's counselor, however, is a without pay. This chapter examines various palliative and preventive health care services available to Israeli women, as well as the relative states of health of men and women in Israel, focusing specifically on reproductive health.

Women's health is part of the first dimension of women's situation described in Chapter 1, involving the basic quality of life—life expectancy, maternal and infant mortality, levels of literacy, fertility rates, and so on. This chapter describes the satisfying achievements made on this level. Nevertheless, an examination of this parameter supports the contention offered in Chapter 1 that women's progress is incidental to general progress on the basic level. This is revealed by the fact that women's particular health needs and concerns currently remain unanswered. Furthermore, a comparative perspective also reveals consistent gaps between the relative situation of men and women in terms of health indicators, to the detriment of women. Whatever progress *has* been made has not been a result of an undertaking for the advancement of women.

As with all the topics covered in this book, information is very much "the name of the game." Until quite recently, not much was known of women's health in Israel (Avgar 1997; Swirski, Knaaneh, and Avgar 1999). Some general conclusions could be made: although women live longer than men, they suffer more sicknesses and chronic illnesses and report lower physical and mental health than men. In terms of research and information, two important developments have taken place: the Israel Women's Network (IWN) together with the Hadassah Institute published a resource book on women's health in Israel, gathering all available information and data on the subject (IWN 1999); and the JDC-Brookdale Institute conducted a national survey, collecting for the first time data on women's health and welfare and women's experiences with the Israeli health care system (Gross and Brammli-Greenberg 2000). The survey was a joint enterprise conducted in cooperation with the U.S. Commonwealth Fund, thus providing for comparative perspective and a broader understanding of the findings. Both initiatives support previous assessments of women's lower health status and stress the importance of continuous research and dissemination of information among health professionals, policy makers, and health care recipients themselves.

General Health Care Services

The foundations for public health care in Israel were laid down in the 1940 National Health Ordinance.[1] In the mid-1990s, two laws relating to public health changed the health care framework. The 1994 National Health Insurance Law establishes a universal right to health services, and the 1996 Patient's Rights Law grants statutory recognition to patients' rights and physicians' duties.[2]

The National Health Insurance Law restructured the Israeli health care system by securing the right of every Israeli resident to health care services, with the principles of "justice, equality, and mutual aid"[3] providing the basis for its enactment. The law ensures the application of these principles by requiring health funds to accept all applicants and provide them with a "basic basket of services."[4] Responsibility for mother-child clinics was to be transferred to the various health funds, but a 1996 amendment was added to maintain the government's direct responsibility for the provision of the clinics and to ensure universal mother and child care irrespective of economic considerations.[5]

The government finances the health services using the budget allocated to it under the law. Every adult is obligated to pay a health tax—a progressive tax based on income—to cover the cost of provision of basic services. Homemakers, or "housewives," however, are exempt from paying the tax. The National Insurance Law defines a "housewife" as a "married woman whose partner is insured and who only provides domestic provisions for their own household, so that she is neither an 'employee' nor 'independent.'"[6] The "housewife" exclusion stems from the fact that the health tax is collected and handled as part of the Social Security system. Since "housewives" have not been paying National Insurance dues according to the National Insurance Law, they are not included in the Social Security databases.

While the new law ensures equality between men and women by charging married working women and men equal membership dues, some married women who work outside their homes pay more for coverage under the new law than they paid under the old law: under the old law families were charged as single units, with married women receiving a 30 percent discount on their dues (Adva Center 1996).

Equality in Health Care

Under the new law, most health care services are included in the basic basket of services. Falling outside the basket, however, is a range of gynecological services including coverage for contraceptives and abortions performed on the grounds of age (the woman being over forty) or extramarital pregnancy (constituting the major cause for legal abortions, for reasons explained in Chapter 11) (Swirski, Ka'naaneh, and Avgar 1999, 13). Also excluded are several medications for treating two gender-related illnesses: breast cancer and osteoporosis. Breast cancer is the major cause of death among young women in Israel (Ifrah 1999), and osteoporosis affects women over sixty-five four times more than it affects men over sixty-five—24 percent and 6 percent respectively (Ben-Moshe, Brodeski, and Rozin 1999, 1). Women's groups and the mass media have helped spark a public outcry over the lack of treatment. In a move perhaps influenced by this uproar, the Gertner Institute for Epidemiology and Health Policy Research, a research institute supported by the Ministry of Health, convened a Consensus Conference to publicly discuss the inclusion of specific medications for osteoporosis (alendronate and raloxifan). The conference took place in December 1999 and its recommendations were presented to the public committee in charge of forming the basic basket of services.[7] In January 2000, the committee decided to include these medications, as well as the expensive Herceptin, a novel anticancer therapy approved by the FDA in 1998 (Hakimian 2000).[8]

Another source of inequality in the health care system is the lack of awareness of gender differences in the symptoms and development of specific maladies such as heart disease. For example, standard cardiac diagnostic tools for heart disease among men are not effective in the diagnosis of women. Heart disease among women develops at a significantly slower rate than among men, and doctors are more reluctant to perform the standard tests on women who present with chest pains. As a result, women are diagnosed at later stages of the disease, when surgery is less likely to be successful. The rate of death from heart disease and complications from bypass surgery among women is two to three times higher than among men (Greenland et al. 1991; Tzivoni 1991; Ra'anan 1998).

Special Health Concerns and Services for Women

Prenatal Health, Birth, and Childcare Services

Mother-child clinics offer high quality, relatively cheap pre- and postnatal care.[9] In 1994, 435 such clinics were in full operation. Despite recent attempts to shift the focus of mother-child clinics from pregnant women to family health, the main focus continues to be on childbearing.

The Ministry of Health has only recently begun to change work and hospitalization conditions in maternity wards. And yet there has been a sharp rise in overall births: 15 percent from 1993 to 1998. The Ministry of Health reported a dramatic 46 percent increase during that five-year period in the number of infants with birth weights of 1,500 grams and less.[10] This sharp rise in births, with its high percentage of infants requiring intensive care, has stretched Israel's maternity wards, delivery rooms, and pediatric intensive care units well beyond capacity. In 1996, the National Council of Midwives and Gynecologists presented a report to the Ministry of Health that exposed serious malfunctions in delivery rooms.[11] Despite the critique, a study of 1,760 women giving birth in hospitals found 70 percent of the women reporting high levels of satisfaction, highest among women who reported a high degree of control in decision-making and intervention and receiving precise information from a medical staff (Ivancovsky et al. 1996).

Geriatric Services and Elderly Women

In 1998, the average life span for Israeli women was 80.3 years, and for men 76.1 years.[12] While women are longer lived than men throughout the industrialized world, Israeli women maintain a smaller life-span advantage than do their counterparts in other countries. Compared with twenty-three other Western countries, Israeli men ranked third for longevity (after Japan and Sweden), while Israeli women came in sixteenth.[13] However, women comprise 57 percent of all Israelis over sixty-five and make up 70 percent of all hospitalized patients in geriatric hospitals (S. Swirski, San-Zangi, and B. Swirski 1996, 14).

Geriatric care is an area of specific concern. The cost of temporary hospitalization for senior citizens is currently covered by the basic basket of services, but the expense of extended hospitalizations of senior citizens is not. The differences in coverage are explained as part of a governmental policy of caring for the "regular elderly" who require nursing care or are mentally frail through the community rather than through geriatric institutions. Researchers advocate care within the community over institutional care, viewing it as both less expensive and qualitatively better than institutional care since it does not require removing the patient from her environment. The National Insurance Law provides a monthly allowance for the elderly (defined as men over sixty-five and women over sixty) who are in need of a personal caretaker. In 1998, women comprised close to 73 percent of the 81,000 recipients of long-term care benefits.[14] One aspect of "communal care" not reflected in statistical findings is that usually the "community" amounts to just one person, either a relative or a professional caregiver. The rise in popularity of professional caregivers has created a profitable new industry in Israel, in which agencies import foreign workers, most of them women from the Philippines. Government allowances for hiring a caretaker are given directly to these agencies, which usually keep half the money as fees for their services (B. Swirski, San-Zangi, and B. Swirski 1996, 19).

Researchers note that elderly women's quality of life is generally worse than that of elderly men (information based on Ben-Moshe, Brodeski, and Rozin 1999). They point to differences in health factors such as chronic disease (such as high blood pressure and osteoporosis), in addition to subjective perceptions of health status: 44 percent of men but only 30 percent of women over sixty-five described their health as being "good" or "very good."

Eating Disorders

As in all industrialized countries, Israeli women and girls are at high risk for eating disorders, with intense pressure to meet an elusive and unhealthy ideal of thinness. For teenagers, Israel seems to be the dieting capital of the world: in 1994, about one in three teenage girls reported dieting to lose weight. This finding put Israel ahead of twenty-three other developed countries for dieting among teenage girls. The writers in *Women's Health in Israel* warn that "before real changes can be brought about, a shift has to take place in the sociocultural values that emphasize extreme thinness in women" (Ifrah 1999, 150).

Mental Health and Psychiatric Hospitalization

In 1995, women comprised 44 percent of all psychiatric hospitalizations. The rate of hospitalized men exceeded the rate of hospitalized women until the ages of 45 (Ifrah 1999, 113). Hospitalization rates for attempted suicide and self-inflicted injury are higher for women than for men of all age groups, except for those over seventy-five, for whom rates are identical. Women comprise 60–65 percent of reported attempted suicides. In the younger age groups, over 80 percent of attempted suicides during 1990–1996 were female. While attempted suicide is reported more frequently among women, rates for accomplished suicides are higher among men. In 1995 for example, 9.4 completed suicides per 100,000 men were reported, compared with 3.7 per 100,000 women (Ifrah 1999, 150–51).

Violence as a Health Factor

Violence against women is recognized as an important factor in women's state of physical and mental health. Most domestic violence takes the form of rape and physical abuse. Contrary to the vague situation in the past, the National Health Law covers any and all medical expenses incurred as a result of physical or sexual violence against women. According to the WHO Regional Office for Europe, Israeli women were ranked in 1992 close to the European Union's average with respect to mortality from homicide and purposeful injury (Ifrah 1999, 19). The 2000 Brookdale survey provided for the first time formal findings of the extent of physical and sexual violence against women, and of domestic violence against women in Israel (Gross and Brammli-Greenberg 2000, 49, 54). According to the survey, 2 percent of all adult women in Israel (34,000) were victims of rape, 4 percent (68,000) were victims of sexual violence, and 8 percent (136,000) were victims of physical violence. More than one in every ten women (11.5 percent) experienced some form of domestic violence, ranging from threats to physical or sexual attacks. This amounts to about 200,000 women, a number often cited by informal estimations of women's organizations and government forums that deal with domestic violence. Gross and Brammli-Greenberg emphasize that these data should be taken as minimum estimates.

The Ministry of Health has established a database in 27 of the 33 general hospitals of women and children admitted to emergency wards with injuries following domestic violence and neglect and who were subsequently referred to social services. In 1998, 1,512 women aged eighteen to sixty-four, 131 women over age sixty-five, and 1,860 children were admitted to emergency rooms as a result of violence. Among women under age sixty-five, the overwhelming majority of the cases (89 percent) were of physical abuse. Among older women (over sixty-five), just over half were cases of physical abuse; 35 percent were cases of neglect or withholding of care. Of the children, just over half (52 percent) were girls. Among younger children (0–5), a slightly higher proportion of children reaching the emergency room (55 percent) were boys, predominantly as a result of neglect and withholding of care. In the six to fourteen age group, 55 percent were girls. The category with the largest sex difference was that of sexual abuse, where twice as many girls as boys were victims. Among adolescents (15–18) girls predominated in all categories of abuse, with the exception of the neglect category (Ifrah 1999, 166–67).

AIDS

The total number of AIDS patients in Israel during 1999 was 622 (494 male and 128 female). That year, 440 of these patients died. There were 2,078 known cases of HIV-positive individuals in Israel in 1999. Of these, 34 percent (707) were women, a definite increase from 1995, when women comprised 26 percent of HIV-positive individuals. Most of these women had contracted the virus outside Israel. Since the first statistical documentation of AIDS in Israel in the early 1980s, the proportion of HIV-positive females has increased significantly, especially since 1992.[15]

Family Planning and Reproduction

Abortions

There are no abortions on demand in Israel, as Israeli law treats abortion as a criminal offense. However, the 1977 Penal Law,[16] sections 312–21, provides for abortions upon the permission of a designated committee in the following cases:

1. The woman is under the legal age for marriage or over 40.
2. The pregnancy is the result of sexual relations forbidden under the criminal code, or of incestuous or extramarital relations.
3. The unborn child will be physically or mentally disabled.
4. The continuation of pregnancy will endanger the life of the mother or may cause her either physical or mental damage.

Originally, the law contained a fifth proviso for approval, termed the "socioeconomic" clause, providing for termination of pregnancy in cases when "the continuation of the pregnancy will gravely harm the woman or her children, for reasons of difficult family or social circumstances of the woman and her company." This clause was the subject of continuing political debate on the basis of religious objection to abortion and was finally repealed in 1979 (Yishai 1997, 217–22).[17] Statistically this repeal has made no difference, and the number of abortions has actually increased. Social concerns have been disguised under the clauses permitting abortions on health grounds (Yishai 1997, 221). There are no criminal sanctions against women who undergo illegal abortions. Although the law penalizes doctors who perform the illegal procedures, criminal proceedings have been extremely rare. Of the committee-approved abortions, only those performed for medical reasons, or when the woman is a minor, are covered by medical insurance as part of the basic basket of health services.

The Committee for Approval of Termination of Pregnancies is composed of two doctors and a social worker, one of whom must be a woman. By 2000, 42 such committees were operating.[18] The only approval required for the abortion is that of the committee, even if the woman concerned is a minor. Upon applying to the committee, the woman seeking the abortion must meet with a social worker, who is instructed by law to explain the physical and mental dangers of abortion.[19] A little-known fact is that the social worker is instructed by the Ministry of Health to attempt to convince the woman to choose an alternative solution to terminating the unwanted pregnancy.[20] The woman must then meet with a doctor, who is also instructed to explain the risks involved in termination of pregnancy, and only then meets with the committee.[21] The committee must review the reports of both the doctor and the social worker before making a decision. In practice, a woman seeking an abortion meets first with the social worker (almost always a woman), and is asked about the circumstances of conception and her contraceptive practices. A study of 13 committees found social workers considered it their duty to convince women to use contraceptives regularly.

Since 1980, the number of legal abortions performed in Israel has fluctuated between an estimated 14,000 and 19,000 a year.[22] The number of abortions performed in 1999 remained within this bracket: 18,785, accounting for 12.2 percent of total known pregnancies that year.[23]

In the second half of the 1990s, a slight change seems to have occurred in the proportions of approvals per application and actual abortions performed. While in the early 1990s, 91 percent of the applications were approved and 94 percent of those approved were actually performed, by 1999 the rate of approval reached 95.6 percent, and the rate of performance 95.5 percent. Central Bureau of Statistics in-depth research into the demographic and social characteristics of applicants to the committees suggests against concluding that the committees' policy has changed, but rather attributes the rate difference to prior selection conducted by the social worker before the application actually reaches the committee.[24] The ratio of the various clauses for approval has remained unchanged: extramarital pregnancy remains the major reason for approving termination of pregnancy, consistently comprising more than 40 percent of the approvals since the late 1980s, reaching more than 50 percent in 1998.[25]

It is difficult to account precisely for the number of illegal abortions in Israel, yet the current estimate of the Israel Family Planning Association stands at 4,000–6,000 abortions per year. Researchers have noted that the numbers have risen significantly following the recent wave of immigration from the former USSR. Many immigrant women are relatively uninformed about birth control and are accustomed to receiving abortions on demand.[26]

Pronatalism and Family Planning in Israel

The family and its reproductive functions occupy a central place in Israeli society. Strong religious influences, Jewish and Islamic, make fertility a major concern of many Israelis. The priority assigned to marriage and childbearing is rooted and deeply ingrained in religious values and in a concern for the continuity of the Jewish people (Berkovitch 1997; Yishai 1997; Fogiel-Bijaoui 1999). Inasmuch as religious and national concerns have been at the heart of the matter, familism and pronatalism have become a major cultural trait of the Israeli society, and childbearing is a prime value. Even immigrants from the former USSR, where the average is one child per family, have internalized the Israeli ethos, reflected in an increased rate of 1.8 children per family.[27]

Notwithstanding the pronatalist ethos, Israel has witnessed over the past twenty-five years a gradual expansion of family planning services in both the public and private health care sectors. Despite fairly universal health care coverage and the broad range of medical assistance provided in the basic basket of services, however, contraceptives continue to fall outside this basket.

The Israel Family Planning Association, a nonprofit association, has been actively engaged in performing services not provided by the health funds or governmental institutions. Since 1981, the association has operated walk-in counseling centers for adolescents facing social, psychological, and gynecological problems. Trained counselors give professional advice concerning contraceptive use, sexual relationships, and pregnancy. Gynecologists give periodic on-site examinations. According to the 1994 study of Health Behaviors in School-Aged Children, about 20 percent of Israeli tenth and eleventh graders reported having already had intercourse; 13 percent of boys and 16 percent of girls said the last time they had had sex was without contraception (Harel, Kanny, and Rahav 1997, 23).

Fertility Rates, Treatments, and Services

The absolute number of live births per year has increased from 80,843 in 1970 to 130,080 in 1998. The fertility rate (the average number of children a woman is expected to have in her lifetime), however, has decreased steadily among all population groups.[28]

The largest drop in fertility occurred among Druze women, from 7.2 in the late 1950s to 3.1 in 1998. The smallest drop was among Jewish women, from 3.6 in the late 1950s to 2.7 in 1998. Among Muslim women, the average fertility rate remains much higher than for Jewish women (2.7 versus 4.8 children in 1998), but still a significant drop from 8.2 in the late 1950s. Within the Jewish population, the largest drop in fertility occurred among women born in Europe and America (from 2.8 in the early 1980s to 2.3 in 1998), and the smallest among women born in Israel of African origins (from around 3 to 2.84). Significantly, the group of women who are Israeli born, whose origins are also Israeli, has actually experienced an increase in birth rates (from 2.7 in the early 1980s to 3 in 1998).[29] While all population groups have experienced consistent decrease in fertility rates from the early 1980s, this trend changed in the mid-1990s, and since then there has been a slow but steady increase back to the rates of the 1980s in all population groups but the Druze.[30] This shift has not yet been given a sociological explanation that would point to its cause, and it is perhaps too early to tell whether the mid-1990s indeed present a turning point.

When examining trends in fertility rates and family planning, special attention should be given to the Jewish ultra-Orthodox community. Economist Eli Berman (1998) found that ultra-Orthodox women's fertility rate increased from 6.5 in the mid-1980s to 7.6 in the mid-1990s. This is translated into a reality that is reflected in such striking data as the following. In the Jerusalem Sha'arei Tzedek hospital, where over 80 percent of the births to ultra-Orthodox women take place every year, about 40 women give birth to their sixteenth or seventeeth child, and about 180 give birth to their twelfth to fifteenth child. Current sociological research attributes this phenomenon to the substantial increase in child benefit subsidies given through the National Insurance Institute, which unproportionately favor the fourth child onward.[31] A 2000 amendment to the 1995 National Insurance Law that further raised subsidies to families with more than five children is causing a heated public debate over the appropriate policy regarding family planning.[32]

The phenomenon of single-motherhood by choice may be slowly but consistently growing. In the late 1970s, births to Jewish single women comprised only 1 percent of the overall births; the rate doubled in 1995; by 1997, births to single women made up 2.5 percent of all births to Jewish women.[33]

Fertility treatment in Israel is highly developed and subsidized. Israel currently boasts a world record of 22 in-vitro fertilization (IVF) clinics, about one such center for every 270,000 inhabitants. In May 1999, four more clinics were in the process of being approved, which would bring the rate to one center for every 230,000 inhabitants.[34] There is no limit to the number of treatments a woman may receive prior to conception, though the basic basket of services limits coverage up to the birth of two live children for a couple. While there is no clear definition of infertility in the regulations defining the basic basket, couples are generally eligible for treatment after one year of sexual relations without contraception failing to result in pregnancy. Although the overall number of deliveries resulting in live births has increased dramatically—from 542 in 1990 to 1,539 in 1995—the proportion of such deliveries to embryo transfers performed has remained a low 14 percent (Ifrah 1999, 43).

The cost covered by medical insurance for one cycle of treatment stood in 1999 at 12,000 NIS (about $2,800).[35] Moreover, unmarried women are now eligible for artificial insemination by donor as well as fertility treatments in accordance with the same provisions that apply to married women.[36]

Israel was the first country to sanction surrogacy and regulate it through the operation of an administrative (not judicial) organ, according to the 1996 Surrogate Motherhood Agreements (Approval of Agreements and Status of Newborn) Law.[37] By October 2000, 78 surrogacy agreements were approved, resulting in the birth of 26 children in 19 childbirths (due to the prevalence of twins). Two other surrogate mothers were pregnant at that time; 25 couples whose agreements had been approved terminated the process midway or completed a surrogacy process that did not result in a pregnancy.[38]

Recently, public attention was raised regarding the fertility treatment industry, when leading fertility clinicians were suspected of abusing (and endangering) patients by harvesting unjustifiably high numbers of ova and trading in them. The police, the Ministry of Health, and several health funds conducted investigations in numerous such complaints, and several civil suits have been filed.[39] The scandal has indeed come as a sad confirmation of the long-raised feminist critique of the new reproductive technologies and their male control, which are turning women into reproductive machines, leaving them no real choice but to succumb to the new technologies (Weisberg 1996).

Women in Health Care

Between 1969 and 1995, the number of women accepted to medical schools in Israel rose significantly, from 24 percent to 48 percent. Israeli women scored comparably to Israeli men in the National Medical Board examinations (Notzer and Brown 1995, 449). At the end of 1993, two-thirds of all doctors and dentists were male; 74 percent among specialists was 74. The highest rate of women specialists was in pediatrics (40 percent) and psychiatry (40 percent), followed by family medicine (35 percent). The lowest was in general surgery (5 percent), followed by obstetrics and gynecology (15 percent). While 43 percent of male doctors were specialists, only 29 percent all female doctors were specialists (Notzer and Brown 1995, 450). By 2000, women made up almost 50 percent of all medical students in Israel, a 10 percent rise in one decade, and comprised 68 percent of third degree medical students.[40]

The mass immigration to Israel from the former USSR has significantly changed the proportion of practicing doctors who are women in Israel, from 30 percent to 36 percent by 1995 (and 35 percent of all practicing dentists). By 2000, almost 37 percent of all practicing doctors in Israel were women (8,781 out of about 24,000),[41] but no woman headed a major hospital, one woman headed a peripheral mental hospital, one served as a deputy head of an intermediate size hospital, and four were administrative directors of hospitals.[42]

Israeli female physicians tend to work in clinics rather than hospitals; are less likely than men to specialize in surgery-related fields but rather concentrate in traditional health specialization such as family, children, and geriatric care. While the proportion of Israeli and American women who specialize in psychiatry and family medicine is similar, the proportion of women in the United States who specialize in internal medicine, children's medicine, surgery, and particularly gynecology, is significantly higher than the proportion of their Israeli counterparts. Although gynecology is predominantly occupied by women in Eastern Europe, the current wave of immigrants from the former USSR did not significantly alter the number of women gynecologists in Israel (Notzer and Brown 1995, 450). As shown in a study by Holzman and Izraeli (1999), examining women's massive entry into internal medicine compared to their low representation in gynecology, women can be expected to remain in the less technologically advanced fields with lower status patient populations, while men move on to occupy the more technologically advanced areas with more potential for profits. A different expression of women's lower status in the medical field is their salaries: women physicians in the government health services earn on average only 78 percent the salary of their male colleagues.[43]

Chapter 5
Education

Education is a prerequisite for success in modern society. Israel provides free compulsory education through high school, and women's status is relatively solid with regard to the elementary level of access to educational facilities, attendance rates, literacy, and even higher education. In this sense, Israeli women seem to fare well on the basic parameter of women's situation. However, as in other areas, the more advanced parameter is somewhat more problematic: classroom dynamics continue to reflect embedded stereotypes; women constitute a majority of students pursuing higher education, but remain a minority of university faculty members, particularly in the higher academic ranks. Thus, the two parameters that inform women's lives are both reflected within the field of education, and their internal gap is clearly expressed.

Once again, paradoxically, while society is aware of gender inequalities and the need for remedy and many initiatives have been undertaken to address the problem of discrimination against women in the field of education, actual progress remains slow. Moreover, Israel's performance on the elementary measures of education is impressive, but does not progress beyond the elementary dimension. Clearly, the potential is not realized. The gap between the parameters is also evident when viewed in comparative perspective: in other developed countries the general improvement of wealth per inhabitant and women's rising level of education have been translated into a higher representation of women in parliament; in Israel no such correlation can be traced (S. Swirski and Yechezkel 1999b, 4).

General and Legal Framework

The Israeli educational system consists of kindergartens, elementary schools, secondary schools (vocational and general), teacher-training institutions, postsecondary schools for continued and vocational studies, colleges, and universities. In addition to formal studies, there is an extensive range of extracurricular activities. Educational policy reflects the needs of Israeli society, including the absorption of immigrant students, the advancement of disadvantaged population groups, and social and academic integration. The state school system consists of two streams: state and state religious (autonomous with respect to pedagogic considerations and curriculum). Of Jewish students, about 75 percent enroll in the state system, and 25 percent in the state religion system. There are also independent "recognized" schools, most of which provide ultra-Orthodox Jewish or Christian religious education. These schools operate as nonprofit organizations financed by the government. The structure of the institutions and content of the studies in the non-Jewish sectors are analogous to those in the Jewish sector, with necessary differences that reflect the different languages and cultures of these populations. This chapter focuses on the Jewish schools within the state school system, which make up the majority of schools in Israel, but also discusses the state religious education and Arab education.

The Israeli education system is financed primarily by the central government and local education authorities. Government expenditure on education has stood at 7.1 percent of the gross domestic product (GDP) in 1998.[1] Critics point out that the budgetary allocation to education has not grown in several years and is realistically identical to the 1996 budget, even though the student population is estimated to have grown by 7.3 percent since 1996 (S. Swirski 1999c, 5). According to the 1997 Long School Day Law,[2] the duration of the school day shall be extended to 8 hours (currently, the six-day school week is about 30 hours). However, this law has only been implemented in peripheral areas thus far, and its budget was cut by 30 percent in 1999 (S. Swirski 1999d, 2).

The law provides equal opportunities for men and women. The 2000 amendment to the 1951 Women's Equal Rights Law[3] provides that "Any woman and man have the equal right to an existence in human dignity, including equality . . . in education." Formal equality is indeed guaranteed in this area. The 1949 Compulsory Education Law[4] applies to all children aged five to fifteen. Education is provided free of charge through age seventeen, and for eighteen-year-olds who have not completed eleventh grade. A 1984 amendment to the law provides free nursery school education for ages three and four. The implementation of this amendment has been postponed annually due to budgetary constraints, however, and in 1999 the Knesset voted on a ten-year gradual implementation plan (S. Swirski 1999a). The Compulsory Education Law was amended yet again in 1991,[5] and section 3B currently includes a prohibition against discrimination in acceptance, placement, and advancement of students. The 1953 State Education Law[6] provides for a six-day school week and determines the content and procedure of state education. It further states that state education is to be based on building a society on the foundations of freedom, equality, tolerance, mutual assistance, and love of mankind. This law applies only to state schools and excludes independent "recognized" schools. The minister of education, however, is authorized under the 1969 School Inspection Law[7] to apply these educational goals to the independent "recognized" schools as well. The 1988 Special Education Law[8] mandates special education for individuals between the ages of three and twenty-one whose capacity for adaptive behavior is limited and who are in need of special education. The 1958 Council for Higher Education Law[9] defines the tasks of the Council for Higher Education, which is responsible for accrediting and authorizing institutions of higher education that award degrees.

Women and Education: Data and Analysis

Illiteracy Rates, Educational Levels, and Matriculation Performance

Educational levels in Israel have been steadily increasing throughout all population groups; the lower the starting point, the more significant the progress made. Within the Jewish population, the median educational levels (the number of completed years of school for which half the population is below and the other half above) for men and women have always been close. In the early 1960s they stood at 8.8 and 7.9 respectively, and in 1998 they rose to 12.4, an identical level for the first time. In the non-Jewish population the gender educational gaps had been much larger. In 1961, non-Jewish men's median educational level was 5.2, while women's was close to zero. In less than four decades, men's level more than doubled, to 11 in 1998. Women's level rose to 10.4, and although the gender and national gaps still remain, when viewing current data in light of the starting point, criticism is somewhat subdued. Moreover, among non-Jewish youth the gender gap is diminishing almost to nothing. In 1998 the median educational level of non-Jewish boys and girls aged fifteen to seventeen was the same (10.6), and the level of eighteen- to twenty-four-year-old women was actually higher than that of men (11.9 and 11.8 respectively).[10]

Parallel to the increase in the population's educational level, illiteracy rates, namely the rate of those with less than one year of schooling, have significantly decreased, in 1999 reaching 2.5 percent in the Jewish population and 7 percent in the non-Jewish population. Still, illiteracy rates are highest among women aged sixty-five and over: 13.1 percent among

Jewish women (compared with 6.4 percent among Jewish men), and the shocking rate of 57.6 percent among non-Jewish women (compared with 26.6 percent among non-Jewish men).[11]

In the Israeli educational system, the first six years of schooling are conducted in elementary primary schools, followed by intermediate and high schools. The secondary education system is made up of technological/vocational and general schools. Toward the end of the intermediate school, students select a particular track by choosing specific subjects studied on enhanced levels on which they take their final matriculation exams. Researchers describe the tracking process as beginning in eighth or ninth grade, when the students are placed, with the guidance of an advisor, in either the technological or general track.

One primary distinction is the differentiation between general and technological or vocational tracks: in 1996, 71 percent of the girls in twelfth grade studied in the general track, compared with only 58 percent of the boys.[12] Despite major differences between technological and vocational schools in terms of human-capital gains, future earnings, and professional status, the two are grouped together for statistical purposes, unlike the general track. In some of the distinctive subjects, there is a striking disproportion. For example, statistics depict machinery or electronics as almost exclusively male subjects (96 percent and 94 percent respectively), while fashion and nursing/paramedics are clearly female dominated at an almost equal percentage rate for women: 97 percent and 89 percent. Interestingly, building and architecture are studied almost equally by men and women (46 percent women), while such subjects as biotechnology, industry, and management have a clear male majority of 63 percent.[13] These differences are a clear indication of the strong gender stratification in the Israeli labor market.

Girls consistently fare better than boys on matriculation examinations. More girls than boys take the exams, and their success rate is higher. In 1999, 86.5 percent of all girls in the twelfth-grade age group were in school, compared with 73.5 percent of the boys. Girls' entitlement to matriculation certificates was also much higher, 48.5 percent of all age groups, compared with 35 percent of the boys.[14] The difference between the general and the technological/vocational tracks is visible here, however; the success rate of boys in the latter is higher than for girls. Of the nearly 39,000 twelfth-grade girls, 58 percent were studying in the general track, compared to 42.1 percent of the 37,500 twelfth-grade boys. Girls fared better on the general track: 64.2 percent were eligible for certificates of matriculation, compared with only 56.4 percent of the boys. Boys, however, fared better on the technological track: 34.7 percent were eligible for certificates, compared with 32.1 percent of the girls.[15]

Further gender differences are apparent from levels of exams taken by both boys and girls. For tenth-grade students, the gap in the mathematics level between girls and boys is quite evident. In 1985, there was more than a 2 : 1 ratio of boys to girls in the five-point (advanced) math matriculation level (Amit and Movshovitz-Hadar 1989). More than a decade later, in 1999, the ratio has changed only a little: 22 percent of the boys who took the math matriculation exam, but only 13.5 percent of the girls took the five-point level (see Table 1).[16] The success rates, though, were generally higher for girls than for boys. However, the achievements of the girls *before* the division into levels (in the tenth grade) are equal to or greater than those of boys: the gap is created only *after* segregation into levels. Hence, girls tend to choose a matriculation level below their actual abilities (Rom 1995b). This impression is supported by data concerning the performance rating of girls and boys in the exams themselves. The differences and gaps in the professions, levels, and achievements of the sexes have been shown to be a direct result of the tracking system (Amit and Movshovitz-Hadar 1989), which may limit access to certain areas in higher education and therefore affect one's chosen profession. Girls consistently tend to take high levels of the matriculation exams in the humanities and social sciences, staying away from mathematics and the natural sciences, although these may be essential for continuing one's higher education. As the math and science level sciences (such as high-point matriculation tests) increase, so does the number of boys in comparison to girls. Statistics from the Ministry of Education, Culture, and Sport (henceforward referred to as the Ministry of Education) show that these gaps are not decreasing in any significant manner.

Success rates for girls are consistently higher than for boys, in both tracks and in all fields, even among the girls who do take the five-point mathematics (96.5 percent and 95.5 percent passes respectively in

TABLE 1. Rates of Examinees, Entitled to Certificates, and Best Achievers in Mathematics Matriculations Examinations, 1999

	Examinees in mathematics matriculation exams		*Entitled to certificates*		*Best achievers*	
	Girls	*Boys*	*Girls*	*Boys*	*Girls*	*Boys*
Total	80.4	77.5	91.7	89.6	45.8	38.6
3 points	59.7	51.8	88.6	84.9	41.2	31
4 points	26.8	26.6	96.2	94.2	51.7	41.9
5 points	13.5	21.7	96.5	95.5	54.7	52.4

Source: Ministry of Education, Matriculation Examinations Data, 1999.

1999), except for management and economics.[17] Even when it comes to passes with distinctions girls, fare better in five-point mathematics (54.7 percent compared with 52.4 percent of the boys).[18] However, while girls do better than boys in the matriculation exams, more boys than girls take enhanced scientific exams (12 percent of the boys and 10 percent of the girls), which are critical for acceptance to universities. Thus, while more girls than boys pass the exams, fewer girls meet the minimum requirements for acceptance to university. In 1999, for example, while 88.2 percent of the boys who passed their exams met these requirements, only 85.6 percent of the girls did so.[19] This marks an improvement since 1996, when only 82.1 percent of girls met the requirements, as opposed to 84.3 percent of boys (Swirski and Yechezkel 1999a).

Like many other areas regarding women's situation in Israel, the need to intervene and implement reforms within the educational system was recognized as early as 1978, with the Namir Commission report (Office of the Prime Minister 1978). The commission recommendations included encouraging female teachers to participate in training on topics such as administration and organization to prepare them for these positions in the future; raising awareness among the teaching staff on the status of women in society, while stressing that their own behavior often results in creating gender stereotypes; integrating the subject of the status of women into social studies courses; and conducting research on the influence of the mainly female constituency of the teaching profession on the students and their development. It was also recommended that they aspire for a male/female balance among the staff responsible for creating educational policy and writing curricula. The report additionally stated the importance of awareness of stereotypes in schoolbooks. Finally, the report called for developing ways to discuss gender equality. Predictably, most of these recommendations are just as relevant today. Nevertheless, progress has been made in some areas, in line with the Namir Commission recommendations.

Classroom dynamics is an important factor in assessing gender differences. Teachers relate differently to boys and girls, often unconsciously, and are more attentive to male students. This can be partly attributed to the fact that behavioral problems are more common among boys; yet the message conveyed to girls is "to be cute and quiet," while the message to boys is "to try harder and improve" (Avrahami-Ainat 1989). Often the children themselves are aware of such discriminatory treatment. For example, a 1989 study of report cards in one school found that teachers had spent more time on the boys' report cards and wrote more specific advice for improvement, thus showing that in general teachers are more familiar and create a stronger bond with male students (Avrahami-Ainat 1989). In attempting to categorically reform classroom dynamics to the advantage of girls, suggestions have been made to create an informal atmosphere through an alternative classroom style that would eliminate the dominating role of boys within the classroom (Hertz Lezrovitz 1995). The theory was that a formal traditional classroom encourages individuality and competition, while the informal setting maximizes participation, cooperation, and equality. The theory was supported by a 1993 study by Dina Chasidov (cited in Hertz Lezrovitz 1995, 266), which examined the effects of the alternative style classroom on students in grades four to six studying mathematics and computers; concluded that while students' achievements were greater overall in the informal setting, the results were most advantageous for girls, whose achievements in the informal classroom exceeded those of the boys.

Less revolutionary initiatives are more reasonable to expect. The Ministry of Education has engaged in numerous activities and educational programs in order to prevent discrimination, central among them being the initiative to eliminate gender stereotypes within schoolbooks. Research conducted on messages conveyed in schoolbooks from 1989 to 1992 (on various subjects and for different age groups) showed women being depicted as emotionally unstable, overly concerned with their appearance, weak, lacking personality, ignorant, jealous, disloyal, dependent, overly inquisitive, and failing to contribute to society. Men were mentioned in schoolbooks three times as often as women, and their contribution to family life and housework was portrayed as minimal. Women's contribution to society was portrayed as incomparable to that of men, and they were often depicted as teachers, nurses, or housewives. Not surprisingly, fewer stereotypes existed in books by female writers (Meler 1995). In 1993, the Ministry of Education issued a new list of criteria for schoolbooks, stressing equality, avoiding gender-characterization, and using neutral, inclusive language to convey inclusiveness.[20]

In recent years attempts have been made to remove stereotypical messages from textbooks used within the Arab sector as well. Fearing opposition, however, the curriculum department for the Arab sector has adopted a gradual rather than a radical feminist approach.[21] Inasmuch as sincere efforts were made to follow these directives, the 1999 State Comptroller Report revealed that the Ministry of Education lacks the means to implement them, and very few schoolbooks actually undergo review. Consequently, the minister of education decided to "lift the advanced censorship" over the schoolbooks, while maintaining the policy of prohibiting the use of books that contain racist or sexist messages.[22]

Stipulations set out by the Ministry of Education in 1987 encourage girls to learn in technological schools. This is partly implemented through cooperation with private educational initiatives, such as the Na'aleh Project. Na'aleh, an intervention program carried out in some middle and high schools, allows for female students, parents, and school staff to work together and make informed decisions about studying sciences, such as mathematics, physics, chemistry, and computers (Rom 1995b).

The importance of women's nongovernmental organizations (NGOs) and private organizations in stimulating action is strongly apparent here. Major development in terms of the Ministry of Education's formal policy took place following a report which accompanied a one-day seminar on equality within the education system, organized and written by the Israel Women's Network (IWN) in 1993. As a result of this initiative, the minister of education declared a policy to encourage equal opportunity for men and women in education. A supervisor on Equality between the Sexes was appointed in the Ministry of Education. A steering committee of the IWN, consisting of experts from different areas of education, works together with the Supervisor to offer advice and provide support. One of the Supervisor's main activities so far has been the publication of a reader titled "A Gender Found Its Equality," which includes many articles, reform programs, and research findings on the issue of gender equality in education (Segen and Katzovitch 1995). Other initiatives include a training program for teachers; seminars to create awareness of gender inequality; raising the awareness of children's magazine editors to hidden messages they might convey; checking schoolbooks and curricula; creating a connection with women's organizations in Israel; and establishing seminars for different audiences (teachers, advisors, administrators).

The highlight of Ministry of Education initiatives in this area has been the IWN-initiated Equality 2000 project, first implemented in 1996 as an experimental project. In its experimental phase the project was a three-year intervention program carried out within four different middle schools, involving ten to fifteen teachers in each school who were specifically trained to deal with issues of gender equality. The program is slowly being implemented in more schools and is rapidly becoming a permanent part of the ministry's curriculum.[23] Its methodology, though, was slightly changed to reach more educators who would act as agents of change. It contains elements of both a research project and an active intervention program and is meant to bring about change in the attitudes and behavior of teachers, advisors, administrators, students, and parents regarding gender equality. Thus, during 1998–2000, new gender-equality departments were opened in thirteen pedagogic centers (nine in the Jewish sector, four in the Arab sector), various intervention programs were conducted in some thirty schools, and short-term seminars on gender equality were held in ten municipalities (six in the Jewish sector, three in the Arab sector, one mixed).[24]

Sex and Family-Life Education

More significant to the general attitude toward gender equality and the promotion of women is the area of sex education and education on family life. Here, as elsewhere in the Ministry of Education, programs seem to flourish. The question is whether and how they are in fact being implemented and passed on to the students.

Since 1987, the Ministry of Education has employed a mandatory program on sex and family-life education for grades 1 through 12. The program concentrates on a variety of topics, such as physical development, body image, sexual identity, femininity/masculinity, gender equality, the family, reproduction, interpersonal relationships, couplehood, and sexual health. It also addresses issues such as date rape, sexual harassment, identification of sexual violence risk factors, and how to seek help when necessary. The program's stated goals include developing a positive perception of human sexuality and sexual identity, providing accurate information appropriate to the students' developmental stage, advancing gender equality and respect, minimizing stereotypes, and strengthening family values and students' awareness and acceptance of varying types of families.[25] The sex education curriculum attempts to make students aware of existing stereotypes and of the ways society encourages boys to "act masculine" and girls to "act feminine."

Separate Education for Boys and Girls: State Religious and Ultra-Orthodox Schools

The place of religion in Israel and its impact on women's lives is separately dealt with elsewhere.[26] An evolutionary process of women's entry into religious practices and realms from which they have previously been excluded is referred to as the "quiet" feminist revolution within modern orthodoxy.[27] Women's education plays a primary part within this quiet revolution, both in the sense of being one of those fields of entry and in the sense of being a major tool in the process. This may be the most interesting and promising feminist process that is currently taking place in Israeli society, and it has already drawn serious scholarly attention (El-Or 1998). Significant as this revolution may be, its scope should not be overplayed: it takes place only within the modern orthodox community, which in Israel parallels the Zionist-religious community, as opposed to the ultra-Orthodox one; moreover, even within the former, it is still confined to a minority group (El-Or 1998). Moreover, while gaining momentum, most of the revolutionary educational developments are taking place at the post high-school level within the realm of private initiatives and are mostly beyond government intervention. At the earlier stages of women's education, which are part of the state education system, things are much slower to change.

One of the points of concern on the international measures is separation of boys and girls in the education system, which may cover discrimination in terms of resources and quality (International Women's Rights Action Watch 1996, 27). The ultra-Orthodox schools have always maintained separation between boys and girls. State religious secondary education has also traditionally been separate, and in the past few years such separation has been increasing in state religious elementary schools as well. In both streams, sex-segregated education entails various curriculum differences, although these do not necessarily imply lesser quality or fewer resources for girls' education. In state religious schools, especially elementary schools, the main difference between the girls' and boys' curricula is in religious subjects.

In 1999, the state religious schools comprised 21 percent of all primary schools and about 18.5 percent of post-primary schools.[28] Regrettably, the Administration for Religious Education does not have exact data on girls' education, but its assumption is that 50 percent of the students are girls. The head of the Administration further estimates that 35 percent of the classes are separate at the elementary level and 90 percent at the high school level, and claims that the budget allocated to girls' institutes is the same as that allocated to boys' institutes.[29] This lack of specific data—written materials and documents—presents serious difficulties for any attempt to describe the situation relating to various aspects of girls' education under the state religious education. This deficiency can be regarded as indicative of the general treatment of girls' education under the state religious stream. This may not necessarily indicate indifference but rather show a sense of confusion as to the appropriate guidelines and leading values in this area, which in itself is indicative of the general gradual process of change religious women are going through.

This gradual process of change is indeed apparent in girls' education as well. For example, change is taking place in the course of religious studies for girls compared to that of boys. The differentiation had always been quite clear: in line with Jewish tradition, girls are precluded from the study of what is known as the Oral Law (Gemara) and are relegated to the study of the Bible, theology, and the parts of religious law specifically relevant to their lives as observant Jewish girls at present, and as women (wives and mothers) in the future. Thus, for example, they have always studied the dietary laws of Orthodox Judaism (kashrut), and the laws concerning "family purity" relating to ritual baths. The highly intellectual course of Gemara studies used to be exclusively designated for boys. In the past few years, a slow change has been taking place in this respect, and more girls' schools have added the study of Gemara to the curriculum. This change, however, is not mandated by the administration of national religious education, but is the independent initiative of individual schools throughout the country. The administrator of the national religious education stated that there is no difference in educational programs for boys and for girls, except with respect to Gemara studies, which girls do not take, with the minor exception of a few high schools for girls.[30] The emphasis on the independent nature of this process is significant, since it relates to the analogous process of girls' entry into continued post-high school Torah learning. This is probably the most significant process within the Zionist-religious circles described by anthropologist Tamar El-Or (1998, 17) as a revolution within orthodoxy. In less than a decade following the late 1980s, about twenty institutes for rigorous high-level Torah and often also Gemara studies for women opened, offering advanced religious studies before or after army or national service.[31] Two of these institutes even offer a program that combines high-level religious studies with army service for young religious women, similar to the arrangement that already exists for young religious men. Moreover, as of 1997 the Ministry of Religion is obligated by the High Court of Justice to give financial support to the women's institutes just as it has always supported the men's yeshivot (institutes of higher Torah learning for men).[32] Perhaps the most far-reaching development is the program for training women to be capable of rendering Halachic (Jewish legal) decisions, currently in the area of family purity and reproduction.[33] These dramatic developments, which occur outside the realm of the state religious education system, will sooner or later undoubtedly transform this system's approach to girls' education as well.

Another gradual change in state religious education is in relation to the educational programs dealing, as a whole, with the issues of sex education, gender equality, and the advancement of women. All these are dealt with under the rubric of family life education, since officially there is no explicit topic of sex education under state religious education.[34] After years of deferral of the subject, in contrast to the awareness raised and programs designed under the general education system, the state religious education system has initiated a program to adapt the main anthology used by the general education system for gender equality education to the framework of the religious educational system. Several other programs have been started, including one for Bat-Mitzvah girls (religious confirmation at age twelve for girls), and another for teachers' training courses. A supervisor on family life education was appointed in January 1996, responsible for social education and education for democracy in the state religious education system. In explaining her goals, the supervisor stressed the needs to integrate modern and present needs with the values of traditional Judaism, aiming at strengthening the traditional forms of family life.

All these developments are taking place only within Zionist-religious or modern-Orthodox circles. Ultra-Orthodox education is totally different. In ultra-Orthodox independent "recognized" schools, which in 1999 comprised 14 percent of the primary schools and 11 percent of the post-primary schools,[35] there is definitely a greater distinction between the curricula of the boys and girls. Education is highly valued in ultra-Orthodox society, and despite strictly defined gender roles, many ultra-Orthodox women finish high school. In "recognized" schools for girls such as Beis Yaakov, girls learn a wide variety of subjects with special attention paid to preparing them for their position in society. While girls are directed to be religious and marry a religious man, they are also encouraged to obtain higher education in certain religious institutions. Interestingly, women's different status in ultra-Orthodox society results in girls being exposed to a more thorough secular education than boys. Boys, who are expected to devote all their time to religious study, do not generally take secular classes after elementary school. Girls, on the other hand, who are not expected or often even allowed to pursue religious studies on a high level, continue to take secular classes through high school (foreign languages, computers, even accounting), all in order to prepare them for their adult roles as both childbearers and childrearers and economic providers (Schiffer 1998, 32). Thus, while according to the ultra-Orthodox terms and values girls are denied access to the tools critical for success, they can be better equipped than boys to fare in the secular world. As girls and women within the ultra-Orthodox community benefit from a more advanced secular education than boys and men, they serve as a bridge between their segregated communities and the rest of society. However, much of girls' education in ultra-Orthodox schools focuses on preparation for their responsibilities as a mothers and housewives, perpetuating their secondary status in ultra-Orthodox society. According to Tamar El-Or (1994), who researched women's position in ultra-Orthodox society, women's education mainly serves as a mechanism that enables the women to justify their inferior position to themselves.

Teachers in the Israeli School System

The teaching profession in Israel is composed primarily of women. As of 1998, more than 80 percent of all teachers in Hebrew education in

Israel were women. Among Arabs, however, the gap between the sexes within the teaching profession is considerably smaller. As the level of educational institution increases, the female majority of teachers decreases. In 1998, women made up 90 percent of teachers in Hebrew elementary schools and 64 percent of teachers in Arab elementary schools. In post-elementary schools, women made up 73 percent in Hebrew schools and only 37 percent in Arab schools. In middle schools, 82 percent of the teachers in Hebrew education and 39 percent in Arab education are women. In high schools, though, only 68 percent of teachers in Hebrew education and 34 percent in Arab education are women.[36]

When the data on the predominance of women in the Jewish education system are added to the data on teachers by subjects,[37] the conclusion is that Jewish Israeli elementary school children have less than a 10 percent overall chance of seeing a man in the position of a schoolteacher, and then only in such fields as physical education or religious subjects.

Despite women's predominance in the teaching profession, their position in the profession is inferior to that of men, as evidenced by comparing salary levels and representation in high-ranking administrative positions. Data supplied by the Treasury Ministry in 2000 on salaries of teachers employed full-time by the Ministry of Education reveal that overall, women earn on average 91 percent of men's salaries. Although a significant improvement from the 87 percent ratio of 1996, this still suggests that steps should to be taken in order to eliminate any trace of inequality.[38] Research conducted in 1993 also proves the differences in the salaries of men and women within the educational system: salaries paid to men are out of proportion to their presence in the school system. For example, in Jewish elementary education, men make up 9.5 percent of the total teachers but 25.5 percent of the highest pay level of the status of second and third degree holders. Similarly, men make up 28.4 percent of the total teachers in Jewish secondary education but 41.4 percent of the highest pay level (Herzog 1993). Similarly, an examination of authoritative administrative positions reveals that the number of men working in educational institutions increases with the level of the position (Herzog 1993).

Higher Education

Gender examination of higher education in Israel offers a complex picture. Women now make up more than half of those pursuing an academic degree, and their share among graduates is constantly rising. Since higher education in Israel, as elsewhere in the Western world, is a crucial entry ticket for a rewarding career, this trend is definitely encouraging. Yet the picture seems a little less optimistic when the gender division is inspected among the types of degrees and qualifications acquired. Women concentrate on the humanities and the social sciences and are underrepresented in the technological fields and in engineering. For example, women make up a mere third of graduates from the prestigious Weizmann Institute of Science.[39]

In 1999, 56.6 percent of undergraduate students in Israel were women.[40] In addition, over 50 percent of all graduate students are women. This percentage exceeds that of all countries except the United States, where the percentages are basically equal to those in Israel as noted in the mid-1990s.[41] In 1993, of the population group aged twenty to twenty-nine, the percentage of women enrolled in university surpassed that of men (10 percent and 8 percent respectively).[42] In 1998–99, 41.3 percent of third degree recipients were women, while among first and the second degree recipients, women comprised 58 percent and 55 percent respectively.[43] According to 1999 figures released by the Israel Central Bureau of Statistics, 50 percent of Ph.D. students and 58 percent of all MA and MSc students were women. As the following statistics indicate, however, women continue to concentrate in the humanities and are less likely to enter fields such as business and mathematics/computers. In 1999, women made up 70.8 percent, 63.8 percent, and 81.2 percent of first degree students in humanities, social science, and paramedical studies respectively, but only 43 percent in sciences and mathematics and—most surprising of all—a mere 23 percent in engineering and architecture. Interestingly, women make up 46.9 percent and 47.3 percent of those studying for the first and second degree in medicine, and a clear majority of 69.7 percent of third degree medical students.[44] In 1999, women comprised 74 percent and 61.5 percent of first degree recipients in the humanities and social sciences respectively, but only 18.8 percent in engineering and architecture. Similarly, women made up 77.6 percent of second degree recipients in the humanities but only 22.8 percent in engineering and architecture. Quite interestingly, though, women made up 48.5 percent of second degree recipients in sciences and mathematics.[45]

The impressive data of women's participation in higher education in Israel come to a halt at participation in the academic staff. In 1998–99, women represented 22.4 percent of senior academic staff financed by the Council for Higher Education budget, while in 1978–79 they represented only 16.2 percent (Hershkovitz 2000). Despite the clear increase in the number of women across the ranks, this progress is slow, and the percentage decreases as the rank increases. Thus, while women constituted almost 39.5 percent of all lecturers, they comprised only 32.2 percent of senior lecturers, 19.9 percent of associate professors, and a mere

8.8 percent of full professors, a modest increase from 7.3 percent in the early 1980s (Hershkovitz 2000). This last point is particularly important, since the rank of full professor is the condition for entering the most important institute in the university, namely the senate, where all the significant academic decisions are made. It is also the condition for holding such posts as dean or rector and for serving on the university's central committees such as the promotion committees—that is, the entitlement for power and decision-making authority.

Women represent a relatively small proportion of senior academic staff in physical sciences, mathematics, computer science, engineering, and agriculture, while they represent a relatively large proportion of the senior academic staff in fields such as the humanities and medicine. Nina Toren of the Hebrew University, who conducted a thorough study of women in the academic staff in Israel, notes that although women are better represented overall in the humanities, they actually fare better in the exact sciences with regard to advancement in the academic ranks. In the humanities, women faculty tend to be far more concentrated at the lower levels, while in the sciences they are more evenly distributed among the academic ranks. Toren attributes this phenomenon to the greater objectivity of evaluation criteria in the sciences (Toren 2000). Toren's study further demonstrates that as the age of the department increases so do the chances of finding women professors in that department. As women's power grows within the department through the number of professors, the number of women in that field of study increases. In addition, larger departments advance more women to the position of professor. It is often claimed that married women with children are not as professionally productive and as a result their professional advancement is postponed or made more difficult to obtain. Toren tested the connection between professional productivity and number of children. Specifically, female professors with more children (three to four), were found to publish more articles. Furthermore, single female professors were the least professionally productive. Although this research was conducted on only 44 professors, it is believed to be relatively accurate, since similar results were obtained in the United States and Scandinavia (Toren 2000).

A somewhat different perspective is suggested by Professor Hershkovitz of the Council on Higher Education, who maintains that the promotion gaps can be partially explained by the differential career patterns of men and women, particularly with respect to obtaining experience abroad. Clear gender differences have been found in spending time abroad, whether for doctoral or postdoctoral studies. For example, among male third degree recipients in physical sciences, 73.4 percent continued their training abroad, with 57 percent staying more than three years. The parallel figures for women were only 37 percent and 14.3 percent respectively (Hershkovitz 2000, chart 4). Hershkovitz asserts that the conventional perception of training abroad as a prime condition for acceptance to the academic staff conflicts with women's family ambitions and roles. The demand for a long stay abroad usually comes when women are in their childbearing years and face much more serious difficulties than men to meet this demand. Consequently, Hershkovitz bravely suggests that this conventional perception of the appropriate training should be reexamined (Hershkovitz 2000, 43).

The glass ceiling in the universities has implications far beyond the academic institutions themselves. The1996–97 membership list from the Israel Academy of Science reveals women's underrepresentation in academia. Of thirty-six members comprising the Natural Science section, only two were women. Of the thirty-one members of the Humanities section, only one was a woman.[46] Another telling statistic is women's lack of representation among recipients of the prestigious annual Israel Award. Throughout the years, women have comprised a mere 11 percent of the recipients of this award, given to Israeli citizens for outstanding achievements in the fields of art, music, literature, science, education, and social and volunteer work. Women's inferior position in academia directly affects their scarcity among Israel Award recipients. This is highlighted upon close examination of the distribution of recipients according to the fields in which they received the prize, revealing that most of the women who were awarded belonged to fields other than academia.[47]

In partial response to this deadlock, and in realization of the need to form a feminist community within academia, women academics in Israel established the Israel Association for Feminist Studies in early 1998. Among its aims is the advancement of gender and feminist research and studies in Israel and the creation of a network of support for those engaging in these fields within Israeli academia. It is also hoped that the association will serve as a vehicle to advance women within the academic world in general.[48]

Chapter 6
The Welfare State

Israel sees itself as a welfare state, that is, a state whose government ensures all its citizens a basic level of income, sustenance, health, shelter, and education as a political right. This chapter particularly relates to Israeli women's welfare and economic situation, in terms that are not covered in other parts of the book. Thus, as family social benefits that are employment-related are discussed extensively in the following chapter, this chapter focuses on social benefits supplied regardless of employment status. Since this subject is closely related to women's economic state in general, the discussion proceeds to address women's poverty in Israel and focuses on some of the groups that are more vulnerable to poverty.

A thorough examination of the welfare system and of women's particular welfare and economic situation demonstrates the general thesis of the book. Women in Israel do not experience high levels of indigence and destitution only because Israel is indeed—to a large extent—a welfare state. Women's overall reasonable economic situation is incidental to Israel's general commitment to its welfare goals, but their particular needs are not being responded to. A general observation of the social security system in Israel leaves no doubt as to the system's prototype recipient: only a productive individual who has participated in the labor force or the family as a whole social unit, which women recipients should be considered to be part of. Women as individuals, stripped of traditional market productivity or traditional family context, are not the natural targets of this system. Gender-specific life situations, such as single motherhood, widowhood, nonremunerative work activities such as care for the elderly or the young, do not receive satisfactory compensation through the system. For example, 16 percent of the women surveyed in the 2000 Brookdale survey reported taking care of an ill or disabled family member, two-thirds of them of a parent (Gross and Brammli-Greenberg 2000). While the levels of poor health estimations, depression, and need for psychological counseling among the women caregivers were much higher than the average, and while their care work often comes at the expense of waged work outside the home, this care work is uncompensated for in any form. Only when the care work is done by a professional caregiver are costs covered by a social security allowance.[1]

Social-economist Barbara Swirski follows this analysis and observes the antithetical message conveyed by the government: promoting a gender equality policy while declining to back up this policy with actual expenditures (Swirski 1999). This is but one more reflection of government performance, as seen in the symbolic reform in the civil service (Maor 2001) and discussed later in the area of gender-based violence against women. Such critical analysis reveals that there is in fact no government commitment to women's advancement. This goal is not perceived as deserving special budgetary allocations. It is true that in recent years Israel's welfare system has experienced a general decline, as part of the economic recession since the 1990s, which affects both men and women. The overall level of social security benefits is low, and people who rely on them alone are very close to the poverty line (Swirski, Konor, and Yechezkel 1999a, 25). However, even within this decline, women, particularly specific groups of women, take a harder blow. Israeli society as whole is undergoing a process of widening inequality and income gaps (Awad, Cohen, and Yaniv 1998), which seriously threaten any commitment to distributive justice (as discussed in detail in Chapter 7). Israel's income gaps have reached the point where the share of the top 20 percent of the population in 1998 was close to 40 percent of the "income pie," leaving only 60 percent to the remaining 80 percent of the population (Swirski, Konor, and Yechezkel 1999a, 7). Within these increasing socioeconomic gaps, women's economic situation is further declining, as a result of their inferior situation in the labor market, which also serves as the starting point for social benefits allocations.[2] In addition, the lack of old age employment pension is a general social problem in Israel, where most employees (estimates vary between 50 and 60 percent) do not have an old-age pension plan.[3] Various attempts have been made in recent years to legislate an obligatory pension law for all workers. Nevertheless, more women than men suffer from lack of an employment pension, since more women retire without ever having participated in the formal labor force, having a pension plan, or accumulating enough pension rights due to their irregular work patterns.

The right to social security is included in many international human rights instruments. Its essence is to secure minimum livelihood for everyone in circumstances that jeopardize one's survival and are beyond one's control (Tomasevski 1998, 13). Universally, women are more often susceptible to such circumstances and are therefore more in need of this right. Since social benefits depend largely on accumulation of employment years or aggregation of salary levels, women's inferiority in the labor market directly diminishes their welfare benefits. Women's presence among social benefits recipients is proportionately much higher than their rate within the population: in 2000, women comprised close to 73 percent of all recipients of long-term care benefits, a figure obviously related to women's higher longevity. Furthermore, while only 12.2 percent of the male recipients of old age pensions also received income supplements, 20 percent of the female recipients received both benefits.[4] This figure already takes into account women's greater longevity, so the difference should be fully attributed to their generally lower working status, on which so much of the social benefit depends. In early 2000, 65.3 percent of all recipients of income support benefits were women.[5] These examples already highlight circumstances of specific concern to women, such as old age and low income; combinations of such circumstances put women in an even more vulnerable state. Thus, while Israel's welfare system guarantees the right to social security, the full scope of this right is far from being conferred on women.

Women and the Welfare State in Israel

The Welfare System in Israel

A welfare state does exist in Israel and has emerged gradually since the state's establishment in 1948. Israel succeeded in building a comprehensive system of social protection, encompassing social insurance and social assistance programs. The cornerstone of social insurance was laid soon after the establishment of the state, through the passage of the 1953 National Insurance Law, later replaced by the 1995 National Insurance Law (Consolidated Version).[6] The social insurance system is extended to include all major contingencies of income loss in modern industrial societies: old age, survivorship (widowed spouses and orphans), disability, childrearing, maternity, unemployment, and work injury. Some benefits are short-term payments replacing wages of those temporarily unemployed (due to dismissal, work injury, giving birth, or military reserve service); but most benefits are long-term payments, aiming to guarantee subsistence to those permanently out of the workforce due to old age or disability, to survivors who remain without a principal breadwinner, and to families facing the economic burden of raising children. All long-term benefits (except child allowances, which are in monetary values) are calculated as a given percentage of the average monthly wage in the economy as defined in the National Insurance Law.[7] The average monthly wage was 5,493 NIS ($1,553) in 1998, 5,890 NIS ($1,413) in 1999, and 6,242 NIS ($1,503) in 2000.

The body responsible for administration of the social insurance programs is the National Insurance Institute (NII), which currently operates under the supervision of the Ministry of Labor and Social Affairs.[8] The NII provides welfare services to residents in need according to the National Insurance Law and is also responsible for payment of benefits under the social assistance program, as directed in the 1980 Income Support Law.[9] This law guarantees minimum subsistence income to all individuals and families of limited means whose benefits are very low or who do not meet the conditions of entitlement to a benefit under the National Insurance Law. As noted, the general improvement in women's situation is closely connected with Israel's welfare system. Notable development in Israel's welfare system took place in 1994–95, with a national program to combat poverty that also led to the enactment of the 1994 Law to Reduce the Scope of Poverty and Income Gaps (Legislative Reforms).[10] This law has had a significant role in lowering the incidence of poverty in general, and among the more vulnerable populations groups in particular, where women's presence is notably higher, and has increased the level of allowances paid to low-income families.[11] However, towards the end of the 1990s the law became less effective (Awad, Cohen, and Yaniv 1998), once again placing the more vulnerable populations at higher risk.

Women and Social Benefits: The Normative Framework

There are no distinctions in the National Insurance Law regarding men and women's NII contributions (premiums), which are set as a percentage of the insured person's income, regardless of gender. However, only housewives, defined as exclusively *women* whose spouses are insured and who do not work outside their home, are exempt from contributions. This gender-based difference limits the choices of couples, discriminates against men who prefer to raise their children while their spouses work outside the home, and reinforces the traditional patriarchal division of labor in the family. This is the most noticeable distinction on the basis of gender in the social security legal framework. Housewives, traditionally, have not been entitled to old age pension in their own right, and have received half their spouses' old age pension. Since 1996, when the law was changed,[12] housewives have received the minimum old age pension (provided they turned 65 after 1996) but are still exempt from contributions and are not covered in all types of insurance. Since housewives are not considered workers by the NII,[13] they are not eligible for income replacement benefits, such as work injuries insurance, maternity leave allowance, unemployment insurance, and insurance of employees (CESCR Report 1997, 74). Moreover, regulations governing old age pension enable accruing an additional 2 percent for each year over ten years of employment, and 5 percent for each year of delay in claiming the pension. These benefits do not apply to housewives; it seems that "home work is not considered work after all" (B. Swirski 1999).

One of the main social benefits women might receive is maternity insurance, which covers a hospitalization grant, a maternity grant, a birth allowance, and a maternity leave allowance. Any woman who gives birth at a hospital is eligible to a maternity grant, set as 20 percent of the average wage on the birth of one child, 100 percent on the birth of twins, and an additional 50 percent for every additional child born in the same birth.[14] A 2000 amendment to the law doubled the maternity grant payable on the birth of a single child, so long as this is the family's fifth child onward, and set it as 40 percent of the average wage.[15] The maternity grant is paid to all women residents or wives of residents, even if they give birth in a hospital outside Israel, and to women working in Israel or wives of men working in Israel, provided they give birth in a hospital in Israel.[16] A 1998 amendment to the National Insurance Law[17] provides for a maternity grant, with adequate adjustments, to those who adopt a child under the age of ten years (when a couple adopts a child, a grant is given to only one of the parents). For multiple births, families receive an additional birth allowance for nine months, equal to 50 percent of the average monthly salary for triplets, 75 percent for quadruple births, and 100 percent for quintuplets (or more).[18] Another benefit under maternity insurance unrelated to employment is the special allowance and benefit, paid to a widower of a woman who died while giving birth or within a year of giving birth.[19] The conditions for eligibility for maternity leave allowance and for risk pregnancy benefit are detailed in Chapter 7, as they are employment-related benefits.

Another major social benefit that is of particular concern for women is the old age and survivors pension.[20] Old age and survivors benefits comprise the largest insurance branch at the NII (34.7 percent of the total benefits paid in 2000).[21] The basic old age benefit amounts to 16 percent and 24 percent of the average wage for a single person or couple respectively (Yaniv 1998). Recipients of old age and survivors benefits who have no other income, or whose income from another source is low, are eligible to receive an income guarantee according to the Income Support Law. In 2000, this amounted to 30.8 percent of all recipients of old age and survivors benefits.[22] Women are eligible to a non-means-tested old age pension at sixty-five, and men at seventy.

Women at sixty and men at sixty-five are eligible following a means test.[23] Of those receiving an old age pension, 61 percent receive it after having accrued insurance coverage, while 21 percent receive pensions in the form of a supplement to the spouse's pension. An additional 18 percent of elderly women, primarily new immigrants who were unable to accrue pension rights in Israel through the NII, receive pensions under special arrangements funded by the Ministry of Finance (general revenues),[24] which went into effect in January 1999.

All elderly people, including housewives, who are limited in functioning and reside in the community (as opposed to an institution), are entitled to a means-tested long-term care benefit.[25] Again, the age of entitlement for women is sixty and for men sixty-five. The conditions for entitlement to the benefit require at least 50 percent medical disability for housewives as compared to 40 percent for other insured persons (Gera 1998). Apparently, NII practice in evaluating the level of a person's disability is also differential, using stricter measures regarding housewives than for other workers.[26]

Every Israeli citizen aged eighteen or over and not yet sixty (women) or sixty-five (men), and whose degree of disability is at least 75 percent is entitled to a means-tested monthly disability pension[27] at the rate of 25 percent the average wage for a single person, with an additional dependent's increment paid for the dependent spouse and children. A housewife, however, is entitled to a dependent's increment for her children only. Other benefits under general disability insurance include attendance allowance, a grant following decease, a disabled child benefit, and a special benefit for a new immigrant (CESCR Report 1997, 67–69).

A major function of the Israeli welfare system is the protection and support of children and their families. The NII, for example, provides child allowances[28] to an insured parent under the law, paid to one of the parents for each child (under age eighteen), and to an insured person who supported a child who is not his or her child for at least twelfth months. The child allowance in a given family increases from the fourth child onward, thus helping large families attain a minimum income necessary for the care and upbringing of their children. A 2000 amendment to the 1995 National Insurance Law further emphasized this by substantially raising the amount of children's allowances paid from the fifth child onward.[29] Research has shown a direct link between rising fertility rates among the Jewish ultra-Orthodox population and the increasing levels of allowances.[30]

A primary social benefit designated to support children and families in need is the 1972 Alimony (Guarantee of Payment) Law,[31] which states that any person who has received a court decision in his or her favor for alimony and who is an Israeli resident may receive this grant directly from the NII according to the court decision, instead of attempting enforcement on the debtor. In practice, due to a combination of religious rules that govern alimony and maintenance and gender income disparities, alimony beneficiaries are always women (99.4 percent of them with children) and the debtors are men. This law is indeed quite revolutionary, enabling entitled people who cannot succeed in implementing court decisions on their own to receive the sums laid down by the courts. In particular, it somewhat eases the plight of divorced women with children and gives some answer to the worldwide phenomenon of "deadbeat fathers." Indeed, in 1998 the NII managed to receive only 43 percent of the total alimony payments from the debtors.[32] In 2001, the alimony allowances stood at 25 percent of the average wage for the alimony of a woman alone (1,741 NIS, approximately $425 per month), 39.8 percent of the average wage for a woman with one child (2,789 NIS, approximately $680), and 49.8 percent for a woman with two children (3,485 NIS, approximately $850).[33] However, as detailed below,[34] most beneficiaries do not receive these amounts, since the law entitles the alimony recipient to receive the lower amount of either the court decision or the alimony rate set in the regulations.

One of the most important social pieces of legislation for women is the 1992 Single-Parent Family Law,[35] which entitles single-parent families to income support and has strengthened the social protection for single-parent families with low income by increasing the level of their means-tested benefit. A significant improvement in their benefits came with the 1994 Law to Reduce the Scope of Poverty and Income Gaps,[36] which has indeed led to a dramatic decrease in the incidence of poverty among single-parent families—almost a third (from 36.8 percent in 1994 to 25.7 percent in 1995). Single-parent families were the major beneficiaries of the program to combat poverty (Awad, Israeli, Shaul, and Yaniv 1996, 150–51). The Single-Parent Family Law has also awarded single parents annual education grants for children aged six to fourteen and has given them priority in vocational training. In addition, the law entitles them to benefits in income tax through special credit points, programs for mortgage payments, and financial help in paying rent. The ideology behind the Single-Parent Family Law was to bring about an equalization of rights among the various types of single-parent families, under the principle of "equal treatment for families with equal needs," regardless whether they were headed by men or women. However, the law had initially defined "single parent" to include only unmarried individuals (whether never-married or divorced) who live alone (not in a relationship of nonmarital cohabitation, as explained in Chapter 11). This obviously left out some of the most needy women, primarily those who are separated from their husbands but not yet divorced, which often means that no property distribution had taken place yet, hence they are sometimes completely deprived of income and property.

The law was amended in 1994,[37] when the definition of "single parent" was broadened to include women or men separated from their spouses for at least two years who have started divorce proceedings and followed them for at least two years; immigrants whose spouses did not immigrate with them and do not have another spouse; and women who are *agunot* according to the narrow National Insurance Law definition of the term. Nonetheless, even the broadened definition has left out numerous groups of vulnerable women: women whose husbands are in jail, women deserted by their husbands, and more. Moreover, as explained in Chapter 11, an *aguna* is a woman whose husband refuses to grant her a bill of divorce. The National Insurance Law defines *aguna* only as a woman whose husband's whereabouts have been unknown for more than two years, or has left Israel without her agreement for more than two years and does not pay her alimony. This is of course a much narrower definition, and when used in the Single-Parent Family Law it obviously leaves out all other *agunot.* Consequently, in an attempt to truly realize the goal of equalization of the minimum level of benefits to families with equal needs, the Law to Reduce the Scope of Poverty and Income Gaps has provided for all individuals who in fact head single-parent families to be eligible to the higher level of income support. This leads to a somewhat strange description referring to "formal" and "informal" single-parent families, who are now put to the same level of subsistence (Awad, Israel, Shaul, and Yaniv 1996, 158). As much as this is indeed a progressive development, the economic situation of single-parent families, primarily of single mothers, continues to be poor.

There are also some differences among single-parent families, between widows on the one hand and divorcees and others on the other. The overall impact of these differences is an apparent preferential treatment of widows over divorcees and others, in terms of higher benefits and developed rehabilitation services to facilitate their entry into the labor market. The differences apparently stem from historic reasons, not ideological ones, as the group of war widows was the prime constituent of single mothers in the NII's early years, and the growing rate of divorcees has presented budgetary problems (Shreibman 2000). However, the resulting effect is a negative incentive to enter or reenter the labor market for divorcees, who—unlike widows—lack appropriate vocational training programs and face the fear of losing most of their benefits if they receive salaries. The importance of facilitative policy toward this group of women cannot be overemphasized, and budgetary constraints, as maintained by the NII, can serve as no excuse. Moreover, there is a gap between the spirit of the law, to truly advance single mothers with their children, and the reality of the law's implementation. Some regulations that were supposed to aid single-parent families as such were in fact applied to the category of all income-support recipients, thus obscuring the particular status of single-parent families as the most vulnerable family units with minor children, and exposing them to any cutbacks that apply to the other groups.[38] In addition, the NII routinely conducts lengthy investigations to verify the "single" status of the mothers, during which allowances are suspended.[39]

The Reality of Women and Social Benefits: Some Data

The only way to examine poverty of women in Israel is through data. I present here, in full force, the "information story": there are no official, published rates of poverty of women in Israel. Throughout the NII Annual Surveys, which routinely include a whole section on "Poverty and Income Inequality in Israel," statistics are not gendered except for those dealing with old age and survivors pensions. Official publications do not answer such simple and basic questions as gender distribution among recipients of income-support benefits or of the total benefits distributed through the NII. However, the information, at least most of it, does exist. When I turned to the NII Research and Planning Administration, I received most of the data I sought, and the following portrayal is indeed mostly based on that information.[40] This obviously is not the way things should work. Information as to actual economic situation of women as a group, and of various included subgroups, should be readily available. Once again, it is impossible to point to a problem or formulate a social policy without actually fathoming its existence and its extent. Moreover, some information is not even available with the NII itself. There are no exact data on the incidence of poverty among single mothers, as distinguished from single-parent families in general, for the very simple reason that the number of observations done on that particular population group is not statistically sufficient.[41] Needless to say, reaching a statistically sufficient level of observations is only a question of awareness and commitment.

However, statistics supplied by the NII show almost no gender-related differences regarding the incidence of poverty among the population at large, and poverty is documented in more or less equal proportions among men and women. While this shows that, in contrast to other Western countries, an overall phenomenon of feminization of poverty has not taken place in Israel, analysis of further statistics reveals that, among specific population groups with higher poverty rates, women's presence is much higher.[42]

The conventional definition of poverty according to the NII is a family whose net income (disposable income after transfer payments such as all social benefits, and after payment of taxes) falls below the defined poverty line. The poverty line in Israel is defined as 50 percent of the median disposable income adjusted to family size. In 1999, of 2,003,000 adult women, 341,500 were living below the poverty line. Of 1,855,000 adult men, 282,700 were living below the poverty line.[43] These statistics show that women constitute 54.7 percent of the persons with income below the poverty line (having constituted 54.3 percent in 1995). Since women constituted 52 percent of the adult population in 1999, the conclusion is that the proportion of women in poverty is only slightly higher than their proportion in general in the population.

Nevertheless, specific groups of women are especially vulnerable to poverty. The pertinent global data here, before examining each group separately, are the differences in poverty rates among families headed by women and families headed by men: In 1995, 25 percent of all families headed by women lived below the poverty line, compared with only 20 percent of families headed by men. Likewise, 22 percent of all families headed by elderly women lived below the poverty line, compared with 14 percent of families headed by elderly men.[44] These initial statistics cover all groups of women more vulnerable to poverty: elderly women, divorced women, single mothers, and more. Let us now turn to examine these particular groups, starting with the elderly.

While NII statistics show that poverty among the elderly in 1998 is in almost equal proportion among men and women, with men's level actually a little higher than women's (15.9 percent for elderly women and 16.3 percent for elderly men decreasing from 18.2 percent and 18.9 percent in 1995), elderly women are still worse off, simply because they live longer, while suffering from poor health conditions. Thus, as noted, women comprised almost 73 percent of all recipients of long-term care benefits in 2000.[45] Particularly disheartening data are that more than half (52.9 percent) of the women recipients of the long-term care benefit lived alone, almost double the rate of the men recipients, of whom 64.4 percent lived with their spouse, and only 27 percent lived alone.[46] Besides, retired women receive lower pensions than retired men, as throughout their working years they earn much less than men. Indeed, while only 12.2 percent of the male recipients of old age pensions also received income supplement, 20 percent of the female recipients received both benefits.[47] Statistics depicting poverty rates reflect the economic situation after the intervention of the state's security net, in the form of social benefits. Therefore, while the bottom line of the incidence of poverty may be more or less the same, the economic state and well-being behind that is undoubtedly different.

The next population group is the increasingly growing group of single mothers: in 2000 they comprised 11.4 percent of all families in Israel, an increase from 8.9 percent in 1993.[48] Moreover, while the annual growth of the general number of families with children in Israel is 2 percent, the annual growth of single-parent families was 6–8 percent throughout the second half of the 1990s. A partial explanation for this growth is immigration from the former USSR; in 2000 the rate of single-parent families among immigrants was 23.2 percent. Of the almost 105,000 single-parent households, in close to a third of them (31,826) the parent was an immigrant who came to Israel after 1990.

The NII annual surveys routinely discuss single-parent families as a separate group. However, they fail to mention that the overwhelming majority of these families (96 percent) are headed by women. In other words, the plight of single-parent families in Israel is the plight of single mothers and their children. The incidence of poverty among single-parent families is much higher than in the general society: in 1997, 28.5 percent of single-parent families were below the poverty line, compared with 16.5 percent of two-parent families with children. This marked increase followed a sharp decline in 1995 and 1996 as a result of the Law to Reduce the Scope of Poverty and Income Gaps. The incidence of poverty among children of single-parent families is even higher, 36.5 percent in 1997, also a marked increase from 28.4 percent in 1996. This means that every third child of a single parent (overwhelmingly single mothers) was below the poverty line. The general incidence of poverty among children in 1997 stood at 21.8 percent, meaning that every fifth child in Israel was below the poverty line. NII researchers explain that the main reasons for the regression in the economic state of single-parent families are gradual erosion in income-support benefits relative to the average wage, and an increase in the rate of single-parent families where the parent is unemployed (Awad, Cohen, and Yaniv 1998, 72). Nevertheless, data from 1998 are more encouraging, as poverty among single-parent families and immigrant families decreased substantially (from 28.5 percent in 1997 to 24.7 percent in 1998 for single-parent families, and from 17.2 percent to 15.1 percent for immigrant families).

No valid statistics investigate the class of single mothers apart from all single-parent families. Even though the two classes almost fully correspond, a separate examination might reveal an even graver situation regarding single mothers and some significant gaps between single fathers and single mothers. One indication of this is the disproportionately high rate of single mothers who received income-support benefits in early 2000. At that time, 40.8 percent of all women receiving income support benefits were single mothers.[49] Another set of statistics to examine with regard to single mothers is statistics regarding women who receive alimony payments, since the two groups correlate strongly: in 1999, 68 percent of the single mothers where women who were divorced, 16 percent were never-married, and 16 percent were widowed.[50] Divorced women consistently comprise 70 percent of the women who receive alimony payments (27 percent of the recipients are women who are separated from their husbands, and 3 percent were never married to their children's father) (Yaniv and Haron 1999, 95–96). Of course, not all single mothers receive alimony payment benefits from the NII. Those who do are among the neediest, as turning to the NII means that the debtor does not pay, either that he is either unable to pay or that the woman creditor does not have the means to start proceedings on her own.[51] Nonetheless, as almost all women receiving alimony payments are women with children (99.4 percent in 1999), data concerning them are not only important in themselves, in describing one of the most vulnerable groups of women, they also add to an understanding of the situation of single mothers in general and shed some light on the economic consequences of divorce for women in Israel.

In 1998, 21,100 women received alimony payments, more than double the number ten years earlier (9,985 in 1988), and an increase of 40 percent from five years earlier in 1993. The overwhelming majority (99.4 percent) were women with children: more than a third had one child, close to a third had two children, almost 20 percent had three children and about 10 percent had four children or more.[52] The most striking finding in the NII statistics is that only 4 percent of the women received the full sum determined in the regulations. Some (15 percent) received a decreased sum due to other sources of income (such as employment), while the majority (over 80 percent) received sums dictated in courts' decisions. This means that the sum decided in the courts is almost always lower than the fixed amount, and, as explained before, the beneficiary is entitled to the lower sum of the two. NII figures reveal that the average sum paid on the basis of a court's judgment was only 20 percent of the average wage, while the average sum paid according to the regulations amounted to 45 percent of the average wage. If all recipients were paid according to the regulations, they would have received double the amount they actually were receiving (Yaniv and Haron 1999, 95–96). Thus, women in this particular group, probably among the most economically impoverished, are in fact denied benefits to which they are entitled by law, due to inexplicable, disgracefully low alimony court judgments. Unfortunately, no empirical research has ever been done on alimony awards in Israel, nor on the socioeconomic profile of women alimony beneficiaries in general or women recipients of NII alimony allowances in particular. Nevertheless, it is difficult to conceive of a plausible explanation for the factor of two disparity between the courts' awards and the amounts in the regulations.

The most recent in-depth NII research on women who receive alimony payments shed some light on this issue (Toledano 1999). Apparently, close to half the alimony benefits recipients had rabbinical court awards in their favor, which tend to be significantly lower than civil court awards (district or family courts, as explained in Chapter 11). The average sum of rabbinical judgments amounted to only 16.9 percent of the average wage, while the average district and in family court awards were 22.2 percent and 26.9 percent respectively (Toledano 1999, table 12). In other words, rabbinical court awards tend to be 30 percent lower than other court awards. This fact, together with the predominance of rabbinical court awards, of course has a significant effect on the overall level of benefits. NII researchers note that the trend toward an increase in the number of women who receive benefits according to court awards rather than regulations is continuing. One explanation is that the sums in the regulations were increased as a result of the 1994–95 plan to combat poverty, whereas court judgments were not increased. Many women who previously received their benefits according to the regulations thus were switched to the court-ordered sums, as they have become lower. In other words, these women have not enjoyed the reformed increased regulations' amounts at all (Toledano 1999, 3).

The NII researchers conclude that all these statistics show that the Alimony Law in fact fails to guarantee minimal subsistence for all the population for which it was intended. Furthermore, the rate of participation in the labor force among women who receive alimony payments is lower than in the general population of women with children: 43 percent compared with 70 percent. Consequently, women whose court alimony payments are low and who lack any other source of income are entitled to income supplement. Indeed, in 1998, more than 40 percent of all women who received alimony payments from the NII also received income support benefits. For those who have been receiving a salary, overall income including salary and alimony payments in 1998 amounted to 57.5 percent of the average wage (Yaniv and Haron 1999, 97).

A major part of the vulnerable economic status of women-headed households is the direct result of the earning gaps between women and men and of women's lower status in the workforce in general. NII statistics clearly show a significantly lower incidence of poverty among families headed by an employee (6.8 percent in 1997, a decline from 7.2 percent in 1996) relative to the general incidence of poverty among families (16.2 percent in 1997, an increase from 16 percent in 1996) (Awad,

Cohen, and Yaniv 1998, 61). Women's higher rate of unemployment, added to their lower wages when employed, is detrimental. This contention is also supported by the breakdown of the incidence of poverty among working men and women. The NII 1996 data revealed that 14 percent of employed Jewish women lived below the poverty line, while the poverty rate for employed Jewish men was only 7 percent.[53]

Chapter 7
The Work Women Do

In looking at the legislative framework alone, Israeli society's awareness of protecting a woman's right and ability to work is impressive. It all seems to be demonstrated by the very progressive, comprehensive legislation which attempts to provide for women's special needs as well as ensure that women are not discriminated against. The developments within the legislative framework also reflect the move from protection of women's maternal rights to the endorsement of parental rights. On deeper reflection, though, this first impression could be gravely doubted. Many of these employment rights of parents are clearly traced back to the protection of maternity and of women's reproductive roles, rather than of women. From a comparative perspective, this development conforms with the worldwide process in which women's reproductive and productive roles were initially combined by giving preference to the former. This policy was gradually revealed to be counterproductive to gender equality and was replaced by policies aimed at protecting "workers with family responsibilities," not women as such (Tomasevski 1998, 11). This development in Israeli law, then, reflects the worldwide trend to further the family and accommodate family responsibilities in the employment market. Comparative statistics demonstrate that, despite overall legislative progress, women's position in the labor market is far from satisfactory and falls below the average for industrial countries in terms of female participation in the workforce, existence of female managers, and females' share of earned income.[1] All in all, the same pattern evident in women's representation in political and public life is seen here too: Israel's performance in these and other measures of women's participation in the labor market and the economy is well below Israel's performance in the general measures of human development.[2]

The present government attitude is even more disturbing. Nowhere is the gap between the normative sphere and the actual situation more apparent than in the area of women's employment. The laws are simply not being enforced, and so the market behaves as if no progressive legislation exists. In that case, the data cannot be said to be surprising. In a ritual that parallels media commotion and public outcry in the wake of yet another cycle of violence against women, politicians and the media are exasperated each year anew in light of the Central Bureau of Statistics (CBS) or the National Insurance Institute findings of vast salary gaps between men and women. This exasperation does not last long and does not translate into budgetary commitment or change of policy. The implementation of long school days has been repeatedly postponed, preschool child care is lacking and costly, and child care expenses are not tax-deductible. All these observations support sociologist Dafna Izraeli's claim that the ongoing gender inequality in the Israeli labor market is inherent in the institutions, processes, and practices of the labor market itself. The labor market is not a neutral social institution. It is a gendered phenomenon, like the careers themselves. They were all structured and constructed around male norms; they fit men's life patterns and benefit workers who abide by them (Izraeli 1999b).

This thesis is further supported by the recurring theme of information. The area of women's employment presents numerous gaps in information. Perhaps most significant in terms of policymaking is the treatment of family-market relationships from the perspective of information collection and analysis. Official statistics do not enable the gathering of information on the effect of in-house child care on women's work patterns. Moreover, family-market relationships are only examined in relation to women's work patterns. The first observation suggests, for instance, demands for tax reform in recognition of child care as an expense. The latter reinforces social perceptions of gender roles within the family and the market and works to rule out any possibility of social change in the direction of increased paternal involvement in childcare. In contrast to the previous criticism regarding economic constraints on women's equal integration into the workforce, this last point hardly requires any economic commitment but rather an awareness of women's predicament and commitment to women's advancement.

Israel is no exception in its failure to consider housewives, stay-at-home mothers, and all the unpaid housework, child care, and other forms of care work for the computation of the gross national product; nor are these included in the CBS workforce statistics. This results in a distorted account of the Israeli workforce, which excludes these women from the statistics and reinforces the view that they do not participate in the economic growth of the country. Bringing in the gender factor and taking into consideration women's house and reproductive work may cause a total revision of economic estimates. Thus, the 1994 World Survey on the Role of Women in Development stressed that women's reproductive work continued to be unremunerated and doubled the men's burden.[3] As Tomasevski (1998, 11) notes, this was the first time the term "work" was used in these surveys to denote childbearing and childrearing. Tomasevski goes on to demonstrate the effect of revising statistical definitions: in India, for instance, the proportion of working women is 13 percent according to a conventional definition, but 88 percent according to a gender-sensitive definition.[4] No similar study has been done in Israel. A time-use survey was conducted in 1991–92 (and not repeated since), and its fascinating findings are described below. However, no national economic policy conclusions were drawn from it, despite the CEDAW committee's recommendation.[5] Izraeli sees this, as well as the ambivalence with which women themselves view their unpaid work, as a reflection of the gendered market economy and relates this to women's general reluctance to negotiate their salaries and benefits (Izraeli 1999b, 179–83).

Another form of work done mostly by women, but not recognized and unaccounted for in the national work statistics, is in the informal sector. Whereas the formal sector is conventionally defined as being comprised of "stable full-time jobs for registered firms," and may also include temporary or part-time workers and workers who work under substandard contracts, the informal sector comprises several categories of workers (Chen 2000, 3). In Israel this includes unsupervised and unreported hired housework and child care, which make up the major part of this industry, as well as unsupervised and unreported sweatshop work. An informal sector that is larger than the formal one is a characteristic of developing countries, while in industrialized countries it is estimated that 85 percent of the workforce is in the formal sector (Chen 2000).

Industrialized countries are characterized by overrepresentation of women in the "contingent workforce" (Chen 2000), defined as workers who lack explicit or implicit contracts for long-term employment or who work minimum hours that vary unsystematically (Polivka and Nardone, 1989)—an expanding phenomenon in many industrialized countries (Ferber and Waldfogel 1996). This phenomenon, too, seems not to have escaped Israel. It has been suggested that over 7 percent of the Israeli workforce consists of temporary work agencies; almost 30 percent of the public sector workers are employed through such agencies, and over 80 percent of them are women (Zohar 1999, 31). Here, too, there are no formal statistics, only estimates given by NGOs (Zohar 1999). These workers are in general more vulnerable to workforce instabilities and cutbacks and lack many of the standard workers' social conditions and benefits. Thus, for example, personnel agencies may "suspend" workers for up to three months until new jobs are located, during which time they receive no salaries or unemployment benefits (Zohar 1999, 32). Pregnant women are particularly vulnerable to such arrangements.[6] Side by side with the growing class of underprivileged "contingent" workers, another class of even more vulnerable workers has recently been emerging in the Israeli labor market, namely foreign workers. Israel's treatment of foreign workers has been the subject of much public and political debate, and several studies have been devoted to it (Natanzon 1999). However, no separate discussion has taken place of women foreign workers and of their particular plight, except in occasional media and newspaper reports, and these women remain similarly absent from the discussion in this chapter, due to a lack of concrete data and information.[7]

From a totally different angle, Israel's "high-tech revolution" of the 1990s has had special implications for women. Although academic research on this area is only beginning, some assessment can already be made. As much as the high-tech industry had seemed to offer an egalitarian, meritocracy-based environment that could enable flexible hours and workplaces, reality has proved this to be a myth. Researchers point to the "visibility" standard, which expects workers to be visible and available well beyond the formal nine hours, and talk about the creation of a "local clock" reflecting the new time norms, in total antithesis to the conventional expectations of a woman who is also a mother (Izraeli 1999b, 168; Rubinstein 2000). Some scholars see this as a direct continuum of the military management culture,[8] while others suggest that it may represent a strategy for obstructing women's entry into the field. Recent research confirms long-held suspicions: men business administration graduates whose credentials are similar to and sometimes even lower than those of women graduates reach substantially more senior positions than do women.[9] This also causes significantly lower rates of women among the "newly high-tech rich," namely, holders of stocks and options in successful start-ups. One can fairly predict that the implications of this new type of gender capital division will be far-reaching and may even undermine much of the feminist economic achievement of the last few decades.

The Normative Framework—Workers as Women

Protection from Discrimination

Until the end of the 1980s, few laws specifically dealt with matters of gender equality in the workplace. The 1964 Equal Pay (Male and Female Employees) Law, replaced in 1996,[10] demanded that male and female workers receive equal pay for equal work. A more general condemnation of discrimination against women can be found in the 1951 Women's Equal Rights Law,[11] which demanded that "one law apply to men and women regarding every legal action." As noted, while it lacked the constitutional status of a Basic Law, the Supreme Court construed it as containing norms of a constitutional nature, and has held that, where possible, other laws should be interpreted so as to conform to its provisions.

One of the few significant precedents relating to gender equality in the workplace previous to the 1980s was the 1973 *Union of Air Steward Staff v. Edna Hazin*[12] case. The National Labor Court held that provisions of a labor agreement preventing women from being promoted to the highest level of air steward, terminating their employment on marriage or pregnancy, and denying paid sick leave during pregnancy for any reason, were null and void. The fact that the court did not utilize the Women's Equal Rights Law, operating instead within the general parameters of contract law, is further demonstration of the practical ineffectiveness of the existing women's rights legislation and its failure to empower general statements with specific remedies (Raday 1995).

The 1987 Equal Retirement Age (Male and Female Employees) Law[13] prohibits employers from forcing early retirement on female workers. The law was passed while the Supreme Court was deciding the case of *Nevo v. The National Labor Court*,[14] in which a female employee sued for nullification of a policy requiring female workers to retire five years earlier than men. Unanimously rejecting the employer's argument that the policy was intended to benefit women and further equality by taking into account their special needs as both mothers and wives, the court held that, while the law did not apply retroactively to the case at hand, the legal situation existing before the passage of the law, specifically the 1951 Women's Equal Rights Law, forbade such discriminatory practices. The law provides that in cases where a collective agreement continues to specify different retirement ages for men and women, female workers retain the option of early retirement. While proponents of this option argue that it is consistent with the conception of substantive equality in the Israeli legal system, it has been widely criticized both by adherents to formalistic notions of equality and by many who express concern for the financial burden imposed on pension funds.

The 1988 Equal Employment Opportunities Law[15] prohibits discrimination in government or private workplaces based on gender, sexual orientation, marital status, parenthood, race, age, religion, nationality, country of birth, or political or other orientation. Protections offered to female employees that take into account their special needs as women or mothers are not to be considered discriminatory, but the law specifies that any such rights offered to working mothers must equally be given to men who either have sole custody of their children, or whose wives work and have chosen not to make use of these provisions.

The 1988 law also recognizes sexual harassment as a form of discrimination in the workplace subject to civil and criminal sanctions. Until the enactment of the 1998 Prevention of Sexual Harassment Law,[16] this was the only law that explicitly dealt with sexual harassment confined to the workplace, and its definition of sexual harassment changed to incorporate that of the new law. A 1995 amendment placed the burden of proof on the employer in civil sexual harassment suits.[17] While the other provisions of the law are limited to those employers who employ more than five workers, the provision forbidding sexual harassment applies to all employers.[18]

The Civil Service Code is another document dealing with the issue of sexual harassment,[19] proscribed as a disciplinary offense in its 1990 supplement in a definition already broader than that in the 1988 Equal Employment Opportunities Law. With respect to sexual harassment between supervisors and workers, the code specified that matters of consent or initiation were irrelevant. A 1995 amendment to the code added the creation of a "hostile working environment" and provided for legal and professional aid to the plaintiff through either the superintendent over discipline or the supervisors on the status of women in each ministry. The general supervisor on the advancement of women in the civil service and the superintendent over discipline in the civil service handle all complaints regarding sexual harassment in the service. The amendment obligates all employees to report any suspicion of sexual harassment. According to the general supervisor, while the overall number of complaints dealt with by the Unit for the Advancement of Women has remained stable, the rate of sexual harassment complaints has increased from 25 percent in 1998 to 45 percent in 1999.[20]

Going back to the 1988 law, a violation of its primary provisions constitutes a criminal offense, punishable by a fine. Unlike its 1981 predecessor, however, which merely criminalized discrimination, the law entitles civil remedies as well. Exclusive jurisdiction is given to the labor courts. Although Israeli contract law generally prefers compensation over interfering in employee-employer relationships, the court is specifically authorized to grant enforcement injunctions in cases where mere compensation would not serve the cause of justice.[21] In deciding whether to grant enforcement injunctions, the court must also consider their potential impact on the various workplace relationships; indeed, very few such injunctions have been granted. Suits may be filed by the worker, by a representative labor organization, or—with the worker's consent—by any other organization dedicated to protecting the rights of that class of worker. Such organizations may also intervene, with the court's permission, and present arguments for the plaintiff. These provisions are particularly important in view of the somewhat ironic tendency of labor organizations to side with employers against the worker whose rights have been violated (Raday 1995, 102–5). Women's organizations, particularly the Israel Women's Network (IWN), have taken advantage of this provision in several cases in attempting to reach favorable precedents.

It took more than a decade to put this law to test: in the 1997 case of *Plotkin v. Izenberg Brothers Ltd*,[22] the National Labor Court accepted an appeal by Ms Plotkin, who had answered a job advertisement and was invited to an interview. During the interview, she was told that women were not suitable for the job, as it entailed being a salesperson outside the office. Having been turned down for the job, Plotkin filed suit with the Regional Labor Court, joined by the IWN. The court found that Plotkin was discriminated against, but awarded her damages in the amount of only a one-month junior employee salary. Her appeal to the National Labor Court was accepted, setting a precedent in terms of appropriate compensation in cases of discrimination. The court rejected the employer's argument that the job was difficult for a woman. Similarly, the employer's argument that he eventually hired a woman for the job was also rejected as irrelevant. Most significantly, the employer's comment to Ms Plotkin was found to be tainted with a stereotypical approach and thus was sufficient, by itself, to render the employer's conduct wrong. As for compensation, the court's purpose was twofold: to compensate Plotkin for her actual damages and to educate the employer, and all other employers, in order to achieve nondiscriminatory, nonstereotypical conduct. The court ordered the employer to pay Ms Plotkin 50,000 NIS ($14,200) in punitive damages.

As for enforcement mechanisms, the 1988 law authorizes the Minister of Labor and Welfare to appoint supervisors who may investigate complaints both by demanding relevant information from the employer in question and by entering the premises of the workplace to question the owners and any other person involved.[23] While the law does authorize the minister to appoint a public council in charge of overseeing implementation of the law, its functions are merely advisory, and it is not authorized to file suits on behalf of workers. Even this weak version of public council has not really been operative, and it ceased functioning in 1993. This absence of a public body that can effectively contribute to enforcement and to defending the rights of individual workers has been widely criticized.

Another impressive—yet almost totally inoperative—law is the 1996 Equal Pay (Male and Female Employees) Law,[24] which expands protection against discrimination by broadening its definition, providing greater access to remedies, and implementing the progressive notion of pay equity. While the 1964 law dealt merely with "salaries," the law now extends to "all other forms of compensation," which previously served as "loopholes" for employers wishing to evade the spirit of the law. While the law previously required employers to pay workers in "essentially equal" positions at the same workplace equal salaries, today's law extends its protection to positions at the same workplace that are "equal in value,"[25] which includes different positions demanding equal qualifications, effort, expertise, and responsibility.[26]

Exclusive jurisdiction over disputes arising under this law is given to the Labor courts. Employees found to have been underpaid according to this law may sue for up to 24 months back wages. Suits may be filed by the employee, by a representative organization, or, with the worker's consent, by a women's rights organization. Class action suits can also be filed by one worker whose rights have been violated on behalf of a number of such workers, a rare option in the Israeli legal system.

Bringing a case based on the new law's provisions requires a sophisticated argument of "occupations analysis," namely a socioeconomic evaluation of the comparable worth of the various occupations. In her elaborate work *Equality by Opportunities and Prohibition of Discrimination in Employment in Israel*, Ruth Ben-Israel (1998, 768–71) explains the impediments faced by any employee who may attempt to use this mechanism. A major obstacle is the probable impossibility of obtaining information about male co-workers' salaries. This may begin to be overcome through case law. In 1999, the Be'er Sheva District Labor Court, in one of the few proceedings ever held under this law, decided that an employer must release information regarding the salaries of male employees in the workplace of the claimant. The court ruled that the principle of equality and the worker's right to sue her employer overcomes the other workers' right to privacy (regarding their salary levels).[27]

Pregnancy, Maternity, and Parenthood Rights

According to the 1954 Employment of Women Law, it is illegal to terminate the employment of a pregnant woman who has been working for the same employer or at the same workplace for at least six months without permission from the minister of labor and welfare, given only where dismissal is unrelated to the woman's pregnancy.[28] Women on maternity leave or high-risk pregnancy sick leave may not be fired under any circumstances or given notice that their employment is to be terminated during that time. Women who have chosen to take an unpaid leave of absence (discussed below) may not be fired during their leave without permission from the minister.[29]

These provisions, however, were significantly lacking in many respects. The minister's discretion in granting permission has been very broadly construed. Female employees were not given protection against dismissal on return to work following leaves of absence, and employers could worsen the working conditions of pregnant female employees, thus in fact forcing them to "voluntarily" quit their jobs. The law was therefore amended in 1998[30] so as extend the protection against dismissal for an additional 45 days on return to work, thus making it less tempting for employers to hire replacements during the employee's absence. A 2000 amendment prohibits the inclusion of the 45-day period within the required period of advance notice prior to dismissal.[31] The 1998 amendment further prohibits any cutback in a pregnant employee's post without permission from the minister on labor and welfare. However, recent data from the supervisor on employment laws in the ministry indicate that 54 percent of the requests are approved.[32]

Another new protection against dismissal adopted recently relates to fertility treatments. While the law allowed workers leave of absence for fertility treatments, it did not prohibit their dismissal; this prohibition is made in a 2001 amendment to the Employment of Women Law.[33] The Employment of Women Law addresses pregnancy, motherhood, and parenthood in various other provisions. A pregnant employee must notify her employer of her condition by the fifth month of her pregnancy. The prohibition against employing a pregnant woman for overtime and night work was replaced by the 1998 amendment, which gives the woman the option to decide, with medical approval, whether to work overtime.[34] Both men and women are allowed to take leaves of absence, characterized as sick leave, while undergoing fertility treatments. Likewise, pregnant women are entitled to paid absences from work for routine medical examinations.[35] Since 2000, the law permits a male worker up to seven days of absence a year on account of his spouse's pregnancy or birthgiving as part of his right to sick leave.[36]

A mandatory twelve-week leave of absence (extended under special medical circumstances) may be taken by the expectant mother at any point after the middle of the seventh month of pregnancy.[37] In 1994 the Knesset amended the National Insurance Law so as to provide women on maternity leave with the full equivalent of their salaries, instead of the 75 percent (untaxable) previously granted.[38] However, the full compensation now given is taxed as regular salary. The main beneficiaries of the amendment are women whose earnings are taxed according to lower tax brackets. In July 1997 the law was amended so as to allow the couple to decide for themselves who would take the second half of the maternity-leave, the six to twelve weeks following the birth of a child, in an ultimate move from maternal to parental rights, as discussed in Chapter 2.[39] These dispositions, along with those concerning unpaid leave of absence and those forbidding the dismissal of workers who benefit from these dispositions, are extended with necessary adjustments to parents upon adoption of a child (the dispositions apply only to one of the parents, with the choice left to their discretion).[40]

A pregnant woman medically confirmed unable to work for a specified period may absent herself from work without affecting her seniority rights.[41] The National Insurance Law[42] previously entitled women on high-risk pregnancy leave to receive the equivalent of their salary from Social Security but only up to 70 percent of the average workforce wage. The law was amended in early 2000, setting the limit at 100 percent of the average wage.[43] Other problems may arise where the employee's medical situation is not severe enough to qualify as "high-risk," but does interfere with her ability to work, or where the nature of her work makes it difficult for her to continue while she is pregnant. The law offers no clear protection, and dismissals have been approved by the minister of labor and welfare despite the requirement that such permission be granted only where dismissal is unrelated to pregnancy.

Following the birth, mothers or fathers who have been employed by the same employer or at the same workplace for at least two years may take an unpaid leave of absence of up to twelve months following their maternity leave, depending on the length of their employment.[44] In addition, for four months following her maternity leave, a woman who works full-time may absent herself from work for one hour each day without affecting her salary.[45] Other laws that seek to protect the needs of parents allow them the freedom to decide which of them will take advantage of the various protections offered. For instance, the 1963 Severance Pay Law provides that an employee who quits his or her job within the first ninth months after childbirth to provide care for the baby is entitled to severance pay, as long as the other parent has not claimed such pay.[46] According to the 1993 Sick Pay (Absence from Work due to Child's Illness) Law, parents may decide which of them will absent him/herself from work for a combined total of eight days a year in order to care for a child under the age of sixteen.[47] According to the 1988 Equal Employment Opportunities Law, any day care services offered to mothers or day care expenditures covered by employers, as well as any shortened work days or absences offered to mothers, must be offered to fathers as well.

Case law has recently been adding force to the legislative movement toward facilitating the accommodation of work and family. Let us examine just two examples, which, while encouraging, should be viewed cautiously, as there always are counterforces and conservative holdings.[48] In a 1999 case, in which the Na'amat women's organization joined the husband-claimant, the Tel Aviv District Labor Court adopted a broad interpretation of a working mother's right to pass her shorter working day privilege to her spouse. The court held that this privilege is reserved for all working mothers, whether hired or self-employed. This interpretation was held to be in accordance with the principles of basic equality as well as with the object of the Equal Employment Opportunities Law. Significantly, the court specifically aimed its decision at encouraging the incorporation of women into high-ranking positions in the workplace.[49] The National Labor Court also had an opportunity to expand parental rights, in a 2000 case which gave a broad interpretation to section 7 of the 1963 Severance Pay Law, providing for severance pay to any employee who quits his or her job during the first nine months after childbirth in order to care for a child. According to the traditional interpretation of this section, severance pay is awarded to a worker who starts a new job as long as the number of hours spent working at the new workplace is significantly lower than at the old one. The National Labor Court held that the worker is entitled to severance pay even in cases where the new place of work is closer to the worker's home, explaining that "it isn't the number of hours worked which is relevant, but the fact that the claimant-mother is physically closer, and thus more available to her baby, should he/she need her."[50]

Enforcement of Employment Legislation

The Department of Supervision of Labor Laws of the Ministry of Labor and Welfare supervises the enforcement of a number of labor laws, including the 1954 Employment of Women Law.[51] Applications to the department can be classified in two categories: complaints from women discharged from their employment during pregnancy, and employers' applications for termination permits. In recent years, the number of applications in both categories has risen steadily, and now reaches around 850 cases per year. The disappointingly high rate of approval of termination of employment during pregnancy has already been noted. Even more disappointing is the steady increase in the approval rate: from 43 percent of the requests in 1994 to 54 percent in 2000.[52] It seems that the protection the law allegedly offers is being circumvented by the very organization that should implement it.

In addition to the Department of Supervision of Labor Laws, the Department of Labor Law Enforcement is also in charge of supervising and enforcing labor legislation. Of the 59 supervisors employed by the department in 1997, only two dealt with the enforcement of the Equal Employment Opportunities Law. These two supervisors were to investigate complaints of sexual harassment and discrimination as detailed in the law. The law also requires all employers to advertise job offers in both male and female grammatical forms. If further proof were needed to claim the futility of the law in its current form, the Department's data reveal that most cases dealt with by the department pertain to job vacancy advertisements (162 of the total 188 in 1996). In 1996, only 23 of the cases involved discrimination (including discrimination on the basis of age and race), 19 of which resulted in no findings. Two cases alone were sexual harassment cases. Ironically, 162 of the cases that pertained to discriminatory advertisements resulted in conclusive findings, and all the employers investigated regarding their advertisements corrected them following the department's verbal or written requests, with no need for prosecution.[53] It seems, then, that the government agency officially ordered to protect female workers from discrimination sees its mission as guarding politically correct speech. In contrast, over the course of 1996, the IWN "Struggle Against Discrimination" hot line received 302 complaints, 42 percent of them regarding discrimination at work, and sexual harassment. In other words, 157 complaints of discrimination prohibited by the Equal Employment Opportunities Law were made to the IWN, seven times more than to the Department of Labor Law Enforcement.[54]

The enforcement division of the ministry seemed to increase its activities, conducting 597 investigations during January to August 2000. However, most cases involved unlawful advertisement and only a few cases involved alleged substantial discrimination. Furthermore, of the cases involving discrimination, no data concerning the number of cases involving discrimination against women are available.[55]

The 1987 Minimum Wage Law[56] sets a minimum wage for the employment of workers in proportion to their scope of employment. It entitles workers earning below the minimum wage level (currently set at 47.5 percent of the average wage) to a wage supplement up to the minimum level, to be paid by their employers. The Minimum Wage Law is enforced through self-initiated employee complaints and through processes initiated by the Department of Labor Law Enforcement. For the purpose of enforcement of this law, the department employs eleven supervisors, divided into five teams in conjunction with the Labor Union, Workers' Council, and workers' hot line, to investigate the worker's wages.

An employer found in violation of the law is issued a warning that ensures payment of back salary. An employer who refuses to pay back salary is prosecuted or fined approximately $750 per employee per month. According to Israel's Report on the Convention on Economic and Social Rights, in 1997 more than 2,500 workplaces employing 45,000 workers were inspected for compliance with the Minimum Wage Law. Violations were found with regard to approximately 2,650 workers, who received compensation totaling NIS 3.3 million. The comparison with data from 1996 points to a fall in the number of violations as well as to a clear improvement in the amounts paid in compensation for these violations (CESCR Pre-Session Working Group 1998, 21–24). Previous research conducted by the Research Department of the Bank of Israel found obedience to the law to be only partial (30 percent), with four times more women than men earning below minimum wage (Palug and Kassir 1994). Critical research points to presently ongoing violations and low levels of obedience (Efroni 1994, 1997).

Social Security Benefits

Israel is a welfare state, and National Insurance is an institution that plays a large role in every citizen's life. The status of a homemaker, and the extent of coverage she is eligible to receive, however, reveals a lot about the way society views her working contribution inside the home. A "homemaker" in Israeli law can only be a woman; therefore, it is entirely appropriate to use the gender-specific term "housewife" here.

The definition of the term "housewife" in the 1995 National Insurance Law (Consolidated Version)[57] varies according to the context in which it is used. A housewife is generally defined as a married woman who is not employed outside the home and is therefore not obligated to pay Social Security. While married men must pay Social Security regardless of their employment status, married women must do so only when they are employed outside the home. The National Insurance Law, therefore, both reinforces the stereotypical gender division of labor and denies legal recognition to the husband who wishes to stay home and tend the household while his wife earns the family's living. Until 1995, a wife who chose to stay home was not eligible for an old-age pension unless she chose voluntary insurance. In 1995, the National Insurance Law was amended to include homemakers in their husband's mandatory coverage, allowing them to receive the minimum old-age pension while still exempting them from contributions. The law, therefore, now gives a certain degree of recognition to the economic contribution of homemakers. "Housewives," however, are still not considered workers: they are not eligible for income replacement benefits such as employment injuries insurance, maternity allowance, or unemployment benefits.[58]

Many of the social security benefits that are not work-related are discussed in Chapter 6. The main work-related social benefit for women is maternity leave allowance. Eligibility for this allowance is conditional on having worked for a certain period of time prior to the birth and having acquired a minimum period of social security payments. In 1998, only half the women who gave birth were eligible for the allowance in terms of working the required amount of months prior to the birth (close to 64,200 women, representing 50.3 percent of all births that year). However, this is more than a 32 percent increase from 1993, explained by the increase in women's general participation in the workforce, as demonstrated below (Eliav 2000, 182–83). Significantly, 94.5 percent of the women who received maternity leave allowance in 1997 were Jewish, even though they constituted only 70.5 percent of women who gave birth that year. This disproportion reflects the huge difference in the rate of Jewish and non-Jewish women's participation in the female workforce: 93 percent and 7 percent respectively in 1997 (Eliav 1998, 186–88).

The main work-related benefit for all workers, men and women alike, is the unemployment benefit, which is given to a person who has worked for 180 days during the year prior to being unemployed. Any person registered at the Employment Service, willing and able to work, who has not been offered work by the service, may receive unemployment benefit. Accordingly, the number of unemployment benefit recipients is always lower than the total number of unemployed persons. The daily unemployment benefit is calculated at rates determined in the law on the basis of the daily average wage of the unemployed person during the last 75 work days of the qualifying period. Significantly, regular National Insurance Institute statistics do not segregate unemployment benefit recipients on the basis of gender. Based on special information given in 1997, women receiving unemployment benefits were only 3.9 percent of the female workforce, while women's unemployment rate was 8 percent. The corresponding figures for men were 2.8 percent benefit recipients and 5.1 percent unemployed.[59] In 1999, the rate of women unemployment recipients was 4.6 percent, while their unemployment rate reached 9.4 percent. This could suggest that many women are unaware of their entitlement to unemployment benefits. Another possible explanation is that women are denied benefits because of an alleged refusal to accept "suitable work"—a refusal that might be based on inability to accommodate irregular work hours with available child care. The law's definition of "suitable work" includes professional, educational, health, and physical considerations, but not familial ones. Labor courts have evidently construed the definition formally, and there are numerous examples of single mothers who lost their right to unemployment benefits due to inability to accept work whose hours conflict with child care arrangements. This was taken by the placement authority as an unjustified refusal to accept "suitable work." While some courts have expressed their discomfort with the resulting loss of benefits, they have mostly felt constrained by the statutory definition and left it to the legislator to change.[60] All this despite a 1996 National Labor Court precedent which explicitly held that a single mother's inability to accept work that would require her to leave home at 6:15 a.m. does not render her "work-resisting."[61]

Several recent legislative amendments have limited the right to unemployment benefits. A 1999 amendment to the 1995 National Insurance Law reduced the amount for unemployment benefits, setting it at the average wage for the first five months of unemployment and two-thirds of the average wage from the sixth month on.[62] Two 2000 amendments reduced the total period of unemployment benefits eligibility in all categories.[63]

Taxes

Some progress toward legal recognition of women's equality has been made in recent years in the area of tax law. The Income Tax Ordinance,[64] as it took effect upon the establishment of the state, viewed the married couple as a single unit for tax purposes, with regard to both the manner in which income was calculated and the procedural obligation to report. The Income Tax Ordinance obligated the man, the automatically designated "household head," to report the joint income of his wife and himself in all instances, and denied any option for separate calculation of income. As a result, it both refused to relate to married women as taxpayers and created a situation in which it was often not economically beneficial for women to seek employment outside the home. While a 1952 amendment to the ordinance[65] offered couples the option of separate calculation where the woman's income derived from her "personal toil," the effect of this change was significantly weakened by a number of subsequent amendments as well as the narrow interpretation of "personal toil" applied by the courts so as to prevent exploitation of this provision.

This combination of denying recognition to married women as taxpayers and strictly restricting separate calculation led to a 1961 attempt to convince the Supreme Court that the requirement of joint calculation violated the 1951 Women's Equal Rights Law. In the Lubinsky case,[66] the Supreme Court rejected this claim on the grounds that the requirement did not discriminate against women as such, but rather represented a legitimate policy decision to view couples as a single tax unit. The court added that the Women's Equal Rights Law lacked the constitutional status necessary to prevent the Knesset from enacting contradictory laws.

In 1989, several private bills designed to amend the situation were submitted to the Knesset. The income tax commissioner agreed to establish a public committee to examine the status of women vis-à-vis income tax.

The committee had the mandate to "recommend changes in the law and work procedures relating to income tax, in order to create legal and procedural equality between spouses." However, its mandate was restricted to recommendations, with no far-reaching economic implications. In July 1990, the committee handed in its report to the commissioner, who adopted most of it and submitted his version to the Finance Committee. In March 1992, the commissioner's proposal was accepted, with some minor modifications, and became amendment number 89 to the Income Tax Ordinance.[67]

In general, the 1992 amendment granted equal recognition to married women as taxpayers and widened the instances where separate calculation would be allowed for husbands and wives. Instead of referring to "husbands" and "wives," the Income Tax Ordinance now differentiates between the "registered spouse" and the "other spouse." It widened and relaxed the conditions allowing women to be designated the "registered spouse" and allowed both spouses to appeal decisions of the tax authorities and receive credit points for dependents. Although the 1992 amendment continues to see the married couple as a single tax unit, it has expanded the instances in which separate calculations are permitted. Separate calculation is now allowed not only for income earned by the "other spouse" in "personal toil," but also for income earned by the "other spouse" at least a year prior to marriage or inherited by that spouse during marriage (Lapidoth 1992).

All in all, the 1992 amendment has not brought the anticipated policy change of complete separation between the spouses' incomes. The main reason for that was the narrow mandate of the committee restricting it to changes with no far-reaching economic consequences. Allowing the child care expenses of a working mother to be tax-deductible, like other similar recommendations, has never been implemented.

Significantly, all these tax arrangements apply solely to couples recognized as officially married. As explained in Chapter 11, the institution of nonmarital cohabitation has special significance as a result of the various religious restrictions on the individual's right to marry. Section 1 of the Income Tax Ordinance explicitly defines "spouse" as a "married person," thus excluding nonmarital cohabitants. Accordingly, couples may prefer, under certain circumstances, to avoid being recognized as officially married, in order to enjoy the lower tax brackets of two separate individuals.

Women as Workers

While the level of women's participation in the labor market has risen dramatically over the years, reaching almost 50 percent of all adult women,[68] the occupational segregation and glass ceiling phenomenon remain entrenched; indeed the salary gap between men and women has increased slightly. Moreover, even the increased participation in the labor market should not be overemphasized as an achievement, since it seems less impressive from a comparative perspective. As noted, the United Nations Human Development Reports show a clear gap between Israel's performance on the Human Development Index and its performance in relation to Gender-Related Development and Empowerment Indices.[69]

Time Use by Women and Men

The perpetual need to reconcile work and family obligations characterizes the career and work patterns of women worldwide. Israel is no exception to the lack of recognition of the economic value of housework and child care, which is mostly done by women and which—when it is recognized—changes the whole perception of the labor gender division. Once again, the information story comes into play here: the only survey that scientifically examines all the work that men and women do on a daily basis was conducted in the early 1990s.[70] Although things may not have changed dramatically since then, it is nonetheless difficult to rely on these figures in an area that has seen such developments as the steady growth of women's employment along with the emergence of new fields of almost unlimited work such as the high-tech industry.

The findings of the time budget survey conducted by the CBS in 1991–92 are indeed fascinating. According to the survey, men devote most of their working time to paid work, more than twice (2.5) as much as women. Women devote most of their working time to unpaid work, almost three times (2.75) as much as men. Women devote 11 percent of their time to care of the home, in contrast to 2 percent of men. Women devote 4.3 percent of their time to care of children, in contrast to 1.4 percent of men. Among the age group of thirty to forty-four, the major part of the time is spent on work (36 percent in general). However, men spend most of it on paid work (28 percent), while women spend most of it on unpaid work (25 percent). Overall, of the total time men and women of all age groups spend on work, 74.4 percent of men's working time is spent on paid work, while 71 percent of women's working time is spent on unpaid work. Anecdotally, men and women spend the same amount of time on sleep (33.6 percent).[71]

Perhaps the most significant observation of this survey is that, even among those in full-time employment, women spend more than twice as much time on unpaid work as men (14.8 percent compared to 6.1 percent), making the total time spent on all work equal for men and women who are employed in full-time jobs (38 percent). Interestingly, of those who are employed in part-time jobs, women spend much more time than men on work in general (33.5 percent and 25.1 percent), since men who work part-time hardly increase their share of unpaid work in the home.[72]

There is a high correlation between the number of children aged zero to seventeen in a household and the amount of time married women spend on unpaid work; as expected, this amount increases in direct proportion to the number of children. Whereas without children a married woman devotes 19 percent of her time to unpaid work, this grows to 31 percent when she has three or more children. Men's work is not correlated to children at all: the amount of unpaid work of married men is small compared to married women (8 percent), and remains small, with no relation to the number of children in the household. Married women with three or more children in the household spend a daily average of 7 hours and 20 minutes on unpaid work, compared to 2 hours by married men with three or more children.[73]

A more recent survey sheds some light on the outcome of the perpetual work-family conflict: the 2000 Brookdale Institute Women's Health Survey examined the connection between a woman's work and her physical and mental health, and particularly her attitude toward accommodating family and work obligations (Gross and Brammli-Greenberg 2000). Not surprisingly, only 23 percent of the women who were satisfied with their accommodations reported a high level of depression, compared with 50 percent of those who were not satisfied with the accommodations they were making. Likewise, of those who were satisfied, 86 percent graded their general health as being good, compared with only 56 percent who were not satisfied. On the more general issue of working conditions and health, the survey revealed that the less control a woman feels she has over her work, the more likely she is to report a high level of depression, and the less likely to report a good health condition. In terms of type of work, a high rate of women who work in menial jobs report a high level of depression (54 percent), compared with only 24 percent of the women who work in "white collar" jobs.

Women's Participation in the Workforce

Women's participation in the workforce has risen steadily, with a yearly increase of about 1 percent, whereas men's participation has remained the same. Women comprised 45.2 percent of the total workforce in 1999 (compared to 33 percent in 1975),[74] and the increase is evident in almost all age groups except for the youngest and the eldest. Jewish women's level of participation is higher than overall women's participation, 52.5 percent in 1999. It is also interesting to note that the level of participation among Jewish women is the highest in the age group thirty-five to forty-four (78.5 percent in 1999).[75] Increase in women's participation is taking place among Arab women as well, though the level of participation within that group was low to begin with (24 percent in 1999, compared to 18.3 percent in 1995 and 16.8 percent in 1994).[76]

A woman's marital status, the number of children she has, and her age all greatly affect participation in the workforce. Consistent with the steady increase in women's overall participation in the workforce, there is a constant increase in level of participation among married women, from only a quarter in 1967 (25.3 percent) to well over half in 1999 (55 percent).[77] In 1998, 41 percent of unmarried women were in the workforce, compared with 53.4 percent of married women and 63.7 percent of divorcees.[78] This is explained by the fact that the group of unmarried includes younger women who are still students. The data that concern the higher participation of divorced women undoubtedly express the more pressing economic needs of this group of women.

Women's participation in the workforce decreases as the number of their children increases and rises with the age of their youngest child. In 1999, 77 percent of all women with one child were in the workforce, compared with 49 percent of those with four children or more; 62 percent of women whose youngest child was less than a year old were in the workforce, compared with 80 percent of those whose youngest child was ten to fourteen.[79] The CBS data do not even examine the variable of the number or age of children on the fathers' level of participation in the workforce—another poignant example of the "information story," or how the actual gathering and processing of information affects social conventions.

The CBS data also examine the variable of employing domestic help and its influence on women's level of participation in the workforce, but not on men's participation. Not surprisingly, the level of participation increases along with the increase of weekly hours of domestic help, from 49 percent among women who do not use any domestic help to 63 percent among those who employ domestic help for seven hours a week, and up to 76 percent of those who employ over sixteen hours a week.[80] These data clearly support the demand for the tax deduction of payments for domestic help. Significantly, though, the data do not differentiate between two greatly different (in cost and time frame) types of domestic help: general household aid and in-house child care. Once again, the questions asked in data-gathering totally manipulate the conclusions. The lack of differentiation also precludes the possibility of connecting these data with the data on women's workplace participation relative to number of children, or to data regarding time spent on child care and house work by men and women. Thus, no truly full picture of women's work patterns, priorities, and concerns is available, just as no full picture of the influence of parenthood (both maternity and paternity) on women's and men's work patterns is possible.

Work Patterns

One of the major differences between working women and men in Israel is in the area of part-time work, defined for statistical purposes as any work between one and thirty-four hours per week, regardless how the work is officially labeled. Significantly, more women worked part-time: in 1999, 67 percent of those who regularly worked part-time were women. Of all working women, 35.9 percent regularly worked part-time, while only 14.5 percent of all working men did so.[81] The most common reason given for women's part-time work is child care and housework (21 percent), significantly coming under the CBS definition of "housewives," which by definition excludes males (thus, there is no way of knowing whether any of the 14.5 percent part-time male workers do so for reason of taking care of children).[82]

Like full-time workers, part-time workers accumulate social benefits relative to the amount of hours they actually work. A part-time worker gains tenure as does a full-time worker, and the prospect of promotion is not negated by part-time work. All these reflect the relative strength of workers' unions, at least in the past. Interestingly, in terms of returns on human capital, women in part-time work are less discriminated against than women in full-time work (Haberfeld 1996).

Women's Careers

Gendered work segregation is clearly seen when comparing the distribution of employed men and women by main "economic activities." Thus, in 1999, of all employed women, 21 percent worked in education, 17 percent in health, welfare and social-work services, 11 percent in manufacturing, 12 percent in trade, 10 percent in business services, and less than 10 percent in each of the other economic activities. The picture is totally different among employed men: 23 percent in manufacturing, 14 percent in trade, 10 percent in construction, 11 percent in business services, and less than 10 percent in each of the other groups. In education and health, welfare and social-work services, where about 40 percent of employed women work, three-fourths of all workers are women. In personal household services, in which only 3 percent of employed women work, they account for 93 percent of all workers.

Work segregation is further evident on examination of the data regarding women's and men's occupations. In 1999, close to 30 percent of employed women were clerical workers (a figure unchanged since 1980) compared to 8 percent of men. More than 22 percent of employed women were agents, sales workers, and service workers (compared to 15 percent of men). More encouraging figures concern the rates of female academic professionals (13 percent) and associate professionals and technicians (20 percent), as they are higher than those for men in these categories (12 percent and 11 percent respectively). However, most women in these occupational categories are teachers, nurses, social workers, and the like, mostly in the public services. The overwhelmingly major occupational category of the employed men is industry, construction, and other skilled workers, where 34 percent of the employed men are concentrated (compared with only 6 percent of the employed women).[83] Women predominate in the following occupations: clerical workers (73 percent), associate professionals and technicians (59 percent), and sales and services workers (54 percent).[84]

The Glass Ceiling

"Glass ceiling" is the term sociologists use to describe the transparent yet unbreakable barrier that obstructs women's rise to top levels in hierarchical institutions, as in employment settings. Comprehensive data documenting the existence of a glass ceiling at all levels of the labor market are difficult to gather, as they necessitate a complete breakdown and analysis of the job structures in all economic branches, both public and private sector. This kind of information is not collected by the CBS. Information control is once again present in full force.

One specific piece of data examined by the CBS and relevant to a discussion of workplace hierarchies concerns male and female workers in managerial positions. Management is not merely an occupation; it represents authority and command (Izraeli 1994). However, these data are indicative of women's overall position in the workforce. According to the CBS 1998 data , 7.9 percent of all working men were managers, compared with only 2.9 percent of working women. Of the total managers, 26,100 out of 116,600 were women (22.4 percent). This represents a certain increase in comparison to the 1990 data for women in management positions (18 percent of all managers: 12,000 out of 66,000). Of all women managers, 8 percent are chief executive officers (CEOs) or directors general, 65 percent are senior managers, and 27 percent are other managers, whereas of all men managers a total of one-third are CEOs/directors general, four times the share of women managers in this category. Of the men managers, 45 percent are senior managers, and 21 percent are other managers.[85] The CBS data further indicate that women comprised more than 25 percent of the increase in total managers during the decade between 1980 and 1990 (Ministry of Labor and Welfare 1991, 3). A comparison with other industrial countries puts Israel's 1995 rate of 19.5 percent female administrators and managers far below the 36.5 percent of industrial countries.[86] In 1998, the annual cost of senior managers in the top 400 corporations traded in the Tel Aviv Stock Exchange was 19 times more than the average wage—rising from 13 times in 1994, and superseding the comparative cost in England, Japan, and Germany (Swirski, Konor, and Yechezkel 1999a, 10).

The Forum of Women Managers in Industry conducted a survey in 1997 on the situation of women in managerial positions. The survey revealed that 45 percent of the companies did not employ women in managerial positions at all, 34 percent employed only one, 16 percent employed between two and four, and only 5 percent employed more than four women in managerial roles.[87] In a previous survey the forum had found that the average age of the female managers in high-tech companies was thirty-nine, and 77 percent of these were married.[88]

Gender stratification in the civil service can also be viewed as a case study of the situation in the labor market. While women made up 62 percent of all workers in the civil service in 1999, less then 12 percent of the top three ranks in the four main classifications of the service (which serve as the main resource for managerial positions) were women.[89] This is a perfect demonstration of the hierarchy inherent in modern bureaucratic organizations referred to by Izraeli (1999b, 171).

Somewhat counter to the impression from this discussion, a survey that examined the attitudes and self-perceptions of women in the employment world found that only 12 percent of the women surveyed see "success" in the workplace as meaning promotion to a managerial post (Natanzon 1997). This could be seen as a protective measure women unconsciously take from probable disappointments, in a manner that resembles the cognitive dissonance mechanism.

Salary and Earning Gaps

According to the CBS 1998 data,[90] in all branches of the labor market, a male employee's average monthly income was 1.63 times higher than that of a female employee, making the female employee's average monthly income about 61 percent of her male counterpart. This is partly explained by the differences in the average weekly work hours—46.4 for men and 35.9 for women. This means, however that while men worked 29 percent more hours per week than women, they earned on average 63 percent more than women. This obviously proves the partiality of the differences in work hours as an explanation of the earning gaps. Furthermore, the data clearly show that a large gap existed in the average income per hour as well, which was 1.21 times higher for men. In other words, women's hourly income is 83 percent of that of men.

A thorough examination of earnings by age, educational level, economic activity, and occupation reveals that even when the relevant variables of women and men employees are the same, the monthly and hourly salary gaps remain constant. For example, male and female scientific workers who work over 45 hours per week, almost matched in terms of hours of work (52.4 for men and 50.4 for women), but their earnings were far from equivalent: the average gross monthly income of women was only 64 percent of the men's, and their hourly income was 72 percent of the men's.

Data from the Ministry of Finance are even more distressing: women's general average monthly income in 1997 was only 55.5 percent of that of men's.[91] National Insurance Institute data confirm the grim picture. Of all male employees in 1998, 10.6 percent earned less than half the average monthly salary, while 14.8 percent of all female workers earned less than that. Of all male workers, 2.9 percent earned four times the average monthly salary, while only 0.3 percent of all female workers earned that amount.[92] Examination of the adult population income survey reveals that in 1996 women made up 57 percent of all employees earning less than the minimum wage.[93] Furthermore, in early 2000 women made up 65.3 percent of all individuals receiving income support benefits.[94]

The United Nations Human Development Reports demonstrate the universality of the phenomenon: the world average share of earned income by female workers was 33.71 percent. Notwithstanding the universality, the dimensions of the gaps differ. Here too, Israel fares much worse than its Human Development Rank: the 1995 share of earned income by female workers in Israel was 33.1 percent, far from the 38.02 percent average of the industrial countries, which Israel is part of according to the General Human Development measures.[95]

The discrimination variable has been well demonstrated in the work of Linda Efroni, an expert in the Israeli labor market who has analyzed gender stratification and salary levels of men and women in several specific public institutions, including the civil service and two large municipalities. According to Efroni, the seniority variable can only explain 2 to 3 percent of the gap, while the rest of the gap among workers in the same occupational classification and level, caused by differences in the allocation of fictitious additional hours and travel allowance, is the result of clearcut discrimination (Efroni 1990). Unpublished data supplied for the CEDAW Report by the Ministry of Finance indicated that the overall salary gaps between men and women in the civil service have decreased somewhat: women's monthly average income relative to that of men rose slightly, from 76 percent to 78 percent between 1996 and 2000. However, in 2000 men still made 1.28 more than women, meaning that the 28 percent gap remained constant since the early 1990s.[96]

Salary levels are not routinely supplied and are generally not publicized. Therefore it was quite unusual and of particular significance when in 1997 the civil service commission took upon itself, at the request of the Knesset Sub-Committee on the Advancement of Women in the Employment and the Economy, to examine salary gaps between men and women in the civil service (Civil Service Commission 1998). Its August 1998 report related to salary data of 1996. It found consistent gaps in all classifications, reaching a 25 percent gap at the administrative classification, with the exception of the professional attorney classification, where women's earnings exceeded men's by 8 percent. Not surprisingly, the report was presented by the Commission as proof that no gender discrimination exists within the civil service with regard to salaries, claiming that when specific ranks are separately examined, the gaps are much smaller.[97]

Once again there is some evidence that women are unaware of these salary gaps. A survey of employed women revealed that half the women believed that their earning level was similar to their men co-workers' (Natanzon 1997). Only 24 percent of the women were aware of salary discrimination.

Child Care

The child care system in Israel is composed of both public and private programs.[98] The operation hours of all day care centers suit the traditional model of a six-day working week, while much of the Israeli market has moved to a five-day week with longer daily hours. Thus, women who work in more demanding and less traditional jobs cannot rely on the day care system and must seek additional or alternative child care solutions. The total places available in the government subsidized day care centers do not satisfy the need. While the number of working women grew by 40 percent between 1990 to 1996, the number of children in those day care centers increased by only 22 percent (Sheffer 1999, 48).

Chapter 8
Political and Public Life

The area of political and public life is the "pure" public sphere. The public/private dichotomy is discussed broadly in Chapter 1, so at this point we ignore the countless debates around the appropriate definitions of this category. All the areas discussed in this chapter—national and regional politics, media, the armed forces, and religion and state relationships—undoubtedly belong to the public sphere. The latter two are also the two main factors unique to women's situation in Israel. Concentration on the public sphere serves as a bridge between the two levels of examination of women's lives: basic health and welfare and participation in public life. Looking at women's participation in public life underscores the gap between the reasonable, even satisfying accomplishments on the basic level and the totally inadequate progress on the more complex level. This is well reflected in a recent evaluation of women's representation in the Israeli parliament and government in comparison with worldwide data, taking into consideration various economic and welfare parameters and research and data from the Human Development Database (Swirski and Yechezkel 1999b).[1] Breaking the surveyed countries into five groups, the evaluation shows that, while gross national product and women's education put Israel among the top quintile, women's representation in parliament and in government puts Israel in the fourth and the third quintiles respectively. Of course, there is nothing really new in this, except that it also highlights the underlying thesis of the incidental nature of the progress made on the basic level, which results from the progress made in Israel on issues of public health, elimination of illiteracy, and other welfare matters in general. The commitment to advance the well-being of people in general has not been matched by a commitment to advance women in particular.

There is a deeper level to this differential attitude. Israel, being a welfare state, perceives the gender-neutral welfare zone as the responsibility of the state. Yet the political sphere is perceived to be the ultimate responsibility, capability, and eligibility of the individual alone. It reflects the ultimate accomplishment of the individual, according to what he or she deserves. With respect to conventional electoral politics, no regulatory interventions for purposes of advancing particular groups can be fathomed. While the area of public life is broader than the scope of the pure political zone, it seems that the culture of merit took over the other areas where a greater degree of regulation and review could be possible. Despite steps in that direction, mainly through the introduction of the affirmative action mechanism into the civil service, implementation is gravely lacking, which only furthers the assertion of lack of commitment.

Probably due to the nature of this subject as a prime indicator of women's status, in addition to the well-known poor representation of women in Israeli politics, this topic has generated much research interest—mostly from a sociological or legal perspective. As elsewhere in the world, it is perhaps the simplest example of attainment of formal equality that ends the legal struggle with the right to vote and be elected, which unfortunately does not lead to any direct further accomplishment (Rhode 1989). The mechanisms of affirmative action, quotas, and the mandatory inclusion of women on lists of government candidates have never been formally implemented in the Israeli political sphere. Although the public at large seems to favor the idea of mandatory fair representation in political parties and within the government (Bar-Tzuri, Fischer, and Hendeles 1996, 10; Charney 1998), it seems that the political sphere is still perceived by politicians themselves as a place of "free competition" where no normative restrictions should enter. This chapter, then, concentrates on sociological description and returns to legal aspects only when getting to other areas of public life, such as the civil service.

The subject of women in politics is in fact broader than what follows in this chapter. A major aspect of women in politics has been dealt with in discussing women's political activism through women's organizations.[2] Borrowing from Hanna Herzog's terminology, the following discussion focuses on women in formal politics (Herzog 1999, 313); however, the separation between the two complementary aspects of women's work in politics should not mislead us into a narrow interpretation of their work. The discussion in this chapter focuses on formal politics, but substantively, when deconstructing the components of political action, women's organizations present an equally political sphere. I decided to separate the two facets of women's political action because I thought it more important to present women's political activism through women's organizations as agents of change, in contrast to government operation for the advancement of women.

Israel is the only Western democracy where military service is compulsory for women as for men (Raday 2000, 190). This chapter seems to be the most appropriate place to include the subject for several reasons, which all come under the understanding of the centrality of the army in Israel's ethos. This centrality, leading sociologists to describe civic-military relations as a "civil military" (Kimmerling 1993, 129), clarifies the inclusion of the military under the general sphere of public life. Moreover, it has led others to claim that the military, with its powerful gender regime, has contributed more to the construction of gender inequality in Israel than any other institution, due to its predominance within Israeli culture and society (Izraeli 1999a).

Women in Israeli Politics

National Politics

The right to vote and be elected was taken for granted at the establishment of the State of Israel, but it was the product of a long struggle (Azaryahu 1977; Fogiel-Bijaoui 1992; Yishai 1997, 61–62). During the pre-state era, Jewish women in Palestine fought against the right-wing ultra-Orthodox movement to attain voting rights. Their struggle seemed to have ended in 1920, when for the first time in history they participated in the elections for the Council of Palestinian Jewry, and 4.5 percent of those elected were women. After the establishment of the State of Israel, women's voting rights were legally reinforced. Formally, there is full equality between men and women regarding the right to vote and to be elected in Israel. Section 5 of the 1958 Basic Law: The Knesset specifically states that every Israeli citizen aged eighteen or older shall be entitled to vote, and Section 6 of the same law states that every Israeli citizen aged twenty-one or older is entitled to run for election.[3]

In terms of voting patterns, there seems to be no noticeable difference between men and women regarding voting turnout at elections; the percentage of men and women voters remains approximately the same (85 percent), among the highest in the democratic world. The Israel Women's Network (IWN) commissioned a comprehensive survey to investigate the potential for both politicians and women themselves of treating women as a distinct interest group; they concluded that the present insignificance of the gender factor in casting a ballot may change, and suggested ways in which this unused variable could empower women (Charney 1998).

Women in Israel operate within political parties under two categories: in specific women's sections and as individual members. Their role is dual, in that they are expected to recruit support for the party among female constituencies as well as to promote women's representation in the party. The significance of women members in Israeli political parties was accentuated when primary elections were first held during the 1992 elections. In the primaries, only the registered members of a certain party may vote in that party's internal elections and can thereby decide who will be the party's candidates to the Knesset. The introduction of primaries as a means for selecting parliamentary candidates resulted in a sharpening of politicians' sensitivity to the public mood. It also stressed the importance of membership in political parties. In a survey recently conducted, only 17 percent of male and 10.9 percent of female respondents reported actual membership in political parties. Moreover, 44.3 percent of the women polled stated that they did not support, nor were they active in any political party (Yishai 1997, 98, 102). The media also has a very important role in publicizing election campaigns. In a poll conducted two months before the 1996 elections, 94 percent of the people interviewed said they received information about female candidates from the media, while only 11 percent reported that they received it from the candidates' public activity. Interestingly, men in general were more aware of female candidates than were women.[4]

In terms of international comparison, Israel does not fare well in women's presence in the legislature. The 1999 elections for the 15th Knesset indeed marked great improvement, with 14 women elected, making it a record 11.6 percent of the Knesset members, in addition to another record of the first Arab woman to be elected, Hussniya Jabara of Meretz.[5] However, the overall record of Israel in this domain has not been encouraging. Indeed, following the 1996 elections, with only 7.5 percent (9 women members), Israel was placed 57th within a list of 94 countries in a Human Development Database survey of women in parliament (Swirski and Yechezkel 1999b, 2). A 1995 World Statistical Survey showed that even within the Middle East region Israel fared only third, superseded by both Iraq and Syria (Tomasevski 1998, 7).

A close examination of the Human Development Reports, discussed in the Introduction, reveals that the low ranking of Israeli women's representation in parliament stands in contradiction to Israel's overall high ranking in national production, wealth per inhabitant, and Human Development Index in general. In other words, Israel fares much better in terms of human development measures, as well as women's education, than in terms of this indicator of gender equality. In contrast, compared with other countries that rank high on the Human Development Index and national production, women in Israel are far below on the level of their representation in the labor market, on the level of their revenue in comparison to that of men, and also on the relatively low number of women in management positions. As noted, these statistics strongly support the thesis that most progress in women's status in Israel for the first forty years of the state's existence has been made on the elementary level of women's lives and has been incidental to Israel's overall socioeconomic advancement. Recall that my definition for the basic parameter of women's lives parallels the measures of the Human Development Index and the one indicator of gender equality where Israel ranks high (women's education, including high education).

One factor raised by other researchers who looked at UN data is the central place of the army in Israeli society and the huge defense budgets (S. Swirski and Yechezkel 1999b, 5–6). Israel's parliamentary makeup, which includes a growing number of religious parties where women are de facto not represented, should also be added to this analysis (see Table 2).[6] Since the early 1980s, there have been no women Members of Knesset (MKs) representing religious parties. Out of 120 seats, presently 27 seats are occupied by religious parties. Thus almost 25 percent of the places in the Israeli parliament are by definition closed to women. In left-wing parties (Ratz, Meretz, Labor), women's representation is higher than in right-wing parties (Likud), a recurring phenomenon in line with the general rule postulating an advantage for women in left-wing parties (Yishai 1997, 29). It is often pointed out that the quota system is in fact a double bind.[7] In practice, the quota often turns to be a maximum rather than a minimum determinant, since women candidates who are elected to the party's list with no external involvement are seen as fulfilling the party's commitment to women's quota, and so those who were to be secured are moved backward (Friedman 1999). Worse still, relying on the quota system and realizing its blocking effect, people who care for women's representation might prefer to actually vote for male candidates, so as not to cause this situation.

Many of the powerful seats and positions in the Knesset have never been assigned to women: there has never been a woman Knesset Speaker, though many women have served as Deputy Speakers (two women held this position during the 15th Knesset); few women have

TABLE 2. Women Elected to Knesset by Party, 1992, 1996, and 1999 (percentages in parentheses)

	Labor		*Likud*		*Meretz (1992: Ratz)*	
	Men	*Women*	*Men*	*Women*	*Men*	*Women*
1999	23	3 (12)	16	3 (16)	6	4 (40)
1996	31	3 (9)	30	2 (6)	7	2 (22)
1992	40	4 (9)	30	2 (6)	4	2 (33)

Source: Israel Women's Network.

been assigned to the two most powerful Knesset committees, the Foreign and Security Affairs Committee and the Finance Committee (Yishai 1997, 31); women have never headed those committees, nor the Law, Constitution, and Legislative Committee. The present Knesset, following the 1999 elections, set a precedent in assigning for the first time two women to the Foreign Affairs and Security Committee. Beyond this, three women head other Knesset committees, and three women head subcommittees (Committee for the Advancement of Women 2000, 10). As in other countries, there are many women on committees responsible for matters associated with traditional women's interests, such as education, welfare, and social services. The Knesset Statistical Report, which quantifies legislative and parliamentary activity, reveals that women's productivity stands in stark contrast to their representation in the Knesset.[8] While women constituted only 7.5 percent of the legislators in the 14th Knesset, they were responsible for 15 percent of the laws passed.[9]

In the most thorough and comprehensive research to date of women in Israeli politics, Yael Yishai claims that women who attain top party positions regard themselves as representing not the female constituency but rather the public at large. Moreover, women MKs often still take pains to emphasize that their political careers are geared toward national ends, rather than toward promulgating women's interests (Yishai 1997). Beginning with the late Prime Minister Golda Meir, Yishai describes women representatives' attitudes toward their own role and toward women's interests in general. She concludes that until about a decade ago women parliamentarians in general have not promoted women's interests by their legislative activity. However, as of the 13th Knesset, "The women [Members of the Knesset], while not exempting themselves from interest in and responsibility for general affairs of state, are acting in their legislative capacity as representatives of women" (Yishai 1997, 31). The establishment and ongoing operation of the Knesset Committee on the Status of Women are no doubt both a reflection and a stimulator of this development. Significant proof of this changing trend is clearly seen in the mentioned Knesset Statistical Report : consistently, 30–50 percent of the bills put forth by women Members of Knesset during the 13th and the 14th Knessets involved women's status.[10]

A Women's Party that might have been the most effective in pushing for reform and advancement of women's status issues has never been able to garner significant support. Ever since Rachel Kagan's membership in the first Knesset and her clear-cut outspoken drive to represent women's interests there, none of the attempts by Women's Parties to make it into the Knesset—in 1977, 1992, 1999—have borne fruit.[11] These failures have been attributed to several factors. First, most adherents have lacked political experience or the willingness to "push" themselves all the way into the Knesset. Second, the different women's parties have unfortunately been plagued by internal rivalries and factionalism (Yishai 1997, 41–44). And third, they have lacked funding.[12] Nevertheless, some have claimed that the parties' first priority in running for election was to raise consciousness, not to win votes. Indeed, women's parties have become a focal symbol for feminism, a token of women's independence in the male-dominated political world. Yet simultaneously, some suggest that the association of the past women's parties with radical feminism—perceived as threatening by many Israelis, men and women alike—has been a deterrent to their success (Yishai 1997, 122).

Women's low representation in the Knesset obviously affects their representation in the government. Since the emergence of the State of Israel, only one woman, Golda Meir, has served as prime minister. Having served in the Knesset since 1949, Meir was elected prime minister in 1969 and held office until 1974. The case of Golda Meir represents a tremendous achievement (even from an international perspective) and, at the same time, a major impediment. The fact that a woman could and did achieve the highest political position possible has reinforced the myth of equality in Israel (Hazelton 1977). Thus it served to conceal claims of inequality and discrimination in Israel, as apparently did Golda Meir herself (Yishai 1997, 36).

A bill to assure a minimum of 25 percent representation of women in the government was introduced by MK and then minister of education Limor Livnat of the Likud party (an opposition party at the time). At the first reading of the bill, in an unprecedented move, the Speaker of the Knesset allowed for another round of votes after the first round resulted in a majority for the bill. The majority included women of the coalition party, though the coalition's formal stand was to oppose the bill. The bill failed on the second round. Significantly, the minister of justice explained his opposition with the argument that it would be an impossible requirement, in light of the entirely male constituency of the religious parties in the Knesset.[13]

One concluding observation: there has never been a woman president in Israel. The Knesset regulation that refers to the president's pension rights defines the president's spouse in the gender-specific term "wife," thus conveying a hidden message of the incomprehensibility of a woman president.[14]

Women in Local Authorities

Women's representation in local authorities has also been extremely limited, notwithstanding the common perception of women's relative advantage and aptness for local politics (Herzog 1994, 7). However, there has been a significant increase in women's representation since the first local elections were held in 1950. In the most comprehensive work to date on women in Israeli local politics, Hanna Herzog traces institutional changes on the municipal level that have made local politics more flexible, thus opening up possibilities for new groups to enter politics, including women. These institutional changes include splitting the ballot between national and local elections, thus enabling the concentration of political competition on local issues alone; the rise in the number of competing lists in municipal elections; and changing the election system itself (Herzog 1994, 10–11). The trend is reflected in the increase in women's representation: from 29 women elected at the 1950 elections (4.2 percent of the total electees) to 240 in the recent 1998 elections (15 percent of the total), an impressive jump from the 1993 total of 11 percent. Overall, women are currently present in 70 percent of the local authorities. Herzog draws attention to the means through which women have now entered the local authorities, pointing to women's extensive use of independent parties, many formed and headed by women. Apparently, most women who headed the lists were eventually elected to the authorities (Herzog 1999, 315).

Until the 1998 elections, only six women had served as heads of local councils and only one was mayor of a city. The 1998 local elections set a precedent in that respect as well: two women were elected mayors of fairly large and central cities (Herzelia and Natanya). Twenty-nine women serve as deputy mayors and two women were elected to head regional authorities.[15] These achievements, unfortunately, are restricted to the Jewish population. Since the establishment of Israel, only one Arab woman has served as a head of a local council (Violet Khouri, elected in 1972 to be the head of the Kfar Yassif Local Council).[16] Only two women were elected in 1998 to Arab municipal councils.[17] This minuscule number is commonly attributed to the familial-patriarchal character of Arab society, which sees the political sphere as a distinctly male domain.[18]

Whether it is on the national or on the local level, researchers note that politics in Israel is still viewed as a public activity more suitable for men, interfering with women's familial roles. The public-private dichotomy is most vivid in this arena. Women are caught in a double bind that rejects their attempts to take on the male characteristics perceived as essential for politics, while denying that their femininity qualifies them to enter politics.

Women in the Media

The world is becoming more and more media-constructed; some claim that the public sphere in particular is no longer a reality, but only a depiction of the reality as constructed by the media (Curran and Gurevitch 1991; Gamason, Croteau, Haynes, and Sasson 1992). It is to be expected, then, that a discussion of women in the media will be included in the broader discussion of women in the public sphere in Israel.

Women in the Media Industry

A discussion of the involvement of women in the Israeli media industry must be separated from a discussion of the *portrayal* of women in Israeli media. Despite the increasing number of women taking over high and low positions in journalism, women continue to be portrayed as victims and sex objects, and as marginal to the important issues, involving themselves in "women's issues" only. Such portrayals of women on TV, on radio, and in newspapers color the public's opinions and define their attitudes.

However, women who *work* in the media are part of a system in which progress in gender equality is clearly being made. In 1989–1990, 44 percent of the 211 new members of the various reporter unions were women. In 1994, 36 out of 136 local papers had female editors (Limor and Caspi 1994, 37–38). In the early 1960s women composed only 7 percent of the journalists associations members; in less than three decades their number rose to 31 percent (Caspi and Limor 1995, 33). In addition, women head the Israel Broadcast Committee and the National Committee for Cable.

Most of Israel's electronic media are under the authority of the Israel Broadcast Authority (IBA). Although women currently hold high-ranking positions in newspapers, radio, and television, the majority of central positions in editing and management remain in the hands of men. A 1997 internal IBA examination revealed that while women made up 41.5 percent of all workers, their rate in journalist and management positions was 10 percent lower than men's. Most significantly, in the senior ranks men made up 80 percent of the department managers and 90 percent of the unit managers (the highest position). In 80 internal tenders issued between 1995 and 1997 for senior IBA positions, there were twice as many men candidates, and only 13 women were selected (Liran-Alper 2000, 200). Data from December 2000 indeed indicate regression: the overall rate of women in the IBA went down to 41 percent, the 12 unit managers in Hebrew and Arabic television and Hebrew radio were all men, and only in Arabic radio, two out of the three unit managers were women; the rate of women among the journalists and reporters in Hebrew television and radio was 27.6 percent and in Arabic television and radio only 15.6 percent.[19]

In 1994, a Second Authority for Television and Radio was established, controlling private broadcasting. Interestingly, the position of women within it is better than in the IBA. Within the Second Authority Council, responsible for policy issues, a third of the members (5 of 15) are women. Within the Second Authority itself, women make up 60 percent of all workers, 50 percent of the senior managers (3 of 6), and 37.5 percent of the rest of the managers are women.

Women's Images and Representation in the Media Industry

A 1995 report by Media Watch's global media monitoring project found a clear discrepancy between the number of male and female journalists and interviewees in Israel as opposed to the 70 other participating countries. Invariably, the numbers for Israel are lower than the global average.[20] Of particular interest is Israel's four-month study by Media Watch, which compared two popular morning radio talk shows, one hosted by a woman, the other by a man. The subject matter of the programs was similar, general discussions on politics, social and cultural issues, medicine, economics, and psychology, with the goal of providing the public with professional information. The study examined, among other issues, the balance between men and women on the shows and concluded that there is a definite discrimination against women guests on both shows: women interviewees made up fewer than 20 percent of the show's guests, and those 20 percent included many who reflected an inferior social position, such as battered women.[21] Women are often presented differently from men on television: they are generally introduced by first name, family status, and a supporting description (wife of, niece of, etc.), whereas men are introduced by title, professional grade, and full name. This holds in the written press as well (Hoffman 1996).

Women are disproportionally portrayed in the media as "victims." The global media-monitoring project focused on the portrayal of women in the media found out that, internationally, 29 percent of the women interviewed or mentioned in television broadcasts were victims, as opposed to 10 percent of men. In Israel, women appeared in the news as victims 65 percent of the time, more than double the world rate.[22] One explanation for this statistic is that bereaved families are often shown on the news (a sad consequence of the violent Middle East reality), and particular attention is often focused on grieving female family members (for further discussion of the presence of women on the news, see Lemish 1995, 125–28).

A study of the representation of women criminals in the Israeli media revealed that media images of male and female offenders differ, the major difference being the attribution of responsibility. Female offenders are very often viewed as erring and misguided creatures who need protection and help, rather than as dangerous criminals, as "pawns" rather than "originators" (Weimann, Rathner, and Fishman 1988).

Television election campaigns have become increasingly popular in Israeli society. In the four election campaigns between 1984 and 1996, female representation was extremely limited. Actual research on the 1996 campaign revealed that only 17 percent of the images in all printed campaign propaganda were of women, up only 1 percent from the 1988 campaign study (Lemish and Tidhar 1988, 1999). Moreover, women generally constituted less than 20 percent of all persons who represented the major parties on television. In the newly formed Arab parties, however, the percentage of women who appeared in their campaign literature reached 55 percent (Lemish and Tidhar 1999). Of all topics in campaign advertisements, only 25 speakers (1.3 percent) dealt directly with the status of women. Violence against women gained much attention in the campaign, highlighting the stereotype of women as victims (Lemish and Tidhar 1999).

Celebrity and Power: Media Women as Agents of Change

Notwithstanding this discouraging picture, in the past several years, there seems to be a gradual change within the IBA and the media at large. More programs dealing with "women's issues" are being aired, mainly on the radio. Perhaps the strongest and most interesting expression of this development is demonstrated in an unprecedented voluntary group formed by leading women from the Israeli media, who joined the Sexual Assault Victims' Help Centers Union. The group Ezrat-Nashim[23]—a double entendre meaning both "Women's Aid" and the women's section in Orthodox synagogues—began a high-profile campaign to increase awareness of the help centers and to raise money and public support for their operation. The journalists used their publicity and authority to appear in various service advertisements to convey the message. A national fund-raising event was held with the participation of numerous public figures and leading performers, which generated close to $100,000 for the help centers. Media coverage was wide, and the campaign's overall success was undeniable: the daily number of calls to the centers increased fivefold (Kormann 1998).

It is indeed justified to view this organization and its operation as women acting as agents of change within the dominant culture. It is significant to note the connection between media, media power, and the issue of sexual violence against women. The medium that is probably the most influential in instituting and reinforcing negative stereotypes and images of women is utilized for their advantage. It is not a coincidence that these women chose to focus on sexual violence against women in general, not on domestic violence. There is a general consensus that the latter subject has gained increased public awareness throughout the 1990s, and some see this as a sign of improvement. However, much media coverage of this issue is tainted with scandal and sensationalism that sometimes even border on pornography.[24] It has often been claimed that such coverage ill serves the fight against domestic violence. Furthermore, the focus on domestic violence reinforces women's conjunction with children, both in making them resemble children in their helplessness and in emphasizing their maternal role.

Women's Representation in Other Spheres of Public Life

Women in the Civil Service

The discussions of the civil service so far have focused more on the nature of the measures taken to improve the overall situation of women and less on the data themselves. It is time to turn to the data.[25] Many civil service employees, particularly in the top ranks, are powerful decision makers and leading executives in the public sector. As the data show, several years after the legislation that mandated affirmative action in rather strong terms, this method is clearly not implemented.

Although women made up 59.4 percent of all civil servants in December 1995, their rate among the top three ranks of senior staff (of the four main classifications that compose the main resource for managers in the civil service) was only 10.5 percent. In 1997, when women made up 61 percent of all civil servants, that rate was still only 14.8 percent, and in October 1999, when women composed 61 percent of all civil servants, it was 16.4 percent. Even if one were tempted to view this as progress, it would be misleading. Between 1993 and 1994, a sharp decline in the percentage of women in top positions took place due to new payment agreements signed. Thus, the slight rise in women's representation in top positions by 1997 was merely a restoration of their position of 1993, which was close to 13 percent. Women's underrepresentation in the top positions correlated with their presence in the lowest ranks (8th rank and below), where their presence only seems to be growing: from 66 percent of all workers in 1997 to 71 percent in 1999. This analysis is supported by an examination of the changes in the proportions of women in the lowest ranks among all women civil servants: while 73 percent of all women workers occupied the lowest ranks of the civil service in 1993, this figure rose to 77 percent in 1997. Men's stratification, on the other hand, is much more even: in 1997, 40 percent of the men civil servants occupied ranks 1–7 (compared to 46 percent in 1993), and 60 percent occupied the lowest ranks (compared to 54 percent in 1993). In 1999, only 2.5 percent of the women civil servants occupied the first three ranks, compared with 7 percent of the men, and only 28 percent of the women (compared with 45 percent of the men) occupied ranks 4–7. In other words, women continue to be overrepresented in the lowest ranks of the service, and women who join the civil service are much more likely than men to cluster at the lowest ranks. Between 1993 and 1999, no woman occupied the highest rank of the administrative or the technical classification, two of the most prestigious classifications in the service.

Formally, the major procedure for occupying positions in the civil service is through tenders. The 1995 affirmative action amendment to the State Service (Appointments) Law[26] specifically referred to this method of appointment. Section 15A first directs the Civil Service Commissioner to actively engage in programs to advance the goal of adequate representation, and then provides for the operation of affirmative action programs in tenders. Although in practice tenders are circumvented through de facto appointments and exemption from the tender requirement, the method continues to play an important role in the operation of the civil service, and so the examination of women's participation in them is of consequence. There are internal and public tenders; the public tender is used only when attempts to find "internal candidates" have failed. The role of public tenders in placing workers to the service is probably higher than expected, and in fact 40 percent of all appointees through tenders in 1997 were appointed through public tenders.[27] In a four-year period there was a more than twofold rise in percentages of female candidates (from 23.2 percent in 1993 to 51.9 percent in 1996) and of women appointed in internal tenders (from 26.1 percent in 1993 to 55.7 percent in 1996). In contrast, the situation in public tenders is far less positive. From a slight increase in the percentage of female candidates and appointees, there was a sharp decline among female candidates (only 30.3 percent), and an even sharper one of those appointed (28.9 percent). Additionally, though women were consistently appointed at a slightly higher rate relative to the rate of women who presented their candidacy (with an exception in 1994 internal tenders), this shifted in the 1996–98 public tenders.[28] The commission explains this general decline by the overall cutbacks imposed on the civil service during 1996. The data from 1997–98 show similar rates of appointment (a candidate's chance to be appointed) for men and women, whereas women's candidacy rate in public tenders remains low (32 percent in 1997 and 38 percent in 1998).[29]

To aggravate the situation, in 1996 an additional regression appeared in the gender composition of the tender committees. As explained in Chapter 3, one of the changes in the Civil Service Code following the

1993 Ben-Israel Committee recommendations was the reinforcement of the required representation of both sexes in tender committees.[30] Although there was indeed a slow decline between 1993 and 1995 in the number of committees composed of men alone, in both internal and public tenders, there was an unexplained increase in their percentage in 1996 (3.9 percent in internal tenders and 30.6 percent in public tenders).

These figures clearly show that no active steps were taken to implement affirmative action. Even if women's success rates correspond to their candidacy rates, this only means that they are no longer subjected to overt discrimination. This is a perfect example of formal equality, where the implementation of substantive equality is desperately needed: the clear words of the law are not being followed, and affirmative action is not employed in tenders.

While many argue that the fault lies in the law itself (Izraeli, forthcoming), I believe that the data presented here substantiate the claim previously made, which places the fault mostly on the implementors of the law. Granted, the law lacks reference to "tenders-circumventing" methods, and this was indeed addressed in the most recent amendment to the law, as we shall shortly see. Nevertheless, the provisions regarding appointments through tenders are clear enough and in my opinion are no less comprehensive than the provisions in the parallel section 18A of the 1975 Government Corporations Law,[31] yet, unlike that law, the provisions are simply not being followed. Quite remarkably, 1999 report does not contain any data on tenders. This is, once again, a reflection of the information problem (indeed, in the sense of the in-formation of information). Bearing in mind that the preceding analysis is mostly based on data from an internal, unpublished report, the familiar pattern of controlling and withholding information can be easily seen, in this case leading to the prevention of claiming discrimination.

Even if the original affirmative action provisions had sufficed, had there been sincere will to advance women, a better equipped law for that purpose is of course a more hopeful option. Indeed, as already mentioned in the previous discussion of women in the civil service, section 15A was amended in December 2000, expanding affirmative action in the civil service.[32] Significantly, the driving motive behind the amendment was the promotion not of women, but rather of minority groups, mostly non-Jewish, who are hardly represented in the civil service. Most important, the amendment mandates the use of affirmative action in all civil service hiring methods. Furthermore, it introduces a quota system, in that it authorizes safeguarding certain positions for women only. The amendment also includes an annual reporting obligation by the civil service commissioner to various organs, including the Knesset Committee on the Status of Women and the Authority for the Advancement of Women, thus implying responsibility in case of nonimplementation or unsatisfactory results.

The Judiciary and the Public Attorneys

The percentage of women in the judiciary is extraordinarily high compared with other areas of public life. In 1996, in all the different courts (Supreme Court, district courts, magistrate courts, labor courts) there were 146 female judges and 229 male judges. The presence of women judges is increasing with the growing number of judges, and in early 2001 there were 200 female judges (including three Christians and one Muslim) of a total of 459 judges (43.6 percent of the judiciary).[33] Although the overall numbers are indeed impressive, the detailed breakdown shows the familiar form of the pyramid structure. Most of the women are at the registrar level, (56 percent of the local courts' registrars, and 82 percent of the labor courts' registrars) and as judges in the magistrate courts (42 percent of all magistrates).[34] Impressively, the number of women justices has recently grown to reach four out of the 14 Supreme Court Justices (28.5 percent) (Committee for the Advancement of Women 2000, 7).

Women's relatively large representation in the judiciary is also evidenced in the public sector of the legal profession. The present state attorney is a woman; her predecessor was the first woman to serve in this role and was later appointed to the Supreme Court. In August 2000, in the state attorney and attorney general offices, there were 325 women lawyers compared with 148 men, and 318 women public service attorneys compared with 163 men.[35] In addition, six of the eight district attorneys were women, as well as the heads of the Criminal Department, the Criminal Department for Special Issues, the Civil Department, the Labor Conflicts Department, the Fiscal Department, and many other senior positions ranking high in the civil service, in much higher proportions that any other ministry or civil service unit. All in all, 16 of the top 20 positions in the public sector of the legal profession are women.[36] Significantly, it seems that the break through the glass ceiling in the civil service legal classification affects salary levels. As seen in Chapter 7, it is the only classification in the service where female workers earn more than their male counterparts on the same levels.

While women's high representation in the prestigious and powerful judicial branch is often celebrated as a significant achievement that proves the success of meritocracy (Raday 1996b), the public legal field should only be taken as an exception that proves the general rule. In fact, the legal field is an exception throughout all its aspects, starting from training, where the data show a high percentage of female law students, often even higher than male law students. Later on, when many male graduates enter the private market of law, female graduates prefer the more secure, less time-demanding public sector and bring with them higher human capital.[37] The Israeli method for selecting judges, through a statutory committee (composed of three supreme court judges, the minister of justice and another minister appointed by the government, two members of the Knesset, and two representatives of the Israeli Bar Association)[38] facilitates the "cleanest" possible process, devoid of political or other unprofessional considerations. No other area of public life provides a matching procedure.

Indeed, one can examine the often neglected peripheral areas of the judicial field, such as the labor courts, where lay people operate as public representatives (representing employees and employers' unions), side by side with the professional judges. Here, reality hits with full force: in 1999, only 12 percent of the worker representatives in the labor courts were women. Significantly, women compose the majority of professional labor judges (60 percent of the judges and 71 percent of the registrars).[39] Needless to say, worker representatives are rather generously compensated for their work.[40]

It seems that skepticism is in place here. Questions have been raised on women judges' "voice" (Gilligan 1999) and on the meaning for justice of their presence on the bench (Beiner 1999). In general, scholars disagree on whether women's greater presence on the bench will improve the legal institution (Solimine and Wheatley 1995), while some suggest that if women reason differently from men, participation by more women judges (and lawyers) has the potential to change judicial decision-making and thereby improve the institution's responsiveness to women and other underprivileged groups (Bogoch 1999). Research on gender and judicial reasoning does not provide unequivocal support to this thesis. Nevertheless, even those who accept that empirical studies show little difference between the overall voting behavior of male and female judges still call for more women in the judiciary, because women's experience as women gives them valuable knowledge, perspective, and understanding that men lack and that are needed in court (Solimine and Wheatley 1995).

Little research has been made in Israel on the gender effect of judicial decision-making. However, Bogoch and Don-Yechiya's comprehensive study, discussed at length in Chapter 2, contradicts intuitive predictions of women judges' greater sensitivity to victims of sexual and domestic violence (1999, 262–65). A more limited statistical study, examining patterns of dissent among Supreme Court Justices along the lines of religiosity, ethnicity, and gender, found no clear connection between these factors and the justices' voting patters (Birnhak and Gussarsky 1999). Qualitative context-analysis research centering on the substantive reasoning, rhetoric, language, and style of the judgments does support the theoretical assumptions about women judges' different voice (Almog 1996; Bilsky 1997; Tirosh 2001). Anecdotal support can also be drawn from cases, such as the recent Mordechai sexual harassment cases, where in both the trial and the appeals courts the minority opinions demanding more severe sentencing were from women.[41]

It seems then that despite lack of substantial empirical evidence, women's growing presence on the bench is a cause for celebration and for a call to even greater participation, in Israel as elsewhere in the world.

Government Corporations

Another area of public life controlled by the government involves government corporations, broadly discussed in Chapter 3. This was the first area where active state involvement introduced affirmative action in order to advance women.[42] The 1993 amendment to the Government Corporations Law made a significant contribution to women's participation in economic and public life in Israel.[43] However, there is a limit to this progress. Data submitted by the Government Corporations Authority indeed indicate an impressive improvement over the years in women's general presence on boards of directors, but are far less encouraging on women's participation as board chairs. In September 1999, 40 percent of the directors were women (235 compared with 364 men), a significant rise even from 1996, when 25.6 percent of the directors were women (198 compared with 575 men). However, there was still only one woman who served as chair of a board of directors, compared with 50 men, and only eight women served as general managers of government corporations, compared with 73 men.[44] Significantly, board chairs are financially rewarded far more substantially than directors are; their annual compensations can amount to $20,000, compared with only $3,000 for directors at the same company.[45]

Women in the Military

Interaction Between Military and Civilian Life

Various researchers have referred to the paradoxical effect of the military on Israeli women's status (Izraeli 1999a). Israel prides itself on being the only Western democracy where women, like men, are conscripted for mandatory service in the military. Given the importance of the army in Israeli society, this represents a mark of gender equality. It must be noted, however, that military service for most women is quite different from that for men. Since its inception, the Israel Defense Force (IDF) has reinforced gender stereotypes by creating and maintaining very different roles for men and women. While progress has been made in the past decade in women's status in the army, with more jobs opening up to them, women continued to be excluded from combat positions until very recently and as a rule could not serve in geographical combat areas. This, more than any other factor, continued to exclude women from the upper echelons of military leadership.

All this may be undergoing a process of change, as the Israeli army presently undergoes what can be confidently described as a quiet revolution. In January 1999, a bill to amend the 1986 Defense Service Law (Consolidated Version), providing for equal military service for men and women, passed first reading, and a year later it became law.[46] A similar provision is included in the amended Women's Equal Rights Law,[47] qualifying equal rights to military positions and assignments by "the substance and nature of the position." Military officials profess that this amendment will result in complete equality in opportunities for placement and positions, as well as in duties that accompany such positions, which will be designated by the defense minister according to the law.[48] This amendment was indeed necessary to create formal equality in men's and women's military service, even though there is currently no legal basis for the army's continuous differentiation between men's and women's military positions. Women's legally shorter service, nevertheless, has hampered their recruitment to certain positions that demand longer training periods. Therefore, an amendment that would enable the army to demand a longer period of service from women who volunteer for the newly opened jobs was essential for facilitating this revolution. The only type of military occupation that remains closed for women's recruitment is infantry combat, as it involves specific physical qualifications which, according to military officials, are beyond women's capabilities. This, they contend, is within the law's legitimate criteria for qualification of the equality mandate.[49]

Among the positions that were traditionally closed for women were those that could entail wartime combat and other occupationsclassified as combat positions. Significantly, the amendment does not mention combat positions, or any other positions for that matter, while the chief of staff has already issued an instruction for inclusion of female soldiers in all combat areas, based on their qualifications alone.[50] Army officials contend that the Israeli public had crossed the constraint of seeing women in combat positions and of risking the possibility of women actually participating in war, with all the implications of such a step. In response to an interviewer question whether Israeli society is "ready for a situation where women may fall in captivity," the chief military personnel officer replied that the Alice Miller case had settled the issue.[51] In the Miller case, detailed below, the High Court of Justice had accepted Miller's petition to be allowed to undergo the examinations necessary to become an air force pilot. It was obvious that the practical consequences of such training would be the potential inclusion of women pilots in wartime combat. However, the issue can hardly be said to have been directly confronted by the court. Moreover, one can rightfully ask whether any discussion of such a sensitive issue in a court's ruling, even if it were a thorough discussion, could be regarded as consummation of the public debate on the subject. Still, army officials keep relying on this ruling as having resolved the dilemma, and the chief of staff has already approved women officers' participation in combat units beyond the border lines.[52] In light of the relative silence in which the current process is being carried out, this rhetoric raises the impression that it is in fact an evasion of a thorny, still unsettled issue, which can be expected to come up in full force in the future.

Thus far, it seems that the only public confrontation of the issue, apart from the Miller case, was during the first reading of the recent amendment to the Defense Service Law. Knesset deliberations can indeed be viewed as a form of public debate, and Knesset protocols present fascinating sociological material, revealing many aspects that are otherwise inaccessible. The particular debate that accompanied this bill's first reading is no exception. Very little was said regarding the sensitive issue of women's participation in actual combat: only two out of the six participants addressed this issue. Member of Knesset Yael Dayan presented one side of the debate. In a straightforward confrontation of what she perceives as "the real issue . . . the very principled and moral problem, back to Ben Gurion's days . . . whether we send women across the enemy lines," Dayan proposed an unequivocal argument of "sameness equality" to this direct question: "human dignity requires thinking in the same manner about men. . . . We have to internalize equality in such a manner, that a woman's blood is no different . . . from a man's blood." The dissent on this issue came from a member of her own party (Labor), Shevach Weiss, former Speaker of the Knesset, who clearly presented an ideology of "difference equality," arguing that "we sometimes need to make distinctions between man and woman. . . . I see this as the peak of feminism. . . . This is no discrimination, it is a protection from unique hazards that are more fatal to women than to men."[53] The lack of others to join in on this issue is no less significant, especially in light of the heated debate concerning women's military service that ensued exactly fifty years before, when the 1949 Defense Service Law was passed (Berkovitch 1997).

This argument in fact epitomizes the sameness/difference debate under liberal feminism, with its somewhat simplistic nature. Totally missing here is the alternative discourse of cultural and radical feminism, which, in this context, could bring forth a more complex attitude towards the subject of women's military service. Such discourse could construct the dilemma as including other possibilities besides treating women like or unlike men, such as changing the whole structure of military service in Israel and turning it into a professional army, or other means that would totally transform the concept of military service, thus also transforming the meaning of women's inclusion or exclusion from service. There is a reason for such notions not to have come up during the legislative deliberations. The legal sphere is not easily adaptable to cultural or radical feminism. As already discussed in Chapter 1, both cultural feminism and radical feminism, each coming from discourses other than law, are difficult to accommodate into the legal discourse. The law, especially when in the form of legislative debate, is too narrow to incorporate them. It seems that such ideas will have to locate an alternative forum of public deliberation where they can more easily be expressed, thus broadening the various perspectives and possibilities. Right now, the ground still belongs to the sameness/difference debate alone.

In order to understand the impact of this dynamic upon the status of Israeli women, it is necessary to understand the social and political significance of the army in Israel. A country preoccupied with security concerns, Israel has invested a tremendous amount in the military, both financially and socially. The army is one of the most important public institutions, a major source for the formation and recruitment of the political, and to a certain extent, economic elite (Izraeli 1997; Yishai 1997). It is an important channel for political recruitment and a recruitment pool for civilian managers in business and industry. On an even more substantive level, Berkovitch contends that "Military service in Israel signifies 'true' citizenship in the fullest sense" (Berkovitch 1997, 610). The marginalization of women within the army, therefore, has tremendous consequences on their status outside the army. The fact that no woman holds a rank higher than brigadier general essentially means that only men define and determine issues of national security (Izraeli 1997, 1999). As prestigious combat positions are virtually the only avenue to the most senior positions in the professional army and to the symbolic rewards and glory associated with them, women's exclusion from combat units means their exclusion from the top ranks of the army.

Quite significantly, the current revolution in women's military service is not presented by army officials in general as a plan to "promote women's status in the army." The amendment too does not address the issue of women's promotions in the army. Rather, it is a plan "to promote women's incorporation into the army," in line with the ideology of "realizing the high-quality human potential needed by the IDF."[54] The chief of staff is the only top army official who openly admits the need to promote women; he has declared his plan to have a woman general participating in the general staff forum during his term.[55] Apart from him, a clear division is made between equalizing women's service and the question of women's status in the army. Once again, questions of women's status are being coopted by the pretense of gender-neutral security concerns. The obvious question regarding the waste of women's human potential is ignored. It seems that the rhetoric of equality (as to actual participation in the military) is now being replaced by gender-neutral rhetoric of human potential and quality factors. Besides the preference for obscuring the nature of the move, it also seems that this effort at concealment foresees future demands for specific advancement of women in the military, and through this gender-neutral rhetoric it is trying to forestall this development before it begins.

The Legal Framework

The 1986 Defense Service Law (Consolidated Version),[56] which replaced the 1949 version of the law, mandates service in the military for both men and women, while differentiating between the sexes regarding their conditions of service. Article 1 states that the law applies to men between ages eighteen and fifty-four and women between eighteen and thirty-eight. Gender-based differentiation is also made with regard to length of mandatory service, the extent of reserve duty obligations, voluntary service, and exemptions. Women are exempt from mandatory service if they are married, pregnant, or mothers. These exemptions may be viewed as reflecting the traditional approach, expressed by then Prime Minister Ben Gurion on the establishment of the state, that the most important contribution a woman can make to the national security is the production of children. Nitza Berkovitch sees this "maternal exemption" as powerful proof of the construction of "the Jewish-Israeli female . . . first and foremost, not as an individual or a citizen, but as a mother and a wife" (Berkovitch 1997, 606). Women may also freely claim exemption based on conscientious objection or religious belief, whereas a man's right to do so is generally subject to the army's discretion. The religious component is a story in itself. In the early years of the state, Ben Gurion made a political pact with the leaders of the ultra-Orthodox community in Israel whereby young men would be allowed to postpone or cancel their service in the army in order to study in religious academies (yeshivas). At the time, the number of those to whom this arrangement applied was not so high, and the concern for the religious communities of Eastern Europe annihilated during the Holocaust seemed to outweigh the security concern. While this arrangement is still in force today, its application is supposedly restricted to a narrow segment of the population, although its continuity has been the subject of a recent High Court of Justice intervention.[57] The 1953 National Service Law[58] provides what may be seen a parallel arrangement for young women who, for religious or conscientious reasons, wish to substitute two years of national service for military service. This provision, however, is not strictly enforced.[59]

The Defense Service Law itself does not differentiate between the duties that may be assigned to men and to women. As of 1987, regulations that limited women's roles in the army were no longer in effect.[60] In practice, however, IDF policy has continued to discourage and forbid women soldiers from combat positions. In 1995, the Supreme Court decided in the landmark Alice Miller case that the IDF could not claim logistical and budgetary constraints as justifications for excluding women from serving as pilots in the air force.[61] Both sides accepted the legitimacy of excluding women from certain combat positions. Indeed, the IDF's original argument was based on its 1970s classification of the position of pilot as combat-related. Relying on the Defense Service Law, the IDF argued that the shorter mandatory service required of women, together with their more limited reserve duty obligations and exemptions for pregnancy and childbirth, interfered with its ability to make efficient use of the resources and funds invested in the training of a pilot.

In three separate majority opinions, the Court rejected this line of reasoning. Justice Mazza, finding for Miller, suggested the army conduct a trial period during which it would admit a limited number of female pilots. Justices Strasburg-Cohen and Dorner (both women) emphasized the importance of providing for women's unique needs, while avoiding discriminatory practices, and held that the army, an organ of the state, can be expected to do so, as demanded by Israeli law of private employers. Significantly, while the army's argument in the early stages of the trial addressed the social and value-related aspects of the petition,[62] it later specifically narrowed the argument to rely on logistical grounds alone. Thus the court has not had an opportunity to express its own opinions on the substantive social concerns. Instead, the decision reads like a treatise on the meaning of equality.

The IDF has taken steps to implement the decision's conclusions within the air force, and female candidates have since joined all pilot-training courses. The first female combat pilot graduated in June 2001, and three women were already serving as navigators at that time.[63] Guidelines have been established to adapt IDF policy to the potential reality of women combat pilots. Perhaps most important, the guidelines provide instructions whereby women pilots will perform combat duties or duties in hostile territory according to the decision of the commanding officer of the air force, under the advisement of the chief of staff. Similar moves were made by the navy, the artillery and border troops.

All these moves were a prelude to the present process of change in women's military service. As of the draft of summer 2000, women recruits have undergone pre-selection like, allowing advance decision of preferences. According to IDF surveys, 37 percent of the women recruits express interest in serving as pilots, a rate similar to that of the men recruits.[64] During 1999 women began training in combat-related occupations, such as border surveillance, task officers, and in armored divisions. The training for these positions is the same for men and women, and women who volunteer for such occupations have to sign up for thirty-months service (compared to the mandatory twenty-one months for women and thirty-six months for men).[65] According to army officials, the reactions thus far are very encouraging, and commanders are interested in adding women soldiers to their troops.[66] At this stage, a somewhat unresolved issue is that of reserve service for women in combat positions. Thus far, no legislative change has been suggested regarding reserve duty exemptions for pregnant women or mothers. Army officials seemed to prefer to defer decision on this issue, although when asked, their "vision of equality" includes the division of reserve duty between spouses, based on their necessity for the army.[67] However, in an official reply to our inquiry, the IDF spokesperson referred to a recent decision, ratified by the chief of staff, concluding that women will serve in the reserve forces until age thirty-eight (thirty for women in combat positions), and pregnant women and mothers will be exempt from this reserve duty.[68]

Women and Men in the Military

Until the late 1990s, all women entered the army through the "Women's Corps" (designated by the acronym Chen, which, significantly, means "charm"). The Women's Corps was created during the War of Independence and was based on a compromise between two competing models—the Palmach model,[69] in which men and women served in mixed units, and the British model, in which women served separately in an auxiliary unit. There is no "Men's Corps" in the army, and all other corps are identified by their functions. Chen has had formal responsibility for all women soldiers with regard to military training (including officer training), job assignments, discipline and judicial matters, and welfare, including protection from sexual harassment. Since 1983, Chen has had a Women's Corps social worker whose job was to assist female soldiers in handling such situations as pregnancy, various sexual issues, and sexual harassment. Since 1997, as part of the overall revolutionary process within the army, the posts of Chen officers in each unit were virtually abolished, and female soldiers are now subject to the command of unit officers for all purposes, including disciplinary and judicial matters. Regional Chen officers remain, and serve as a resort for female soldiers who face problems such as sexual harassment, gender-based discrimination, or gynecological problems. Until 1987, the rank of the Chen commanding officer (CO) was that of colonel. After intense public pressure from women's organizations and women MKs, the rank was raised to brigadier general, one rank below the CO of personnel. However, there is only one woman of that rank, and no woman is of high enough rank to participate in General Staff meetings on a regular basis.[70] The Chen CO, who reports to the chief of personnel, is rarely consulted on matters of general relevance to women: she was not party to the decisions to cut women's military service from twenty-four to twenty-two and then twenty-one months.

Indeed there has been much circular logic in the deeply gendered nature of the military. The clearly defined gender roles restricted the army's flexibility in its assignment of women. This in turn limited women's usefulness to the military, which, in the face of budget cuts, became the justification for shortening women's military service. Women's shorter military service then made it not cost-effective to invest in their training, which reduced their usefulness even further. The end result was that most women began to seem increasingly dispensable (Izraeli 1997). Once again, this circular logic seems to have been presently broken in light of the legal reform, which enables lengthening the service of women who volunteer for combat positions.

In certain areas, such as the technical branches, women's participation remains low despite the army's willingness to accept them into such positions. This is mainly because few enlisted have the pre-army training necessary to fill these positions effectively, and their short service makes it not cost-effective for the army to train them. The army has recently become involved in various projects designed to encourage women to enter technological fields.[71]

Women's inferior status in the military is clearly reflected in data relating to ranks and promotions. Figure 1 compares the 1996 proportion of women officers during mandatory service to the total number of officers throughout the various corps. As can be expected, certain corps are dominated by women officers while others have few or no women. In

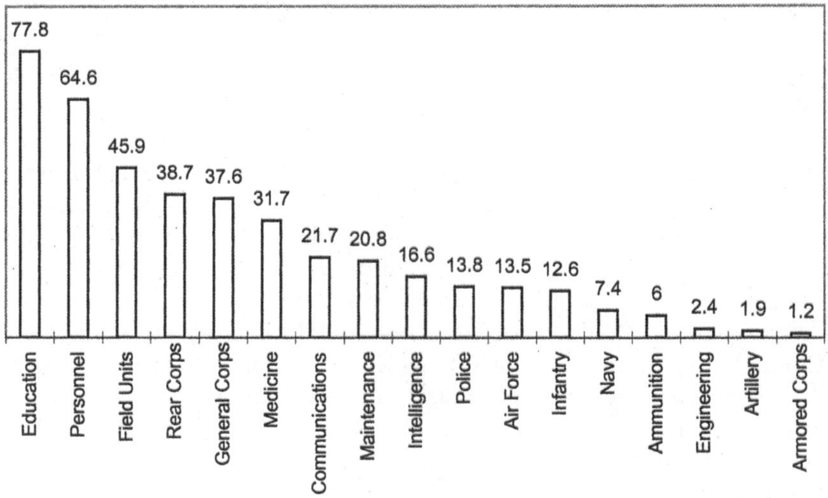

Figure 1. Percent of women officers in service (mandatory and career) by corps, 1996. Source: data provided by an IDF spokesperson (on file with the author).

the Education and Personnel Corps, for example, women make up well over half the total number of officers. In the Field Units Corps they constitute nearly half, while in the General and Rear Corps they make up about a third. The corps with virtually no women officers include Engineering, Tanks, and Artillery.

Will the ongoing present revolution impact the differences in rank attained? As put by women MKs to the Chen CO and the head of mandatory personnel planning, this is a clear question of affirmative action.[72] Women have traditionally suffered from slower promotions than men, in addition to their disadvantage in lacking combat experience. For example, various positions, while not actually involving combat, have traditionally been viewed as requiring previous combat experience and have thus been closed, de facto, to women as well. These included chief educational officer, intelligence CO, personnel CO, military spokesperson, chief medical officer, chief mental health officer, chief military prosecutor, and president of the appeals court. If the ideology behind the current changes were explicitly geared for the advancement of women, then these changes could rightly be expected to remove the de facto barrier from those high-ranking noncombat positions and propose a somewhat faster track of promotion for women who enter the newly opened combat positions. At the current pace of women's promotions, even as women enter combat occupations that enable faster and more certain promotions, it will be a very long time before they are eligible for the top of the hierarchy.

Here, however, the military officials once again resorted to the rhetoric of formal equality, leaving it to due course and the regular progression of things. The Chen CO admitted there was no concrete plan for reaching a minimum number of high-ranking women officers. The most proposed to be done was to actively seek and locate women in the middle ranks who would be eligible for promotions. These responses, described by members of the committee as vague and evasive, fit well with their strong rejection of seeing the current changes as having an objective of women's advancement. In the larger framework of this book, these developments can be viewed as presenting the recurrent theme of progress intertwined with hindrance under the guise of objectivity and gender neutrality.

Sexual Harassment in the Army

The army, a hierarchical institution based on discipline and camaraderie and an institution where the status of women remains problematic, provides an atmosphere conducive to sexual harassment. It should come as no surprise, then, that the two main episodes concerning sexual harassment that have recently come to the public attention have involved present or past high-ranking military officials. Both the Mordechai and the Galili affairs, discussed at length in the following chapter, should be seen as typical outcomes of the military establishment, and have led to endless media reports of women's similar experiences from their past military service.

Sexual harassment of women in the military remains an all too common experience, though the army is now undergoing a process of change in its treatment of sexual harassment. Several developments have prompted this change, including the enactment of the 1998 Sexual Harassment Law; the Galili and the Mordechai affairs; and the intense pressure from the Knesset Committee on the Status of Women as well as by other women's organizations. Thus, for example, the committee's insistence has led to the publication of a semi-annual report on sexual harassment in the army that includes the number of complaints and their outcomes, thus precluding any possibility of cover-up.

All female conscripts are encouraged to view sexual harassment as the fault of the perpetrator, and to come forward and report the incidents. Confidentiality is ensured, and the soldier's right to choose which of the available services she turns to is emphasized. Various services, such as a hot line for sexual harassment complaints and a counseling program, have been in place since 1996, and a new chief of staff instruction on sexual harassment (including a broad definition of the term) came into effect in April 2000.[73] Where the harasser is the victim's commander there need not be an objection on the victim's part to support charges of harassment. The instruction also obligates commanders to report to the military police all instances of grave physical harassment which come to their attention, even if the victim refuses to complain. Investigation by the police is at its discretion, where in other cases it is conditional upon the victim's consent.

A 1994 internal Chen report on sexual harassment in the military found that most incidents of sexual harassment and indecent acts resulted in absurdly low fines imposed on the perpetrator. The report was not published, but several of its findings reached the press and caused public outcry. A soldier found in a disciplinary proceeding to have attempted forced intercourse with a woman soldier was fined 100 NIS (the equivalent of approximately $30). Another, who demanded sexual favors in exchange for benefits, was given a fourteen-day suspended sentence. The very fact that soldiers accused of such harassment are dealt with within the disciplinary as opposed to the criminal framework of the military was criticized. As a consequence, efforts were made within Chen to ensure that punishments for sexual harassment reflect the severity of the offense, and in some cases, sentences of eight years imprisonment have been imposed. Moreover, more complaints—54.7 percent in 1999—are now transferred to the military police.[74] Most significant is the change of policy regarding the punishments imposed on career soldiers convicted of sexual harassment, who are now to be discharged from the army. Current data confirm implementation of this change: in the first half of 1999, out of 35 convictions in sexual harassment of career soldiers, 30 were discharged from service. During that period, a total of 134 complaints of sexual harassment were processed, a rate similar to that of the previous year.[75] The impressive figure, though, relates to the years 1997–98: during these two years, there was an increase of 43 percent in complaints of sexual harassment in the army compared with 1996. Significantly, five involved male on male sexual harassment, one was a case of male harassment by a female, and one of female on female harassment.[76]

Despite these developments, the chief military prosecutor declined to specify any concrete data concerning punishment of sexual offenses, preferring to resort to the vague rhetoric of harsher measurements against the perpetrators.[77] It can be legitimately assumed that, had there been a reason to be proud of the data, the subject would not have been evaded.

The Allocation of Resources: The Battle over the Budget

The battle over the budget represents the "information story" in its full force. Budgetary review is always an elusive task. In order for it actually to take place, far-reaching prerequisites are needed, which no government establishment is keen on supplying. These include transparency and disclosure in policy decisions and their implementation, full and free flow of information regarding the executive branch's operation, and use of clear and comprehensible terminology. In fact, the most capable organ to produce such a review is the Ministry of Finance itself, since it alone has the necessary information and is in control of all these prerequisites. No other agency can claim such knowledge and control.

The reality is that government policy and its implementation are far from being transparent, information on government operation is not disclosed on a regular basis and is often hard to obtain, and budgetary books and other documents are written in a style comprehensible only to a very few experts and government officials.[78] The government itself does not engage in budgetary review from a general social or gender-specific perspective. There is no formal overview of budgetary needs regarding women, nor is there a formal annual comparative review of allocation of resources toward particular needs of women. Thus, the government does not supply the means to monitor its budgetary commitment or expenditure for the advancement of women. It seems that an honest and total commitment to implement all the human rights conventions Israel has ratified would demand an official comprehensive budgetary analysis and assessment of present and future expenditures to realize their goals. Refraining from such a task might stem from fear of the resulting account and its implications.

Moreover, very often even the examination of a particular program or plan is impossible due to lack of reliable and clear budgetary information on its implementation or lack thereof. Allocation of resources, budgetary commitment, and priorities are perhaps the most significant indicators of government sincerity in promotion of gender equality and advancement of women. Decisions regarding the cutting of the "budgetary pie" are a prime battlefield for social interests and goals such as the advancement of women. Unlike other social interest groups, women's interests and concerns do not enjoy political patronage by any distinct political party or government ministry. Hence it is mostly the Committee on the Status of Women that leads the battle for larger pieces of the pie, or rather, for maintaining their size and not cutting them down.[79]

The task of analyzing this battlefield and engaging in a budgetary review becomes difficult. It would have to rely on secondary and unofficial sources, in addition to partial official information that is only occasionally available. Thus, much as I would have liked to provide a thorough and comprehensive gender-sensitive budgetary analysis, a concrete attempt in that direction—to the extent that is at all possible—would be an endeavor well beyond the scope of this work. The following discussion accordingly is only a partial observation of government allocation of resources and changes made within it. Whenever possible, use was made of official information provided by government ministries in response to inquiries. The major source of information was the Adva Center, a nongovernmental research and policy center on social and welfare issues that also focuses on gender.[80]

Obviously, all budgetary decisions influence women, just as they affect all other citizens. The battle over the budget in terms of promoting women's interests usually takes place in the areas that clearly cater to women's specific needs, such as resources allocated for combating violence against women or for subsidizing day care centers. However, many other areas also affect women's situation in no lesser force. Thus, for example, any cutback in health care resources has a greater negative impact on women than on men, both as consumers and as employees. In most families, women are the primary caretakers of the family's health, and so partake of a larger share as consumers of the health care system; many of the new and costly health technologies relate to women's particular health needs; and the health care system is one of the largest employers of women (Swirski 1999c). Similarly, any decrease in the educational budget adversely affects women more than men since about three-quarters of the teachers are women, and teaching is the major occupation among employed women.[81]

The major source of budgetary allocations for distinct women's issues is the Ministry of Labor and Welfare. It is therefore the most pertinent agency to examine when one wants to appraise the level of commitment to women's advancement. Generally, as explained by Adva Research Center, the Ministry of Labor and Welfare is one of the few ministries whose budget did not shrink during 1996–2000; it in fact enjoyed a 15 percent increase (Swirski et al. 2000, 9). Of the departments that experienced significant budgetary growth, the one of particular relevance for women is the Department on Women's Employment, which is—quite tellingly—responsible for the operation of day care centers. Once again, the message that child care is women's prime responsibility and is essentially indivisible from women's employment could not be conveyed in more apparent form. Budget-wise, this department enjoyed a 10 percent increase in 2000, but only after three years of much more moderate increases that lagged behind the growth in the population of children ages four and under (Swirski et al. 1999b, 14). Another department with relevance to women's concerns is the Department for Adult Training, which offers vocational training programs during which the participants are eligible to receive unemployment or income support benefits. Although between 1996 and 2000 the number of unemployed increased by close to 40 percent as Israel went into recession, the department's budget went up by only 10 percent (Swirski et al. 2000, 14). Probably the most significant budgetary allocation in terms of women's welfare and advancement is the ministry's financial support of organizations for prevention of sexual and domestic violence against women and for treatment of its victims. Support to these organizations reached about $4 million in 2000 (a mere 0.45 percent of the ministry's total budget), a steady increase amounting to close to forty times the budget in 1990. Nonetheless, the ministry's allocation for battered women's shelters in 2000 was lower than in 1999. On the other hand, the ministry's subsidy for Centers for the Treatment and Prevention of Domestic Violence has been constantly increasing, including in the 2000 budget.[82] Two other government sources support these purposes, the local authorities and the Estates Fund, which operates under the Ministry of Justice. The total government financial support for these purposes in 2000 amounted to slightly over $5 million.[83]

The area of prevention of violence against women (discussed in further detail in the following chapter), particularly of domestic violence, can be examined as a case study in the dynamics of the battle over the budget. In November 1998 the inter-ministerial committee established to deal with the problem presented a comprehensive concluding report with integrative proposals across the spectrum of all agencies and institutions involved in handling domestic violence. The estimated overall cost of these proposals was $50 million. In April 1999 the government adopted the report's recommendations, deciding on a gradual implementation over several years.[84] The government resolution was not quite followed, and it was not at all clear whether the necessary amounts for the most urgent needs (amounting to only $3 million) were in fact included in the upcoming budget.[85] On the eve of the approval of the 2000 budget, a request to allocate the funds for more immediate projects was put to the Knesset Finance Committee (see Swirski et al. 2000, 19). This was eventually approved, with the intention of continuing the same level of allocation into subsequent years.[86] Moreover, it was granted matching funds of $3 million by various other government ministries (see Swirski et al. 2001). While this could be presented as indicating some level of commitment, it is nonetheless a far cry from what the committee recommended and represents a de facto rejection of its report.

Religion-State Integration and Its Effect on Women

Next to the armed forces, religion is the other factor that is uniquely important to the situation of women in Israel.[87] The place of religion in Israel has been acknowledged, here and elsewhere, as a primary factor informing the position of women, to their detriment (Yuval-Davis 1985; Safir 1993; Raday 1996a). To follow the discussion here we need to go back a little bit, to the CEDAW convention. International law allows states to make a legal commitment to implement a convention while reserving the right not to apply some of its requirements or even principles with which they cannot comply, all this in order to enhance global acceptance of human rights obligations. However, much controversy has been created regarding reservations to the CEDAW convention, since in many cases they appear contrary to its very aim (Tomasevski 1998, 14–16). That is primarily so with regard to reservations on religious grounds, which mostly apply to countries which apply Shari'a law. Some countries submitted reservations concerning the very obligation to eliminate gender discrimination.[88] It also applies to reservations on religious grounds that were made to Article 16 on Marriage and Family and to Article 7 on Political and Public Life, such as the ones made by Israel. The reservation to Article 7 declares:

> The State of Israel hereby expresses its reservation with regard to Article 7(b) of the Convention concerning the appointment of women to serve as judges of religious courts where this is prohibited by the laws of any of the religious communities in Israel. Otherwise, the said Article is fully implemented in Israel, in view of the fact that women take a prominent part in all aspects of public life.[89]

The reservation seems to take, as a working assumption, a religious prohibition against women serving as judges in religious courts. However, Jewish law cannot be said to categorically prohibit women from serving as religious judges. Consequently, Israel should perhaps withdraw this reservation or at least qualify its tone.[90] Withdrawing the reservation, though, would subject Israel to demands to actively promote women's representation in religious courts. Interestingly, it seems that drafters of the reservation felt somewhat uncomfortable with its implications and saw fit to defend the State of Israel in pointing out, rather cynically, Israel's compliance otherwise with Article 7, which is supposedly reflected in the "prominent part" women take in "all aspects of public life"

The two areas of family life and political and public life indeed present the obvious main areas of concern for discrimination against women on religious grounds. Officially, then, these are the only areas where the place of religion in Israel hampers women's advancement. I argue that the effect on women of the involvement of religion within Israel's polity and ethos is much vaster then that. What makes the religion factor so significant to the situation of women in Israel is indeed the formal integration of religion and state, particularly the rule of religious law over issues of family law and the legal consequences of this rule (Strum 1989; Raday 1993). This is the strongest expression of the influence of religion over women's lives. Nevertheless, apart from this formal and clearest effect, religion influences women's lives in other ways in Israel. Some are direct or indirect results of formal status that religion is given in family law and other areas; some have nothing to do with such formal status and are clear expressions of sociocultural norms. I term these semiformal and informal expressions of the religion and state relationship in Israel, and discuss them now as a case study of the effect of religion on the situation of women in Israel. The formal expressions of religion and state integration in Israel, primarily the rule of religious law over family matters and its ripple effect, are extensively discussed in Chapter 11.

Semiformal Expressions of Religion-State Integration

Semiformal expressions of the interconnection between religion and state in Israel concerning women are defined here as instances where women's rights, concerns, and interests are effectively prejudiced as an indirect result of the rule of religious law in matters of marriage and divorce, or of another formal-legal integration of religion and state. The clearest semiformal expressions are reflected in the physical space where religious law governs, namely the religious courts, and relate to the actual possibility for women to participate equally with men in all levels of their operation.

Starting from the highest level of participation, namely that of judges, both the 1955 Rabbinical Judges (Dayanim) Law and the 1962 Druze Courts Law[91] have been interpreted by Jewish, Muslim, and Druze religious leaders to mean that only men can serve as judges in these courts. Bearing in mind the fascinating process that the observant Jewish community is undergoing in terms of women's entry into the world of religious learning (as discussed in Chapter 5), and the formation of such feminist organizations as Kolech (see Chapter 3), this may not remain the case for long. The observant Jewish community is undergoing an evolution, perhaps even a quiet revolution, with respect to women's learning (El-Or 1998). As more and more women master the halachic (Jewish law) knowledge and its developmental tools, and as the drive toward inclusion gains force, demands can be expected for women to be included into the actual halachic process as recognized by the state in the very form of rabbinical judges.[92] From the constitutional perspective, this will bring about an unprecedented entanglement of civil law in religious matters. Rabbinical courts have formal jurisdiction within the Israeli legal system; they are subject to supervision by state officials (such as within the Ministry of Religion) and their appointments are regulated by the civil law; and they are also subject to the scrutiny of the High Court of Justice. Therefore it can be assumed that, if and when demands for inclusion are made by women, the civil legal system—through the High Court of Justice—will have to intervene. I see this as an unprecedented intervention because none of the conflicts involving women's demands for inclusion into the religious sphere so far have presented such an acute tension between women's right to equal participation and unsettled interpretation of Halacha,[93] in a setting that is under the overall control of the civil system and in a matter that distinctively affects women as a whole.

However, as already mentioned, the pattern of subordinating gender equality to religious demands has once again taken its toll in the 2000 amendment to the 1951 Women's Equal Rights Law.[94] This amendment not only maintained its original qualification that excluded the law from applying to the area of marriage and divorce, but added another qualification for religious reasons. The qualification applies to the novel affirmative action norm that was introduced in the amendment and exempts it from applying to religious roles, including religious judicial roles. Thus, quite ironically, the former discussion has turned moot through the act of the civil legislature, which closed a window of opportunity that the religious community had started to open. Indeed, the effects of this qualifications are already seen in a High Court of Justice decision that dismissed two petitions filed against the appointment of a qadi (Muslim court judge). One involved claims by a female candidate arguing the importance of the appointment of a female qadi for promoting the principles of gender equality and adequate representation in public posts. In dismissing the petition, the court also relied on this very qualification to the Women's Rights Law, accepting the argument that it specifically precludes the adequate representation principle from applying to religious courts.[95]

The case of women's certification as rabbinical advocates seems similar to the previous analysis. But despite the external resemblance, the substantive issues are quite different, primarily because the case of rabbinical advocates does not raise such serious and deep halachic contention or perhaps even any halachic controversy. The issue of women representing clients in rabbinical courts presents a most interesting and significant development. Certified attorneys, male or female, can always represent clients in rabbinical and other religious courts in any and all matters. Both rabbinical and Muslim courts have also recognized the competence of rabbinical or Shari'a advocates, who were allowed to represent clients in the relevant religious courts, regardless whether they were certified attorneys. The 1967 Rabbinical Advocates Regulations[96] originally applied to men alone, since graduation from a yeshiva was a primary condition for qualification as a candidate to the profession. The law was amended in 1991 to include graduates of other educational institutions of higher learning recognized by the Chief Rabbinical Court. It was not until 1994, after an institute for higher Torah learning for women petitioned the High Court of Justice, that the Chief Rabbinical Court decided on the criteria for its recognition.[97] The High Court of Justice reviewed those criteria, and found that some were intended to make it impossible for women students to qualify for candidacy and therefore were discriminatory and void. Several dozen religiously committed women have since passed the examinations and are now functioning as rabbinical advocates. Not surprisingly, they primarily represent female clientele, and their performance can often be perceived to be feminist in nature (Shamir, Shitrai, and Elias 1997). Although this accomplishment has not significantly opened the doors of rabbinical courts to women (since female attorneys could always represent clients there), and despite its narrow scope that does not pertain to the actual halachic process, this development should not be underestimated. Even while recognizing the substantive differences in the nature of the halachic question in the two cases, the achievement presents a concrete accomplishment on at least two levels, one geared toward women themselves, and the other toward the religious establishment as a whole. On the former level, this move has led to the creation of a cadre of women committed to serving the interests of female litigants. On the latter, it has crossed the barrier against women's formal functioning within the halachic world. This may have invaluable ramifications for the future struggle over women as rabbinical judges.

Following two landmark Supreme Court decisions in 1988, women were granted the right to participate in the committee for selection of municipal chief rabbis and the right to participate in municipal religious councils. In *Poraz v. Tel Aviv Mayor*,[98] the Supreme Court allowed women to participate in the committee for the selection of the Tel Aviv Chief Rabbi, emphasizing that exclusion of women from serving on political committees that deal with religious matters constitutes discrimination and is therefore void. In *Shakdiel v. Minister of Religious Affairs*,[99] the Supreme Court granted Leah Shakdiel, one of the pioneering Orthodox feminist activists, the right to be elected to the religious council of the city Yeruham in southern Israel. In both cases, which were decided close together in time, the court emphasized the secular nature of the disputed positions and functions. Almost a decade after the Supreme

Court decision, women still have great difficulties in getting elected to municipal religious councils.[100]

The ongoing case of the Women of the Wall serves as an opposite illustration of the effect of religion on Jewish women. In December 1988, women representing all religious streams in Judaism prayed together and read from a Torah scroll in the women's section of the Western Wall while wearing prayer shawls—all practices traditionally reserved for men alone. The group were interrupted, attacked, and dispersed by ultra-Orthodox men and women. In March 1989, the group petitioned the High Court of Justice after being violently attacked even when they tried to pray without prayer shawls and Torah scrolls. In December 1989, the minister of religion amended the 1981 Regulations on the Protection of Sacred Places for the Jewish People to include a prohibition on religious ritual at the Western Wall that offends the feelings of those praying there.[101] The petitioners then amended their petition to include the nullification of this amendment. The court gave a majority decision in January 1994, denying the petitions but recommending the establishment of a government committee to fully investigate the subject.[102] After many delays, deliberations of several committees, and two sets of elections in Israel, the bottom line recommendation was that the women be allowed to pray in the manner they wish, but in a secluded section of the Wall that is removed from the main public area and serves as an archeological garden. The women objected to this solution, in principle and for practical reasons. A further ruling in May 2000 accepting the women's position was met with criticism from religious circles and the passage of a preliminary reading of an ultra-Orthodox party's bill to impose a seven-year jail sentence to any woman praying at the Wall adorned with the traditionally male prayer shawl and phylacteries, or reading aloud from the Torah. Significantly, there has been little sympathy or understanding in the media for the women's cause, perhaps expressing Israeli society's general hostility to feminist causes (Lahav 2000). The case of the Women of the Wall is still pending, and their struggle is not yet over (for a detailed description and analysis, see Sered 1997; Lahav 2000; Halperin-Kaddari 2000b).

Informal Expressions

Informal expressions of the interconnection between religion and state in Israel concerning women include episodes where women's rights, concerns, and interests are being effectively prejudiced with no relation whatsoever to the rule of religious law over marriage and divorce or to any other formal or legal integration of religion and state. Examples of such informal expressions of the interconnection between religion and state in Israel abound. Perhaps the most obvious one has to do with the highest form of the public sphere, political participation. As explained at the beginning of the chapter, some of that public political space is inherently closed to women inasmuch as it is occupied by religious parties that view politics and leadership roles as exclusively male. Even in the local elections, the ultra-Orthodox parties demanded the exclusion of women as a condition for a joint campaign with the more moderate National Religious Party (Herzog 1999, 321). Thus, with no formal or legal sanctioning, women are partially precluded from political integration. One could of course argue that there is a place for formal involvement, from the exact opposite direction: the state should actively prohibit such exclusively male-represented political parties. This approach implies actual state intrusion into what is usually perceived as the "internal affairs" of the community, albeit a religious community. It challenges the basic definition of the question as one internal to a community (Minow 1989). Moreover, it suggests that the state can legitimately impose certain values, such as gender equality, on all its citizens (Tamir 1998; Okin 1999). These are all aspects of the intense debate on pluralism, multiculturalism, and cultural relativism that has been going on in Israeli society in recent years (Mautner, Sagi, and Shamir 1998; Rabinovich 1995; Simons 1995), though with not much attention devoted to explicit feminist concerns. Although this specific example has not yet been directly confronted, a position such as that of Frances Raday, who argues against promotion of multiculturalism at the expense of women's rights and gender equality, could perhaps lead to legitimization of state regulation of religious political associations (Raday 1996a). An opposite, more communitarian and cultural relativist approach would obviously lead to firm rejection of such a suggestion.

The next example perhaps demonstrates the best case study of the feminist-multicultural dilemma in the Israeli context. In July 1997 the Ministry of Traffic adopted a trial policy of sex serve mainly the ultra-Orthodox population in Jerusalem and Bnei-Brak.[103] While maintaining each passenger's personal option for mixed seating, the policy sanctioned the voluntary ordering of the ultra-Orthodox population to direct separate embarking, debarking, and seating. The voluntary arrangement would provide for men to enter and sit at the front of the buses, while women were to occupy the back. The committee on whose recommendations the policy was adopted apparently included only one woman, and among the sixteen representatives of the bus companies and ultra-Orthodox community, only one woman was present.[104] Immediately following the ministry's decision, the IWN appealed to the High Court of Justice, arguing the policy to be discriminatory against women, physically and symbolically relegating them to the rear part of society.

Relying on the famous holding in the U.S. Supreme Court case of *Brown v. Board of Education*,[105] the IWN argued that such a "separate but equal" arrangement violates the principle of gender equality. The state's response to the appeal clearly demonstrates the ideology of multiculturalism. In emphasizing the initiative as coming from the religious community and mostly directed at that community alone, the voluntary acceptance of the policy by the community, the overall satisfaction of the passengers, and the lack of any complaint by passengers, the state denied the network's contention of gender discrimination altogether.

In a hearing three years after the appeal, following quite a few delays, the IWN was practically convinced by the High Court of Justice to withdraw the appeal. In so doing, one can speculate that the court has indicated its hesitancy to confront the delicate subject of multiculturalism, and its apprehension at being once again blamed for intruding into religious affairs and circumventing religious freedoms of closed communities.[106]

The overall expressions of the influence of state and religion on women's lives in Israel result in a combined effect of oppression of women, both in the private and in the public sphere. Unequal power within the family results in women's subordination in the private sphere, while power is all too often denied to women in the public sphere. While the formal integration of religion and state in Israel is central to this, the semiformal and informal expressions of these relationships are no less significant. In the current political situation, structural change regarding the various expressions outlined in this chapter are rather improbable. The only venue for reform at present seems to lie in the internal mobilization of women within the religious community itself. The Orthodox feminist movement represents the potential for social, institutional, and even normative reform of the religious community. Although this movement is still confined to the moderate segment of the Orthodox community, and even there faces tremendous internal opposition, it nonetheless signals the possibility of internal change, where no formal external pressure is imposed.

Part III
Power Politics, Body Politics, and Radical Feminism

Chapter 9
Violence Against Women

Among those life situations that are unique to women, gender-based violence against women is perhaps the most negative and poses the strongest claim against traditional liberal feminist analysis. Gender-based violence, particularly sexual violence, mostly happens to women and not to men, and it is done to women by men. Women, predominately, are raped, and raped by men. Liberal legal feminism's sameness/difference theories lack the analytic tools that would place rape and other forms of sexual violence against women on women's political agenda. The most they could offer is that women are raped because they are different from men, but that would not advance the cause at all. Reconceptualized by radical feminism's dominance theory, however, sexual violence against women and domestic violence can clearly be explained as disparate power relations between the powerful dominating man and the powerless subordinated woman (Barnett 1998, 170). In terms of the public/private split and radical feminism's critique and rejection of it, this is where the private becomes public, and turns into a political issue.

As an interesting point of reference, it should come as no surprise to learn that violence against women, in any form, was not dealt with by the drafters of the CEDAW convention in 1979. In the late 1970s, violence against women, domestic violence in particular, had only begun to be revealed and acknowledged. While international women's rights scholars such as Rebecca Cook see the CEDAW convention as moving "from a sex-neutral norm that requires equal treatment of men and women, usually measured by how men are treated, to one that recognizes the fact that the particular nature of discrimination against women is worthy of a legal response" (Cook 1993, 239), it seems that with respect to the phenomenon of gender-based violence against women the convention still reflects the conventional liberal legal feminism that reigned at that time. The emergence of radical feminism from the periphery to the center of feminist discourse came along with the revelation of the universal phenomenon of domestic violence against women.[1] This is of course no coincidence. Liberal feminism lacks the theoretical tools to confront gender-based domestic violence and violence against women openly as the most extreme expressions of patriarchy and as phenomena of control and subordination, simply because this vocabulary is not part of its discourse (Barnett 1998, 170–72). It takes radical feminism's vocabulary and tools to face these issues systematically and openly. Going back to the CEDAW convention, the omission of gender-based violence against women was a reflection of careful political consideration (IWRAW 1996, 8). Only during the eighth and eleventh sessions of CEDAW, in 1989 and 1992, did the committee adopt General Recommendations 12 and 19 to deal directly with violence against women.[2]

In a sense, gender-based violence against women epitomizes the whole thesis of this book. No other subject captures all the paradoxes of the situation of women in Israel. No other subject has undergone such broad legal reforms (Shachar 1998, 116) or earned so much government attention and action—with so little improvement in result.[3] Major legal and operational developments have taken place in both areas that comprise this subject—sexual violence against women and gender-based domestic violence—yet, although these reforms aim to reduce the level of violence against women, empirical data do not point in that direction. However, these reforms can also strive to achieve other goals beyond the immediate and actual reduction of violence against women, such as increasing awareness of the problem, changing the attitudes of law-enforcement agencies, improving the care of victims, and so on. Here, the empirical data render a more complex impression. While public awareness may have been raised and the treatment of the victims somewhat improved, it is doubtful whether law enforcement agencies of all fronts have indeed internalized the changing attitudes. It seems that normative reforms have progressed faster than the attitudes of the social agents whose job is to implement them.

Strong evidence of the failure of implementation is found in a recent evaluation study, *Police Intervention in Intimate Violence*, by criminologists Zvi Eisikovits and Avi Griffel of Haifa University, commissioned by the Ministry of Internal Security (Eisikovits and Griffel 1998).[4] Perhaps the most remarkable statistical finding of the research is that, of 1000 cases analyzed, only 14.5 percent of the suspects were actually put to trial, only 6 percent were convicted, and only 1.2 percent of the total (12 of 995) were sent to jail. In addition, in only 8 percent of the cases was there referral to treatment. Eisikovits and Griffel note that since the stated policy is that the main police role in intervention is to execute judgment against the accused, and, as a supplementing intervention, to refer the couple to treatment, their findings prove that the police are only partially successful in attaining these two goals. The study focused on the police, but the findings are no less relevant to the evaluation of the judiciary's treatment of domestic violence.

Gender-based violence against women can be taken as a case study in several ways. First, it is the area that has undergone the largest amount of new and reforming legislation: much of the normative progress (legislative and judicial) made in this area conforms with suggestions classically made as part of the radical feminist critique of traditional criminal law.[5] Bearing in mind the earlier reference to radical feminism, this is indeed the area in which a theoretical move in the direction of radical feminism is best evidenced. Yet this also demonstrates the limitations of such ideological developments on the normative layer, when they have only weak pragmatic underpinnings and not enough ideological and conceptual infrastructure on the sociological layer. In other words, it reveals a deeper dimension to the familiar gap in the reality of women in Israel. This is the gap between the advancing ideology of the legal system as reflected "on the books," and the stranded ideology of the operation and implementation of the "law in action." It seems that this gap is one of the major reasons for the overall failure of the reforms. Radical feminism (or any feminism, for that matter) cannot be decreed from above without accompanying educational work. Support for this claim can be found in Eisikovits and Griffel's research on police attitudes to domestic violence against women, which found, among other things, partial legitimization of men's violence against their spouses, despite all the educational and instructive work done in the area in the past years. Their findings are corroborated by a series of smaller scale surveys done by criminologist Efrat Shoham, who also compared the attitudes of regular police investigators to those of the specially trained investigators who are part of the national investigative system focusing solely on domestic violence that was established in 1998,[6] revealing that even the latter still maintain some prejudice against women complainants and show some sense of reluctance in their role in handling domestic violence (Shoham, forthcoming).

On the operational level there are numerous commissions and committees, producing various recommendations and suggestions, leading to the formation of many new plans and programs; in reality, nothing changes. The absence of budgetary back-up is easily seen when examining such necessities as financing shelters for battered women.[7] Perhaps a beginning of realizing this can be detected in the conclusions and recommendations of a report by the most recent committee on violence against women within the family (Inter-Ministerial Committee 1998).[8] For the first time, the committee truly examined the situation on almost all government and operational fronts, and many of its recommendations are indeed geared at a broad spectrum that cuts across various government ministries and organs.

As for increased public awareness and attentiveness, here too the paradox is evident. First, public attention to this subject, mainly through the media, focuses mostly on the graphic and pornographic aspects of this terrible reality rather than stemming from feminist ideology or theory. Furthermore, while awareness does seem to be increasing, media coverage and public debate seem to be more willing to address violence against women within the family rather than sexual violence against women as such. The discourse then usually takes the angle of the gender-neutral "domestic violence," enabling the blurring of the clear gender-specific nature of the phenomenon. Second, this increased awareness too has not produced any real change in women's reality. It sometimes seems that both public and government reaction are merely lip service. At the end of the day, this is one of the two main areas in which women's organizations have begun, and still carry on doing, much of the mundane, everyday work.[9]

Sexual harassment is one particular area where growing public awareness seems to be more than just "lip service" and presents the beginning of a concrete change of perceptions. This subject has undergone major normative change with the 1998 enactment of the Prevention of Sexual Harassment Law[10] and several high-profile cases of sexual harassment. The joint effect of two such affairs could be well described as "collective consciousness raising," as was eloquently put by Deborah Rhode in relation to the Anita Hill-Clarence Thomas hearings (Rhode 1992). One, perhaps the more significant in gaining public attention and causing public debate, involves allegations by several women against Yitzhak Mordechai, then serving as minister of transportation, a leading Israeli politician, head of the Center Party, former IDF commander of the northern region and candidate to the post of chief of staff. Some of the allegations concerned incidents that occurred when Mordechai was still a high-ranking army official, while the one put by the woman who first stepped forward related to the more recent period of Mordechai's political career. In July 2000, Mordechai's parliamentary immunity was lifted and he was indicted on two counts of sex offenses. His trial opened in October 2000. In March 2001 he was found guilty in two of the three charges and faced a maximum sentence of seven years in prison. In April 2001 a split panel of three judges gave him an eighteen-month suspended sentence. The two male judges wrote that they weighed Mordechai's public achievements and military past in determining the sentence, whereas the dissenting judge, a woman, gave him four months in prison and a year of suspended sentence. Both the state and Mordechai appealed.[11] A little more than six months later (very fast by Israeli standards), the court of appeals gave its decision: it unanimously rejected Mordechai's appeal on his main conviction, but was split with respect to his second conviction (accepted) and the state's appeal on the lenient punishment (rejected). On both issues, the dissenting judge—who represented harsher treatment of Mordechai—was a woman.[12]

The public debate surrounding this affair could be taken as a case study of social change. On the one hand, there were segments in the media and in the general society, generally all male, who expressed bafflement, confusion, and lack of understanding of the legal norms, as well as sympathy to Mordechai, who in their eyes was simply behaving according to age-old social norms.[13] On the other hand, the media cited many women telling their own experiences of "age-old social norms," leaving no doubt that the "rules of the game" have changed.[14] On the basis of the way this affair has been handled in the media, the public contention that accompanied it, and the wave of sexual harassment complaint reports that ensued, a radical reviewer of Israel society could safely label it as the beginning of open war between the sexes in Israel.

Going back to the overall subject of gender-based violence against women, this area is also illuminating for the "information story" theme, that is, the way information and the lack thereof condition the handling of the subject matter. Until 1995, there was absolutely no way of assessing the extent of violence against women within the family, since there was no separate coding for family relations between victim and perpetrator in police files. This was only a symptom of the overall trivializing attitude toward this problem. While police attitudes may have changed, other authorities have not internalized the message. Thus, no data on violence against women within the family are available from welfare services in local municipalities, since no separate code for violence exists. Apparently, violent relationships are included under "unstable marital relations" in welfare authorities' records (Interministerial Committee 1998, 10). The hidden message of this classification is that violence is a regular part of deteriorating relationships, perhaps even caused by their deterioration. In a similar vein, there is still no way of assessing the extent of overall violence against women from police or state attorney records, since no routine separation is made between violence against women and violence in general.[15] How can a comprehensive program to address gender-based violence against women be developed when no statistics exist? How can any claim about the growing phenomenon of gender-based violence against women be made when the official police record "shows" that there is no such thing?

In fact, law enforcement or welfare agencies' data show only part of the picture due to underreporting in this area, particularly in domestic violence cases. It was not until 2000 that a scientific assessment of the extent of domestic violence against women became available, through a first-ever national survey conducted by the JDC-Brookdale Institute, collecting data on women's health and welfare state, and within that on the particular phenomenon of domestic violence against women (Gross and Brammli-Greenberg 2000).[16] In addition, until the Eisikovits and Griffel study of 1998, no scientific examination of criminal proceedings on domestic violence existed (that is, the statistical final outcome of complaints to the police), and there still is no similar investigation as to civil proceedings in this area (discussed in detail below). Once again, without concrete knowledge of the facts, how can any honest evaluation be made of the efficiency and sufficiency of the various authorities' handling of this problem?

Sexual Violence—Legal Aspects: Transition and Reform

Legislative Reforms

Tremendous strides have been made by the Israeli legal system in combating sex crimes over the past decade. In 1988, 1989, and 1990, the 1977 Penal Law was amended[17] in a manner that could best be described as shifting from the traditional, moralistic protection of female genitalia toward the protection of individuals and their human dignity against violent crimes of a sexual nature.

Thus, the previously narrowly defined crime of rape, which protected only women from vaginal penetration, was broadened so as to protect all individuals from violent penetration of any kind. The reform also clarified the question of marital rape, previously recognized by case law as illegal, it was not clearly prohibited by the statutory definition of rape. The law as worded until 1988 retained the traditional common law requirement that an act of intercourse be "illegal" in order to qualify as rape—in other words, that the act involve extramarital intercourse. The courts, which disapproved of this distinction even before the legislative reform of 1988, interpreted "illegal" as referring to the personal religious law applicable to the individual in question. As Jewish religious law prohibits marital rape, this provision was effectively circumvented in cases of marital rape among Jews.[18] It was not until the reform, however, that a clear territorial legal stance was taken and applied to all citizens of Israel.

Perhaps most significantly, the 1988–90 reform replaced the prohibition against having sexual intercourse with a woman "against her will" with a prohibition, still worded in negative terms, against sexual intercourse without a woman's free consent ("by free consent"). The amendment has been welcomed as instituting a positive requirement that intercourse be consensual. This change, far from semantic, has had a tremendous impact both on the way rape is viewed by society and on the way the criminal prohibition is applied by the courts. Whereas merely forbidding intercourse against a woman's will implies that a woman needs to actively express her opposition to the act in order for it to qualify as rape, positively requiring consent assumes that no individual may presume another willing to engage in sexual activity unless such consent is expressed. The change may be taken to imply an abandonment of the chauvinistic assumption that when a woman says "no" she really means "yes," or even that women who do not consent to intercourse "really" enjoy it.[19] While consent according to the amendment need not be explicit, it must at least be implied.

The most recent and somewhat unexpected legislative amendment took place in June 2001. It amended the actual definition of rape in section 345(a)(1) of the Penal Law, removing its major part ("by use of force, infliction of physical suffering, exertion of pressure or threats of the above, whether these were done against a woman herself or against another individual"), leaving only the requirement that the penetration of a woman's sexual organ be done without her free consent. Apparently, the rest of the definition that detailed possible causes for the lack of the woman's free will (such as "the use of force") was seemed redundant, especially in light of recent case law that had already interpreted the penetration itself as constituting "the use of force."[20] A differentiation is made between *rape*, for which the maximum punishment is sixteen years imprisonment, and *aggravated rape*, for which up to twenty years may be imposed. Aggravated rape consists of any of the above acts, in which the rapist threatens the use of weapons, causes severe bodily or emotional damage or causes pregnancy, abuses the woman before, during, or after the act, or commits the rape in the presence of others who are there in order to participate, actively or passively, in the commission of the rape. Similarly, the rape of a minor under age sixteen is considered aggravated rape.

As for the age of consent, while consensual intercourse with minors under age fourteen is considered rape, consensual intercourse with minors between ages fourteen to sixteen is defined as a separate offense punishable by up to five years imprisonment. Exception is made for those rare instances in which a minor under sixteen is married.[21] A separate exception is made in section 353 for circumstances where the age gap between the minor and the accused does not exceed three years, the minor has agreed to the act, and it was done "as part of regular loving relationships with no abuse of status by the accused." Sexual relations with minors aged sixteen to eighteen, where the perpetrator exploits a position of authority or a relationship of dependence, or where the perpetrator offers false promises of marriage, are similarly punishable by up to five years in prison.

An important provision, specific to sexual offenses, states that the criminal liability of one who causes a sexual offense to be committed is equal to that of the individual who actually commits the offense. This provision, which recognizes the criminality of passive participation in acts of rape, may serve to increase societal awareness of rape as a crime deeply connected to general social norms and perceptions of women as sexual objects.

The 1989 and 1990 reforms also transformed the law's treatment of sexual violence against family members, by designating a whole new and detailed section for this purpose. Section 351 of the 1977 Penal Law specifically prohibits the commission of sexual offenses against family members (for which the law provides a wide definition) who are minors, and provides severe maximal punishments comparable to those specified for aggravated rape. The 1989 reform also introduced mandatory reporting requirements to the police or welfare officers by an individual responsible for a minor, or who is in a position specified by the law regarding a minor (e.g., a teacher), who has reasonable basis to suspect that a violent, sexual, or abusive offense or neglect had been committed against the minor. The 1971 Evidence Ordinance (New Version)[22] was also amended to exclude violent crimes from the rule that provides testimonial immunity for spouses, parents, and children from testifying against each other. In addition, the law was amended in 1996[23] to extend the statute of limitations on sexual crimes committed against minors by parents, guardians, or other family members. According to the amendment, the statute of limitations on such crimes only begins when the minor reaches age eighteen. The section stipulates, however, that where ten or more years have passed since the crime was committed, the approval of the attorney general is required before it may be prosecuted. This is obviously a clear exception to the rules of limitation that favor the "finality" of the law. It expresses the recognition that in this area of criminality, the victim needs enormous emotional powers to be able to face the abuser, and the process of gathering these powers may continue well into the victim's maturity. It also recognizes that conviction in these cases is not necessarily done for the traditional criminological purposes of deterrence, or for abstract justice, but rather for the purpose of the victim's emotional rehabilitation.

What distinguishes the crime of rape from most other criminal offenses is the weight placed on the victim's state of mind in determining the guilt of the accused. With the exception of intercourse with minors, it is the issue of the victim's consent that determines whether rape has in fact taken place. Questions of evidence, therefore, take on special importance. The balance that must be struck between the rights of the accused and of the victim requires that the evidentiary requirements both encourage victims to come forward and ensure that alleged perpetrators are given a fair trial. The extent to which rape is unique in this regard is controversial. Some have pointed out the similarity between the crime of rape and the crime of assault, both of which depend on lack of consent on the part of the victim and both of which may often hang on the word of the victim against the word of the perpetrator. Arguing that a double standard is applied in differentiating between these two offenses, many suggest that, were it not for societal prejudice, the evidentiary requirements in both instances would be identical. Others, pointing to the stigma and emotional involvement attached to forced sexual intercourse, argue that the distinction is justified (Harel and Vagner 1997).

Various steps have been taken to encourage and protect rape victims who do choose to come forward. In 1988, Section 2A was added to the 1957 Procedural Amendment Law (Questioning of Witnesses),[24] forbidding courts to allow victims of sexual crimes to be asked about their sexual history. In 1995, the Knesset passed an additional amendment to the above law, the 1995 Procedural Amendment Law (Amendment No. 2) (Questioning of Witnesses),[25] authorizing courts to order that the testimony of a complainant in a sexual offense be given in the accused's absence. This must be done in cases where the court believes that the complainant or the complainant's testimony may otherwise be harmed.[26]

As of 1998, the whole subject of sexual harassment is separately dealt with in the 1998 Prevention of Sexual Harassment Law,[27] whose ideology, contents, and process of legislation can be taken as symbolizing the changes presently taking place in Israeli feminism. Until 1998, sexual harassment was mostly conceptualized as a form of prohibited discrimination in the workplace within the 1988 Equal Employment Opportunities Law[28] and was only treated in passing in the Penal Law with no specific reference to sexual harassment as such. The new law, resulting from mutual efforts of women's organizations, the Knesset Committee on the Status of Women, and women from academia, now makes sexual harassment both a criminal and a civil offense, not limited to the workplace context at all. The more dramatic innovation goes to the change in conception of sexual harassment. Unusual in the context of criminal or civil legislation, the law states its aim as preserving the dignity and privacy of the person harassed and at the promotion of gender equality. The concept of sexual harassment as an offense against the woman's dignity and liberty was strongly advocated by the promoters of the new law and was indeed embedded into its first section. One of the central figures behind this law, law professor Orit Kamir, has suggested that the concept of "dignity and liberty" is more fitting and suitable in contemporary Israeli society, certainly more than the traditional measures of offenses through the problematic legal concept of "reasonable person," which was much more susceptible to subjective and relative interpretations (Kamir 1998).[29] Sexual harassment is broadly defined to include unwanted sexual advances, requests for sexual favors, and any sexual verbal or physical conduct that demands such behavior or that conditions promotion or benefit upon such behavior. In order to be considered as harassment, the advances and the references must have been specifically rejected by the harassed person, unless they were made in the context of hierarchical working relationships, medical treatment, or psychological therapy, or the harassed is a minor or a "helpless" person as defined in the penal law. In these latter cases, even consensual sexual advances or relations may be considered harassment. No harm needs to be proved in order to bring a criminal complaint or file a civil suit. The court may order up to 50,000 NIS in damages (approximately $12,000) even without proof of harm. The law applies to the army as well as to academia. Its innovation includes obligating employers to take steps to prevent sexual harassment in the workplace, including setting up of a mechanism for processing complaints, and the publication of regulations for this purpose.

Somewhat related to the legislation on sexual harassment is the 2001 Stalking Law,[30] proposed by four women MKs, which provides for issuing a prohibitive injunction against a person who engages in stalking but does not make stalking a criminal offense.

Sentencing presents another important lens for examining the dynamics of the transition. While the high maximal punishments provided for in the 1977 Penal Law represent a clear condemnation of sexual violence, the sentences imposed rarely constitute more than a fifth of the maximum in practice (Bogoch and Don-Yechiya 1999).[31] As awareness of light sentencing increased, public disapproval led mostly by women's organizations called for legislative restrictions on judges' discretion in sentencing. A 1998 amendment[32] instituted a minimum punishment for those convicted of rape, indecent acts, and sex crimes against family members, constituting a quarter of the maximum that may be imposed. Courts may still impose the minimum imprisonment in the form of a suspended sentence without demanding any special and mitigating circumstances. It has been suggested that the resort to suspended sentences as a way of circumventing the minimum punishment may have escaped the attention of the minimum punishment proponents, who probably intended that the punishment be only in the form of actual imprisonment (Kannai 2000, 724–25).

Judicial Rejoinder

Sentencing is of course only one expression of the judicial role in law-making, and probably the least central of them. More significant is the judiciary's role as interpreter of substantive law. In this respect, the various statutory reforms of 1988–90 have been paralleled by significant changes in the attitude of the court system toward perpetrators and victims of sexual offenses. The Shomrat case[33] in particular has been welcomed as a turning point in the judiciary's treatment of rape. In 1993, the Supreme Court decided this tragic incident involving the gang-rape of a fourteen-year-old girl by a group of boys aged seventeen and up, who were all members of the same kibbutz (collective settlement), Shomrat. For several consecutive days, the group of boys forced her to have sexual intercourse with them, using various physical and emotional pressure tactics. In a policy decision that could be viewed as epitomizing all that had been lacking in the criminal justice system's response to rape, the state originally decided to refrain from prosecuting on the grounds that there was no "public interest" in doing so. The matter was eventually brought to court, partly due to a massive public outcry. The district court, finding there to be a reasonable doubt as to their guilt, acquitted the group of seven boys. The prosecution appealed to the Supreme Court against the acquittal of four of them.

The Supreme Court decision has been recognized as a turning point in handling rape cases. Explicitly declaring rape to be a crime against the human dignity of the victim, and rejecting stereotypical notions of women's sexuality that promote a forgiving attitude toward those who rape "loose" women, the court adopted a strong stance against the relevance of a woman's sexual history as evidence of her consent in the instance at hand. Similarly, the court laid down clear guidelines consistent with the laws of evidence, prohibiting the admission of *any* evidence relating to the victim's sexual history. The court also explicitly acknowledged the tendency of rape victims to refrain from coming forward with their complaints, holding that such delays in coming forward, when reasonably explained under the circumstances, do not impact upon the credibility of the victim as a witness.

Recognizing that the crime of rape, as defined in the 1977 Penal Law (prior to the June 2001 amendment), required the use of force or the exertion of pressure against the victim, the court held that such force need not be either immediate or severe. The court also recognized that the amended law, which no longer speaks of the woman's *will* but rather requires her *consent*, plainly does not demand that the victim actively resist the attempt, especially where it is clear that the victim is too frightened to do so. Justice Heshin likened the sexual relationship to a contract that requires offer and acceptance, holding that where the law speaks of consent rather than will, it demands active consent and not simply lack of opposition. Just as no contract would be valid where one party said "no" and was assumed by the other to mean "yes," so too no man may justify nonconsensual sex by claiming that the woman's "no" meant "yes." The court accepted the state's appeal with respect to four of the accused boys and sent the case back to the district court for sentencing. During oral arguments at the sentencing stage, the defense lawyers did not fail to raise the typical argument of military service, this time asking the court not to hamper the boys' future military service.[34] Three of the boys were sentenced to fifteen months actual imprisonment and twenty-one months suspended sentence each, while the fourth was sentenced to one year of actual imprisonment and one year suspended sentence.[35]

In April 1996, the Supreme Court decided the case of *The State of Israel v. Biton and Others*.[36] With facts painfully similar to those of the Shomrat rape, the case involved an insecure and vulnerable fourteen-year-old girl who was sexually exploited by her "boyfriend" and his friends. Questions regarding why the victim allowed herself to be subjected to such treatment were dismissed as illegitimate by the Supreme Court, which held that the perpetrators' exploitation of victim's fear of abandonment and then later her fear of public shame clearly explained the victim's inability to extricate herself from the situation.

Although the Shomrat case was relatively recent, many other cases since have relied upon and implemented its progressive approach. In these two cases the court emphasized the fact that victims' delays in coming forward with testimony regarding sexual assault should generally not damage their reliability as witnesses.[37]

Family Gender-Based Violence—Legal Aspects: Transition and Reform

Gender-based domestic violence epitomizes the paradoxes of women's situation in Israel. It has undergone no less fundamental legal reforms and has generated more government action and plans, yet so far the situation seems only to have worsened. The paradox here seems to be even greater, since the general impression is that people are very much aware of this problem and that it is being taken care of. It has almost become fashionable to address, so much so that any self-aware politician deems it necessary to mention it as part of the agenda for action. This ambiguous attitude is best reflected in the yearly march, on Women's Day, of male politicians to a battered women's shelter, taking advantage of a photo opportunity with women whose identity is concealed, pledging to increase the fight against domestic violence.[38] It seems that in Israel the association of Women's Day with the plight of battered women is not a reflection of any deep appreciation of the relationship between feminist critique of the patriarchal family and the struggle to expose violence against women within the family. If it were, the whole attitude toward this subject would be different, and leaders would not stop by the shelters one day a year, but would be truly concerned with these women's suffering all year round, and would form the way to uproot it from the bottom.

This, however, would demand much more thorough thinking and planning, that might ultimately lead to radical legal changes in the overall family structure, including the partial control of religious law over this area, far beyond what any contemporary leader would be willing to endorse. It would also demand a total revision of the labor market so as to reinstitute women as central, not marginal constituents within it. This also has never been an explicit goal of any Israeli government. Furthermore, it would order a total revision of budgetary priorities, so that all the progressive programs and plans submitted by one committee after another could finally be implemented. In light of the diminishing allocations for welfare needs, this is hardly a realistic goal. Thus, what is left to do is to handle the outcome of the predicament, but not its causes. To sum up, this whole process can be described as resulting from yet another paradox: the relative success in raising awareness and consciousness of the problem has led to government and leadership involvement in treating it, which in turn has translated into an overall impasse in this area. It is as if the government had "appropriated" these issues from the women's organizations, who were of course the first ones to alert the public awareness to them, only to provide mostly superficial solutions that bring favorable public opinion but leave the basic problems intact and also leave much of the mundane tedious work to women's organizations. To understand all this, we now turn to a chronological description of the developments in this area.

Legislative Reforms

In 1989, the Karp Committee, headed by the Deputy Attorney General Yehudit Karp, published a comprehensive report dealing with the phenomenon of domestic violence (Karp Committee 1989). The report distinguished three possible societal responses to violence in the family:

"legal-criminal," "therapeutic-social," and "object oriented." The report suggested a comprehensive integration of all three approaches that would acknowledge the criminal and violent nature of domestic violence as well as the need to treat it as a distinct phenomenon. It also recommended various measures to clarify the criminal nature of such abuse, encourage various government and social institutions to cooperate in order to treat the problem, and provide victims with emergency access to remedies that could provide immediate protection.

The most important result to come of the report's findings was the passage of the 1991 Prevention of Violence in the Family Law.[39] Until then, a woman wishing to obtain a restraining order could do so only in the context of her applicable personal law, as a consequence of the general rule of personal-religious law in the area of family law. Since Jewish law recognizes as part of a woman's right to marital support her right to "safe and peaceful housing," Jewish women were able to request restraining orders within general marital support suits. The effectiveness of this option was severely impaired both by its limited application to women recognized as officially married and eligible for marital support and by its complicated and lengthy procedural requirements. While requests could be made in either the rabbinical or the district courts, the rabbinical court's emphasis on reconciliation deterred it from granting restraining orders in the vast majority of cases. Most cases were therefore brought to the civil court system. In 1982, the civil court system, reacting to what it perceived as overuse of the remedy as a weapon in divorce battles, and wary of potential violations of alleged abusers' rights, established strict and unrealistic tests for its application.[40]

The 1991 Prevention of Violence in the Family Law operates independently of personal family law and creates a "protective injunction" designed to provide immediate protection for those subjected to domestic violence. The law, which explicitly preserves the existing legal situation, has been interpreted by the Supreme Court as adding to the options already available according to personal law.[41] Worded in gender-neutral language so as to protect "family members" from domestic violence, the law considerably broadens the definition of "family," to include various relationships, past and present, within which such violence may occur. The law also explicitly defines "spouse" as including nonmarital cohabitants. Offering jurisdiction over the granting of protective injunctions to the magistrate's courts, the law also broadens the choice of jurisdictions available to the requesting party. After much debate, a 1998 amendment[42] also gave religious courts the jurisdiction to grant protective injunctions. It was often asserted that women from ultra-Orthodox communities hesitate in turning to civil courts, and this amendment would ease their plight (Parliamentary Investigative Committee 1996, 17–18). However, some claim that giving religious courts jurisdiction over such life-threatening situations, with hardly any training and guidance, leads to more harm than benefit.[43]

The law recognizes the profound emotional distress of the abused individual and hence empowers the attorney general and police prosecutors to intervene on behalf of adults who are unable to act. This unique provision, which allows for action to be taken by individuals other than the adult victim, implies the acknowledgment of the helplessness characterized as "Battered Women's Syndrome," which often prevents abused women from actively seeking intervention. Recognition of this problem is supported by the 1975 National Health Regulations (Notification of Suspected Violence),[44] which requires various health care providers to notify the police of suspected violence against their patients. The most recent step in this direction is found in a 2001 amendment to the Prevention of Violence in the Family Law, requiring all professionals dealing with victims of spousal violence (including social workers, health professionals, police officers, lawyers, and chaplains) to notify their clients of all legal and support options available to them.[45] In an attempt to ensure that victims who wish to come forward are not averted from doing so, the law provides that the protections it offers may not be forfeited and that consent to injunction violations by the requesting party do not exempt the violator from liability. Steps have therefore been taken within the police to ensure that cases pertaining to women who later withdraw their complaints are not closed.[46]

When discussing the law's treatment of the problem of domestic gender-based violence, it is important to distinguish between criminal and civil proceedings. One of the significant aspects of the 1991 Prevention of Violence in the Family Law is its civil characteristic. The victim of domestic violence can pursue immediate help within the civil court system, and her relief is not contingent on filing a formal complaint with the police. The separation between these two spheres, and the availability of immediate relief in the civil sphere, reflect a deep comprehension of the predicaments and dilemmas of victims of domestic violence. This separation, however, is also a problematic feature in the legal treatment of domestic violence, as discussed later. At this point, I turn to examine the criminal sphere of handling gender-based family violence. A 1996 reform of the laws of criminal procedure[47] specifically includes reasonable suspicion that an individual committed an act of violence against a family member as grounds for immediate arrest and provides the court in which he is charged with the power to arrest him until the end of the trial, if the charges concern violence against family members. Furthermore, if a suspect is released on bail, he must deposit any weapon he may own with the police.[48] A 1996 amendment to the Penal Law[49] makes further progress in recognizing abusive violence within the family as a special and uniquely severe form of assault: it defines violence against family members as a special offense and provides a maximum punishment that is double the usual maximum for assault. Moreover, a 2000 amendment has set a minimum punishment for grave acts of assault and violence against family members, equal to a fifth of the maximum that may be imposed.[50] There are no data yet on the effect this reform has had since its adoption.

In line with the move toward a more treatment-based approach, both the 1991 Prevention of Violence in the Family Law and the 1977 Penal Law were amended in 1996,[51] so as to allow courts to require abusive individuals to undergo therapy. Courts are also provided with the option of ordering therapy without conviction in relevant criminal trials.

The availability of weapons has been found to increase the risk and probability that an attack will occur.[52] The 1949 Weapon Law was amended in 1997,[53] so that a court that convicts an individual of any violent crime is not to refuse the prosecution's request to suspend whatever weapon license that individual might have, or to deposit that weapon with the police. Any refusal of such a request must be accounted for with special reasons. The amendment, however, does not address the issue of individuals who are members of the security forces or who are issued weapons in order to perform their annual reserve duty in the army.

An important step in the direction of easing the plight of victims of domestic violence was taken in 1995, when the 1973 Legal Aid Regulations were amended so as to expressly cover domestic violence among the matters for which legal aid may be obtained under the 1972 Legal Aid Law.[54] Requests for legal aid in matters of domestic violence have priority over other requests in all other areas.[55] Another development worth mentioning is the 1995 Recompensation Law (Child Orphaned due to Domestic Violence),[56] which was passed to ensure that where one of a child's parents is killed by the other, the child will be provided for financially.

Another recent law, representing significant achievement for women's NGOs and reflecting change of attitude and policy of law enforcement agencies toward victims, is the 2001 Victims of Offenses' Rights Law, passed in March 2001.[57] The law grants a long list of rights, with special emphasis on victims of violence and sexual offenses, including the right to protection at every stage of criminal proceedings, to be notified on the proceedings' developments, to be notified on the perpetrator's arrest or release from arrest, to be accompanied during investigations, to express an opinion prior to a delay in proceedings, plea bargain, parole or clemency, and more. Until the passage of this law, the interests of victims of physical violence, especially sexual violence, were referred to only in internal directives issued to individual prosecutors.[58]

Two recent legislative developments attempt to aid battered women on the economic level. The first (mentioned in Chapter 7) is the 2000 amendment to the Employment of Women Law,[59] aimed at protecting women who are absent from work because they are hiding in shelters from being fired. The second is the 2001 amendment to the 1992 Single Parent Families Law,[60] which provides that women who stay more than 90 days in battered women's shelters and have started divorce proceedings are defined as "single parents" and therefore eligible for several welfare benefits.

Unprecedented legislative energy has been put into the area of violence against women within the family. No other substantive area (except finances and budgetary legislation) has witnessed such rapid development and such intensive legislative work. The most recent inter-ministerial committee, mentioned above, has also made several proposals to amend the current statutory situation (Inter-Ministerial Committee 1998, 62–67). This time, however, it is clear that most proposals are necessary not to correct purely legal problems, but rather to address problems with the implementation of the existing laws. These can be grouped into two classes: those caused by lack of understanding of the nature of such situations by the courts or law enforcement agencies and those caused by mere lack of resources due to "budgetary constraints." Of the former, a typical example is the rejection of a request for a protective injunction based on the written forms alone, without hearing the requesting party.[61] As for the latter the overburdening of social workers on the one hand, and of courts on the other, make it almost impossible to implement the procedures for ordering therapy or for hastening the judicial handling of these cases.

Judicial Rejoinder

Perhaps one of the greatest problems in the implementation of the law has been lack of awareness among judges of the issue of domestic violence. It is difficult to support this assertion scientifically, apart from examination of actual judicial products, that is, cases, in both their outcomes and their substantive content. It is perhaps worth mentioning a more anecdotal observation, made by Judge Yehudit Schtoffman, former Tel Aviv and Central District deputy president of family courts, at a conference on domestic violence, when she admitted the difficulty people in judicial positions have in accepting the existence of situations of inequality.[62] Anecdotal as it may be, this is a very interesting observation that sheds original light on what often seems to be inexplicable lack of understanding on the part of the judiciary. Nevertheless, the overall change of attitude reflected in the passage of the 1991 Prevention of Violence in the Family Law may sometimes be observed in the judiciary as well. In the 1995 case of *Carmela Buhbut v. The State of Israel*,[63] a woman sentenced to seven years imprisonment by the district court for killing her abusive husband successfully challenged the severity of her punishment. While the case was unique in that even the prosecution felt it necessary to describe the extent and nature of the abuse in the writ of indictment, the ruling represents an awareness of Battered Women's Syndrome and of the need for individuals other than the victim of abuse to take action.[64] The sentence was reduced to three years, and efforts of various public figures, including MKs, have since succeeded in having Ms Buhbut paroled.[65] A recent amendment to the 1977 Penal Law allows courts to impose lenient sentences on victims of severe abuse who have been convicted of murdering the perpetrators of the abuse.

The Buhbut case reflects a deep understanding of the plight of the battered woman and of the intricate dynamics of the gender power imbalance in the family. Not all cases though, demonstrate such an understanding. *Azualus v. The State of Israel*[66] is one example of a court's treatment of a murder case as an isolated incident rather than as part of a phenomenon that victimizes women (Kamir 1997, 181–83). In this case, a man who was convicted of killing his wife and her lover on actually witnessing an instance of their already known infidelity was found to have been "provoked" in a manner negating the "malice aforethought" required of him to be guilty of murder. He was convicted of manslaughter.

Sexual Violence Against Women: Facts and Figures

It is difficult to obtain precise statistics on annual incidents concerning sexual violence. As elsewhere in the world, most cases go unreported. Until very recently the only available statistics were police records, which cover only those few who actually report the attacks and are always qualified—even by the police—as not reflecting the actual situation, and statistics from the help centers (rape crisis centers) around the country. The 2000 JDC-Brookdale survey allows for the first time a more accurate impression of the real situation. Unlike previous statistics, the data here reflect self-reporting of a nationally representative sample of adult women (i.e., over twenty-two years old) regardless whether they turned to official authorities or help services; even so, the researchers qualify their findings, warning that this too is a minimal estimation. According to the survey, 2 percent of adult women in Israel (34,000 women) had at some time been victims of rape, 4 percent (68,000) were victims of sexual violence, and 8 percent (136,000) were victims of physical violence. Significantly, only a third of the rape victims, a third of the sexual violence victims, and 42 percent of the physical violence victims had sought medical aid (Gross and Brammli-Greenberg 2000, 49–52). This sheds some light on the victims' reluctance to step forward and seek help and can also give some indication on the unreliability of formal reporting statistics.

Not a formal authoritative institute, but still involving some degree of exposure on the part of the victims, the Help Centers Union also supplies important data that give a fuller picture than the police's data. The Israeli Sexual Assault Victim's Help Centers Union, established in 1990, operates as the umbrella organization for nine help centers throughout the country, including one that specifically serves ultra-Orthodox Jewish women and two especially geared toward serving Arabic-speaking women. The Union's annual reports show a consistent increase in women's appeals for help; this is conventionally explained as reflecting a combination of increasing violence against women and growing awareness on the women's part. Figure 2 depicts the increase in requests in general and for assistance following sexual assaults; because the help centers also serve as information centers and as a resource women in for other situations of distress, the figure also shows the increase in general help center requests.

In an attempt to assess the extent of sexual violence against women, police data can only serve as an indication of the trend taking place, and not of its actual scope. In this respect, the overall direction is of increase in the number of sexual violence cases in general and of grave sexual

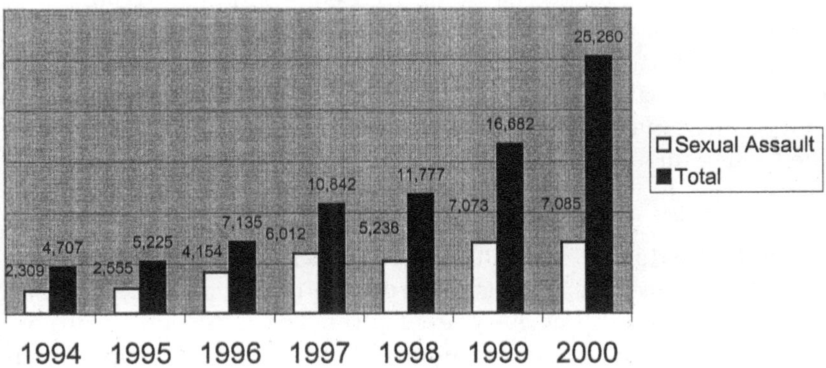

Figure 2. Appeals to help centers, 1994–2000. Source: Help Centers Union, *Sexual Violence in Israel*, 2000.

offenses (defined as rape or forced indecent acts) cases in particular. Between 1996 and 1999, the annual number of overall sexual violence complaints rose by almost 40 percent, from 2,848 to 3,959. The number of grave sexual offenses rose by 31 percent (from 2,157 to 2,819); the number of rape complaints alone increased from 480 to 649.

Following the pattern established in Israel of government reliance on women's organizations for providing social services for women (see Chapter 3), the Help Centers Union serves the most important role in the area of sexual violence against women.[67] In fact, it was this void of social support services that prompted the establishment of the first help center, in 1978, following the suicide of a rape victim. Her suicide note said she could not bear living after what she had been through, during both the rape and the complaint to the police (Eilam 1993, 313–14). Besides providing 24-hour emergency hot lines, individual assistance, and support groups, the Israeli Sexual Assault Victim's Help Centers Union works to increase public and political awareness of the phenomenon of sexual violence and to lobby on behalf of victims.

In 1996, the Union collaborated with the Israel Women's Network (IWN) in promoting the establishment of a Victim's Witness Assistance Program, though it is constantly under threat of closing down for lack of funding. The program, developed in conjunction with both the State Prosecutor's Office and the police, coordinates meetings between different agencies to ensure that the victim receives the emotional, legal, and economic aid appropriate to her needs. During its two and a half years of operation, 150 victims received assistance and support throughout criminal proceedings. Prosecutors have attributed successful prosecutions to the project, finding that the emotional support the victims received made them better witnesses, and this enabled the prosecutors to concentrate on their professional role alone (Kormann 1998, 5).

The whole range of treatment and help services for victims of sexual violence is basically left to NGOs. Not surprisingly, most of the help centers' operational budget comes from the private sector, mostly from independent fund-raising. The major source of government subsidy for the Help Centers Union comes from the budget of the Ministry of Labor and Welfare. In 1997, the centers received one-time grants and contributions totaling 1,066,000 NIS, as part of a government campaign. This amount, one-third of the 1997 expenditures of the centers, allowed them to deal with the dramatic increase in the number of applicants compared with the previous year's figures. The most significant raise came during 2000, when the ministry's subsidy to the Help Centers Union increased fivefold, to $600,000, making it 35 percent of the Help Centers Union's operational budget.[68] This move—attributed by some to a successful public opinion campaign—is even more significant since the contribution is a specially designated item in the ministry's budget so that it is no longer up to ministry officials whether and how much to allocate.[69]

Law Enforcement Agency Handling of Sex Crimes Against Women

The basic police guidelines for handling rape complaints have been used since 1981 with no formal changes.[70] They note that police officers must carry out the necessary investigations while considering the victim's suffering and preserving both her dignity and her privacy. Only relevant and necessary questions are to be asked, and the investigation should, if possible, be handled by a female police officer who has specialized in the area. The victim is to be brought to the hospital for medical examination, regardless of what hour she arrives at the station. In appreciation of the sensitivity of these issues in the Arab community, further internal instructions were issued, requiring investigation by a trained female officer and forbidding a police officer to handle cases involving a family member or friend. In 1998, two Arab women investigators were trained to serve the Arab population. However, only one of them concentrated on violence against women alone.[71]

Police Practices and Sentencing for Sex Crimes

In terms of law enforcement data such as rates of prosecution, convictions, and sentencing, no official statistics are regularly available. The only data routinely collected by the police regard the initial classification of the complaint as one in which an investigation file is being opened (CR—Case Record) or as one in which no further proceedings are taking place (NP—No Proceedings). A gradual improvement can be traced here, after years of criticizing the police for too readily classifying sexual violence complaints as NP cases. In 1999, only 15 percent of sexual violence complaints were classified as NP, a decrease from 20 percent in 1997 and 32 percent in 1995.[72] Regular police records, however, do not supply the final outcome of such criminal proceedings, thus precluding the possibility of ongoing evaluation of law enforcement.

The information problem with relation to judicial handling of sexual violence against women was partially mended in a comprehensive study of gender bias in the courtroom, conducted during 1992–96 (Bogoch and Don-Yechiya 1999).[73] The findings demonstrate that sex crimes continue to be treated in a way similar to other bodily harm offenses, despite legislative reforms. As previously mentioned, maximum prison sentences for sexual crimes were increased significantly by the legislative reform of 1988–90, and in 1998 minimum punishment for sexual violence was established. The research was conducted prior to the 1998 amendment, and its findings emphasized the need for reform.

The average sentence for prison inmates was a little over a year and a half in offenses for which the range of punishment was from five years to life. The average for sexual offenses was two years; bodily harm warranted a year and a half. Defendants overall tended to be sentenced to an average of one fifth of the maximum for the offense they were convicted of. In offenses against life, the average sentence was approximately half the maximum. In sexual offenses, it was only 15 percent of the maximum and in bodily harm offenses slightly less.

Gender-Based Domestic Violence: Facts and Figures

Until very recently, statistics pertaining to the number of battered women in Israel were only estimates. According to conservative estimates, approximately 10 percent of married Israeli women are subject to domestic violence (150,000–200,000 women), 7 percent of them on an ongoing basis (Inter-Ministerial Committee 1998, 10). The JDC-Brookdale 2000 survey actually confirms those estimates. From interviewing a nationally representative sample of 850 women aged twenty-two and over, the researchers conclude that approximately 200,000 women in Israel (11 percent of the female adult population) have been victims of violence at least once by their spouse, and approximately 67,000 (4 percent of the population) have been victims of domestic violence during the year prior to the survey (Gross and Brammli-Greenberg 2000). Reports of domestic violence are higher in the United States, where 32 percent of women (one in three) reported having been the victim of spousal violence at some time. It could be that, in addition to actual higher levels of domestic violence, American women are more aware and more open to reporting and responding to such surveys.

The survey also provided analysis of its scope among various population groups. While significant rates of violence were found among all strata of society, the rate was higher among those with low education. Of women who had not graduated from high school, 19 percent reported having at some time been the victim of spousal abuse, while 11 percent of high school graduates and 5 percent of the women with higher education reported the same.

Police records show a ant rise in complaints of domestic violence.[74] Thus, in 1998, the police received a total of 21,912 complaints of domestic violence submitted by women, 76 percent of all domestic violence reports (compared to 14,706 complaints in 1995, also 76 percent of all domestic violence reports). These alarming numbers continue to grow; 22,540 files of domestic violence were opened in 1999, 194 of which dealt with severe spousal sexual violence against women, which falls into the categories of forced rape or forced indecent acts (an increase from 113 such incidents reported in 1995).[75]

In light of all these numbers, data from the Ministry of Health national database mentioned in Chapter 4 are particularly alarming. The data show a mere 1,472 hospital reports of battered women admitted for medical care in 1999. This figure clearly reflects a very low detection rate of domestic violence incidents and calls for the initiation of appropriate educational and training programs, also discussed in Chapter 4.[76]

Domestic violence is a threat to a woman's very existence. Between 1990 and November 1998 a total of 113 women in Israel were killed by their spouses, an average—as cynically put by the Inter-Ministerial Committee–of more than one woman each month (Inter-Ministerial Committee 1998, 10). The Parliamentary Investigative Committee on the Murder of Women by Their Spouses, established in March 1995 in response to a particularly high rise in such cases, conducted a study of 77 cases. The committee noted in general a number of areas in which society's handling of domestic violence needed improvement, especially in the lack of coordination among the various government bodies dealing with the problem. In 17 percent (13) of the cases, there were previous police complaints or files of domestic violence involving the perpetrator, while in 25 percent of the cases various state bodies (either the police or welfare agencies) were aware of conflict between the spouses, and in 21 percent they specifically knew of domestic violence (Parliamentary Investigative Committee 1996, 26–30).

Law Enforcement Agency Handling of Domestic Violence

It took more than thirty years for the state to accept the fact that Israeli families are no different from families elsewhere in the world and Israeli men no better than others.[77] Since the first scornful reactions to the attempt to put domestic violence against women on the national agenda,[78] formal attitudes and treatment have come a long way, mostly in the manner of investigative and self-checking committees. The latest of these committees, the Inter-Ministerial Committee to Tackle the Problem of Domestic Violence, whose report coincided with the publication of the findings of yet another significant initiative in this area (the empirical research of Eisikovits and Griffel), may indeed represent some change of perception. The potential change is with regard to both its perception of its own role and operation, and its far-reaching proposals, but true change on the state level will only come about once these proposals are implemented, that is, once resources are allocated toward this particular area. In order to understand the weight of this committee, a survey of its predecessors is in place.

The first admission of a problem came thirty years after the state's establishment, in 1977, with the publication of a report summarizing the manner in which complaints regarding domestic violence were handled by the police (Israel Police 1977). The report showed that police action was directed primarily toward "peace-making" between the spouses rather than toward enforcing criminal law and bringing abusive husbands to justice. In response to these findings, the police issued guidelines, but a 1984 report showed that despite these guidelines, very little was changed (Avni 1984).

The turning point came in 1989, when the Karp Committee published a comprehensive report dealing with the phenomenon of domestic violence and police response (Karp Committee 1989).[79] In addition to serving as the basis for various legal reforms, contained in the 1991 Law for the Prevention of Violence in the Family, the report prompted a complete reevaluation of the treatment of domestic violence by the police.

Most important, internal police guidelines to implement the Karp report in letter and spirit were promulgated.[80] Emphasizing the criminal nature of domestic violence and the obligation of the police to refrain from becoming involved in the substance of the conflict, the guidelines direct the police to give complaints of domestic violence high priority and stress the importance of cooperation with welfare authorities. A decision to close the criminal file altogether can only be made in certain conditions (including a complainant's request, on her own initiative, in the presence of a police officer and not in the presence of the suspect, to cancel her complaint). Nevertheless, the withdrawal of complaints by battered women who have been threatened or who wish to continue living with their abusive husbands has remained a recurring problem.

The guidelines also contain various instructions on handling the prosecution and advise that as a rule the prosecution should strive to obtain the maximum sentences for severe instances of sexual violence. Prosecutors are similarly instructed to consider plea bargaining where it may be difficult to obtain a conviction, or where the trial itself may cause additional harm to the victim. Perhaps not surprisingly, the case of these guidelines joins the typical chain of remarkably progressive legal norms whose implementation lags behind.

In 1992 the state comptroller included in its 42nd annual report a study of the phenomenon of domestic violence and the way it is treated by the police. Coming approximately one and a half years after the implementation of the 1990 guidelines, the report focused on the extent to which these guidelines really succeeded in alleviating the problems discussed in the 1989 Karp report. The report noted some improvement in the situation, but found implementation of the guidelines to be significantly lacking. Victims' requests to revoke their complaints were routinely accepted over the telephone; little attention was given to the need for a medical examination to be performed on the victim directly following the violent incident; the number of files closed on the grounds of lack of public interest continued, despite the guidelines, to be disproportionately high; and many files were simply classified as NP. The report also pointed to a lack of effective coordination between the police and social services, and to the need for more members of the police force to undergo training on the specific issue of domestic violence (State Comptroller 1992, 542–55).

Like a story that repeats itself, several years later a series of new studies (Eisikovits and Griffel 1998; Shoham 1999; Shoham and Regev 2000; Shoham forthcoming) showed that, once again, little had changed. Eisikovits and Griffel supply concrete statistics supporting the claim of stalemate, in addition to thorough analysis of police personnel's own attitudes and perceptions of domestic violence against women.[81] The bottom line of the study is that the professed goals of the police in this area are not achieved. A careful examination of the statistical findings proves lack of implementation, perhaps even failure, at almost all stages of police involvement in the cases, except for the initial stage of opening a police file, that is, initiating criminal proceedings.[82] Despite wide authorization given to make arrests in cases of violence against women, arrests were made in only 9 percent of the cases during all levels of handling, and the police arrested the suspect on the scene in only 6 percent of them. This astonishing finding is further contrasted by the views expressed by the police personnel themselves, 75 percent of whom believe it is the police's duty to arrest a man who beats his wife, and 87 percent of whom actually state they routinely arrest the man when arriving at the scene of the violence against the woman (Eisikovits and Griffel 1998).

This study as well as Shoham's studies focus on the actual attitude of police personnel as reflected from the routine handling of the files themselves, through quantitative evaluation of questionnaires, and through careful analysis of in-depth interviews. Interestingly, none of the studies addressed gender as a significant variable in the characteristics of police personnel, and their identification as "policemen" seems to be taken for granted. This oversight may be questionable, in light of the fact that women now make up 21 percent of the permanent police force and 30 percent of the investigations department force.[83] Most alarming is the finding of partial legitimization of wife battery. Eisikovits and Griffel's study reveal that 7.7 percent of police personnel agree that "sometimes the woman deserves to be beaten," 9.3 percent believe that "a man is allowed to beat his wife only if she cheats on him," 17 percent believe that "a woman who keeps quiet will forestall beatings from herself," and 26 percent(!) believe that "sometimes, the woman causes the man to beat her."[84] Their in-depth interviews support this distressing impression and reveal a common bias: the woman is sometimes perceived as cunning, vengeful, foolish, and weak, while the man is sometimes perceived as merely lacking in understanding, innocently slipping, and even deserving apology for enforcing the law upon him (Eisikovits and Griffel 1998, 79–82).

Shoham's research relates to two different groups of police personnel. Her early study, a 1997 survey with a 1999 follow-up, addressed regular police force personnel; the more recent study compared the attitudes of officers from the special domestic violence unit (discussed below) to those of other officers. The study of regular police personnel reveals that very little had changed in the second part of the 1990s, despite the police's constant educational efforts.[85] Shoham found that in 1998, 40 percent of the policemen still view the violence as related to the manner in which the woman fulfills her domestic roles, and half of them believe that the family's sustenance is the man's responsibility and a mother of young children should stay home. Policemen's general perception of women was found to be particularly demeaning: 63 percent describe women as unreliable and easy to manipulate. Perhaps most alarming is the finding that a third of the policemen believe that a woman's infidelity justifies violence. The more recent study of the special units' investigators is more encouraging.[86] The comparison between the specially trained and general investigators shows greater commitment by the former to deal with domestic violence and significantly less prejudice against women complainants. For example, while half the general investigators believe that many of the women file false complaints, only 20 percent of the special investigators share that view. Nevertheless, the findings are probably not as reassuring as one would have hoped from such experienced and specially trained personnel. Thus, half of them share the view that public pressure in this area leads to injustice against the men, and 28 percent believe that domestic violence is not police's business to deal with (Shoham forthcoming).

Another study by Shoham gives what may be described as the mirror image of these findings, the side of the women victims of domestic violence. In this study Shoham interviewed 90 married women who had complained of violent behavior by their husbands at five police stations in central Israel during 1998. The most distressing findings were that 89 percent of them described their apprehension in turning to the police and 78 percent felt tremendous fear in doing so. Half of them thought the police officer who received the complaint sided more with the abusive husband, and only 37 percent believed the police officer understood their situation. Forty percent of the women maintained that their rights had not been explained to them by the police, thus sadly proving once again the nonimplementation of the 1990 guidelines (Shoham 2000).

The findings of these studies coincided with the publication of the 1998 Inter-Ministerial Committee's report on handling the problem of domestic violence (Inter-Ministerial Committee 1998).[87] The first true attempt to integrate all the bodies involved in handling this problem, the report proposes a list of thorough reforms, including further legislative amendments, thorough professional training, information gathering and monitoring, development of risk-evaluation tools, educational programs, services for special needs population groups, policies on civil and military weapon holding, and cooperation on the local level. The overall budget requested for implementing these recommendations was approximately $50 million. While this committee's recommendations cannot be said to have been "buried" in "non-action," neither can they be described as being implemented. The pace of less than 10 percent annual budgetary allocation can hardly be described as implementation of the recommendations.

Prior to the issuance of these recommendations, and in response to previous criticisms, a national investigative system focusing solely on domestic violence was established in 1998 in all police stations, supposedly consisting of 170 specially trained investigators. Nine of the positions were reserved for Arab women investigators in stations that serve the Arab community. It is not clear, however, whether these positions have indeed been filled.[88] Furthermore, as criminologist Efrat Shoham found, 18 of the trained investigators were not assigned to the posts they had been trained for, and 44 were transferred to other duties and replaced by only 36 inexperienced officers (Shoham forthcoming).

The judiciary is an integral part of the law enforcement bodies, and the role it plays in the system is no less crucial than that of the police. Unlike the police, though, the Israeli courts enjoy a high level of confidence and are often perceived as beyond scrutiny. Generally, no empirical research—government or academic—is readily available on sentencing for specific offenses, and qualitative analysis and evaluation of cases and of courtroom discussions have only lately appeared.[89] With no concrete information, it is hard to make claims. The general sense that there are not enough convictions and that sentences are too light, which is shared by the police, remains a sense alone, with little available empirical support.[90] Bogoch and Don-Yechiya (1999) somewhat substantiated this sense in finding that lower sentences tend to be imposed for nonsexual domestic violence than for nonsexual violence against strangers. Eisikovits and Griffel's findings are limited to conviction rates and prison sentences from the overall total of complaints to the police. The only relevant piece of date in that respect is the finding that the most common sentence for those convicted was a suspended prison term (in 65 percent of the convictions, compared to 22 percent sentenced to actual prison terms) (Eisikovits and Griffel 1998, 119). On the civil side of the proceedings, however, as part of the Prevention of Violence in the Family Law, an increase in restraining orders is evident.[91] But these orders, as explained before, only serve as "first aid" and in no way reflect the criminality of the phenomenon.

Governmental and Nongovernmental Services and Shelters

Shelters for battered women in Israel have always been founded and provided by women's organizations. The first shelter for battered women was established in Haifa in 1977 (Swirski 1993b, 322). The founding of the shelters was perceived not just as an essential lifesaving action, but also as a feminist educational enterprise (Swirski 1993a, 299). Over time, however,

> the focus of activity became narrower, more and more devoted to the day-to-day running of the institution—albeit an alternative one—and to taking maximum advantage of government bureaucracies in order to benefit the shelter or its residents, rather than all women or even all battered women. While shelters reach women that other feminist organizations do not reach—Arab women, Oriental, or Mizrachi Jewish women, women from poor towns and other peripheral areas—their impact has been limited by routinization. (B. Swirski 1993a, 300)

This interesting analysis is indeed relevant to other areas of feminist activities as well, which have gradually been "taken over" by government initiatives, perhaps achieving some progress on concrete issues, yet leaving them bare of feminist convictions, and thus obstructing any further mobilization.

There are currently 13 such shelters throughout the country; the average shelter has housing capacity for 12 to 15 women and their children (Konor 2000). The number of shelters and their geographical distribution do not meet the needs of the thousands of victims of domestic abuse, at least two-thirds of whom are annually rejected due to lack of space. The establishment of these shelters was financed by various nonprofit organizations alone. The ongoing upkeep expenses of the shelters are partially funded by the Ministry of Labor and Welfare and local authorities. Until 1995, approximately 50 percent of the expenses were covered by the ministry. Since 1997, the ministry formed a new scale of subsidizing the shelters, and their operational expenses are now divided between the Ministry of Labor and Welfare, the local authority, and the operating NGO (Konor 2000, 3–6).

Other auxiliary forms of immediate help are the (currently) ten hot lines, for victims of domestic violence in general and for battered women in particular, operated by various women's organizations with the participation of the Women and Girls' Service of the Ministry of Labor and Welfare. The national line takes around 5,000 calls a year, and the ten municipal lines served 7,000 callers in 1997 (Inter-Ministerial Committee 1998, 26–27).

The secondary institutions under the "umbrella" of protection, and perhaps the primary ones in prevention, are the Centers for the Treatment and Prevention of Domestic Violence, established by the Ministry of Labor and Welfare, which operate with various degrees of cooperation with women's organizations. The services provided include diagnosis for the parties involved, individual, couple, family, and group therapy, preventive intervention, and training sessions for relevant professionals. In 1994 there were nine centers; by 1995, the number had nearly doubled to fifteen. There are currently twenty-five centers throughout the country, about half of them run in collaboration with various women's organizations, and ten run primarily by the ministry.[92] Most centers (70 percent) routinely report a budget deficit (Konor 2000, 13–15). A tremendous growth in the number of families treated can be attributed to the increase in the number of centers available and to greater awareness of the problem throughout the public. The results of the treatment have been very positive, and according to reports from the centers, in most cases the violence either stopped altogether or decreased significantly.[93]

One unique treatment program is a hostel for battering men. Noam Home, established in 1997, houses twelve men at a time, each for a period of four months. The project was started as a special "experiment project" under the National Insurance Institute, and showed remarkable success according to its evaluators. Nevertheless, it is constantly under the threat of elimination due to budget cutbacks (Inter-Ministerial Committee 1998, 104–5). By the end of 2000, the evaluation stage was over; half the 130 graduates of the program were surveyed, and their violent behavior was found to have ceased.[94]

The 1998 Inter-Ministerial Committee report examined the operation of all these services, and included many proposals for improvement. It is worthwhile to note the lack of a directive that would mandate special training in domestic violence during health care and health professions studies (Inter-Ministerial Committee 1998, 27; Parliamentary Investigative Committee 1996, 12).[95] All this explains the findings of the JDC-Brookdale 2000 survey, concluding that the health system in general fails these women, as detailed in Chapter 4 (Gross and Brammli-Greenberg 2000, 54–56). The findings are particularly alarming since community-based health services such as family health clinics and mother-child clinics could provide means for identifying victims and offering help without compelling the woman herself to actively seek the help. Thus, the health system—often the most crucial resource in spotting a woman's vulnerability and directing her toward help—too often fails her, leaving her once again isolated and abandoned.

Chapter 10
The Exploitation of Women

It is, of course, no coincidence that this chapter follows the discussion of sexual violence against women and gender-based violence within the family. The theoretical connection between all these subjects has already been discussed, and is strongly supported by empirical evidence that links sexual child abuse with adult prostitution.[1] Radical feminism supplies the analytic tool for understanding all these as reflecting different facets of male dominance through its control of female sexuality, thereby maintaining sex inequality and patriarchy. Susan Brownmiller's words are particularly strong with regards to prostitution:

> Legalized prostitution . . . institutionalizes the concept that it is a man's monetary right, if not his divine right, to gain access to the female body and that sex is a female service that should not be denied from the civilized man. Perpetuation of the concept that the "powerful male impulse" must be satisfied with immediacy by a cooperative class of women, set apart and licensed for this purpose, is part and parcel of the mass psychology of rape. (Brownmiller 1975, 392)

Even if one does not accept the direct link put here between institutionalized, regulated prostitution and rape, the suggestion is nevertheless important, and helpful in contemplating the reality of these phenomena, and the underlying social conventions that they share.

On the theoretical level, liberal feminism's sameness/difference theory cannot explain sexually specific issues such as prostitution and pornography, discussed here. Both issues are "the expression of power of (privileged) men—economic, physical, sexual—over (underprivileged) subordinated women" (Barnett 1998, 171). In the introduction to the previous chapter, I pointed to the significance of considering these subjects together. On the more pragmatic level, when examining prostitution, trafficking in women, and pornography in light of the previous subjects, the similarities and differences that come out with respect to law, policy, and reality may lend support to radical feminist critique and analysis. Similar to previous subjects, the area of prostitution reveals the familiar gap between the law on the books and the law in action. Here, however, the gap goes beyond mere nonimplementation and actually leads to a de facto implementation of a peculiar combination of prohibitionist and regulatory approaches, instead of the abolitionist approach professed in the law itself. Furthermore, here we cannot talk of a paradox of seemingly intense doing on the state's behalf that produces depressingly few results, simply because until very recently (2000) there was hardly any mention, let alone planned action, in this area. When these observations are viewed in light of other indications, such as the suggestion of an intentional lack of enforcement on the part of the police and the inexplicable tardiness in passing a comprehensive bill to amend the law, the inference could be rather alarming. One could even suggest that the state prefers to act where women's victimization is undisputed (domestic violence and to a lesser degree sexual violence), while in an area such as this women are perceived as guilty participators in criminal activity, who neither need nor deserve any protection. Such a differential attitude can only be made when all these subjects are regarded as unrelated. If this analysis is right, the pertinence of radical feminism is unequivocal. First and foremost, radical feminism supplies the tools to analyze these phenomena in terms of power politics, which seems extremely appropriate given the Israeli reality delineated below. In light of the denial and neglect that characterized views on sexual exploitation until not long ago, their recognition as interrelated and interconnected should lead to a consistent policy of implementation and treatment. Moreover, radical feminism should be adopted here, since only when all these elements are recognized as different expressions of male dominance in a patriarchal society can the demand for major educational efforts to change perceptions regarding women, women's bodies and sexuality, and men's and women's power relations be made. In short, elimination of patriarchy is a prerequisite for the elimination of prostitution, human trafficking, and other forms of sexual exploitation.

Sexual objectification and exploitation are not merely the result of having power, but the purposeful means through which power is achieved. "Sex," writes Andrea Dworkin in her celebrated "Against the Male Flood" (1985, 17), "is the material means through which the subordination is accomplished. Pornography is the institution of male dominance that sexualizes hierarchy, objectification, submission, and violence. As such, pornography creates inequality, not as artifact but as a system of social reality." According to this stance, once egalitarianism is achieved, sexual exploitation and objectification can be expected to disappear, not just equally practiced between the sexes. Assuming egalitarianism means at least the end of dominance and subordination, sexual exploitation as the measures for gaining power and control is inconceivable in a nonhierarchical world.

Moving on from theory, sociological and criminological research seem undecided on the effects of pornography on male sexual violence. However, it is clear that a distinction should be made between pornographic expressions of sexual violence and exploitation and nonaggressive pornographic images. According to Donnerstein and Linz, leading authorities in this area, "There is no evidence for any 'harm'-related effects from sexually explicit materials. But research may support potential harmful effects from aggressive materials. Aggressive images are the issue, not sexual images. The message about violence and the sexualized nature of violence is crucial" (1996, 510). Radical feminism's theoretic definition and description of pornography clearly correspond with this empirical analysis and conclusion. For purposes of the current discussion, the overall connection between all the issues discussed in these two chapters is once again made clear through radical feminism's critique of patriarchy.

This chapter first addresses the general social and political framework in which prostitution takes place in Israel. It then describes the normative framework, pointing to changes proposed, and some implemented, along the way, and then moves to describe the mundane reality of prostitution in Israel. The description concludes with the painful subject of the involvement of minors in prostitution, and rehabilitation services for girls. The chapter ends with a discussion of pornography, which is—as succinctly put by two Israeli abolitionist activists—the PR of violence against women.[2]

Questions of Policy

Growing Awareness

Prostitution and trafficking in women are particularly sensitive and difficult issues in Israel because of the combination of traditional and religious ideas that also translate into political power. This mixture of mostly conflicting considerations and interests, on top of perplexities toward women's status in general and sexuality in particular, leads to lack of clear policy and indeterminate law enforcement in this area. This too frequently results in degradation of the women who engage in prostitution. The perplexity and indetermination expressed at this subject have grown in the past few years, when it evidently took on the aggravating facet of trafficking in women. Some point to another complicating factor that has to do with the increasing numbers of foreign and illegal workers. They believe that this population increases the "demand" for "sex services," which causes the "supply" to grow through increased trafficking in women.[3] Even if one objects to this offensive analysis, it cannot be denied that much of the current clientele of prostitution are foreign workers. In fact, this line of explanation was even admitted by a high ranking official in the Israeli police.[4] In the following pages I try to assess government policy as well as public attitude toward sexual exploitation using various legal and nonlegal sources.

Until fairly recently, one could hardly talk about a "government policy" regarding prostitution. It was only during 2000 that some change in public and government attitudes took place, leading to the beginning of policy formation in the police as well. This change can be attributed partly to the investigation and publication of a report by Amnesty International concerning the trafficking of women from the former USSR into Israel's sex industry (Amnesty International 2000), and the publication in July 2001 of the U.S. State Department Trafficking in Persons Report.[5]

Once again, international attention did not fail to produce internal self-reflection.[6] The Amnesty International report stirred public interest and concern and has led to several discussions in the Knesset Committee on the Status of Women. It probably contributed to the establishment of a Parliamentary Investigative Committee on Trafficking in Women in June 2000, as well as the establishment in January 2001 of an Inter-Ministerial Committee for outlining recommendations to face the phenomenon of trafficking, both on the criminal level and on the level of treating the women victims of the phenomenon. All these developments have probably also had some effect on speeding the passage of a significant amendment to the 1977 Penal Law concerning prostitution and trafficking. This amendment, first introduced in July 1997 and passed in August 2000, includes a new, explicit prohibition on trafficking in people, making it punishable by up to 16 years imprisonment.[7] Further concern for women engaged in the sex industry was caused by a series of arsons of brothels during the summer of 2000, which led to the tragic death of three women who had been sleeping in one house. The suspect arrested was said to have acted from religious zealousness.[8]

Even these developments take a very long time to lead to true changes in policy and law enforcement. A typical example of this was the lack of any response to Amnesty International's inquiries to such officials as the prime minister, minister of internal security, minister of justice, and others (Amnesty International 2000, 6). Following the publication of Amnesty International's report, both the minister of justice and the police investigations head evaded direct confrontation by attributing the grave reality to the lack of specific prohibitions on trafficking in women.[9] The impression they gave was that, once the anticipated legislation passed, the problem would be solved. However, there were enough legal means to employ even prior to legislative change; this seems to suggest that what was lacking (and probably is still lacking) was the commitment and will to the means available. That this was the case until quite recently was confirmed in a joint meeting of the Knesset Committee on Foreign Workers and the Subcommittee on Violence Against Women in February 2000, by none other than the minister of internal security, who admitted that "trafficking in women has not been defined as a target within the Police Commander's targets."[10]

The year 2000 may have been a turning point in government attitude toward this subject. In June the heads of the Police Investigations and Intelligence Departments issued an internal circular delineating for the first time guidelines for initiating police investigations on prostitution and trafficking, defining the subject as a priority category and naming eight police representatives across the world to encourage cooperation with international police forces.[11]

There have never been official estimations of the extent of prostitution and trafficking of women in Israel. Although the Israeli government publicly acknowledged the growth of trafficking,[12] the actual magnitude is unclear. In 1997, the Israel Women's Network (IWN) held a five-month investigation into the trafficking of women into Israel. The research involved over 50 interviews with officials, prostitutes, academics, and nongovernmental organizations (NGOs) throughout the country. One interviewee, sociologist and expert on prostitution Esther Eilam, cofounder of "We Are Worthy,"[13] estimated the total numbers of prostitutes in Israel as between 8,000 and 10,000; another, Efraim Ehrlich, commander of the Tel Aviv Vice Squad, estimated the number of prostitutes who work in Tel Aviv as between 800 and 1,000 (Israel Women's Network 1997, 2–3). The truth is probably somewhere between these two extreme estimations. The Amnesty International report also emphasizes the lack of formal statistics on the extent of the phenomenon (Amnesty International 2000, 4–5).

This is a typical expression of what I called "the information story," namely the dynamics and the politics of the formation of information. The lack of official data implies concealment and denial, as if no information means no problem. Official estimates and information are perceived as rendering formal recognition of the existence of the phenomenon. Indeed, as the process of formal recognition began, primarily through Israel's participation in international forums dealing with trafficking of women and children, sources of formal information started developing, including Israel's reports to these forums and working papers of various Knesset committees. The stories told in the growing body of court cases constitute another type of official information, on which I elaborate later. As much as the courts hinder efforts to suppress trafficking, often by lenient sentences, they nevertheless serve as a unique platform for the "construction of legitimate legal knowledge," as phrased by Villmoare (1999, 457).

Policy Reflection in Legal Norms and Their Implementation

In terms of formal state policy as reflected in legislation, the Israeli legislature adopted an abolitionist approach regarding prostitution; that is, prostitution itself is not regarded as a crime, but all related activities such as procurement or managing a brothel are defined as crimes. In reality, however, there has never been a clear and definite policy toward the issue of prostitution in Israel, at least not until very recently. An attempt to establish such a policy took place in February 1975, when the justice minister had appointed a committee, headed by Judge Hadassah Ben-Eato (later appointed, as acting justice, to be the second woman justice to the Supreme Court) to present recommendations for legal reforms in the area of prostitution. The committee presented its recommendations in April 1977 (Ministry of Justice 1977). In principle, the committee recommended continuing the abolitionist approach. Realizing, however, that prostitution cannot be abolished altogether, the recommendations related only to those provisions which make it impossible, under the existing framework, to engage in prostitution without violating the law. Thus, the committee recommended decriminalizing engagement in prostitution in one's own home or in a separate hotel room, so long as it does not create a public disturbance or involve minors in any way. Overall, the committee concentrated on preventing women from entering prostitution and hardening the legal and actual treatment of procurers. Following this line, the committee emphasized the need to enhance rehabilitation efforts for women who engage or are about to engage in prostitution. Consequently, the committee recommended establishing an additional offense of hindering such rehabilitation efforts, directed specifically at procurers. In line with its approach to confront the procurers, the committee recommended amending the definition of solicitation to circumvent its narrow interpretation in the courts, so that it need not include the actual occurrence of prostitution. With respect to clients, the committee specifically recommended proceeding against clients who in the process of seeking prostitution services violate such provisions as section 210 of the 1977 Penal Law, discussed below.[14]

As could be expected, none of the committee's recommendations was ever adopted as such. Moreover, the reality of law enforcement in this area totally contradicts the committee's ideology. Not only were the sections penalizing procurers rarely enforced, the prostitutes themselves were often arrested for related practices that constituted felonies, and more recently for illegal stay in Israel. This has led to a de facto implementation of a peculiar combination of prohibitionist and regulatory approach, instead of the abolitionist approach reflected in the law. Prostitution itself was effectively penalized, while the business of prostitution was effectively left untouched; hence it could actually be described as being regulated.

This enforcement policy has led to the revictimization of the women, this time by the state. Abandoned by the establishment, the women's only recourse comes from NGOs. The Hot Line for Migrant Workers and the Awareness Center presented a report to the UN Commission on Human Rights in March 2001 on trafficking in persons in Israel, which serves as an important source of informal information.[15] The Hotline for Migrant Workers is the only NGO with direct contact to the victims of trafficking, and operates a legal department to represent them. The Awareness Center is a member of the International Abolitionist Federation.

Since the operation of the Ben-Eato committee there have been several unsuccessful bills to amend the legal framework. A specific piece of legislation, often forgotten, is a notification by the general director of the Ministry of Health in January 1988, declaring any person who engages in prostitution a potential HIV carrier.[16] According to previous regulations, all such suspect persons must undergo a biannual HIV test.[17] Apparently, these provisions concerning people who engage in prostitution have never been enforced.[18]

The Legal Framework

Legislative Aspects

The current legal framework of prostitution in Israel was enacted in 1962, when the British Mandate's 1936 arrangement was repealed.[19] The 1962 reform presented some major changes, such as the deletion of the definition of a "place of prostitution" where prostitution was allowed, and the introduction of an absolute prohibition over the use of a place for the purposes of engaging in prostitution. As explained further below, this is not the only manner in which the legal system makes actual engagement in prostitution impossible without violating the law.

The major crime associated with prostitution is "procurement," legally defined as living off the profits, or taking all or some profits from a woman who engages in prostitution, and solicitation of a woman to engage in prostitution. Prior to the recent amendment, the old sections 199–201 of the 1977 Penal Law provided that such criminal involvement was punishable by five years in prison, and up to seven years under aggravated circumstances.[20] Case law, however, has interpreted solicitation as proven engagement in prostitution, thus making it much more difficult to prosecute for solicitation.[21] Under the old section 202, soliciting a woman to leave her home with the intention of engaging her in prostitution was punishable by five years imprisonment, and up to seven years in the case of a minor. Soliciting a woman to leave the country (i.e., Israel) for the same purpose was also punishable by seven years imprisonment. The main accomplishment of the August 2000 amendment was the introduction of a specific and explicit prohibition on trafficking in humans, defined as "the selling or purchasing of a person for the purposes of engaging the person in prostitution"[22] and punishable by sixteen years imprisonment. The punishments for procurement and other related offenses were made more severe, particularly where aggravating circumstances exist.[23] Cases of minors' involvement have a dividing line between minors under or over fourteen, the former leading to double the original length of imprisonment, the latter to an additional two to five years.[24] The offense previously under section 202 was expended to include the solicitation of a person to leave his or her state of residence in order to engage him or her in prostitution, regardless which state that is, in addition to increasing the maximal punishment for that offense to ten years.[25] Significantly, the amendment does not introduce any new commitment to actually help the women and protect them from their abusers.

Prior to this amendment it was often asserted that there was no specific legislation in Israel that forbade human trafficking and no law against buying or selling human beings in Israel (Israel Women's Network 1997, 21). This assertion could only apply to the period before the 1951 Woman's Equal Rights Law was reformed in early 2000, since it included the specific right of a woman "to protection from violence, sexual harassment, sexual exploitation and traffic in her body."[26] However, there was always a provision that seems extraordinarily fit to extreme cases of trafficking, found under the heading of "Offenses Against Liberty." Section 374 of the 1977 Penal Law states that abducting a person with the intention of—among other things—engaging that person in prostitution, or knowing that the abducted person will be thus engaged (by others), is punishable by up to 20 years imprisonment.[27] Perhaps not surprisingly, a computerized search of all court cases reveals that very few charges were ever made under this provision in relation to trafficking in women. Notwithstanding the legal difficulties of proving the intention or knowledge required for conviction under this provision, it seems that some of the harshest cases described in the various NGO reports and documents could have been prosecuted under it.

The history of the recent amendment is particularly interesting and tells much about official policy and attitude toward this subject. As already mentioned, the amendment originated in a 1997 government bill to comprehensively amend "Prostitution, Sex, and Obscenity Offenses."[28] The main areas the bill sought to reform were addressing the involvement of minors in prostitution and in the pornography industry, adapting the laws against pornography to technological advancements, and amending the provisions regarding prostitution to include male prostitution.[29] In addition, the bill proposed to amend section 202(2) to extend to the solicitation of a person to leave his or her state of residence so as to engage him or her in prostitution, regardless which state that is. Significantly, all the proposed amendments regarding pornographic publications and sex tourism involving minors were passed in 1998, but none of the proposals regarding prostitution were. Moreover, the lack of specific provision prohibiting the actual sale of human beings remained unattended even in that bill, and was added only much later as a private reservation by MK Yael Dayan. The conceptual message that came out of the previous lacuna is that no such trade in humans normatively existed. As put by a district attorney prosecutor, "Selling of women is viewed by the court as no different than prostitution. When I went to the court I tried to explain to the judge that the Knesset never imagined that this slave trade could happen here and therefore never made a law against it" (Israel Women's Network 1997, 22). The amendment has no doubt put an end to this problematic concept, but it is too early to tell whether it will indeed change the daily reality of women in the Israeli sex industry.

While the message sent with respect to trafficking in women is clear, the amendment sends mixed messages with respect to the women themselves. In the past, detained prostitutes were usually released after several hours but were sometimes charged for "enticement of others to engage in indecent acts in public places," a felony punishable by never months in prison. This provision, never intended to serve as a regulation of prostitution, was repealed in the recent amendment, but other provisions that had also served to indict prostitutes still remain in place. One is section 216(a)(5), which prohibits "loitering." Another criminal offense directly applicable to women who engage in prostitution, added in 1975 for the explicit purpose of combating the spread of prostitution, is section 215(c), which states that being in a place for the purpose of engaging in prostitution, in circumstances that pose disturbance to neighbors or obstruction of traffic, is punishable by up to one year in prison.[30] As a result prostitutes were further relegated to the margins of society, geographically and socially, notwithstanding the fact that in principle prostitution itself is not a criminal activity. With the expansion of trafficking in women, the obvious ground for arresting them is their illegal stay in Israel. The bottom line is that, from the formal legal perspective, the practice of arresting prostitutes can continue. Whether that will be the case depends on policy decisions which have yet to be formed.[31]

To conclude the discussion of the normative framework, attention should be paid to several changes made by the 2000 amendment on this subject, some of which have already been mentioned. In particular, the amendment repealed some important sections, among them mandatory imprisonment for perpetrators. This was a highly unusual provision in the context of Israeli criminal law, and could be taken to indicate the gravity attributed by the legislature to these crimes. In fact, this provision has remained a dead letter. Courts, with the support of the police and the prosecution, tend to convict managers of such "massage institutes" in the less serious crime of keeping a place for prostitution purposes, which does not impose mandatory imprisonment. Moreover, the provision had been interpreted as nonetheless enabling probation without conviction. For all these reasons it was felt that there is no point in leaving this provision in place. Similarly, the law had previously offered means to criminally charge the clientele of the sex industry, at least theoretically. Section 210 of the 1977 Penal Law stated that approaching a minor under sixteen or an adult woman with indecent insinuations is punishable by up to three months in prison. This section, however, had never actually been enforced.[32] Indeed, it was repealed by the amendment with no accompanying explanation.[33] On the other hand, a specific prohibition on accepting sexual services from a minor was added, with the severe punishment of three years imprisonment.[34] This is in line with the stricter attitude towards involvement of minors in the sex industry and the stronger commitment to protect minors from abuse and exploitation, as reflected in the other provisions added in this amendment, and in the 1998 amendment concerning pornography and minors' involvement in it. Also relevant to the sad reality of minors' involvement in the sexual industry is the move to a gender-neutral language in all the law's provisions that deal with prostitution. Prior to the amendment, the law only recognized female prostitution and addressed women alone in relation to prostitution. The amendment replaced all references to "a woman" with references to "a person."

Implementation and Enforcement

The uneasy sense of selective enforcement that effectively criminalizes and punishes prostitutes, while overlooking the organized operation that abuses them, is strengthened by the data. Whereas the general impression thus far is that prostitution-related offenses alone are rarely enforced against women, so long as no other criminal aspects are involved, the data supplied by the police shown in Table 3 indicate otherwise.

The gender perspective is indeed illuminating here. What clearly stands out in the table is the overwhelming majority of women convicted of keeping and managing a place for purposes of prostitution. The general impression to the contrary, which is reflected, for example, in the Turgemann case discussed below,[35] is supported by the superintendent of the only women's prison in Israel, according to whom all prisoners involved in prostitution were convicted of other crimes, never for prostitution-related offenses alone.[36] The conviction data, however, prove this impression to be wrong. A probable explanation for this seeming discrepancy is that no actual imprisonment terms are imposed on the convicted women. Still, a sense of uneasiness is further sustained in light of another disturbing point—the disproportionately low number of convictions in procurement, a male-dominated crime, compared with the increasing number of convictions in keeping a place for the purposes of prostitution, a female-dominated crime. In 1994, almost twice as many men were convicted of procurement, and in 1995 their number was almost four times that of the women convicted under this crime. The opposite happened with the crime of keeping a place for prostitution purposes: in 1994 almost three times as many and in 1995 more than twice as many women as men were convicted under this crime. The most significant data are the total number of convictions for managing a

TABLE 3. Convictions in Prostitution-Related Crimes, 1994–1995

	1994			*1995*		
Offense	*Men* *n (%)*	*Women* *n (%)*	*Total* *n (%)*	*Men* *n (%)*	*Women* *n (%)*	*Total* *n (%)*
Procurement	30 (62.5)	18 (37.5)	48 (100)	42 (79.2)	11 (20.8)	53 (100)
Solicitation to engage in prostitution	3 (75)	1 (25)	4 (100)	15 (88.2)	2 (11.8)	17 (100)
Solicitation to prostitute	8 (72.7)	3 (27.3)	11 (100)	12 (70.5)	5 (29.5)	17 (100)
Keeping a brothel	49 (25)	147 (75)	196 (100)	106 (31.3)	232 (68.7)	338 (100)
Solicitation of minors	42 (100)	—	42 (100)	44 (95.6)	2 (4.4)	46 (100)

Source: Based on unpublished police data contained in a letter from Oded Brook, legal counselor to the Ministry of Internal Defense, dated December 16, 1996 (on file with the author).

brothel: it was more than four times the number of convictions for procurement in 1994 and more than six times in 1995. While no recent data of convictions could be obtained, Table 4 depicts the distribution of files opened in these offenses along gender lines, proving that the pattern repeats itself:

More recent data in another form also confirm the sense of selective enforcement and contradicts police claims of a stronger stand against exploitation and trafficking in women.[37] Between 1997 and 2000, only 17 percent (273 of 1,606) of police files opened for prostitution-related crimes (including procurement, solicitation to prostitute and engage in prostitution, keeping a place of prostitution, kidnapping for the purpose of prostitution, and—since mid-2000—trafficking) were indeed brought to trial. For the more specifically male-dominated crime of procurement, only 180 files were opened in the first place and only 25 (14 percent) were brought to trial. However, for the more specifically female-dominated crime of managing a brothel, 1,226 files were opened and as many as 327 (27 percent) were brought to trial. Of the total files opened, 38 percent were in the prosecution offices awaiting decision on prosecution. Some of those could still go to trial. Nonetheless, comparing the number of cases tried with the number pending proceedings indicates that close to half the opened files do not even get to the prosecution. When this is considered against the information concerning women's arrests and deportations discussed below, the disturbing impression is indeed of selective, gender-discriminatory enforcement resulting in penalizing the victims.

Notwithstanding the data discussed here, the information problem exists in full force, despite the impression to the contrary. The point is that while some data are available, they are only partial and cannot supply the full picture: until August 2000 there has not been one specific offense of trafficking in humans, and there was no way of knowing how many of the cases actually involved selling women. In addition, it was and still is possible that other cases of trafficking were tried under other related offenses, such as kidnapping or battery and assault. Prior to the 2000 amendment, there was no consistent policy of charges in these cases. It is hoped that the legislative change will also enable a more accurate impression of both the extent of the phenomenon and the level of enforcement.

Obviously, selective enforcement does not come out of nowhere but is the result of official instructions, which capture the unsettled policy issue discussed here. In January 1994, the state attorney issued internal instructions to the police, which are still in place, noting the need to clarify the policy regarding the spread of "massage parlors" and "escort services," to commence investigations under each of the following cir-

TABLE 4. Files Opened in Prostitution-Related Crimes, 1997–1999

Offense	1997			1998			1999		
	Men *n (%)*	*Women* *n (%)*	*Total* *n (%)*	*Men* *n (%)*	*Women* *n (%)*	*Total* *n (%)*	*Men* *n (%)*	*Women* *n (%)*	*Total* *n (%)*
Procurement	21 (87.5)	3 (12.5)	24 (100)	36 (72)	14 (28)	50 (100)	27 (57)	20 (43)	47 (100)
Solicitation to engage in prostitution	4 (57.1)	3 (42.9)	7 (100)	8 (53.4)	7 (46.6)	15 (100)	23 (85)	4 (15)	27 (100)
Solicitation to prostitute	9 (75)	3 (25)	12 (100)	9 (75)	3 (25)	12 (100)	16 (88)	2 (12)	17 (100)
Keeping a brothel	106 (47.3)	118 (52.7)	224 (100)	100 (37.2)	169 (62.8)	269 (100)	221 (55)	184 (45)	405 (100)
Solicitation of minors	—	—	—	0	1 (100)	1 (100)	—	—	—

Source: Based on unpublished data provided by chief superintendent David Sagiv, Department of Statistics, Israel Police, dated December 6, 2000 (on file with the author).

cumstances: minors involved in prostitution; manipulation of persons into engaging in prostitution; severe abuse of women who engage in prostitution by their procurers (including blackmail and violence); and additional criminal activity, such as drug abuse. When one of these circumstances occurs in relation to these prostitution-related offenses, the state attorney's office shall consider pressing charges.[38]

Apparently, these instructions have been closely followed by the police. According to the commander of the Tel Aviv Vice Squad, 90 percent of the raids that take place are authorized due to complaints by neighbors. In an interview with the IWN Report, he added that the women must give evidence before police can arrest the procurers, but since women usually refuse to talk, the procurers remain unscathed. This has led to an absurdity in which the prostitutes were given no protection and were sent to prison as illegal aliens (if non-Israelis) until the trial, since their testimony was crucial, while their procurers went free. In most cases, the procurers were not even arrested but simply held for interrogation. A more suspicious explanation was offered by criminologist Menachem Amir, who believes that the police allow brothels to operate in return for information from the operators about other criminal activity. In other words, the operators and procurers work as informers. Occasional raids are necessary, according to Amir, to show the groups that they are under surveillance (Israel Women's Network 1997, 20–21). This explanation is supported by the contention of the Ministry of Interior's senior official, who charges that the police are reluctant to conduct their own investigations against the procurers, instead relying on the testimony of the women, who are usually too afraid to testify (Israel Women's Network 1997, 24). As for the need to protect the women, the situation is less hopeful, although this too may begin to change, as suggestions for a thorough revision in the authorities' attitude were being formed by the inter-ministerial committee mentioned above.[39] The committee's approach is more victim-oriented and calls for providing the foreign women with shelter and protection in a special hostel during the period of giving evidence and before being deported.

Judicial Rejoinder

The overall attitude of courts toward prostitution is negative, describing it as immoral and corrupt.[40] Attitude toward the women who engage in prostitution is more complex and varies with each case. In the less typical cases, some sympathy is expressed toward these women, and there is recognition of their harsh circumstances and their need to be protected from abuse and exploitation through appropriate legislation.[41] It seems that this empathic attitude is growing in recent years, as more atrocious cases reach the courts. More often, however, prostitutes are portrayed as untrustworthy witnesses and sometimes as deficient mothers.[42]

Most of the cases that directly involve prostitution-related crimes are settled on the case level and do not get to the appellate level. A recent Supreme Court case, *Turgemann v. The State of Israel*,[43] might not set precedent in the area, but it manages to convey, mainly through the dissenting opinion, the ambivalence with which the judiciary and society at large treat this phenomenon. The appellant, a woman, was convicted of procurement and of keeping and managing a place for prostitution and was sentenced to six months imprisonment (with an additional twelve-month suspended sentence) to be served in community service. Her appeal on the sentencing was based on the argument of unjust selective and discriminatory enforcement against her, while the general official policy is to be oblivious to such "massage institutes" as hers. The majority had rejected this argument, while strongly criticizing the police policy of selective enforcement. The long and elaborate dissenting opinion of Justice Heshin had accepted this argument, framing it in jurisprudential rule-of-law terms and seeing the existing policy of nonenforcement as if it were actually part of the normative framework. While accepting the basic claims of the woman in that case, emphasizing the fair and voluntary relationships that existed between her and the women who worked for her, Justice Heshin nevertheless concluded by stressing her inferiority and her repugnant occupation. Moreover, when criticizing the police for its selective enforcement, the judge neglected to point out the necessity of intervention to prevent abuse and exploitation of women by their procurers.

The references in the Turgemann case to police's nonenforcement is of course firmly grounded in reality. The nonenforcement practice, however, has another side to it, namely the side of the judiciary. In the rare cases where procurers are prosecuted, their sentences are light, and the police are well aware of that, as put by the commander of the Tel Aviv Vice Squad: "It is the policy of the courts not to put the pimps in jail" (Israel Women's Network 1997, 21). Most procurers who are eventually convicted are sentenced to community service, and actual imprisonment is highly unusual. Even taking into consideration the difficulty in obtaining testimony from the women, who mostly fear for their lives and the lives of their families back home, the level of punishment is extremely low (Israel Women's Network 1997, 21–25). A recent case, *The State of Israel v. Avitan*,[44] in which a procurer was sentenced to thirteen years imprisonment, is an exception to the rule, although the facts of the case, horrifying as they are, are painfully typical of many others. Avitan was convicted of kidnapping a foreign woman in order to engage her in prostitution, imprisoning her, raping her, and engaging her in prostitution. The woman was six months pregnant when she was literally purchased by Avitan from an unknown person. The judge's description of the woman's conditions in captivity are particularly empathic, noting her vulnerability as an alien deprived of all her rights and dignity by the convict. The judge also hinted to the woman's justified conclusion as to the convict's ties with the local police. In light of the detailed exploitation and cruelty, one would have expected the maximum punishment to be issued on the convict. Nevertheless, the judges were apparently of the opinion that thirteen years (two-thirds of the maximum) constituted a severe enough sentence. Interestingly, in the Supreme Court case they referred to in justifying the severity of the sentence, Chief Justice Barak had admitted the court's willingness to increase a sentence of fifteen years put on a procurer in even more abhorrent circumstances, if only the state had appealed the lightness of the sentence.[45]

As Justice Heshin in his dissent in the Turgemann case[46] summarized the situation, there is an overall lenient attitude toward the perpetrators, except in the most serious cases of exploitation, and even then the sentences are mild.

Evaluation of the Actual Situation

Criticism of the leniency of the courts is undoubtedly justified. However, the courts now serve as a special forum which gives recognition to victims' stories and turn them into official legal truth and reality. This is a fascinating process, especially since those stories were denied by the authorities for too long and were not given any legitimate space to be heard. The only ones who heard the victims before were the NGOs, who started revealing the horror the women went through. Perhaps their most important contribution was in giving the women a voice, quite literally, since so often their stories could not be understood for reasons of language. By recording the women's narratives in their own words, they were in fact employing the storytelling method that has been used by critical race scholars and third-generation legal feminists in recent years (Villmoare 1999, 456–59). This was indeed the typical case of "non-expert" voices attempting to illuminate women's unknown experiences through their narratives. However, they were hardly heard, and even when heard, they were too often ignored and put aside. The processing of their stories through courts' decisions is a totally new phase. It turns them into legitimate legal knowledge, and supplies them with the official approval of legal truth. To some extent, this could happen only through the participation of the NGOs, as demonstrated in the case of *Zaritzkia v. The Minister of Interior.*[47] This case revealed the intricate methods employed by the procurers, who send lawyers to represent women who are detained and awaiting deportation and arrange for their release on bail. The aim, of course, is to avoid losing the women, recapture them, and continue prostituting them. This was recounted to the court by the Hot Line for Migrant Workers, which was granted the status of amicus curiae. The hot line's version was adopted by the court with no reservations, thus rendering it true in the eyes of the court and turning it into an "official narrative." This is particularly significant since the hot line, like other NGOs working in this area, is often portrayed by official authorities as an unreliable source of information.

Thus, the distressing picture portrayed in the following pages uses the women's stories as they were incorporated into recent court cases and told in newspapers as well as in several NGO reports such as those of the IWN, Amnesty International, and more recently the March 2001 Hot Line and Awareness Center Report to the UN Commission on Human Rights. There is ample evidence that trafficking in women in Israel has become a multimillion dollar industry and a sophisticated business operation. Every year, hundreds of women from the former Soviet Union are brought to Israel to work illegally. Many are trafficked by well-organized Mafia networks in the former Soviet Union and in Israel. Their passports, which are usually falsified, are taken away almost immediately on arrival. They are sometimes given approximately $5 per day for food, but usually receive no share of the profit made through them. Those who resist are beaten and raped. They work night and day under constant supervision. They are isolated, held in debt bondage, and forbidden to quit until their "contract" is completed.

From reading the women's testimonies and personal stories, it is clear that they remain where they are out of fear. They are told that should they escape, they will be found and punished and their families back home will suffer grave consequences. Their illegal status makes them vulnerable to manipulation and threat. These women are especially vulnerable to sexual abuse, physical abuse, and even murder. They do not know the language, have no connections in Israel, and are unaware of their basic rights, which makes them practically slaves. They cannot turn to the police, and even if they are arrested most refuse to speak or testify in court. The occasional police raids mostly serve as documentation checks and end up in deportation. The deportation process starts with the women being taken to Neve Tirza women's prison, where they await deportation. In 1998, 459 women were deported, in 1999, 253, and in the first half of 2000, 122.[48] A deportee may be detained for several weeks, depending on the time needed to verify her identity and prepare the necessary documentation for deportation. Ironically, their stay at Neve Tirza may be prolonged in the rare cases when they are willing to testify against their procurers, since even a procedure for an advanced hearing may take a few months.[49] Keeping women waiting for deportation is indeed doubtful from an international human rights perspective, and it may be in violation of international norms, such as those contained in the International Covenant on Civil and Political Rights, that require states to guarantee the right to liberty, to provide legal redress to every form of violation of human rights, and to maintain separation of civil detainees from criminal prisoners.[50] Likewise, the practice of prolonging the women's detention for the sole purpose of testifying against their abusers is in fact a form of punishment with no legal basis. The UN Human Rights Committee has indeed criticized Israel for de facto punishing the trafficked women with deportation instead of offering them protection and legal redress.[51] As awareness of the problematic nature of handling the women is growing, alternatives are beginning to be formed. Apart from the suggestions of the interministerial committee to create a hostel for deportees, the police are apparently already financing the stay of some women out of prison, provided they are willing to testify in court (State of Israel 2001).[52]

Involvement of Minors in Prostitution

Particularly sensitive and unheeded until quite recently is the involvement of minors in prostitution, forced prostitution, and the trafficking of women. All the numbers in this area are in dispute, and there are no formal statistics in any of the issues involved. The actual phenomenon of minor girls forced into prostitution is also disputed by official authorities (CECSECI Report 1997, 47). However, a change in attitude toward the involvement of minor girls can be detected since the August 1996 Stockholm World Congress Against Commercial Sexual Exploitation of Children.[53] In a manner that often repeats itself, international focus on a particular human rights problem applied external pressure and prompted an internal process of investigation and consideration. One explicit result of this focus is the 1998 amendment of section 15(b) of the 1977 Penal Law,[54] designed to combat outgoing "sex tourism" with minors.

The issue of minors' involvement in prostitution is dealt with under the general provisions of the 1977 Penal Law in the sections constituting aggravated circumstances.[55] Most significant is the amendment's addition of the prohibition to engage in prostitution with a minor, punishable by three years imprisonment.[56] Another related legislative change, to combat child sex tourism, had already passed in 1998.[57] The amendment establishes extraterritorial jurisdiction for prostitution-related crimes against minors and makes it possible to bring the perpetrators to trial in Israel for crimes committed elsewhere.

Illegal commerce and sexual exploitation of children has indeed become a disturbing phenomenon that increasingly occupies Israeli policymakers and police. Some NGOs are devoted to work in the area of child prostitution, the most prominent being ELEM (Organization for Youth in Distress), which deals solely with minors. Recently, as a result of the rising awareness of this problem on the global level as well as in Israel, other NGOs who deal with children's rights have joined in efforts to combat child prostitution.[58] ELEM was involved in investigating the scope of child prostitution from 1994 to 1997 and obtained some of its findings from personal accounts and testimonies of girls in treatment and rehabilitation programs. The study was conducted as part of the operation of the Committee for the Examination of Commercial Sexual Exploitation of Children in Israel (CECSECI) and was presented to the Deputy Attorney General in 1997.[59] After four months of field work as part of its Children of the Night project, ELEM researchers concluded that hundreds of young people are involved in prostitution, and while it was difficult to determine exact ages, some were clearly minors. Furthermore, it was evident that a pattern could be traced behind the entrance of girls in distress into prostitution and the sex industry (CECSECI Report 1997). In general, a gradual yet unmistakable development of sexual exploitation in Israel was noted, leading to an estimated range from several dozens to several hundreds of girls directly involved in some degree of prostitution, some of them as young as eleven or twelve (CESCECI Report 1997, 33–34).

Pornography

From a radical feminist perspective, the prostitution and pornography industries revealed male dominance. There is a close connection underlying these two fields: both are the most blatant expressions of women's reduction into sexual objects, entitled to no respect or autonomy, to be used for the sexual arousal of male consumers (Barnett 1998, 167–72). Pornography should be viewed as a practice that abuses the media by depicting distorted, demeaning, and dehumanizing images mostly of women, and it is directly linked to gender-based violence against women (MacKinnon 1987, 175; Morgan 1977; Brownmiller 1975). Women are mostly forced into prostitution or the pornography industry due to their economic vulnerability, which is also an expression of male dominance. The radical feminist approach supplies the tools to analyze these phenomena, which only happen to women (or to equally underprivileged and vulnerable men), on political terms. Liberal feminism with its sameness/difference approach "would leave pornography at the level of recognition of women's difference as a causal explanation for a phenomenon which is predominantly an expression of power relationship" (Barnett 1998, 172). When it comes to pornography, liberal feminism would often also be preoccupied with the guarantee of free speech in the First Amendment to the U.S. Constitution. Free speech issues also seem to accompany handling pornography in Israeli law, although not to the extent that the debate has evolved in the United States. Moreover, the 1998 amendment to the law reveals the possible beginning of the conceptualization of the subject as one of power relations.

Israeli law has dealt with pornography in several pieces of legislation besides the 1977 Penal Law, including legislation authorizing the Council for Scrutiny of Films and Plays to restrict the display of such materials for reasons of moral offense or corruption. However, the difficulty of striking a balance between freedom of expression and protection from pornography has resulted in abolishing the censorship of plays in the 1991 reforms,[60] and the censorship of films was effectively undermined in a recent Supreme Court ruling, making it largely inapplicable. It should be noted that the operation of the Council for Scrutiny only covers the "official" or "legal" broadcasting and cinema display, to the obvious exclusion of a growing market of hard-core pornographic videocassettes freely traded in sex shops and "videomat" street machines. The operation of these is covered by the general provisions of the Penal Law, which has undergone some important changes and reforms.

Until 1991, section 214 of the Penal Law prohibited the selling, possession, printing, display, or publication of pornographic materials. For that purpose, pornography was defined as material that potentially corrupts morality, but case law has added the criteria of obscene materials that lack any sort of artistic value. A 1990–91 reform to the Penal Law[61] shifted the focus from immorality to a clearer separation between the private and public sphere, where protection from offensive materials would be guaranteed, and increased emphasis was placed on the dignity of the person. For example, section 214Ab(2), enacted in 1990, prohibits the representation of persons in a humiliating or degrading sexual manner or in a manner that depicts the person as an available sexual object. Other provisions of the 1991 version of section 214 specifically outlaw the publication of obscene material or its preparation for publication, and obscene performances in public places or any other place accessible to persons under eighteen years of age. These violations are punishable by up to three years imprisonment. In 1998,[62] the definition of the terms "publication" and "publish" were broadened to include computer materials and the dispensation of materials through the use of computers, including the Internet and other modes of computer communications. On the other hand, mere possession of pornographic materials, except those involving minors,[63] is no longer prohibited, thus emphasizing non-intrusion into the private sphere of the individual.

The emphasis on the public-private division here obviously implicates liberal legal feminism, as is the rhetoric of the person's "dignity." Power politics, which do not accept the border between the private and public sphere, are not reflected in this framework. Moreover, while the 1990–91 reforms may overall conform with feminist notions in general, the truth is that they were mostly the result of religious lobbying. Thus, the definition of "offensive representation" for this purpose includes, in addition to the mentioned section 214Ab(2), a picture of a nude body or any intimate body part of a man or a woman, a picture depicting sexual relations or sexual violence, or of a partially nude man or woman, or containing material offensive to the moral feelings of the public, a picture which corrupts the public morality, or is harmful to minors or their education.[64] Perhaps the other reform, that of 1998, does reflect a different conceptualization, one that perceives the power relations and abuse of power inherent in this area. The chronicle of how this amendment came about also sheds light on its perception of the subject.

The 1998 reform was prompted by global politics, and by the need of the State of Israel to comply with international concerns and initiatives. Public opinion worldwide, shocked at revelations on the extent of international trafficking in minors and minors' involvement in prostitution and in sex tourism, led to the convening of a World Congress Against Commercial Sexual Exploitation of Children in Stockholm, in August 1996. The preparations for this congress stimulated a process of inquiry and examination of this issue in Israel.[65] One concrete result of this process was a 1997 bill to considerably reform the Penal Law in relation to prostitution and pornography.[66] In 1998, the bill was partially passed.[67] Significantly, of the substantive provisions relating to prostitution and the contents of pornography, it was mostly those that dealt with minors that passed. Thus, until this reform, only the actual use of a minor (under eighteen) in a pornographic publication or presentation was punishable by up to five years imprisonment. Realizing the growing phenomenon of pedophile networks, their advanced technological operation, and the extent of the harm they cause, the law now also prohibits the mere possession of such pornographic materials (including computer materials) that contain minors or images of minors, even for personal use.[68] This new offense is punishable by up to three years imprisonment; the former offense of the use of a minor for pornographic publication or presentation was separated into two different offenses: publication, punishable by up to five years imprisonment; and preparation of such publication, or the use of a minor in a live show, punishable by up to seven years imprisonment. When these are done by the minor's guardian, or with the guardian's consent, the maximum sentence of the guardian is ten years imprisonment. Another form of publication, which brings pornography and prostitution together, is the advertising of sex services. The 1998 reform explicitly prohibited, for the first time, any advertising of prostitution services by minors, including such services rendered outside Israel,[69] an offense punishable by up to five years imprisonment. Advertising of adult prostitution services is also prohibited now and is punishable by up to sic months imprisonment, except in special publications that are separate from other publications, marked as such, and given only upon specific request.

Nonetheless, true ideological change is judged by enforcement in practice. Here we are faced with the familiar gap between the law-on-the-books and its enforcement, the typical theme that runs throughout this book. Thus, for example, police data show that between 1996 and 19999 only 19 files were opened for "publication of obscene materials."[70] Similarly, as a casual glance weekend editions of daily newspapers clearly shows, the restriction of advertising adult prostitution in separate issues is not enforced at all. The blatant indifference with regard to these laws was powerfully demonstrated in an original experiment undertaken by an abolitionist activist, who pretended to be a potential advertiser of sex services of "his workers."[71] He faced no problem from the newspapers personnel, who did not even attempt to verify his identity or his alleged "merchandise." A simple calculation of the aggregate profits of such advertisements for only one national newspaper reaches the annual sum of $8 million.

In light of the ease of publishing such advertisements and the casual manner in which they appear within regular commercial ads, as if women can be bought and sold just like cars or houses, the announcement of police investigations against newspaper publishers is particularly interesting. Apparently, at least one criminal file against the editors of two national newspapers has been opened, but its processing seemed to be moving very slowly.[72] It seems that the reason for this has more to do with policy than with budgetary constraints. It may indicate lack of internalization of the prohibitory attitude reflected in the law, or perhaps even disagreement as to the point where it strikes a balance between freedom of expression and protection from pornography, and it certainly points to the perception of the subject matter as one of power politics instead of the traditional free speech representation.

Chapter 11
The Halachic Trap: Marriage and Family Life

Feminist legal writing has exposed the institution of the patriarchal family as a prime locus of domination and control of women by men, and revealed its legal regulation as a system that enables and reinforces male supremacy (Fineman 1992; Okin 1989; Olsen 1984). The patriarchal family is seen as the epitome of the social-legal construction of the public/private split. This ideology considers the world to be naturally divided into two spheres: a public sphere, usually taken to include work and politics, inhabited by men, and a personal sphere, encompassing home and the family life, deemed to be the realm of women (Polan 1993, 422). In constructing the family as the ultimate private sphere, laws granted men considerable power over their wives. Women could not count on legal protection in the home, since as the private realm, it was perceived to be outside the law's or society's authority to regulate (Olsen 1985). Moreover, by structuring the functions and the operation of the family along clear and immutable gender lines, the law braced women's confinement into the home, and sanctioned their roles as childbearers and childrearers.

Family law in Israel is governed by the principle of religious personal law in family matters.[1] This means that matters concerning personal status (marriage, divorce, support) are determined according to the religious affiliation of the parties involved (Halperin-Kaddari 1994). Religious laws are generally traditional and patriarchal in nature, and a common feature to most of these systems is their prejudiced perceptions of women's nature and role, which leads to discriminatory treatment of women in these matters (Okin 1999, 12–13).

While the principle of personal law is presently intertwined with the debate over religion and state relations in Israel and has come to represent the focal point of Israel's identity as a state for the Jewish people, it originates from the four hundred years of Ottoman rule in Palestine. The Ottoman regime, which regarded family matters as internal private affairs to be governed by religious law, and simultaneously held that only Muslims have the right to be governed by the Shari'a (Muslim religious law), had allowed those the Ottoman regime regarded as "nations" to be governed by their own religious laws. The succeeding rulers, the British, left the situation as it was. This remained the State of Israel's legal approach toward family and personal status in its formative period and in the present legal system (Rubinstein 1991, 204–8). Socially and politically, the rule of religious law over marriage and divorce has come to symbolize religious coercion in Israel, and it is generating growing resistance by those opposed to any religious practice, by those who oppose the official monopoly of Orthodox Judaism over religious practice, by those whom religious law precludes from marrying each other (Rosen-Zvi 1990; Shifman 1995b), and by feminists (Shalev 1995a; Yishai 1997). Nevertheless, a change in the near future seems inconceivable. The maintenance of religious law in matters of marriage and divorce is still considered a basic tenet in the Israeli polity in general and in the delicate construction of Jewish identity in particular. It has been taken for granted by many as a natural expression of the Jewish identity of the state and as an acceptable political price for the maintenance of internal peace and unity by many others (Levi, Levinson, and Katz, 1993).[2] Although practical and legal subterfuges of the principle of religious law are recently gaining more weight and legitimacy, Israeli law is still a long way from overriding the status quo and introducing civil marriage and divorce (Shifman 1999, 278). Moreover, it is these very subterfuge mechanisms, in the mitigating effect they have on the coercion, that may very well postpone the overall introduction of civil marriage in Israel.

Due to this principle of personal law, the legal situation in Israel in the area of marriage and divorce can be described as violating the precept of gender equality in family life in all three stages of marriage (in entry to marriage, during marriage, on dissolution of marriage) (Shalev 1995a). In a nutshell, it conceives marriage as a one-sided transaction in which the man betroths the woman and not the opposite, which sanctions inequality and discrimination regarding spousal obligations and rights toward each other during the course of marriage, and sanctions harsh limitations over the process of divorce and inequalities with respect to it, to the detriment of women. Furthermore, it also violates the principle of freedom in marriage contained in other international human-rights instruments, in putting broad religious restrictions on eligibility to marry.

Unlike previous chapters, where my custom was to open with the normative description and analysis and then to proceed to the sociological discussion, here I have chosen the opposite course. This is primarily because this subject is the most heavily regulated and has therefore generated the richest legal materials of the subjects covered in this book. Part of the reason for that is the complexity of the legal arrangements due to the complicated relationships of civil and religious laws in this area. For some reason, which could also be related to the previous observation, very few sociological and empiric studies have been conducted on families in Israel in general. In addition, my own specialization in family law has no doubt attributed to this decision. Consequently, this chapter begins by supplying brief sociological background on families in Israel, including some demographic data, and continues with a legal discussion. The legal discussion first addresses the conventional Jewish marriage and divorce laws, including limitations on marriage such as bigamy and minimum marital age, and proceeds to address alternatives to religious marriage, including the uniquely broad Israeli legal institute of nonmarital cohabitation, and the subject of same-sex couples. The discussion continues along the lines of monetary consequences of marriage (mainly property distribution), and moves on to briefly address parents and children. Specific topics such as names, single-parent families, and new reproductive technologies conclude the discussion.[3] Domestic violence is extensively covered in the second part of Chapter 9, within the general discussion of gender-based violence against women. In terms of reference to religious law, the discussion and analysis focus on Jewish law. Specifically narrow descriptions are made to Shari'a and Druze family laws.

The Family in Israel: Social Observations and Demographic Data

Israel is a family-oriented society. Familism, the normative family's centrality in the lives of the individual and the collective (Fogiel-Bijaoui 1999, 113), is one of the central characteristics of Israeli society (Shamgar-Hendelman and Bar-Yosef 1991; Peres and Katz 1991). Using various sets of demographic data that sociologists take to reflect familism, sociologist Sylvia Fogiel-Bijaoui concludes in a comprehensive study of familism and family perceptions in Israeli society that Israel ranks first among twenty-one post-industrial states in which, like Israel, women's educational level and workforce participation have significantly increased in the past twenty years. Relative to the other states in the study, marriage rates in Israel remain high, divorce rates are low, and birth rates are significantly higher (Fogiel-Bijaoui 1999, 130–34). In further analyzing specific religious and ethnic population groups,

Fogiel-Bijaoui claims that familism in Israel is not limited to groups who "have not yet Westernized," but is the common normative framework of the institute of family in Israel.

The familial characteristic of Israeli society is indeed reflected in data such as the high marital status percentages and low percentages of unmarried and never-married men and women in different age groups.[4] Even the phenomenon of cohabitation among young adults, which is growing in Israel as elsewhere in the Western world, is generally found to be just a transition stage before formal marriage takes place (Belosh-Kleinman and Sharlin 1999). Overall, throughout the different population groups, as Israelis get older, those who never marry are an increasing minority. Quite significantly, more women over 40 (both Jewish and Muslim) relative to men over 40 never got married (e.g., 3.2 percent of Jewish women aged fifty-five to sixty-four compared to 2.8 percent of Jewish men that age). Even more significant for the general state of women is the fact that more women who were married are presently not married (either divorced or widowed): almost 30 percent of the Jewish women aged fifty-five to sixty-four) and more than 60 percent of Jewish women over sixty-five are unmarried, compared to only 12 percent and 22.3 percent of Jewish men of those ages. The translation of this into actual numbers is particularly telling: in 1997 there were exactly twice as many divorced women as divorced men (116,600 and 58,400 respectively). In other words, divorced men are clearly much more likely to remarry than are divorced women.[5]

Another indication of the centrality of family life in Israeli society is the relatively low marriage age, especially that of women, compared to other Western societies. While median marriage age for Jewish women and men between 1970 and 1997 has gone up from 21.6 to 24.4 and 24.4 to 27 respectively,[6] it is still lower than in other postindustrial countries (Fogiel-Bijaoui 1999, 137). Median marriage ages are lower among Muslim and Druze Israelis (25.1 and 25 for Muslim and Druze men, respectively, and 20.3 for both Muslim and Druze women) and highest among Christian men (28.2), though, interestingly, Christian women's median marriage age is much lower: 23. The overall trend in all population groups is the rising of marriage ages for both women and men.

Birth rates (discussed in detail in Chapter 4) are also an important factor in determining society's familism (Peres and Katz 1980). While fertility rates in all population groups in Israel have dramatically decreased,[7] they remain significantly higher than in other postindustrial countries, and have even risen since the mid-1990s. In 1997, Israel ranked third within the 45 countries with high human development according to the United Nations Development Program, with a total fertility rate of 2.93, the same as Kuwait and Bahrain and less than Qatar

(3.7) and the United Arab Emirates (3.4). Having children in Israel is a constructed part of the Jewish-Arab conflict and is expressed in terms of "the demographic balance," reflecting the national requirement to have more children (Berkovitch 1997; Izraeli 1997; Yishai 1997) and assigning women the role of "bearers of the collective" (Yuval-Davis 1980).

Increasing divorce rates send a somewhat different message from the previous indicators regarding Israel's familism. Between 1975 and 1998, while the total Jewish population in Israel grew by 62 percent, the number of divorces almost tripled (from 2,857 divorces to 8,186).[8] Figure 3 clearly shows the significant growth in the rates of divorcing persons per 1,000 married men and women. However, the total divorce rate per 1,000 people (1.7) still remains low relative to other post-industrial countries (Fogiel-Bijaoui 1999, 130–34). This explains the somewhat surprisingly low percentage of divorced persons in the population: in 1997, of all men and women over fifteen only 3.5 percent of the men and 6.6 percent of the women were divorced.[9]

Official and published marriage and divorce rates in Israel do not present the full picture, especially with regard to marriage. The Central Bureau of Statistics (CBS) reports only cases of marriage recounted by the official marriage and divorce registrars in Israel, namely the formally recognized religious authorities (which is, for Jewish people, the Orthodox Rabbinate), since there are no civil marriages and divorces in Israel.[10] These obviously exclude the alternative forms of marriage men-

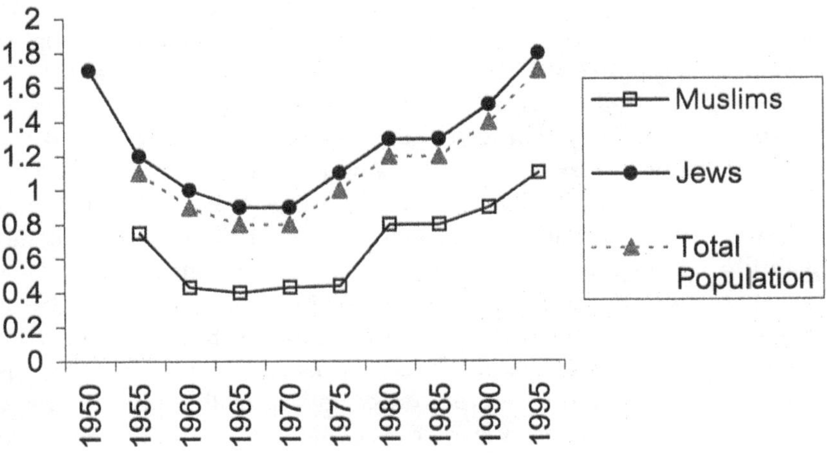

Figure 3. Divorce rates by religion, 1950–1995. Source: Central Bureau of Statistics, *Statistical Abstract of Israel*, 2000.

tioned below, some of which, such as conducting civil marriage out of Israel, are actually recognized as valid for purposes of registration by the Ministry of Interior. In other words, CBS published data do not correlate with Ministry of Interior data, which are unpublished. Moreover, none of these statistics cover nonmarital cohabitation.

Divorce rates are more reflective of the full picture. Since obtaining a foreign divorce that will be recognized for purposes of registration is a legally complex procedure, even couples who were married under civil law outside Israel generally go through a religious divorce in Israel to change their status from married to unmarried and be able to remarry. However, the growing phenomenon of nonmarital cohabitation is not reflected here either. Unmarried couples who separate after years of living together are not included in these data, even though the process they go through is certainly akin to formal divorce, both emotionally and even legally to some extent (in terms of child custody or property distribution) but lacks the officially recognized form of divorce.

In order to get a fuller scope of marriage for Israelis, I obtained some unpublished data from the Ministry of Interior.[11] These data relate to marriages of Israeli citizens conducted out of Israel and registered by the Ministry of Interior (the reason for this double registration is explained later). In order for such a marriage to be registered, an official document of marriage has to be presented to the registrar, thus precluding any form of "private marriage" such as through a lawyer's administered contract or a private religious ceremony. One such set of data reveals that in 1997–98, 13,447 Israeli men and women were civilly married outside Israel, compared with 155,496 men and women who were officially married in Israel. This means that CBS data on marriages miss the real number of marriages of Israelis by at least 8 percent.[12]

About half of all marriages conducted outside Israel take place in Cyprus and Paraguay. Half were marriages between two Jews, and the rest were mostly mixed marriages between Jew and non-Jew.[13] This brings in the political debate behind the whole question of civil marriages in Israel. As much as it relates to social and political struggles against religious coercion in general, it is also strongly related to the struggle against the monopoly of Orthodox Judaism over the practice of religion in particular. One such demonstration of that struggle is conducting a civil marriage out of Israel, after having conducted a religious but non-Orthodox (and therefore unrecognized by the state) marriage ceremony in Israel. Thus, one good example of the growing resistance to the Orthodox monopoly is a comprehensive practical guide issued by the Center for Jewish Pluralism of the Reform Movement in Israel, listing all possibilities for civil marriages out of Israel, including a detailed description of all formal requirements for obtaining marriage license in each state (Center for Jewish Pluralism 1999).

Family Law in Israel: Jurisdictional and Legal Split

Family law in Israel is a uniquely complex system in the Western legal world, in that it combines civil and religious legal systems simultaneously governing the same geographical and demographic unit (Shifman 1995c; Rosen-Zvi 1990). In a sense, it is a special case of legal pluralism (Halperin-Kaddari 1997a) derived from the rule of personal religious law in family matters, which is embedded in the Palestine Order-in-Council (1922–47),[14] still in force today. It is this rule that is responsible for the singular attribute of family law in Israel, namely the jurisdictional and legal split. The split is characterized by the following two features: the parties to the cases are governed by personal (religious) law, and both legal rules and jurisdiction in this area are divided between the civil and religious systems. These features have created a problematic phenomenon known as the "race for jurisdiction" (Shava 1972; Rosen-Zvi 1989). This race develops when each side in a divorce proceeding seeks to gain advantage by petitioning the forum that is perceived to be more favorable in matters under concurrent jurisdiction. In general, the relief offered by religious courts tends to favor the husband, while that by civil courts tends to favor the wife (Shifman 1995c; Rosen-Zvi 1990). Filing a suit in one forum stops the jurisdictional race and prevents the matter from being addressed in the competing arena.[15] Thus, there is a built-in incentive to initiate legal proceedings immediately upon the first sign of marital crisis (Halperin-Kaddari 1994).

Seizing jurisdiction is indeed crucial, since the differences between the two tribunals are substantial, even though both theoretically apply the same laws (Rosen-Zvi 1989).[16] According to the 1953 Rabbinical Courts Jurisdiction (Marriage and Divorce) Law,[17] rabbinical courts have exclusive jurisdiction in matters of marriage and divorce, which are completely governed by religious law. However, all other matters that are related to divorce disputes, from child custody and support through property claims, are under the jurisdiction of the civil court, unless they are properly "attached" to a divorce suit filed in the rabbinical court. Thus, the jurisdiction of the civil court may be obstructed by filing for divorce in the rabbinical court, and "attaching" all other disputed issues to it, according to Section 3 of the Rabbinical Courts Law. The outcomes of disputes depend on the forum in which they are heard, both because rabbinical tribunals apply religious rules of procedure and evidence, and, mostly, because these tribunals generally ignore substantive civil law, even when it specifically includes religious courts in its application

(Maoz 1985; Halperin-Kaddari 1997a). The consequences of this are much harsher on women than on men. For example, rabbinical courts refuse to apply the egalitarian community property rule, and rule according to the principle of separate property, which distributes property according to the formal title.[18] In addition, support awards for both wife and children are overall much lower in rabbinical than in civil courts, as demonstrated in Chapter 6.

Realizing the problematic enforcement of religious law and jurisdiction over nonreligious people, and the injustices caused mainly to women in rabbinical courts, civil courts—mainly through the High Court of Justice—have engaged in a gradual and consistent process of narrowing the scope of religious law and jurisdiction, starting as early as in the late 1950s. In the early 1990s, parallel to the overall "constitutional revolution" that Israel has allegedly been undergoing, the High Court of Justice began to subject religious courts to the basic norms and principles that govern the civil legal system (Halperin-Kaddari 2001). Thus, for example, while property claims were originally deemed to be under the exclusive jurisdiction of rabbinical courts and governed by religious law, they were gradually drawn into civil courts and were subject to civil (contract and property) law,[19] until the whole process culminated in a 1994 ruling that subjected the rabbinical court to the civil principles of equality and mandated that it rule according to the civil rule of community property, which gives the husband and the wife equal shares in the marital property.[20] In addition, the civil system has also been developing civil courses of alternative forms of intimate relationships that would be accorded various degrees of recognition by the state.

Until 1995, jurisdiction was also divided within the civil system itself. The 1995 Family Court Law[21] established a new family law division within the magistrate courts. The family courts became responsible for all family matters under the jurisdiction of the civil system. While the establishment of the family court system has not formally affected the jurisdictional split between the religious and the civil judiciaries, it does carry significant informal consequences for the power struggle between them. Officials in the rabbinical courts have been reported to warn against losing ground to the family courts.[22] In addition to simplifying the proceedings by the consolidation of all the civil suits under one roof, the Family Court Law also sought to introduce less formal proceedings that are more amenable to family disputes. The Family Court Law specifically permits the court to disregard the regular civil rules of procedure and to employ whatever procedure promotes justice.[23] In addition, the Family Court Law provided for the establishment of new Family Court Service Units in every Family Court, to supply auxiliary services as needed on referral by the court.[24] One service provided by family court services is the possibility of resolving family disputes through mediation. Ranging from the management of emergency cases in small-scale mediation sessions to handling the full range of disputed issues, these units provide a hybrid physically out-of-court mediation service under the auspices and supervision of the court (Ben-Rabi and Shmaia-Yadgar 2000). In the three years following their establishment, family court service units have handled approximately 7,600 cases.[25] By the end of 2000 they were staffed with 30 specially trained social workers, vis-à-vis 33 family court judges, in nine of the ten family courts in the country.[26]

Marriage and Divorce

Marriage According to Jewish Law

Any discussion that mentions Jewish law without actually going into and analyzing the law itself is problematic, since Jewish law, perhaps more than any other religious legal system, is pluralistic (Berkowitz 1983; Roth 1986; Sagi 1996). It is therefore misleading to present Jewish law as a monolithic normative system a claim a certain representation of Jewish law on a particular issue as an ultimate portrayal of the Jewish law on that issue. Since Jewish law is not a central theme of this book, the discussion here pertains to a description of the law as it is understood and applied by contemporary rabbinical courts in Israel, narrowed to a specific reading of Jewish law, which in my understanding is sadly the conventional interpretation of Jewish law, as it is understood and practiced under Orthodox Judaism today.[27] Applicable Jewish law in Israel is in fact the Orthodox interpretation of Jewish law, and rabbinical courts are exclusively Orthodox. Therefore, the conclusions I draw below are certainly relevant to Jewish women in Israel. This discussion by no means exhausts the possibilities within Jewish law at large, nor the potential for progressive interpretation that does exist within Orthodox Judaism itself.

Under Jewish law, men and women are in general equally free to choose their spouses. The limitations on marriage, drawn from religious laws and sanctioned by the Israeli civil system, apply almost equally to men and women. Under Jewish law, neither a Jewish man nor a Jewish woman can marry a non-Jew. One of the broadest limitations on eligibility to marry under Jewish law applies to men of the "priestly" class (*kohanim*), who cannot marry a divorced woman or a convert to Judaism. Regarding consent to marriage, Jewish law may sometimes presume marriage for women to be preferable to nonmarriage (Halperin-Kaddari, forthcoming), and accordingly there have been cases where women's unexpressed or unclear choice regarding the marriage was taken as consent (Shershevsky 1993). No parallel cases can take place regarding men's consent, since marriage is in fact a unilateral act on the part of the man who betrothes the woman, in a legal transaction that corresponds to acquisition (Wegner 1988).

The status of men and women during marriage is far from equal. As a traditional patriarchal system, Jewish law strongly adheres to strict gender roles in the family. The differential treatment in the religious laws carries legal implications under the Israeli legal systems, most of it in the areas of spousal support and grounds for divorce. However, Jewish law adopts a double standard with respect to sexual behavior of men and women in general, and of married men and married women in particular. While a married man's sexual relationships with a woman other than his wife hardly carries any legal consequence, except for the very rare possibility of considering this to be a ground for divorce (Halperin 1989), a married woman's sexual relations with a man other than her husband carry extremely harsh consequences: she is to be immediately divorced while losing all her monetary rights otherwise acquired according to the Jewish law. She is prohibited from later marrying either her former husband or the man with whom she had "committed adultery," and any child that results from the adulterous relationships is considered a "bastard" (*mamzer*) who is precluded from marrying within the Jewish community, except for a convert or a *mamzer* like him/herself (Haut 1983; Shershevsky 1993). These grave and unequal consequences of women's extramarital relations profoundly implicate women's position within the divorce process, which is the main form of discrimination against women under Jewish law.

Divorce and the Agunah Problem

What distinguishes Jewish marriage and divorce rules from other legal and religious systems is that both marriage and divorce are autonomous, voluntary acts of two individuals, not legal actions constructed by the external judicial or religious organ. Neither marriage nor divorce can be constituted for the couple. Divorce is promulgated by the spouses' own act either through the mutual consent of both parties or after proof of "faults" (grounds for divorce). The judicial acts, however, are only declaratory, not constitutive, and the rabbinical courts' involvement in divorce cases amounts to determining whether the husband or wife is under any degree of obligation to grant or accept the divorce. The rabbinical courts' incompetence in processing divorce is clearly reflected in unpublished data detailing the number of annual petitions of divorce (both contested and uncontested) compared with the number of actual divorces: in 1998, the number of divorces promulgated amounted to only 48 percent of the total petitions (8,435 and 17,564 respectively), while 47 percent of the petitions were in fact petitions to ratify a divorce agreement, thus reflecting mutual consent to divorce![28] Another set of data confirms this: of 1,630 contested divorce cases decided in the Jerusalem Rabbinical Court in 1998, in only 234 (14.4 percent) was the petition accepted.[29] Where there is no consent, no divorce can be processed, since contemporary rabbinical courts perceive themselves incompetent to annul marriages, although Jewish law does provide for this mechanism under certain circumstances (Freiman 1945; Berkovits 1966; Elon 1978, 686–712).

Although in principle both parties' free will is needed for the bill of divorce (*get*) to be valid, the wife's consent can be circumvented with no consequences on the get's validity, while the husband's voluntary provision of the get is an absolute prerequisite without which the divorce is invalid (Haut 1983; Rosen-Zvi 1990; Halperin-Kaddari 2000a). Invalidity of the *get* means that the wife is still a married woman, so that any sexual relations she may later conduct would still be considered adulterous, with the harsh consequences explained above. Thus, as a rule, the husband has almost absolute control over the *get*, which the wife categorically requires in order to divorce.

The preceding survey also explains the rabbinical courts' hesitation and reluctance in issuing decisions obligating or even compelling men to grant divorce. Rabbinical courts may use several terms of ordering divorce, from the very lenient recommendation to divorce, to the harshest term permitting coercion under very rare circumstances. Each term permits varying degree of sanctions against the recalcitrant party, and the highest category of coercion permits the incarceration of the recalcitrant husband.[30] However, divorce claims against women are easily accepted by rabbinical courts, and women are ordered to accept the *get*. Similar claims against men, under similar circumstances, rarely produce an order to grant the *get*.[31] Contemporary rabbinical courts tend to refrain from compelling a man to divorce (Zilberg 1957, 108–10; Falk 1973). A man's violence toward his wife can theoretically constitute a halachically valid ground for divorce; however, some authorities have indicated the need for special aggravating circumstances or prior warnings and witnesses to the violence, so that contemporary rabbinical courts feel that this does not constitute a legitimate ground for coercing divorce, but only for recommending that the husband give the *get* (Frishtik 1991). According to Rabbi Ben-Dahan, the Rabbinical Courts Administrator, each year there are about ten orders to compel divorce upon husbands.[32] In light of the number of annual petitions for divorce, this number is minuscule.

The rabbinical courts, then, are apprehensive about the validity of the *get,* which is dependent on the man's "free will," and usually prefer to deal with a recommendation for divorce and send the parties to negotiate its terms. This leads the way for a common course of negotiation, which generally results in the woman buying her way out of the marriage by paying whatever the husband demands in terms of property rights, child support, and so on. Women who refuse to pay for their freedom to remarry have no recourse in the Israeli legal system. They are *agunot,* women who are "chained" or "anchored" to their husbands, with no relief available in the religious or civil system.[33] Thus, divorces are almost always based on prior agreements between the parties.[34] These agreements, which commonly cover all aspects of the divorce, are usually negotiated outside the rabbinical or civil courts, although they require ratification by either court. The ratifying court, however, does not engage in substantive scrutiny of the terms of the agreement (Rosen-Zvi 1990; Shifman 1995c).[35] Thus, the power imbalance is not remedied by the judicial system. More often than not it is the husband who translates this advantage into monetary concessions from his wife. In many cases, the civil legal system is the one that conditions property distribution upon prior arrangement of the *get,* so that the wife cannot even execute the right to her share of the property, even if she decides to put off the *get.*[36]

There is another category of women who are restrained from remarriage due to the laws of levirate marriages: under Jewish law, if a man dies childless, his widow is allowed to marry another man only after she is "freed" by her deceased husband's brother from her obligation to marry him (Haut 1983; Shershevsky 1993). Contemporary Jewish law in fact prohibits actual levirate marriage but still necessitates the process of "freeing" the widow (*halitza*) from her "bond" to her deceased husband's brother. In these circumstances, the widow's freedom to remarry depends on the deceased's brother cooperation, and there are cases of money being demanded in exchange for *halitza.* In cases where the brother is under thirteen, the minimum age of marriage under Jewish law, the widow must wait until he reaches thirteen to go through the process of *halitza.* According to data supplied by the Administrator of the Rabbinical Courts, there were twenty such cases of women in need of *halitza* on average a year during the 1990s.[37]

A major step forward with regard to the *aguna* problem did occur in Israel in 1995, when the 1995 Rabbinical Courts (Enforcement of Divorce Decrees) (Temporary Measures) Law was passed.[38] This law uses a mechanism in Jewish law to indirectly compel recalcitrant husbands to grant divorces. In past times this was done by denying them social status, through ostracizing and excommunication. The contemporary "translation" of this mechanism is suspension of one or more of the following unrelated rights and benefits: the right to leave the country, hold a driver's license, hold a passport, hold a bank account, practice as a professional where a license is needed, be nominated to public office, or be eligible for parole in case the husband is a convict. The harshest form of restraining order available through this law is the incarceration of the recalcitrant husband.[39] Problematic as this may seem from a secular liberal perspective, it may be the only mode of solution that can combine Jewish legal principles in a nontraditional framework.

It is still somewhat too early to evaluate the actual effect of this law. The Administrator of the Rabbinical Courts, however, claims that in many cases there is no need for actual sanctions, since the mere threat of using them is enough to propel the husbands to grant the required bills of divorce. If so, this may indicate a breakthrough in the problem of *agunot* and the deadlock of divorces in Israel. However, actual data supplied by the Administrator of the Rabbinical Courts show a definitely less encouraging picture. Through the first four years of its usage, from May 1995 to May 1999, only 163 restraining orders were issued, a small number in light of the number of yearly petitions for divorce. Moreover, one rabbinical court of the twelve operating in the country has consistently issued half of all restraining orders: 76 of a total 163.[40] In other words, making use of this mechanism is dependent upon the personal conviction of the religious judge as to its halachic legitimacy. Furthermore, on the practical level, still fewer than half the cases where restraining orders are issued actually result in a divorce: 71 of 163. This is not to say that the rest have been futile, as proceedings may still be taking place. According to the Administrator of the Rabbinical Courts, it usually takes a period of up to nine months for the sanctions to have an effect on the husband and make him grant the get.

The Ripple Effect of Formal Application of the Halachic Code of Marriage and Divorce

The plight of the *aguna* is indeed the most extreme expression of women's inferiority under Jewish family law. However, a deeper reflection of the law reveals that this is but one reflection of the structural inferiority into the system (Halperin-Kaddari, 2000a). The discriminatory process of divorce often leads women to give up their legal property and monetary rights, so as not to get into the intolerable position of *aguna*. The consequences of this on divorced women's economic vulnerability are clearly seen in Chapter 6.

Nonetheless, discrimination at the end of marriage is only part of the picture. Jewish law perceives marriage as a system of mutual rights and responsibilities, clearly based on traditional separate spheres gender ideologies (Levinson 1990; Lazarus-Yafeh 1988). The husband works outside the home and is responsible for the wife's sustenance, while the wife works inside the home and is responsible for all the housework and childcare, and is also obligated to personally serve the husband. In addition, any property the wife may have had upon marriage becomes subject to her husband's management and her earnings are put against her right to support (Meiselman 1978).[41] Similarly, the code of double standard Jewish law posits for moral and sexual behavior on married men and women also carries grave economic consequences for women. According to this code, as a direct result of the wife's unilateral consecration to her husband as part of her betrothal to him, total sexual fidelity is demanded only of the wife, not of the husband, who can in fact engage in extramarital relationships without fear of legal repercussions (Greenberg 1991).[42] In this sense, the economic relationship of the couple is intimately related to their intimate relationship. All this may have reflected gender balancing and mutuality appropriate to the social and economic conditions of the time when it was designed (Berman 1976; Biale 1984; Hauptman 1998), however its application to present social norms can have devastating effects on women.

Women's awareness of their inferiority projects onto their self-perception and perception of their marital relationship. As the family is the basic unit of socialization, these perceptions structure the socialization process of children within the family (Okin 1989). The summary of the law presented above demonstrates that in a sense, the vices of the patriarchal family, which, at present, are generally a reflection of strong social norms, are in fact normatively sanctioned under Jewish religious law, and are consequently part of the Israeli legal system itself. Thus, for example, the well-known circular interaction between the women's economic dependency within the "private" family and their secondary position within the "public" market is clearly endorsed under the law itself. The difference in wage patterns presented in Chapter 7 can thus be seen not just as a reflection of social norms but as an expression of the legal order.

Restrictions on the Right to Marry: Minimum Marital Age

The 1950 Marriage Age Law[43] states that the minimum marital age for women is seventeen except in rare cases. A 1998 amendment set a minimum marriage age for men(not been set before) at seventeen.[44] The minimal age requirement is accompanied by provisions that make the arrangement of underage marriages a criminal offense punishable by up to two years imprisonment for the person who arranges the marriage and the person who performs the ceremony. The law provides that the mere fact that a marriage was conducted in violation of this law is a ground for divorce, but does not state that such marriages are invalid. The simple reason for this omission is, once again, the hold of religious laws over marriages. Jewish law regards marriages of minors beyond a certain age—which usually coincides with puberty (12.5 for girls and 13 for boys)—as valid. Under the peculiar Israeli arrangement of jurisdiction and law in family matters, it is obvious that the secular legislature cannot interfere with actual marital validity, determinations that are under exclusive jurisdiction and rule of religious laws.[45] The provision that supposedly adds violation of this law as a ground for divorce is of no real effect for the same reason.

Article 5 of the law provides for two alternative grounds for judicial permission of underage marriage. The first relates to circumstances under which the underage woman is pregnant from or has given birth to the child of the man whom she asks permission to marry. No age limit is attached to this ground for exception. The 1998 amendment added a parallel case in the form of circumstances under which the woman the underage man wishes to marry is pregnant or has given birth to his child. The second ground for permission relates to unspecified "special circumstances" that would justify immediate marriage, provided the woman or man is over sixteen years old. In one leading case, then Justice Barak firmly stated that a community's custom and tradition do not justify marital exception, since it is those very traditions and customs that the Marriage Age Law has set to abolish.[46]

The lack of a minimum age regarding the first ground for exception was vividly demonstrated in a 1994 case, in which a fourteen-and-a-half-year-old girl, seven months into her pregnancy, petitioned for permission to marry the father of her future child, a twenty-four-year-old man, her former teacher. The petition was denied by the district court, and her appeal to the Supreme Court was reluctantly accepted by Chief Justice Shamgar.[47] Justice Shamgar's main reason for accepting the appeal was the lack of a better alternative, since it was too late for abortion at that point, and the girl was firm in her desire to keep the child and not give it up to adoption. Chief Justice Shamgar also pointed out, somewhat oddly, that unless the couple officially marry, the man could be accused of statutory rape (according to section 346(a) of the 1977 Penal Law[48]). Statutory rape, which applies to intercourse with girls aged fourteen to sixteen, is hence vindicated by marriage, even though the minimum age for marriage is seventeen. Even the Penal Law, however, had not foreseen the possibility of marriage of a girl under age fourteen, and consequently section 345(a)(3) states that intercourse with a girl under that age is considered rape under any circumstances. Justice Shamgar ignored the dangerous implications of such a rationale, according to which a man who statutorily rapes a young girl can exonerate his criminal act by marrying her.

Despite the criminal sanctions, the phenomenon of minors' marriages has not been eliminated altogether, as the CBS data clearly show: in 1998, out of 40,137 brides, 1,883 were under seventeen (close to 5 percent, an improvement from the 6 percent in 1994). Of these, 412 were Jewish, 16 were Christian, 131 were Druze, and the overwhelming majority—1,323—were Muslim; 125 were under sixteen, more than double the number from 1997.[49] Information as to the number of judicial permits issued each year for minor marriages according to Section 5 of the law has been very difficult to obtain, since this legal procedure is not coded separately from all other family legal procedures. Once again, we are faced with the familiar information problem: child marriage is a social problem that gravely affects girls and is widespread among certain population groups. Strong correlation exists between the practice of child marriage and women's low social status. If the authorities are indeed committed to finding out the extent of the phenomenon in order to combat it, there should be nothing easier than comparing the number of judicial permits for underage marriage with the number of married women under seventeen every year. A separate coding for the procedure of judicial permits to underage marriage requires only awareness of the problem and commitment to eradicate it. Since these conditions, unfortunately, do not seem to exist, special efforts had to made to manually sort out the relevant judicial records.[50] When comparing the data eventually supplied by the Department of Judicial Statistics in the Courts Administration with the CBS data for married women under seventeen in various years,[51] a predictable discrepancy between the numbers of judicial permits actually obtained and the number of minor marriages actually performed clearly exists: in Israel in 1994, 2,140 women under seventeen were married, but only 65 petitions for judicial permits for underage marriages were brought to courts.[52] During almost three years, January 1997 to November 2000, only 122 petitions for judicial permits were brought and 89 permissions were granted (an approval rate of 73 percent), while about 1,800 women under seventeen were married in each of these years alone!

This fact obviously confirms the long-held impression that many of the minors' marriages take place without a judicial permit. Furthermore, when judicial permits are sought, they are apparently given quite liberally: the rate of approvals during the first half of the 1990s stood at 80 percent, and decreased slightly in the late 1990s to 73 percent.[53] Undoubtedly, the various legislative interventions into the religious laws and into the practice of religious laws and norms within various population groups, particularly the Arab and the Bedouin populations, are not being enforced. While this area would seem to invite debates over multiculturalism and over the feminist-multicultural dichotomy (Okin 1999; Halperin-Kaddari 2000b), no such discourse seems to have been developed here, and the grave data presented here are reflective not of a conscious multicultural stance, but rather of neglect and apathy.

Restrictions on the Right to Marry: Bigamy

Bigamy is a particular form of discrimination against women. Under Jewish law, a man may be married to more than one wife, but a woman can never be married to more than one man. While Jewish law was amended about a thousand years ago to include a prohibition against taking a second wife or divorcing a wife against her free will, such practices still carry legally valid consequences after the fact (Shershevsky 1993; Haut 1983). Since questions of marriage and divorce are determined by religious law alone, the secular legislature could not have decreed bigamous marriages to be invalid, but could instead only operate against them through criminal law. Section 176 of the 1977 Penal Law makes bigamy a criminal offense punishable by five years imprisonment. Sections 181–82 prohibit forcing divorce upon one's wife with no judicial decree of divorce and make the arrangement of such prohibited marriages or divorces a criminal offense as well.

Sections 179–80, however, provide exceptions for the rule against bigamy. Section 180 applies to all individuals whose religious affiliation is other than Jewish, citing incapacitation of one's spouse or seven years of absence thereof as permitting marriage to another person. Section 179 applies only to Jewish people, providing impunity to a person whose second bigamous marriage was permitted by a rabbinical court's judgment that was later approved by one hundred rabbis and by the chief of the Grand Rabbinical Court. Criminal law, therefore, yields to religious law on this issue. Needless to say, the said impunity can only apply to second marriages of men. According to Jewish law, a permit to take a second wife is issued under various circumstances, similar to those that serve as grounds for divorce. According to the administrator of the rabbinical courts, throughout the first half of the 1990s, an average of 11 permits to marry a second wife were issued each year.[54]

There is no way to describe this normative framework but as a comprised approval by the secular legal system of the discriminatory treatment toward women under Jewish family law, which enhances women's inferior status in family law in Israel. In the 1971 Boronovsky case,[55] Justice Haim Cohen, who argued that section 179 of the Penal Code sanctions discrimination against Jewish women and should therefore be narrowly interpreted, was rejected and remained in the minority. This legal regulation has not been challenged in courts.

Alternatives to Religious Marriage

Civil Marriage Outside Israel

The various restrictions on the right to marry and the exclusivity of religious forms of marriages in Israel have led many to search for and develop alternative forms of marriage. Most common among them is the civil marriage either outside of Israel, or by proxy, where that method is recognized by the marrying state. These marriages are generally registered by the Ministry of Interior.[56] However, the actual legal validity of such marriages between two individuals who are Israeli citizens and reside in Israel according to private international law rules is doubtful (Shava 1991). The Israeli Supreme Court has repeatedly managed to avoid the issue, in light of its political sensitivity. Recently, Judge Porat of the Tel Aviv District Court has declared such a proxy marriage of an Israeli couple to be invalid under the rules of private international law in Israel. Consequently, the wife was found to have no right to support from her husband.[57] Israeli constitutional law has developed a well-established distinction between two levels. The first is administrative-formal aspects of personal status without an examination of the validity of that status; the second is the substantive legal validity of the status. Formal registration by the Ministry of Interior belongs to the first level, while Judge Porat's decision belongs to the second, and mainly affects the couple's internal relationships. These can easily be taken care of through an expressed, or even an implied, contract. Paradoxically, it is the former level that interests most alternative-seekers, since that is the level that includes the registration of marital status in the Population Registrar in the Ministry of Interior, which carries immeasurable significance.

Pragmatically, registration as a married couple is more important for most people than is according substantial validity to their union. The registration guarantees, for example, social benefits to officially married couples. As early as the beginning of the 1960s, the High Court of Justice instructed the Ministry of Interior to register civil marriages in the Population Registrar, making their status equal to that of marriages officially conducted in Israel for all purposes.[58] Thus, civilly married couples are just as eligible for all economic benefits from the state as are as those who were formally married in religious marriage in Israel, their inheritance rights are the same, and in principle the same marital property laws apply to both groups. Even the question of spousal support that was mentioned in the Brochovitch case, which theoretically requires the determination of the marriage's validity, could be managed without actually going into that. In 1994, the Supreme Court decided the Cahana case,[59] in which it suggested the possibility of reading into the relationships an implied contract that applies all the ordinary obligations and rights that arise under formal valid marriages. For some reason, this venue was not pursued by the claimant or the court in the Brochovitch case.

Nonmarital Cohabitation

Israel is probably one of the most progressive countries with respect to the recognition given to forms of family life without formal marital ties (henceforth referred to as nonmarital cohabitation or partnership) (Lifshitz 2002). The existence of an elaborate liberal system of nonmarital cohabitation side by side with a strict and traditional system of formal marriage and divorce may seem paradoxical at first, but upon reflection this proves to be inevitable (Rosen-Zvi 1990). The two systems in fact supplement each other: the progressive system of nonmarital cohabitation is both an inevitable consequence of the conservative and inflexible system of religious formal marriage and divorce, and a remedy that enables the endurance of that system. While the progressive and liberal characteristic of this system has recently been questioned (Lifshitz 2002), it is nonetheless quite fair to say that, had it not been for the system of nonmarital cohabitation, the sustenance of the principle of personal law would have been politically much more difficult, if not impossible.

The Israeli legal system recognizes the state of nonmarital cohabitation or partnership, and attaches to it a bundle of rights with some obligations that taken together amount to the creation of a virtually parallel institute to that of formal marriage: economic rights of nonmarital partners have been equated to those of married couples for purposes of pensions, social security benefits, residents' protection against eviction, damage awards under torts law,[60] and more. In terms of law of inheritance, a qualification was added to the recognition of nonmarital partnership, namely, that neither one of the two is "married to another person." This requirement that "no prior marriage exists" applies only to inheritance.

Another reflection of the more substantive level of recognition is found in some pieces of legislation that impose the same obligations and duties upon nonmarital partners as those that are imposed upon married couples. These include obligations and duties in the area of family violence and duty of care toward minors in the family. In those areas, which mainly apply to relations with other family members in which the

State has a legitimate interest, the relationship between the nonmarital partners is constructed as equal to those of married couples. The legislature, however, has not gone as far as imposing mutual positive obligations upon the partners toward each other. Therefore, there is no statutory obligation of support. Nevertheless, case law has held that such an obligation could be construed as an implied commitment under the circumstances.[61] Similarly, case law has also held that the rule of community property that was developed by the Supreme Court to regulate the area of marital property prior to the enactment of the 1973 Spouses (Property Relations) Law equally applies to nonmarital partners.[62]

Notwithstanding the broad scope of recognition, there are still some areas in which such relationships are not equated to those of formal marriage. There is no consistent ideology behind these distinctions, and they are mostly the result of traditional formalistic judicial interpretation, which can be expected to change. Such areas include, among other things, the provision of impunity from spousal testimony in criminal proceedings, the right of spousal entry to Israel according to the 1952 Entry Into Israel Law,[63] and the right to adopt a child together in Israel, as distinguished from out-of-state adoptions. The prospect of change was substantiated in a precedent-setting case in which Chief Justice Barak recognized nonmarital couples to be eligible for tort damages, notwithstanding the language of the law that was previously interpreted to exclude such forms of relationships.[64]

Same-Sex Couples

The broad approval of nonmarital cohabitation has had an undeniable effect on the possibility of legal recognition of same-sex couples. This was clearly seen in the most significant step thus far in that direction, namely the precedent-setting Danilovitch case,[65] in which El-Al, the Israeli national airline, was ordered to award an air steward's homosexual partner the same benefit, in the form of a free ticket, awarded for a heterosexual partner, married or not. The Danilovitch holding was made possible as a result of two developments in the Israeli legal system: first, a 1992 amendment to the 1988 Equal Employment Opportunities Law that added sexual orientation as a prohibited ground for employment discrimination;[66] and second, the widespread recognition of nonmarital partnerships (Shifman 1995b; Harel 1996; Yonay 1998). These two developments allowed (then) Justice Barak to hold the homosexual steward eligible for the same work benefits as his colleagues, while expressly maintaining that this does not amount to recognition of the homosexual partners as "spouses" and rejecting the claim that this move constructs them as a family. A narrow reading of Justice Barak's holding indeed confines it to the realm of employment rights, where a clear prohibition on discrimination on the basis of sexual orientation exists. However, the whole rhetoric of the decision and its underlying rationale clearly put same-sex couples on the same level as heterosexual couples as intimate unions deserving recognition and support.

Since the Danilovitch case, no court proceeding has produced final outcomes that could test that holding's applicability to the realm of family relations.[67] A highly publicized suit by a homosexual partner of a high-ranking Israel Defense Forces (IDF) officer against the army to accord him the same benefits as a female widow produced conflicting outcomes on the first level of proceedings, and their appeals from both sides had ended in a compromise with no judicial decision.[68]

The most pertinent cases on this question, in Israel as elsewhere in the world, are cases involving children of same-sex couples, usually lesbian couples. This subject arose in the late 1990s, and several developments have taken place since then. The first one relates to equal access of lesbian women to new reproductive technologies for purposes of constructing a family. As explained later, the procedures of artificial insemination and in vitro fertilization in Israel are regulated in the 1987 Public Health (In Vitro Fertilization) Regulation and in an administrative directive issues by the director general of the Ministry of Health.[69] Both directives limited single women's access to the reproductive technologies and required that they undergo psychological or social worker evaluation before treatment. These regulations were challenged in 1997 by several women and by a lesbian couple, claiming they were discriminatory. The High Court of Justice accepted the appeal, declared the regulations to be void, and ordered the Ministry of Justice to publish an administrative directive mandating equal access to reproductive treatments.[70] The decision was celebrated by the lesbian feminist community as legitimizing lesbian motherhood.[71]

The most recent legal victory in that direction has been the High Court of Justice's decision to register a lesbian partner of a biological mother as the child's second mother, based on a prior adoption order issued in California.[72] While the majority holding, from two women justices (of the three presently sitting in the Supreme Court), was careful to emphasize the narrow and almost technical basis of the decision, namely, the lack of the registrar's discretion to refuse the registration according to a foreign adoption order, the social policy implications of the decision cannot be ignored. It is true that the registration is only administrative and has no substantive validity,[73] and legally the court's decision has nothing to do with substantive recognition of lesbian nonbiological motherhood; nonetheless, in granting the second mother registration, the court does declare that at least officially, if not legally, "this child does have two mothers" (Polikoff 1990). Once again, as with the Danilovitch case, the narrow legal holding carries much broader social ramifications. And similar to the reactions following the Danilovitch decision, this case was met with much criticism and public outcry, mainly from religious political circles, and the state attorney requested a rehearing of the case. The rehearing was granted in April 2001, but the Ministry of Interior's motion to uphold the registration until the final decision in the rehearing was dismissed.[74]

In a substantive challenge to the traditional concept of family and motherhood, a lesbian couple who have together been raising three children born to them through artificial insemination have been pursuing legal recognition of their mutual parenthood over the children through a second-mother adoption order. During the course of their legal battle, Judge Yehudit Schtofman, then deputy president of Tel Aviv and Center Family Court, issued a guardian order for each woman over the biological children of her partner.[75] On the other hand, their petition for joint second-parent adoptions was rejected by the family court.[76] Their appeal to the district court was denied in a 2 : 1 decision, with the majority (two male judges, Deputy President Porat and Judge Mishali) holding that the remedy the couple seeks is beyond the courts' prerogative, and the minority (female Judge Saviona Rotlevi) holding that "the best interest of the children" in this case demands the approval of the second mother adoption.[77] Confrontation of lesbian motherhood is present in another pending case, coming from an altogether different angle. That case concerns a lesbian woman's petition for visitation rights over a child born to her ex-partner prior to their breaking up, claiming to be a nonbiological mother. The biological mother's motion to the family court to dismiss the claim was rejected, as was her appeal on that decision; both the family court and the district appellate court saw the family court as the appropriate forum to decide the case since it involves custodian and visitation issues pertaining to the child and to the child's welfare.[78]

Legal developments regarding same-sex couples have taken place in the administrative arena as well. Thus, for example, in response to the a 1998 petition by the association for Civil Rights in Israel (ACRI), the Civil Service Commission adopted a new policy regarding beneficiaries' rights, providing cohabitants of deceased civil servants with beneficiaries' rights regardless of their sex.[79] Likewise, in early 2000 the Ministry of Interior awarded homosexual foreign partners of Israeli citizens resident status.[80]

It seems that the overall trend in Israeli society and in the legal system is toward growing recognition of gay and lesbian couples. Alon Harel has suggested that, ironically, it is Israeli society's conservative nature that has enabled these far-reaching developments, since "homosexuality was not perceived as a major threat to family values" (Harel 2000, 445). Following this line of thinking, the recent legal challenges on the family front do seem to pose such a threat. However, as one of the women who had gained the approval of the High Court of Justice to be registered as the child's second mother put it, when lesbian couples have children, they are welcomed to the Israeli society almost on an equal basis. Through reproducing, their union is being legitimized, and they are perceived as joining in with the national familial ethos.[81]

Parents and Children

Child Custody

The 1962 Legal Capacity and Guardianship Law,[82] which regulates issues of child custody, among other things, is a territorial law, meaning that it applies to all individuals notwithstanding their religious affiliation, and binds all judicial tribunals, religious or not. The law provides for equal responsibility of both parents toward their children and directs them to act in any matter "in the best interest of the child." Recognition of both parents as equal natural guardians of their children was already expressed in the 1951 Women's Equal Rights Law,[83] in an attempt to end the discriminatory treatment of Muslim women's rights toward their children upon termination of marriage, whether by divorce or by the husband's death.

Confirming the equality of both parents' guardianship over their children, the law, however, sets a "tender years presumption," imposing a rule of maternal preference whenever children under six are involved. Loss of maternal preference can occur under very rare and extreme circumstances of maternal unfitness. In general, most courts tend to favor maternal custody, even when older children are involved (Shifman 1995c). It is important to emphasize, however, that the rule of the best interest of the child is formally the governing norm in all cases, and the maternal preference is perceived to be just an implementation of this rule. Significantly, the evolution in the legal norms that eliminated maternal preference and replaced it by gender-neutral rules of custody that has taken place in most Western countries over the past few decades has skipped Israel, and the topic has never become subject to intensive public debate.[84] This remains the case despite the gradual increase in cases of divorce with children: from 45 percent of all divorces during the 1960s to over 66 percent during the 1990s (Katz and Peres 1996, 494). During 1999, the parents of close to 10,000 children in Israel (0.5 percent of all children in Israel) were divorced, making the average number of children per divorcing couple 2.0.[85]

Rabbinical courts may obtain jurisdiction in child custody cases through the "rule of attachment,"[86] which comes into play when either spouse sues for divorce, provided there is no prior motion for child custody in the civil court. Although rabbinical courts are equally bound by the law and by the best-interests-of-the-child principle embedded in it, child custody cases are in reality often among those that are the most difficult to resolve in terms of jurisdictional conflict. Rabbinical courts do not abide by the law's directives if these conflict with the courts' religious convictions. This may take place under circumstances in which one of the parents, usually the mother, is religiously defiant while the other maintains a religious lifestyle. Rabbinical courts have denied mothers under such circumstances custody over their children, phrasing their decisions in the "best-interests-of-the-child" terminology. The women's petitions to the High Court of Justice have usually been accepted.[87] Nonetheless, the potential for abuse of the rule of attachment is very high, and the incentive to present false indications as to a supposedly religious lifestyle is great.

Child Support

The 1995 Family Laws Amendment (Maintenance) Law[88] refers to an individual's religious law as the law governing child and spousal support. According to Jewish law, the major legally binding obligation for child support is over the father, while the mother only owes a residual duty of "charity," which is less binding. The scope of the father's primary obligation, however, is narrow and refers only to the very necessities of life. Once the child reaches age fifteen, the father's obligation also becomes one of charity and not law (Shershevsky 1993). Furthermore, a 1981 amendment to the law provides that the child support obligation on both parents be relative to each parent's income. In practice, civil courts usually hold the father responsible for a considerably larger portion of the child's estimated needs, unless the mother's economic situation enables her to contribute more, bearing in mind that it is ordinarily the mother, as the custodial parent, who tends to the child's everyday needs.[89] Several Supreme Court cases in recent years have raised the age of obligatory child support until the child finishes military or national service. The scope of the obligation, though, is to be about a third af the scope of the obligation toward children age eighteen.[90]

The problem of "deadbeat dads" is not unfamiliar in Israel. What is unique to Israel is the welfare system developed to ease the plight of women with children whose fathers default on their support payments, by assuring their minimum payment through the National Insurance Institute (NII). However, in 1998 the NII managed to receive only 43 percent of the total alimony payments from the debtors. While this welfare mechanism indeed alleviates some of the economic consequences of marital breakdown for women and children, the situation of divorced women with children in Israel is still poor, as detailed in Chapter 6. Some explanation for this may be found in the spousal support rules, to which we now turn.

Monetary Consequences of Marriage and Divorce

Spousal Support

Spousal support according to Jewish law, which controls this area according to the 1959 Family Laws Amendment (Maintenance) Law, strongly reflects the traditional patriarchal perceptions of gender roles. In principle, the husband is obligated to support his wife, while she, in return, is obligated to give him such services as housework and care of his children, in addition to such personal services as "making his bed and pouring his cup."[91] She must also give him monetary returns she may earn for doing work that is customary among women of her position to do. It is only under very rare circumstances, such as extreme gaps in economic status, that a woman would be obligated to support her husband, and even then her obligation would be considered "charity," with very weak powers of enforcement. The scope of the husband's obligation, on the other hand, is determined according to the standard of living the wife had enjoyed prior to the crisis, and according to the husband's economic potential. However, the evolving social norms regarding married women's work for wages were construed in such a way that any money the wife earns is to deducted from the amount of support. Consequently, in many cases where the wife's salary is not minimal she is advised not to sue for support, since the difference between her own earnings and the amount her husband would be obligated to pay her would not be worth the litigation involved.

There are several circumstances under which a woman may lose her right to be supported according to Jewish law, most of which arise out of "misconduct" on her part: refusal to engage in sexual relations with her husband, evidence of her "misbehavior" with other men, and any other deviation from the sexual code of conduct required of wives under Jewish law (Halperin-Kaddari 2000a). Another ground for losing her right to support is if she leaves the marital home with no justified reason. Determination of what counts as a "justified reason" is obviously value-laden and depends on the forum that hears the case. Thus, for example, a husband's violence toward his wife should unequivocally be perceived as a justified reason, and it is indeed so perceived by the family civil court. Rabbinical courts, however, may evaluate the circumstances differently, and accordingly arrive at different conclusions (Rosen-Zvi 1990). Under Jewish law, as well as under the supplementing provisions of the Family Laws Amendment (Maintenance) Law, spousal support is limited to the period of formal marriage alone, and there is no continuous support obligation whatsoever after divorce. There is no doubt that this lack of alimony after divorce greatly contributes to the grave economic consequences of divorce for women. This could have been redressed by adapting the division of property award to reflect husbands' usually greater earning capacity, which wives would no longer benefit from after divorce. Unfortunately, earning potential is not yet recognized by Israeli law as part of the marital assets in which both spouses have an equal share.

Distribution of Marital Property upon Divorce

Property distribution is the ultimate example of the civil system's attempts to narrow down the rabbinical system's law and jurisdiction, in order to improve women's position and oppose their discriminatory treatment under religious law. Rooted in social norms that are totally alien to contemporary times, Jewish law provides for most of the woman's property to be transferred to her husband, either to his ownership or to his management. Upon marital breakdown, the wife is only entitled to the property which she had brought into the marriage, in form or in value, but not to any assets that may have been accumulated in the husband's name during the marriage. She is also entitled to a specific sum of money to which the husband contracted upon her betrothal, known as the *ketubah* (Shershevsky 1993; Haut 1983). These rules carry devastating consequences in times where more and more women are left economically independent after divorce, when that independence is based on the intolerably small part of the formally joint property. Realizing this, and following the 1951 Women's Equal Rights Law, which (as interpreted by the court) practically annulled the husband's rule over the wife's property, the Supreme Court gradually drew the subject of marital property out of rabbinical and into civil law and jurisdiction.[92]

Distribution of marital property under Israeli law is governed by a shared as opposed to a separate property regime. There are, however, two parallel legal arrangements of that regime, due to delayed legislation that compelled the courts to provide solutions during the legislative vacuum. The first arrangement is the community property rule, developed in the Supreme Court's rulings since the early 1960s, which constructs a general presumption that both spouses have an equal share in the marital property. The trend in recent years has been to broaden the scope of shared property to include even "private assets" that belonged to either spouse prior to the marriage or that either spouse has inherited.[93] The second arrangement is the one included in the 1973 Spouses (Property Relations).[94] This arrangement applies to all couples married after 1974, and provides that the marital property (excluding "private assets") be equally divided on divorce or death, unless the couple expressly contracted otherwise and had their contract ratified by a family court, rabbinical court, marriage registrar, or notary. The judicial "community property rule" applies to all couples married before 1974 and to nonmarital cohabitants as well.

In principle, the rule of community property dictates equal sharing not only in property assets and rights, but also in debts and obligations, when these have accrued in relation to the communal property and are not personal in nature. So far the trend in case law has been to make it rather difficult for creditors to prove the communal nature of the debts. Under both arrangements the exact scope of the community property is not entirely settled. More specifically, the inclusion of assets that come under the definition of "the new property" (Glendon 1981) is still undecided (Mendelson 1995). Regarding such assets as pension rights, case law has made significant strides in the direction of their inclusion in shared property,[95] and they are routinely being distributed between divorcing couples just like traditional property as part of divorce agreements, on the basis of which most couples are divorced.[96] Regarding such assets as earning potential and goodwill, however, there is much more hesitation and even resistance from the courts. Nonconsideration of these factors has long been signaled as a prime cause for the disastrous economic consequences of divorce for women and children (Weitzman and MacLean 1991; McLindon 1987). Unfortunately, no empirical research has ever been conducted in Israel to ascertain the economic consequences of divorce, and it can only be assumed, in light of international research, that Israeli women fare worse. This is due to their weaker power regarding divorce, which is inherent in the Israeli legal system of divorce, and the lack of post-divorce alimony.

The Property Relations Law conditions property distribution on the end of the marriage, through either death or divorce, while the judicial rule of community property is not limited by any prior condition and could theoretically take place at any point during the marriage on either party's request. The law's conditioning of the property distribution upon prior divorce opens up the way for withholding the divorce in order to extract a better property settlement or draw other concessions from the opposing party. In light of the rules of divorce under Jewish law, the husband controls the divorce, and can therefore control and delay the property distribution by withholding the divorce (Rosen-Zvi 1990; Halperin-Kaddari 2000a). These observations obviously relate to the previous discussion of the *aguna* problem,[97] and add another distressing dimension to the structured possibility of extortion that is built into the rules of divorce under Jewish law and, apparently, is unfortunately fortified rather than rectified, under the civil legal system.[98]

Numerous bills to amend the distorted outcome of the law have been suggested through the years, proposing to separate the procedure of property distribution and the divorce. None passed as a law, mainly due to religious objection,[99] based on the fear that allowing for property division prior to divorce would encourage couples to be practically separated without arranging for the formal get. This, of course, could lead women who are still formally married, to engage in intimate relations with other men, and could result in creating a greater problem of *mamzerim.*[100] All these concerns were brought into the open by Chief Justice Shamgar in the 1995 Ya'acobi case,[101] which was supposed to end the disparity between the two legal arrangements of property distribution but only added to the confusion. Nonetheless, it seems that civil courts now tend to enable the distribution of property even prior to the divorce, despite the express wording of the law (Shifman 1996). This move will eventually result in subjecting all couples to the judicial rule of community property, bypassing the problematic arrangements of the Property Relations Law.

Property distribution could still come under the jurisdiction of the rabbinical courts if properly "attached" to a divorce suit.[102] Thus, women who were entitled to half the marital property according to the civil law were often left with nothing if their case reached the rabbinical court and all the family property was registered on their husbands' names. This, however, was changed in the 1994 precedent-setting Bavli case,[103] which not only applied the judicial rule of community property to religious courts but also subjected them to any and all principles of civil law beyond the specific matters of personal status, where religious law continues to govern (Halperin-Kaddari 1994, 1997a). While this decision has intensified the tension between the religious and civil system, it is doubtful whether rabbinical courts can abide by this ruling, and the race for jurisdiction will probably continue until the next intervention by the High Court of Justice (Shifman 1995b, 80; Halperin-Kaddari 2001, 146–53).

Names Law

Until 1996, Section 6 of the 1956 Names Law[104] stated that as a rule a married woman takes her husband's surname upon marriage, although she may keep her own name or add it to her husband's. In practice, however, women's names were automatically changed upon registration of marriage. In February 1996 the law was amended, and Section 6 now neutrally refers to both men and women. Upon marriage, a person may now retain his or her former name; choose the spouse's surname; add the spouse's surname to the person's former name, select a new surname identical to one chosen by his or her spouse, or add it to the former name. In addition, a provision that had previously mandated that a change in the surname of married couples be made by the husband and wife together, adopting only one new name, has been removed.

However, even when no budgetary concerns are involved, progressive laws are difficult to implement, and more than four years after the law was amended, regulations for implementing this reform had still not been promulgated. It is probably not irrelevant to mention that the Ministry of Interior is traditionally run by one of the religious parties, and regulations, obviously, are promulgated by the minister. It seems that once again, the High Court of Justice's intervention will be sought in order to enforce the legislation.

The law's 1996 amendment confirmed a 1993 case, *Efrat v. The Population Registrar*,[105] in which the Ministry of Interior was instructed to register the change of name of a woman to the surname of her nonmarital spouse. Justice Barak, who delivered the case, went into a long discussion about the legal and social attitudes toward nonmarital partnerships and concluded that it is in the public interest to encourage such forms of family life as equally important as "formal," legally married families.

As to children's surnames, Section 3 states that a child acquires his or her parents' surname. If married parents have different surnames, then, as a rule, the child acquires the father's, unless both parents agree that the child would acquire the mother's name or both names. This provision was not changed in the 1996 reform. Furthermore, a child born to unmarried parents acquires the mother's name, unless both parents agree that the child would acquire the father's name, or if the parents were living together as nonmarital cohabitants. This last point is strongly related to the next topic, that of single mothers.

Single Mothers

Economic aspects of single-headed families are discussed in Chapter 6, concentrating on their poor situation and on the welfare system's means to redress it. The Israeli legal system has indeed recognized the growing phenomenon of single-parent families, 95.6 percent of whom are headed by women (Eliav 2000), and accords them a variety of social benefits and aid. The proportion of single-parent families among all families is indeed growing fast, from comprising 8.9 percent of all families in 1993 to 11 percent in 1999. Moreover, the rate of their annual growth is four times larger than that of families in general (8 percent versus 2 percent respectively in 1998). The phenomenon of single-parent families headed by women is mostly the result of divorce (68 percent of all single mothers in 1999), then of widowhood (16 percent), and only marginally the result of choosing motherhood without marriage (16 percent of all single mothers in 1999). Nevertheless, single motherhood by choice may be slowly, but consistently growing: while in the late 1970s, births to Jewish single women comprised only 1 percent of the overall births, this rate was doubled in 1995, and by 1998 births to single women made up 2.5 percent of all births to Jewish women.[106]

The 1992 Single-Parent Family Law[107] expresses society's recognition of the special needs of these family units and tends to their economic and social welfare. It is doubtful, nonetheless, whether this expression can be said to reflect a complete recognition of single mothers and their children as normative families within the Israeli legal system and Israeli society. The most far-reaching precedent in terms of the concept of family as including single-headed families is a 1996 decision of the Haifa District Court regarding an internal dispute in a northern kibbutz over the question of eligibility to new housing units.[108] The district court voided a decision taken by the kibbutz members not to include a single mother with her minor child among the eligible member families, notwithstanding her seniority, since she and her child were not considered a "family." The court asserted that the single-parent family unit is as much a "family" as a two-parent family. Other expressions of the inclusion of single mothers and their children in the conception of the normative family are found in the context of access to new reproductive technologies: this can be interpreted as symbolizing the legitimization of single motherhood by choice.

New Reproductive Technology and Surrogacy

Along with Israel's familism comes Israel's pro-natalist ethos, which is reflected, for instance, in Israel's boasting a world record number of fertility clinics per capita and in generously subsidizing fertility treatments.[109] This "fertility ethos" has been critically observed by many scholars, pointing out the great pressure on women with fertility problems to endlessly try all the technology available, and to the media's role in celebrating women who strive to attain maternity (Solomon 1993). Recent legal developments have complemented this ethos, and along the way, have unexpectedly added to Israel's family law's patriarchal attribute.

The 1996 Surrogate Motherhood Agreements (Approval of Agreements and Status of Newborn) Law[110] made Israel only the third jurisdiction in the world, after the U.S. states of New Hampshire and Virginia, not only to positively sanction, but also to heavily regulate, surrogacy. Israel, though, is the only jurisdiction that regulates surrogacy through an administrative (and not judicial) organ (Halperin-Kaddari 1999). Following a 1992 petition to the High Court of Justice on restrictions posed by the Public Health In Vitro Fertilization Regulations (IVF Regulations),[111] a public multiprofessional commission headed by Justice Aloni was formed to consider all aspects of reproductive technologies in Israel and make recommendations for their regulation.[112] The only principle adopted from the commission's recommendations was the establishment of a statutory committee that would serve as a supervisory and approving medium for altruistic surrogacy. The basic principle enunciated by the law is that full surrogacy[113] is permitted only under very specific conditions. Furthermore, the whole procedure is legal only if a surrogacy agreement is approved by a statutory committee composed of seven members of relevant professions (physicians, social workers, and the like) and a religious official of the contracting couple's religion. The imperative substantive conditions, which are primarily based on halachic considerations, are that the surrogate be an unmarried woman (with provision for exceptions in rare circumstances); that there be no family relationship between her and the designated parents; that the surrogate's religion be the same as the designated mother's religion; and that the sperm be the designated father's sperm.[114] Apart from these religiously based restrictions, all parties to the surrogacy agreement must be of full age and residents of Israel, and the designated parents probably must be married, excluding nonmarital cohabitants.[115] The surrogacy agreement is approved only on a medical evaluation as to the inability of the designated mother to become pregnant or carry a pregnancy. The committee may approve monthly payments to the carrying mother to cover actual costs in addition to compensation for suffering, loss of time, income, or earning capacity, or any other reasonable compensation. No payment beyond this compensation is allowed.

The law, in principle, views the designated parents as the legal parents of the resulting child. To formalize this principle, the designated parents must apply for a "parenthood order" within a week of the child's birth (for circumstances and restrictions, see Halperin-Kaddari 1999). By October 2000, 26 babies had been born to 19 women who served as surrogates (including several pairs of twins), and two pregnancies were in progress.[116]

Incorporating halachic considerations into the social-legal arrangements of the new reproductive technologies has had some unintended patriarchal consequences to the detriment of women (Halperin-Kaddari 1999). This is particularly evident in the Surrogacy Law's mandating that the sperm used in surrogacy must always be the contracting husband's sperm, while no such requirement applies to the egg, which may originate from the contracting designated mother or may come from a donor, so long as it is not the surrogate's egg. In other words, surrogacy is not an option for those couples where the wife ovulates but is unable to carry the pregnancy and the husband is totally infertile. This distorted outcome conveys the message that genetic relation to the woman is not as important as genetic relation to the man. Even though this is certainly not the reason behind this specific arrangement—rather, it was prompted by a specifically stringent halachic opinion regarding the problem of *mamzerut*—I do maintain that preferring the stringent halachic opinion while disregarding its implication is in itself troublesome and is a reflection of the deeply engrained unconscious patriarchal values of Israel's society. The resulting arrangement is clearly geared toward facilitating reproduction, while safeguarding religious considerations but overlooking women's possible interests and concerns. This particularly difficult upshot comes on top of the significant fact that throughout the public debate that preceded the passage of this law, at no point was the option of prohibiting surrogacy altogether seriously contemplated. The Israel Women's Network (IWN) was the only voice heard backing this position, but it was virtually silenced within the official forums of the public debate, such as the Aloni Commission or the Knesset Welfare Committee who was in charge of preparing the law.

Non-Jewish Religious Systems of Family Law

References to social practices involving family structure and customs are also found under Chapter 12, as part of the general discussion of non-Jewish women.

Muslim Family Law

The position of Muslim women in Israel in matters of personal status is precarious on two main levels. Muslim courts, which held broad exclusive jurisdiction at all levels under Ottoman rule, maintained exclusive jurisdiction over all issues of personal status, including paternity claims spousal and child support, until late 2001.[117] Consequently, Muslim women have had fewer options than women of other religious groups for turning to the civil system. More substantially, in the Muslim courts themselves the status of women is undermined by the applicable law, the substantive Shari'a (Islamic) law, which is highly discriminating toward women (Layish 1995; Churi 1996; Abdo 1997). Application of the substantive law is heavily influenced by the patriarchal social structure and cultural norms of Arab society in Israel (Abdo 1997).

A trend similar to the one demonstrated above regarding the civil system's encroachment on the religious system's law and jurisdiction is also traced here.[118] While theoretically respecting the essential principle of exclusive jurisdiction, the civil system has worked—with mixed success—to influence and limit the bounds of Shari'a as it applies to Muslim Israelis. The process in this context, though, takes on a more complex angle, on top of the religious-secular confrontation: many have denounced the intervention of civil law into the exclusive realm of the Muslim courts as an example of national religious coercion, arguing that the Muslim system of law is dynamic and very efficient and must be left to its own creative devices. A typical opinion is that of Qadi Ahmad H. Natour, president of the High Shari'a Court of Appeal, who argued that both through judicial activism and through the guidelines and proclamations of the Shari'a Court of Appeals to the Shari'a courts, the Muslim court system in Israel has managed to "shake off the dust from the Shari'a rules and show to the extent to which the Shari'a religious laws are perceptive, far-reaching, and also substantive."[119]

Muslim law discriminates against women in marriage itself. While in effect the marriage of a Muslim man to a non-Muslim women is valid under Muslim law, a Muslim woman cannot marry a non-Muslim man. Moreover, the option of polygamy is available only to men, who may marry up to four wives (Layish 1995). But it is especially Muslim divorce law that is discriminatory toward women. While a man may divorce his wife of his mere volition simply by saying "talaq" (you are divorced), with no judicial intervention or supervision at all, this option is not available to women. Indeed, a Muslim woman may obtain divorce only through judicial decree, provided this option has been guaranteed to her in her marriage contract, and only on limited grounds such as the husband's marriage to another woman or his ceasing to provide for her. Israeli law has attempted to remedy these inequalities in marriage and divorce by criminalizing both polygamy and the talaq unilateral and unsupervised divorce. Although the secular legislature's intervention has indeed reduced the frequency of their occurrence, these practices are still common among Muslims, and the law that prohibits them is not enforced.

Discrimination in the area of marriage and divorce is complemented by discrimination in the area of parents and children law. Shari'a law, for instance, grants guardianship of children to the mother only until a certain age, after which the guardianship is transferred to the father. The 1951 Women's Equal Rights Law[120] had attempted to end this discrimination by designating both parents as equal guardians of their children. Concerning issues of paternity and unwed mothers, Muslim law traditionally recognizes no paternal ties between a child born out of wedlock and his or her father and thus denies the child of such an "illegitimate union" any rights deriving from this biological tie. While paternity has always been under the exclusive jurisdiction of Shari'a courts (and thus governed by Muslim law), a 1995 case[121] brought about a major change regarding the position of Muslim unwed mothers and their children. By introducing into Israeli jurisprudence the concept of "civil paternity"—namely paternity established upon biological-factual grounds and not determined by the marital status of the child's parents—the Supreme Court has opened the door to ordering a father to pay child support to children born out of wedlock. In a forceful opinion, Justice Heshin recounted the intolerable position of an "illegitimate" Muslim and based his disregard of the religious courts' exclusive jurisdiction on these matters on their refusal to grant the legal consequences of paternity to the child-father relationship as a refusal to exercise jurisdiction in that matter, thus allowing the secular courts to take the case.

In 1996 a coalition for Equality in Arab Women's Personal Status Laws, consisting of several Arab women's associations together with the IWN and ACRI, joined efforts to confer jurisdiction to civil courts, to parallel the jurisdictional choice Muslim women have in divorce disputes to that of Jewish women. These attempts have generated much opposition, mainly from Muslim religious leaders—all men. A typical reaction is that of Qadi Natour, calling it a "big mistake of almost historical proportions" and explaining that "the personal law is structured on the Qur'an and not on the personal opinion of one jurist or another from any particular historical period. Shari'a for Muslims is a part of their identity."[122] These last words reflect the crux of the matter. Struggling to advance the position of Muslim women in the area of family law is not just a struggle between the familiar progressive civil system and the patriarchal religious system, but also within the national political conflict in Israel. And that makes it a much more complex struggle. By the end of the 14th Knesset's term, the proposed reform passed first reading, and the 15th Knesset eventually passed it as a law in November 2001.[123] While this dramatic reform in Shari'a jurisdiction opens the way for Muslim women to turn to civil courts, it also opens a new "race for jurisdiction" similar to the notorious rabbinical-civil race. It also remains to be seen whether Muslim women are socially and politically able to use this new option.

Druze Family Law

Druze religious courts were established by the 1962 Druze Courts Act,[124] granting them exclusive jurisdiction over Druze marriage and divorce.

Other family matters are in principle under the jurisdiction of the civil courts, but Druze courts can in fact obtain jurisdiction over them by means of consent of all the parties involved. Besides setting up the court system and determining its jurisdiction, the 1962 law is also instrumental in making the Personal Status Law Relating to Druze, which originates in Lebanon, compatible to the guidelines of Israeli law. With respect to insuring the status of women, there have been far fewer clashes between Druze courts and Israeli secular legislature in comparison with those encountered by other religious communities in Israel. Druze religious family law is indeed far more progressive in terms of women's status. However, critics claim that Druze religious courts in Israel do not always adhere to the "pure" law, and that in practice they often apply prevailing custom, which is influenced by patriarchal social norms (Layish 1998; Sa'b 1998).

Contrary to both Jewish and Muslim laws, Druze law forbids polygamy. Furthermore, Druze law on divorce can be said to be "one of the most progressive in the Middle East."[125] It indeed confers women equal rights to divorce their husbands. Moreover, a woman has the right to distribute her property under a will, with complete testimonial freedom guaranteed. However, the Druze religious courts tend to reconcile the parties of a divorce procedure in order to give them the opportunity to reconsider, with the divorce being granted only when all attempts fail. This, in effect, almost always functions in favor of the husband. Indeed, it is the wife who mostly endures court pressure to give up on her dowry or other material benefits so that the divorce may be granted. Thus, despite the clear direction of Druze law in trying to promote the interests and status of women, the reality more often than not contradicts this theoretical egalitarian approach (Layish 1998; Sa'b 1998). Furthermore, with respect to children, the position of Druze women is far from progressive. The mother is regarded as the appropriate custodian only until her son reaches age seven, and her daughter age nine. After that, the father is obligated to take them. Moreover, the mother's custody over her children is conditioned upon her characteristics and behavior, and in reality she may lose her children upon remarrying, even if the remarriage is not religiously prohibited (Dana, forthcoming).

A new empirical study of Druze court files sheds more light on the reality of Druze family law (Dana, forthcoming). An examination of all divorce cases in one Druze court during 1983, 1988, and 1998 revealed that 81 percent of the divorces were uncontested. Of the contested cases, women initiated 12 percent of the proceedings, while men brought only 7 percent of the cases. In a different area, that of wills and inheritance, the study confirms the contentions of the gap between the progressive legal norm and its noncompliance. Of 60 inheritance cases in 1998, concessions on the part of the female heirs were made in 44. Thus, while the law grants equal inheritance rights, the social norms impel the women (daughters and widows of the deceased) to forgo their rights in favor of male heirs.

Chapter 12
Multiple Voices

Third-generation legal feminism incorporates into the feminist critique of law theories of multiplicities of voice, identity politics and postmodernism. Rejecting a monolithic portrayal of the "woman's point of view," scholars like Mari Matsuda and Kimberly Crenshaw demonstrated that much feminist legal writing was guilty of the same universal or essential outlook for which feminists had called liberal legalism to account (Matsuda 1989; Crenshaw 1995). In exposing the hegemonic perspective that characterized earlier feminist legal scholarship, third-generation legal scholars introduced the concepts of intersectionality and multiple discrimination. Women's identities are constructed of more than their sex or gender. Their race and class matter as well. Black women's experiences are different from white women's experiences. Likewise, Israeli Arab women's experiences are totally different from those of Jewish women, and Mizrachi women's experiences are different from those of Ashkenazi women.[1] Israel's society has always consisted of many groups, but their differences were ostensibly belittled and even denied under the myth of the "melting pot" in the case of Jews, or, for political reasons, in the case of non-Jews. It has taken several generations for Israeli society to accept the reality of multiculturalism, and it will take many more years before it can embrace and celebrate its variety and differences (Kimmerling 1998). In this chapter I hope to make a modest contribution to the creation of a more complex, nuanced, and critical analysis of Israeli society in general, and of the construction of women's roles in particular. This chapter, then, addresses different groups of women, who in one sense or another challenge the hegemonic perspective of the Jewish Ashkenazi woman.

The Israeli feminist movement has also had difficulty grappling with difference. The first Israeli women who developed a feminist consciousness and a commitment to feminist change belonged to the hegemonic Ashkenazi elite. They were aware of the need to assert that the Israeli

Woman must be seen as separate form, and in political conflict with, the Israeli Man; yet, at the same time, these same women glossed over the differences within the feminist "unity of women" (Dahan-Kalev 1999). It is only in the past few years that Israeli women have begun, tentatively and hesitantly, to deconstruct the term "Israeli Woman" and to address the intersections of religion, ethnicity, social class, sexual preference, and gender, and their implications. Thus, like its counterparts throughout the world, the Israeli feminist movement is beginning to cope with the inherent tension between universalism and particularism, between the universal woman and global feminism and the varied experiences of women within each society, and calls for the development of multicultural feminism have been emerging (Shadmi 1993; Eilam 1994; Shochat 1995, 1996).[2] These events are no doubt influenced not only by developments within feminism outside Israel, but also by the parallel process from collectivism to individualism that Israeli society is undergoing as a whole (Eisenstadt 1985; Mautner 1993, 122–41). Multicultural perspectives are also emerging on the national front. The feminist movement has been criticized for ignoring the plight of Arab Palestinian women within Israeli society. Multiculturalism also poses an appeal for cultural relativism. In other words, while multiculturalism has challenged the feminist cause to broaden its perspectives, it now poses a critical challenge to feminism by questioning its borders and daring it to be tolerant of cultural practices that might be inconsistent with cultural relativism.[3]

This book does not claim to reflect a pluralistic, multicultural perspective; like most works on women in Israel, it has been authored by a woman whose perspective is that of the hegemonic (Ashkenazi elite) Jewish perspective. Yet, consistent with a multicultural perspective, I do accept the premise that women from different communities face different problems and that these difficulties stem largely from different socially constructed positions and policies. This chapter describes several different populations of women in Israeli society. I have chosen to present these disparate groups of women together in this chapter for two reasons. All women whose lives are (however briefly and incompletely) described here experience multiple layers of marginality: as women in Israel; as members of deprived or minority groups in Israeli society, whose historical narrative and current story have yet to be included in Israel's hegemonic discourse; and, most of them, also as women within their own subgroup.[4] By their very marginality and difference, these women challenge the hegemonic dominant culture. By introducing new content into public discussion, by forcing awareness of their situation, they protest against the existing order (Shiran 1993, 304). Nevertheless, the discussion here is far from being exhaustive, not only within each group's story, but also with respect to groups who are absent from this chapter to begin with.

In the Introduction, I discussed the politics and power of information. Nowhere is this dynamic more obvious than in this chapter. There is a dearth of some types of information regarding specific disadvantaged groups, such as Bedouin, Druze, or Jewish Ethiopian women. I believe that this under-study reflects the social, political, economic, and even anthropological marginality and invisibility of these women. The implications of such invisibility are clearest when discussing policy formation. With little information and no gender perspective, there is no empirical basis for demands for legal, political, or economic reforms. I believe that the lack of comprehensive sociolegal research on women in Israel justifies a work that centers on the hegemonic group. However, by presenting an initial sociolegal assessment of the different groups within Israeli society, I simultaneously hope to challenge that very hegemonic perspective, and to point to areas where research, analysis, and understanding are lacking. Ten years ago, I believe, such a chapter would not have been written; five years from now, when such a chapter is written it will be fuller, richer, and more critical.

Jewish Women Challenge the Hegemonic Perspective

Mizrachi Women

The vast majority of Mizrachi Jews came to Israel in large immigration waves between 1948 and 1955. In the past, these immigrants were usually referred to as Sephardim, a historical term relating to the possible historical and geographical origins (Sepharad means Spain). The term "Mizrachi," which has come into use in the past few years, reveals a political awareness, including a deliberate emphasis on the opposition of "occident" to "orient." The very use of the term is thus not merely descriptive, but an assertion of legal, economic, and cultural rights, and a demand for recognition of the multicultural reality of Israeli society.

The Zionist ethos, associated with the Occident and modern nationalism, subordinated the Mizrachi Jews as a social-political entity to the secular, nontraditional, democratic, anti-Diaspora program for the formation of Israeli society. In this context, the Mizrachi entity is, and has been since the establishment of the State of Israel, the dominated, non-Israeli "other" (Ben-Rephael 1989; Peres 1977). The situation of Mizrachi women has paralleled the overall situation of Mizrachi Jews with regard to Ashkenazi Jews in general and Ashkenazi women in particular. Severe social stratification, economic and sociopolitical, has existed since the early years of the state, and all social indicators point to increasing gaps between the groups. The imbalance does not exist only at the socioeconomic level; it has been transposed into almost all organizational power relations, including those within the feminist movement's structure and discourse. Aware neither of their socially constructed power nor of its abuse, Ashkenazi women, the initial leaders of Israel's feminist movement, presumed to speak for the Israeli Woman, ignoring conflicts and contradictions between subgroups of women. Thus, they continued to subordinate or exclude all women who did not identify with or were not part of this view. Ashkenazi leaders of the feminist movement, in asserting their rights as women, denied feminists from other groups their "demand for their own right to individual conscience and judgment" (Dahan-Kalev 1997, 34). In a process that sadly resembles the experience of women of color within U.S. feminism, Ashkenazi women were aware of their own oppression by men but blind to their own oppression of Mizrachi women. Ashkenazi women leaders have failed to recognize that the circles of oppression surrounding Mizrachi women are wider than those surrounding men. Indeed, for many non-Ashkenazi or non-elite women, the direct experience of oppression comes not necessarily from oppressive men, but rather from a child's female teacher, the female (usually Ashkenazi) boss, the mother of the child she watches over, or the women in whose houses she cooks and cleans (Dahan-Kalev 1999, 245; Dagan 1996, 30; Shochat 1996).

The agenda of the Israeli feminist movement, contend Mizrachi feminists, reflects a lack of awareness and perpetuated discrimination. The Ashkenazi elite has tended to put issues such as lesbianism and Palestinian suffering, as well as issues related to middle- and upper middle-class women, before those of the root concerns of Mizrachi women. The right of women to be pilots, argue Mizrachi feminist activists, has nothing to do with the root concerns of Mizrachi women, which include low income and poverty, housing, education, and the sociocultural deprivation inherent in Israel's geographical periphery. Furthermore, by focusing on careerism as an expression of self and professional choice, feminists have ignored the differences in opportunities for education, personal fulfillment, and professional opportunities that divide women. Feminism in Israel, they accuse, has limited itself to one social class (Honig-Parnas 1996).

Parallel to the larger society, feminist organizations in Israel have been governed by the dominant, Ashkenazi sections of society, which control the economic, political, and social spheres and have made only limited attempts to include Mizrachi women in leadership roles (Dahan-Kalev 1997). Thus, most Mizrachi feminists have gradually been supporting separatist groups, asserting that, like women everywhere, women in Israel are simultaneously united as women and divided by ethnicity, class privilege, and prejudice within and across gender (Honig-Parnas 1996). At the 1994 Israeli feminist conference, an event in Israel, the reproduction of inequality became clear. Mizrachi women charged that they were expected to be obedient "followers" and were denied a chance to raise issues of concern specific to Mizrachi women; moreover, they accused, the Ashkenazi leadership expected them to lay down a feminist infrastructure at the grassroots level among their own ethnic group. Thus, the few Mizrachi women who were involved in the conference planning were held responsible when only limited numbers of Mizrachi women and when and when the issues they raised seemed irrelevant or politically incorrect to the sensibilities of Ashkenazi women. The resulting conflicts brought the tension between universalism and particularism to the attention of the feminist movement in particular, and Israeli society in general. As a result, Mizrachi feminist activists organized a separatist conference under the title "We Are Here and This Is Ours."[5] In recent years, the affirmation of a Mizrachi voice in the feminist movement has been stridently vocal (Dahan-Kalev 1997, 33), and several Mizrachi feminist grassroots organizations have been established to deal with the specific problems of Mizrachi women. HILA (Public Committee for Education), for example, is an organization devoted to improving neighborhood schools, empowering families in their dealings with the educational system, and reducing the disproportionate numbers of Mizrachi children referred to special educational programs and projects.

In the Introduction, I discussed two parameters of analysis. The first reflects the basic quality of women's lives, including their life expectancy, maternal and infant mortality, levels of literacy, marital age, and so on. With regard to this parameter, most statistical studies of Jewish women reveal few differences between Mizrachi and Ashkenazi women. There are however, great differences on the second, more complex and also more telling parameter—participation of women in public life and in the workplace, wage equity, educational opportunities, and so forth—analogous to the general ethnic gap within the Jewish population. Gaps between the two population groups point to a clear, persistent, and growing advantage of Ashkenazi men over Mizrachi men and of Ashkenazi women over Mizrachi women. De jure, Mizrachi women do not face any unique or particular impediments to equality that do not similarly impede the path of other Jewish women. Yet this is where the compound discrimination comes into effect. Furthermore, recalling the information story, there are many areas in which no specific data about Mizrachi women exist. In other words, very often there is no statistical intersection of ethnicity and gender, as data are segregated either by gender or by ethnicity, in perfect demonstration of standpoint feminism's claims.

The following socioeconomic data reveal only part of the story, but they are in themselves quite striking. In 1992, the average income of a Mizrachi Jewish employee was only 68 percent of an Ashkenazi employee's income. While the average income of Ashkenazi women reached 49 percent of Ashkenazi men, Mizrachi women's income reached only 39 percent (Haberfeld and Cohen 1995). In 1997, an Ashkenazi employee earned 1.6 times more on average than a Mizrachi employee (Swirski, Konor, and Yechezkel 1999a, 8), and these wage gaps are widening (Cohen 1998). In 1999, 51.5 percent of Ashkenazi families but only 37.9 percent of Mizrachi families had only one child; 4.8 percent of Ashkenazi families but 11.7 percent of Mizrachi families had between four and five children.[6]

In 1999, 74.7 percent of Mizrachi women had completed only 12 years of school or less compared with only 50.4 percent of Ashkenazi women; 16.1 percent of Mizrachi women had finished 13–15 years of education and only 9 percent had completed 16 years or more, compared with 23.9 percent of Ashkenazi women and 25.7 percent respectively of Ashkenazi women.[7] In 1999, the percentage of Mizrachi men in academic professions (that is, requiring an academic degree) was 6 percent, less than a third of the percentage of Ashkenazi men—19.4 percent. Notably the gap between the women was smaller; Mizrachi women working in academic professionals composed 17.6 percent compared with 24.4 percent of Ashkenazi women.[8] Furthermore, Mizrachi students composed only 25 percent of all Jewish students, while their rate within the age group twenty to twenty-four was 46 percent. Notably, Mizrachi women's rate among all Mizrachi students was higher than that of Ashkenazi women: 57 percent and 52 percent respectively.[9]

Lesbian Women

Lesbian activists point to the unique pressures felt by lesbians within Israeli Jewish society, particularly the pressure to be heterosexual mothers. Most scholars point to history and Jewish religious tradition as the sources of this, citing the Holocaust and Israel's repeated wars as well as Judaism's well-delineated gender roles. Jewish tradition emphasizes the importance of marriage and procreation, with an extreme rejection of homosexuality as "an abomination" (Oppenheimer 1993). Within society, homophobic attitudes as well as social norms encourage women to find their identity, security, and social role in marriage. Lesbianism challenges the traditional definition of gender role expectations by challenging the necessity for a male counterpart; it also challenges the traditional patriarchal assumptions of male supremacy (Oppenheimer 1993). An interesting collection of personal stories of Israeli lesbians appeared in 1995 (Moore 1995). Significantly, while many contributors to the volume identified themselves in full, the volume was published in London, in English. This can be taken as symbolically implying that such exposure is still easier, and perhaps more welcome, far from home.

The political and social visibility and assertiveness of Israel's lesbian community has grown consistently in the past twenty-five years. The Society for the Protection of Personal Rights, for both gays and lesbians, has been active since 1976, and led a successful battle for the decriminalization of homosexuality in 1988 (Yonay 1998; Harel 2000). In 1986, lesbian activists established CLAF (Community of Lesbian Feminists). Today it is a vocal, well-organized representative organization that maintains connections with allied and related international NGOs. CLAF publishes a regular newsletter.[10] Championed by MK Yael Dayan, who is also head of the Knesset Committee on the Status of Women, gay rights organizations including CLAF have produced several seminal public events that have been well covered by the media, including a successful protest of an attempt by Israel's national TV to censor or cancel a program dealing with teenage homosexuality.[11] Homophobic comments by public figures or in the media are almost immediately countered by spokespersons for CLAF and the Society for Protection of Personal Rights, as well as by numerous others who have not identified themselves as members of the gay or homosexual community. In addition to a hotline and mutual consciousness-raising and support, representatives of CLAF frequently lecture to schools and youth groups regarding individual rights and sexual differences. Members of CLAF have organized a feminist lesbian theater group and workshops for social workers, teachers, and others.[12] An important initiative by CLAF was a 1999 publication in Hebrew of a reader containing translation of several classic writings on homosexuality and lesbianism, in relation to homosexual adolescents as well as couples and parenthood. The editors of the reader emphasize the acute need for Hebrew materials for professionals, for parents, and for the homosexual community itself (Baum and Maran 1999).

Increasing individualism, concomitant with growing acceptance of individual human and civil rights, have led to increased recognition of the validity of alternative assertions of self. Also, although it is still politically powerful, it would appear that the religious establishment has lost much of its ability to set social norms for the secular majority of Israeli society (Yonay 1998). In the Israeli armed forces, no laws or regulations discriminate against gays or lesbians; in fact, several high-ranking, well-known and well-regarded officers, including a former (now deceased) chief medical officer, have been openly gay.[13] Given the social impact and importance of the IDF, this has contributed significantly to an amelioration of homophobic attitudes. Since most legal issues involving the gay and lesbian community in Israel have mainly concerned legal battles involving lesbian motherhood and families, they are discussed in detail in Chapter 11. One of the conclusions there, relying on the impressive legal achievements in the area of reproduction, was that lesbian mothers are more readily accepted in Israeli society with its familial ethos.

Immigrant Women from Ethiopia

During the 1980s, Israel absorbed immigrants from two main countries: Ethiopia and the former Soviet Union. The 50,000 Ethiopian immigrants have called for special attention in Israeli and Jewish consciousness because of their difference and the heroic operations taken to achieve their immigration.

Several factors have joined in forming the condition of the Ethiopian women immigrants: the general condition of women in Israeli society, the immigration process and difficulties in the transition into Israeli society; and above all the culture gap between Ethiopian and Israeli societies.[14] The family structure in Ethiopia was traditional and patriarchal, with a set hierarchy and strict rules. The division of labor between man and woman was clear, with men controlling the household financial resources, making decisions, and being the sole providers and family representative. Handicrafts such as weaving and pottery were mainly done by men. Women were responsible for the household, raising the children, and assisting the men in working the land. Certain social arrangements in Ethiopia, however, were intended for the protection of women's rights, some of which have been lost during the absorption into Israeli society. These included preserving the woman's maiden name after marriage; equal right in acquiring aid from the community during a marital dispute; equal right to divorce; right to have a resting period during menstruation and after birth. Furthermore, every woman in Ethiopia had one or two "protectors," usually her husband's friends, who were in charge of protecting her from being hurt by her husband.

The majority of Ethiopian Jews did not take part in the educational system in Ethiopia. Among the few who did, women were a minority. Once in Israel, the condition of the younger women differs from that of the older women, in that they participate in various educational institutions. The dropout rate is higher among men than women in all the educational institutions. In high schools, the dropout rate among the Ethiopian community as a whole (6.2 percent) is higher than among the Israeli population (3.5 percent), and the boys' dropout rate is more than double that of the girls (9 percent and 3.5 percent respectively) (Lifshitz, Noam, and Habib 1998, 55).

The role changes within the family that took place upon immigration to Israel are a source of tension in the home. Generally, the men are threatened by these changes which signify loss of their previous uncontested control, and they try to preserve the previous family structure, whereas the women are interested in adopting the new changes. When conflicts arise, women more than men tend to find aid in the social institutions in Israeli society. These institutions represent equal rights for both sexes and are run mostly by women. The men prefer to seek aid in the traditional manner by turning to mediation by relatives and elders who represent the traditional Ethiopian social order and are run by men. There is a relatively large number of Ethiopian single mothers, a phenomenon that did not exist in the community in Ethiopia. Divorced or widowed women in Ethiopia would go back to their original families. In Israel, the original families are financially incapable of absorbing the single women. In addition to financial and parental difficulties, these women are exposed to harassment by men from the community, including their former husbands.[15]

One of the most important parameters measuring the success of an immigrant community is its integration into the workforce. Several studies were conducted by the Brookdale Institute during the 1990s to evaluate this. These studies were conducted among men and women of various ages who had participated in various studies and job-training programs offered to Ethiopian immigrants by the Brookdale Institute. The studies were conducted as a tool to measure and evaluate the effectiveness of the different programs.[16]

Many efforts are invested in vocational training for Ethiopian immigrants in order to equip them with the knowledge and skills needed in Israeli industry. Special programs are geared for adults, with emphasis on job training, and for youth, with emphasis on both job training and social integration. Allocation of vocational training resources is problematic in terms of women's participation, since state-funded professional job training is given to the family member who is regarded by the authorities as the family provider. In most cases, the family representative and provider is male, thereby leaving the female under his patronage. Furthermore, vocational training is characterized by a sex-biased occupational division. Study programs in absorption centers offer different workshops for men and women. Women are offered workshops training them for domestic occupations such as childcare and house chores, whereas men are trained for occupations outside the home. Nevertheless, where there are no male family members, female immigrants receive equal job training (Hertzog 1998).

Finally, one aspect seems to be completely changed since emigration to Israel. In an academic study published in 1997, Ethiopian Jewish women immigrants to Israel reported that ritual female genital mutilation (FGM) was normative in their culture in Ethiopia, but expressed no desire to continue the custom in Israel (Grisaru, Lazer, and Belmaker 1997). The study reports the total cessation of the custom among this community after immigration to Israel.

Non-Jewish Women

Non-Jewish women must simultaneously deal with both aspects of their marginality: the national, political, social, and cultural oppression they feel they experience at the hands of the Israeli majority and their inferior status in Palestinian society.[17] Furthermore, as some have noted, the two may be connected: having lost control over their land and status in the 1948 war for Israel's independence, only one domain remained for Palestinian men to dominate — their families. Thus, these two dimensions of marginality may be inextricably linked, and for Palestinian women, national and social liberation may be very closely interrelated (Hasan 1993). The Israeli Declaration of Independence, which promises not to discriminate according to age, sex, religion, or nationality, ostensibly guarantees equal rights to Israeli Palestinians. Yet, as I discuss below, they face a wide array of formal, as well as informal, laws and regulations, and both de jure and de facto discrimination.

Non-Jews comprise 21 percent of Israel's population,[18] and they have higher birthrates and larger percentages of young children. When discussing the Palestinian population in Israel, it is important to distinguish between urban and rural dwellers. Palestinian urban women consistently enjoy a more prominent status in most realms of life than do those who reside in villages. However, it is similarly important to note that over 90 percent of Israeli Palestinian women live in villages (Fares 1996). Most Arab villages are located at Israel's geographic periphery, far from the centers of economic activity. In the past, agriculture was an integral source of income for Palestinian villages; this meant that women played a leading role in the economy while maintaining their traditional roles as housewives. However, due to the expropriation of farmlands and the overall decrease in the viability of farming in Israel, the main economic focus of the villages has shifted to employment in the cities, leaving a vacuum for Arab women. While many village men moved into the modern work sector, the women were not allowed to and did not leave their traditional roles. Thus, women remained at home, assuming a consumptive rather than a productive role, with little or no tangible compensation (Fares 1996, 3–5).

Following the two parameters I delineated in the Introduction, it is necessary to state that gaps exist between Jewish and non-Jewish women not only on the more complex parameters such as participation in the workplace, wage equity, and educational opportunities, but even at the basic levels of life expectancy, maternal and infant mortality, literacy, marital age and so on. These gaps have already been described throughout many chapters in this book. Perhaps most strikingly, according to the National Insurance Institute, over 21 percent of the poor families in Israel are non-Jewish, almost double the rate of non-Jewish families within Israeli families in general.[19]

Indeed, the basic health parameter is a significant variable informing Palestinian Israeli women's lives in Israel. Prior to the enactment of the 1994 National Health Insurance Law,[20] nearly a third of the Arab villages lacked health clinics altogether or were severely underserved. For example, in the Palestinian city of Um al-Fahem, with a population of 27,000, the General Health Fund provided only one gynecologist for its 18,000 members. Under the current health law, the government has adopted the policy of encouraging the Health Funds to accept members who live in Israel's peripheral areas, such as Um al-Fahem. This policy is meant to bring about a significant improvement in the health services provided to women.[21] Indeed, a greater proportion of Arabs (71 percent) than Jews (34 percent) perceived an improvement in Health Fund services following the new health law. Furthermore, in 1997 nearly all the Arabs (99 percent) reported having a regular family physician, an impressive increase from 63 percent in 1995 (Farfel and Yuval 1999). However, in 1998, on almost all measures of women's health, Palestinian women did not fare well when compared to their Jewish counterparts. Palestinian women have a life expectancy of 77.7 years, as compared to 80.7 years for Jewish women.[22] In 1997, eight of the nine municipalities with the highest infant mortality rates were municipalities in which the majority of the population was Palestinian.[23] Overall, in 1999 the infant mortality rate for Jews was 4.9 and for Palestinians 9 per 1,000 live births.[24] In terms of comparative birth rates, the general decrease and its extent are described in Chapter 4. Among Palestinian women themselves, a study conducted in 1996 reveals a negative correlation between fertility rate and educational advancement and a positive correlation between number of years between births and the level of education (Sabatello, Adler, Shtarkshall, and Peritz 1996). In 1999, the fertility rate among village women was 6.71, compared to 3.84 among city women. Arab women of Jerusalem were found to be exceptional in terms of this correlation, and their fertility rates (4.15) were significantly higher than the fertility rates in other Arab cities.[25]

The JDC-Brookdale 2000 study gives further evidence to Palestinian women's poorer health conditions (Gross and Brammli-Greenberg 2000). Higher rates of Arab women said that at least once during the previous year they had not received medical care when they believed they required it (41 percent, compared to about 10 percent among Jewish women); had not seen a specialist when they believed they needed it (57 percent versus 20 percent); and had not bought medication due to cost (29 percent versus about 15 percent). A higher proportion of women with a high level of depression exists in the Arab sector (45 percent of Arabic-speaking women interviewed,[26] compared to 34 percent of the survey's Hebrew-speaking subjects). Moreover, 39 percent of Arabic-speaking women suffering from a high level of depression were not diagnosed as such by a physician (compared to 28 percent of Hebrew-speaking women). In general, Arab women express a relatively low level of appreciation for their doctors and visit them less often than do Jewish women; 64 percent of the Arabs saw a gynecologist regularly, compared to 83 percent of Jewish women. Most of the Arab women (60 percent) preferred a female gynecologist, compared to 33 percent of the Jewish women. However, an astoundingly low percentage of Arab women are treated by female doctors (8 percent), compared to 49 percent of Jewish women. Among Arab women, 22 percent (versus 8 percent of Jewish women) do not feel comfortable talking to their family doctor about issues relating to their health.

Another major factor in Palestinian women's position in society is their presence in the labor market: while women's participation in the workforce reached 47.3 percent in 1999,[27] Arab women's reached only 24 percent.[28] According to traditional Palestinian norms, village women are largely confined to their homes; moreover, since a husband's authority is manifested and maintained by his ability to control the family finances, many men do not allow their wives to work outside the home. In the villages, especially in large families, single women are considered an integral source of income to the family, but are expected to donate their entire salaries to their families. In upper-class sectors of Palestinian society, the degree of independence a single woman enjoys is directly related to her parents' status and their attitude toward their daughters as autonomous beings. Thus, while both upper-class and lower-class single women work out of the home, upper-class women do so because of positive attitudes toward their abilities and roles as workers, while lower-class women are employed strictly for financial reasons. Single women of both groups enjoy a greater degree of freedom than their married counterparts (Fares 1996, 23). Statistics clearly reflect that labor force participation of Palestinian and Druze women peaks at ages eighteen to twenty-four, then declines with marriage and/or the birth of a first child. However, it is not just cultural and social internal norms that hamper Palestinian women's entry to the workforce. The local social and economic infrastructure in Palestinian villages has also had a deleterious effect on the scope of women's employment opportunities. The Palestinian villages are usually satellites of nearby Jewish cities and villages from which the Palestinians receive their goods and services. Consequently, these villages have not developed their own commercial centers or institutions, which would provide jobs, particularly for the female workforce. Most of the industrial ventures within the villages are small private ventures, which cannot absorb significant numbers of workers (Fares 1996, 7). Furthermore, many Palestinian women, especially older, less educated rural women, are not fluent in Hebrew, which further limits their employment opportunities (26).

The quoted formal employment statistics are somewhat misleading, as many women, in particular women from the villages, do not register at the Employment Bureau and consequently neither appear in these statistics nor receive unemployment benefits. Furthermore, among the working women, many work in the informal sector, primarily in the textile industry, for less than the minimum wage (Chen 2000, 3). They are thus vulnerable to long-term unemployment as the Israeli economy becomes increasingly high-tech and sophisticated and unskilled labor requirements are exported to the surrounding poorer countries. There is also evidence that young Palestinian girls, aged twelve and thirteen, are illegally employed in sweatshops and seasonal agricultural work (Morcos 1999).

The conditions of Arab (Palestinian Israeli) women who work for wages outside their homes are far from satisfactory. A 1998 survey on the conditions of women working in the private section in Nazareth, the largest employer for Arab women, revealed that 61 percent of the women were paid less than the minimal wage, 72 percent had no legal contract, and only 35 percent received overtime payment. When asked what and how much the minimum wage was, only 30 percent of the women could answer correctly.[29] These are all characteristic of the informal employment sector. Furthermore, research on the connection between place of inhabitancy and salary levels, based on Central Bureau of Statistics data from 1997, revealed that among the 72 percent of the municipalities and townships in which women earned less than the general average wage earned by women (75 percent of the average wage earned by men), all 71 Arab municipalities and townships were included (Swirski 2000, 4).

Much of the information concerning Palestinian women in Israel is covered in the previous chapters. For this reason I do not discuss education here, except for one point, which I think sheds a pessimistic light over the relative progress of Palestinian students noted in Chapter 5. According to a 1999 Sikkuy (A Chance) Association report, the rate of Arabs among academic staff, which numbers approximately 5,000 people, is extremely low, as only 50 (1 percent) Arabs are members of the academic staff.[30] In light of this reality, a special Program (Maof) has been set up to encourage the promotion of young outstanding scientists within the Arab Israeli sector, with the explicit intention of integrating them within academia at the rank of lecturer, including three years financing and a commitment of permanent integration into the standard framework. During the six cycles of the program since 1996, there have been 36 candidates and 26 admissions—only four of them women.[31] This is indeed a discouraging figure. As women academics also serve as role models and as agents of change, there is little hope for further progress when they are so few.

Lastly, there is the painful subject of violence against women. Palestinian feminist scholars have internally described the Palestinian society as a "dense network of webs, whose purpose is to reproduce the patriarchal social system. This network will be woven and expanded into a tangle of bonds and chains, which will condition and shape her spirit, supervise her education and rearing, and transform her into one of the mainstays of the patriarchy" (Hasan 1993, 66). Palestinian society is characterized by sharp gendered divisions and imposes social norms of modesty, reticence, sexual "purity," and self-negation on women. The patriarchal structure of Palestinian society is translated into cultural, legal, and sociopolitical practices that disempower women, subordinate them, and weaken their status (Shalhoub-Kevorkian 1997).

This inferior status is clearest in Palestinian tradition of "family honor," meaning that a Palestinian man's honor resides in the body of his wife, daughter, or sister. All women must follow certain rules of behavior, which are subject to the discretion of their male relatives. These rules are interpreted subjectively by each family. A woman who is perceived by her family to have violated this code is subject to punishment, which varies at the discretion of the male relatives. Punishments can range from locking a woman at home to insulting and beating her to murder. Furthermore, if anything happens to the women, it is deemed not to have affected her personally, as she is no more than a receptacle for the honor of her family (Hasan 1993, 1999). Thus, murder for "family honor," states an inter-ministerial report, is legitimized and the murdered woman is considered responsible for her own death (Inter-Ministerial Committee, 1998, 112). According to Palestinian activists, at least 50 women were murdered in the name of upholding their "family's honor"during the 1990s.[32] No official data exist on this issue. Furthermore, Palestinian feminist activists have contended that the dominant Jewish culture has collaborated with the patriarchal leadership of the Palestinian community, gaining support or acquiescence of Palestinian men through their agreement not to disrupt "cultural norms." Palestinian women thus become pawns in a political conflict which they have no power to influence (Hasan 1999).

Traditional marriage patterns add to the women's vulnerability. Nearly 47 percent of marriages within the Palestinian population are among relatives, often for the purpose of maintaining ownership over land (Morcos 1999). Furthermore, although Israeli law forbids marriage of a minor until age seventeen, in many cases girl-child marriages are arranged by male relatives who simply do not register the marriage with the Ministry of Interior until the child is of age. As noted above, all issues of "personal status" are under the sole jurisdiction of the respective religious courts, and the implications for Jewish women have been detailed. The religious tenets are unequivocal regarding women's principal roles as mothers and wives; and, in addition, the religious prohibition of extramarital sexual relations leads to the adoption of extremely stringent familial, cultural, and social sanctions regarding daughters (Shalhoub-Kevorkian 1997).

Until recently, there were few data available regarding the extent of violence against women within the Palestinian community. Palestinian women are loath to report such violence. Often, the reporting itself can cause the violence to escalate. Furthermore, many women, especially those who are less educated, do not feel capable of turning to the dominant, Jewish, authorities. In addition, some of the provisions that serve other women well do not provide adequate recourse for Palestinian women. For example, as noted above, the law provides for restraining orders against husbands who are suspected of abusing their wives or families. Yet, in the Palestinian community an overwhelming percentage of women live with their husbands' families, often in the same house. Needless to say, this often creates an untenable situation for the abused women (Shalhoub-Kevorkian 1997). Here too the JDC-Brookdale 2000 survey serves as an unprecedented source of information (Gross and Brammli-Greenberg 2000). The survey confirms previous estimations and concludes that the rates of domestic violence incidents are highest within the Palestinian population (17 percent, compared to 14 percent within the Jewish sector). Furthermore, Palestinian women are less likely to discuss domestic violence incidents with medical professionals. Indeed, very few Palestinian women turn to help centers, as reflected in their data: in 2000, for instance, only 199 Palestinian women did so, a mere 2.8 percent of all applicants that year.[33] Official police data also show the relatively low rate of Palestinian complainants on domestic violence against women.[34] Thus, for example, in 1999 Palestinian women's complaints constituted only 12 percent of total complaints of domestic violence against women (an increase from 10 percent in 1996l. Interestingly, the rate of increase was higher among Palestinian than among Jewish women: 1.35 and 1.1 between 1996 and 1999).

Since January 1999, the police have adopted a policy of hiring Arabic-speaking female investigators in areas where there are large concentrations of Palestinians, to work with women who do turn to the police; however, not all posts have been filled.[35] There is currently one shelter for battered women in the Palestinian sector and another in formation. The shelter accepted 82 women with 167 children during 1998–99, but 139 women were turned away for lack of space.[36] The existing shelter is fully paid for by the national budget and run by a nonprofit feminist NGO. In addition, the state provides shelter and transitional apartments for girls and adolescents. Feminist activists maintain several Arabic-speaking hotlines for adolescents, rape victims, victims of spouse abuse, and so on.

Due to the intricate relationship between religion and cultural, socioeconomic, and political status, I discuss two Arab subgroups, the Bedouins and the Druze, separately.

Bedouin Women

Approximately 100,000 Bedouins live in the southern Israeli desert (Negev) region. Half of them live in one of seven Bedouin towns that were officially founded and recognized by the state; the remaining half are scattered across the desert, living in villages and seminomadic encampments. The authorities considered these "unrecognized" villages and encampments, in which nearly 50,000 Bedouin live on a permanent or semipermanent basis. However, due to the official Israeli policy to induce the Bedouin community to move into government-planned settlements, these communities are not accorded any official status: they are excluded from government maps, have no local councils, do not belong to other local governing bodies, and receive no government services such as electricity, telephone lines, water, educational facilities, paved roads, sewage facilities, or health services (Shamir 1999, 473–96).

Bedouin society is currently undergoing a severe cultural and political crisis. The government-sponsored transition of Bedouin communities from seminomadic lifestyles to permanent residences, together with exposure to the dominant, largely westernized Israeli society, have had extensive social, political, and economic effects on the Bedouin community and have weakened many age-old customs. As a result, the status of women is also undergoing a rapid change (Tal 1995). The weakening of traditional life has left a vacuum in the lives of Bedouin women that has yet to be filled by new forms of activity; the women are unequipped and unable to enter into the labor market, and the traditional forms of production are no longer relevant. They are unemployed and often unemployable, although they are not recognized as such and are not entitled to unemployment benefits. Women have thus undergone a transition from a productive to a consumptive role, leading to a gradual loss of respect and status in the family unit. Furthermore, in many instances a woman's education may be higher than that of her husband, and she may be the one who comes in contact with the surrounding, dominant, modern Jewish society. At the same time, she experiences tremendous pressures from the patriarchal society, which demands that she continue to maintain the traditional way of life (Abu-Saad 1995, 1996). This transitional state is evident in all spheres of women's lives, reflecting a dialectic process of hesitant progress (in education, for example), hampered by difficult, well-embedded traditional practices (for example, polygamous marriages).

The very basic health parameter is a firm indication of the Bedouin society's poor conditions. The strongest manifestation is perhaps the data on infant mortality, always much higher in the Bedouin community compared to the total rate in Israel. For example, in Rahat, the largest of the officially recognized Bedouin towns in the Negev, there were 12.1 deaths per 1,000 live births in 1996, compared to 4.5 among the Negev's Jewish population and the national figure, 6.3. Major causes of death of Bedouin infants were congenital anomalies (mostly attributed to marriages among relatives), premature births, respiratory distress syndrome, and infectious diseases.[37] From a broader perspective, a survey conducted by Ben-Gurion University researchers in 1999 among a representative sample of 202 Bedouin women (and a control group of 526 Jewish women) revealed higher rates of repetitive unitary tract infections, anemia, and respiratory disorders reported by Bedouin women, as well as higher rates of exposure to family violence. Likewise, more Bedouin women reported depression and low self-esteem, the former in connection to family violence and the latter in connection to a spouse's unemployment (36 percent of the Bedouin women reported unemployment of their spouses). The average number of children per Bedouin women who participated in the survey was 5.8, 14.4 percent were pregnant at the time, and 55 percent reported being pregnant the year before the survey. The average marital age was 18.6, 60 percent reported being married to a relative, and 35 percent reported being married in polygamous marriages.

Bedouin society's indigent state is further reflected through low participation in the labor force and high presence among welfare services recipients. The average monthly wage of a female Bedouin employee is only 50 percent of that of a Jewish female employee and 29 percent of a

Jewish male employee (a male Bedouin employee's monthly wage is 55.8 percent of a male Jewish employee).[38] The low per capita income in Bedouin families is reflected in the large number of recipients of income support benefits, almost six times higher than the national rate.

Taking all this information as background, let us now turn to the issue of education, both as an indication and reflection of the basic parameters and as a predictor of future direction. As indicated above, this subject demonstrates the dialectic process of progress and regression the Bedouin society is experiencing, particularly with respect to women's status. All Bedouin children are entitled, under the 1949 Compulsory Education Law,[39] to a public school education comparable to that provided throughout Israel. However, historically, schools were not widely developed in the Bedouin community as they did not fit the needs or patterns of the seminomadic way of life where literacy was not a priority; nor were national resources allocated to the needs of such unrecognized villages. Consequently, the Bedouin educational system did not develop at the same pace as the general Israeli educational system. Bedouin schools still have the highest dropout rates and the lowest levels of student achievement in Israel (Abu-Saad 1994, 1996). In general, six of ten Bedouin pupils in the Negev drop out of school, and only two per 1,000 Negev Bedouin have university degrees.[40]

The issue of girls' education is especially problematic. Given the expectation that girls will continue to carry out their traditional roles, together with the fact that families preferred not to risk their reputations by allowing their women and girls to travel alone and mix with men from other tribes, there was initially little interest in girls' education. The Bedouin community's outlook on women's education began to change as a result of exposure and interaction with both the modern Jewish community in Israel, and the Palestinian communities in the Occupied Territories. Still, the higher dropout rates for Bedouin girls remain a problem. Recent data show that throughout grades 1 through 9 the boys make up more than half (51.4 percent) of the total number of pupils, except in grades 4 and 8. In the ninth grade boys already make up 53.7 percent of the pupils. In the unrecognized localities the situation is even worse: girls make up only 43.7 percent of ninth graders.[41] However, there is some development regarding the Bedouin attitude to education, particularly to girls' education, so that experts now contend that most Bedouins believe in the importance of education and are not against educating their daughters. The problem is not attitude but economics, since parents are unable to finance their children's academic studies. Consequently, special programs to encourage Bedouin women into academic studies, such as one developed by Ben-Gurion University of the Negev, are of particular significance.[42] Some progress in t women's participation in academic studies can indeed be discerned. In 1998, four of eighteen Bedouin graduates were women, while until 1990 there was only one woman graduate of a total of thirty-eight.[43]

Rising educational levels always indicate progress and advancement, but within Bedouin society this might carry a double-edged effect. Higher educational levels do not necessary carry higher salary levels when there are little employment opportunities to begin with. Moreover, they may paradoxically hamper women's marriage opportunities and lead to educated women becoming second and third wives in polygamous marriages. Polygamy, although forbidden by Israeli civil law, is common among Bedouins. Bedouin men manage to circumvent the law by marrying one wife legally and the rest traditionally, later claiming the other wives to be maintained as "concubines." Sha'ria courts recognize the concubines as legal wives and grant them divorces as well (Al-Atawneh 1993). There is ample evidence that in recent decades polygamy has become more popular and more widely practiced. Exposure to Israeli society has encouraged Bedouin men to expect to marry partners who share their more Western outlook and posses a similar educational background. However, they still seek the traditional roles that they are accustomed to. Thus, men may choose to marry several women, in order to meet their contradictory expectations for both traditional and modern roles. A woman's educational level may also be a deterrent to marriage. Often, an educated woman is perceived as culturally undesirable because she has not maintained her traditional role as a woman; in fact, the woman's level of education may be a predictor of polygamous marriage. Often, an educated woman will also be married off as a second or third wife, although it would appear that her level of education serves as a positive variable in her status within the polygamous marriage. A study conducted in Rahat in 1993 revealed that the average marrying age of legal wives in monogamous marriages is 18.3 years. The average marrying age of the first wife in polygamous marriages is 20.5 and that of the other wives is 24 (Al-Atawneh 1993). Also in Rahat, while wives in monogamous marriages received an average of 4.4 years of education and additional wives in polygamous marriages received an average of 3.5 years of education, first wives in polygamous marriages were found to have received only 0.7 years of education on average. Education was found to increase self-esteem among Bedouin women in monogamous marriages, although educated women in polygamous marriages were found to be more frustrated by their marriage arrangements because of their awareness of their educational and professional potential.

Although data are scarce and incomplete, many experts have noted what may be a particularly high incidence of violence against Bedouin women (Inter-Ministerial Committee 1998, 100). Furthermore, the level of violence is significantly higher in polygamous than in monogamous families.[44] Formal social services are often located a great distance away, and many women are prohibited from even leaving their homes and encampments. Furthermore, the solutions which the laws against violence provide for battered women are largely inappropriate for Bedouin women who suffer from violence. If they were to take out a restraining order against their husbands, they would be socially, and perhaps physically, excommunicated; they could also be at risk for an escalation of the violence, and only a rare few have the skills to live in a transitional home by themselves in a city, or to escape to a shelter for battered women. A woman who runs away from her home and community may well be putting herself in danger; several cases of women who were murdered by their families after they escaped to battered women's shelters have been reported in the media (Inter-Ministerial Committee 1998).

Particularly sensitive and unattended to in terms of state policy is the issue of female genital mutilation. The subject is not officially addressed by police or legal authorities, or even by health authorities.[45] The existing information is based on independent academic research. FGM, traditionally referred to as "purification," has been found to be a normative practice in several Bedouin tribes in southern Israel. In 1992, 21 Bedouin women aged sixteen to forty-five years, from six different tribes, were interviewed regarding the FGM they had experienced. They reported that they, as well as their sisters and all the women in their close and extended families, had undergone FGM, usually between the ages of twelve and seventeen. Medical reports from examinations of thirty-seven women reveal that the FGM did not include clitoridectomy; however, all the women reported bleeding and pain at the time and three reported that they had required medical attention. All reported pain during intercourse. Yet most of the women interviewed said that they approved of the practice and intended to perform FGM on their daughters, usually under the pressure to maintain tradition. There is evidence that with education, support for the practice declines (Asali et al. 1995). The practice of FGM is "strictly a woman's issue," done in secrecy to women by women, with no involvement of men whatever. It has been described as "inextricably associated with key Bedouin-Arab construction of womanhood" (Al-Krenawi and Wiesel-Lev 1999, 433). Another study was conducted in 1998 to find out the attitudes toward and the perceived psychosocial impact of the practice upon women who have undergone FGM. The researchers interviewed twelve women who had experienced the ritual, and twelve who had not. The ritual was performed without preparation, under poor medical conditions, and without anesthetics. One of the most striking findings is that "feelings of fear, shame, and helplessness are created out of this experience, even among those . . . who spoke positively about the value of their circumcision" (Al-Krenawi and Wiesel-Lev 1999, 438). The researchers rightly contend that this subject "cannot be addressed merely as a 'feminist issue'" (Al-Krenawi and Wiesel-Lev 1999, 440), but is a human rights issue. It seems that the lack of official policy toward the phenomenon and the lack of response to inquiries[46] indicate a sense of indetermination on the part of the government. A major cause for this indetermination is probably the familiar feminist-multicultural dilemma, often attributed to these kinds of cases,[47] where the problematic, offensive, and dangerous practices occur in the context of cultural and religious custom. However, as a dangerous health practice, which is also life threatening, it is wrong to address this particular ritual in this theoretic context, and the government should fulfill its duty to protect all its citizens from bodily mutilation, according, for example, to CEDAW and to the World Health Organization's decisions.[48]

Druze Women

An insular, small (less than 100,000) community comprising only 1.6 percent of the total Israeli population, the Druze live in villages in the northern part of the country, mainly in mountainous regions. Although popularly considered part of the general "Arab" (that is, non-Jewish) population, they in fact adhere to a distinct religion, carry a different history, and maintain different social norms and practices. The precepts of their religion, however, are kept in secret (Saleh 1998, 35). Their association with the larger Muslim society stems in part from one of their principles of conduct, the *taqiyya*, which has been described as "concealment of the Druze religion and Druze beliefs; outward acceptance of the religion within whose orbit one lives; going along with the dominant majority; sitting on the fence or adopting a neutral position . . . (in political matters) if possible, and if not, joining the side which seems likely to win" (Layish 1985, 246). This principle also seems to explain the fact that in contrast to other non-Jewish minorities in Israel, Druze males serve in the Israeli army.

Partly as a result of these factors, research on the Druze community in general and Druze women in particular is quite scarce. The small size of the community and the lack of cooperation on its part have made it difficult to conduct fieldwork and empirical research, and the secrecy surrounding its formal structure has only recently began to fade. Thus, the information problem is strongly evident here. While anecdotal information can be found in the personal impressions of the few research workers who have connections in the community and from occasional media coverage, it can hardly be substantiated by concrete data and empirical research. For example, the only statistical information relating to women with specific reference to Druze as a special category, and not as part of the "Muslim," "Muslims and Others," or simply "Others" population groups, has to do with marriage patterns and fertility rates.[49] Otherwise, no formal statistics exist with separate reference to such parameters as women's health, education, exposure to violence, or participation in the workforce.

Notwithstanding these reservations, the fading of the veil of secrecy from Druze religion and law enabled a closer examination of women's legal status as reflected in the Druze family law. After conducting a thorough research of the legal norms and their implementation by the Druze religious courts, law professor Aharon Layish concluded that "The Druze family is subject to tensions . . . which originate from an almost unbridgeable gap between a surprisingly progressive legal norm and a conservative customary one" (Layish 1982, xviii). Druze formal law indeed puts women in a much better position than do most religious legal systems, but, as we saw in chapter 11, the formal law is often circumvented by custom, as courts tend to preserve the pattern of the "patrilineal, patriarchal, and patrilocal" extended family (Layish 1982, xix). Likewise, beyond the area of family law and family life, Druze women have in practice few social or political rights within their community, notwithstanding their theoretical equality with respect to religious practice and opportunity for religious leadership roles (Dana 1998b, 47). Women are generally expected to remain at home, not to study or work outside, and religious leaders have repeatedly ruled that women should not be allowed to drive. In a poignant demonstration of the extent of the Druzes' "sensitivity" to "female chastity," Layish tells of the Spiritual Leadership rulings against miniskirts and cinema visits for women, as well as the official waiver of the requirement of Druze women's photographs on identity cards and other official documents (Layish 1982, 21). Druze women's educational levels remain low; in most communities, high schools are regional, and families object to girls traveling far from home and attending coeducational schools. Thus, Druze women's participation in the labor market is low, and those who do work out of their home work at low-paid, menial, and often seasonal jobs. Consequently, they have few personal or social resources (Layish 1982, 20–22; Dana 1998a, 218). Frequently, they are unable to avail themselves of resources provided by the state, such as vocational training, adult education, and so on.

Although women reveal anecdotally what may be high levels of wife abuse and both stranger and acquaintance rape, levels of reporting appear to be very low. Most experts attribute this to fear of retaliatory violence if women complain and "humiliate their community." Similarly, workers in rape crisis centers reveal that although they receive many referrals due to incest and other forms of intra-family child abuse, social norms prevent removal of either father or child from the home, and the community has been unable to establish alternative resources, such as foster homes.[50] The Druze concept of a "woman's honor" intensifies this distress. Layish (1982, 21) cites religious leaders' statements about woman's honor being more important than one's life, and rulings of female chastity as a condition for the integrity of marriage. There have indeed been several cases in recent years of Druze women's murders by family members on the ground of "defilement of honor."[51]

Nevertheless, like Bedouin society, Druze society is in transition, and women's status has been described as the "sharpest expression of the undergoing mini-revolution in the lives of the young Druze" (Dana 1998a, 218). As evidence accumulates about young women's slow but consistently growing level of education, their changing perception of gender roles in the family and otherwise, and other illustrations of social change, the situation and status of Druze women will undoubtedly continue to stand at the forefront of the Druze community and challenge its traditional norms.

Conclusion

The course of advancement of women in Israel started while the myth of gender equality in Israel still reigned. Even when some appreciation of the "women's problem" was evident, the conduct chosen by policymakers reflected the legal liberalism perception of formal equality.[1] It is only in recent years that a change can be located, reflecting a deeper change in feminist cognition, or rather an attempt to locate an alternative to the liberal legal feminist approach.

Is there hope, in these troubled times for Israel and Israeli society, for change in the status of women? While the preceding chapters provide a rather depressing account, they do offer some prospect for development from a perspective of feminist theories of the law. One of my conclusions has been that through the legal sphere the whole process of advancement of women in Israel can indeed be characterized as movement, sometimes actual and sometimes still needed, from the first generation of feminist legal theories, liberal legal feminism, which mostly holds to formal definitions of equality, to second generation, namely cultural and radical feminist theories, that may require an altogether different conception of the relationship between law and society.

In the judicial arena, the traditional field of analysis for Israeli legal scholarship, these developments started with precedent-setting cases prohibiting a lower retirement age for women and guaranteeing women's right to participate in municipal religious councils. They culminated in more precedents approving and directing the use of affirmative action in government corporations; ordering the Israel Defense Forces (IDF) to recruit women for pilot-training courses; and eventually expanding affirmative action to all areas of public life. Along the way, there were also precedent-setting criminal cases that expanded women's protection from rape and admitted the existence of the battered women's syndrome, as well as cases in other areas of law. Israel's High Court of Justice has definitely moved forward, not only in terms of women's formal rights but also in terms of understanding its own social role in promoting them. But when looking for indications of change on the state's part, I think the true story is the legislative story, much more than the judicial one. The Israeli Supreme Court (which also sits as the High Court of Justice) does not choose its cases. In this sense, the social agenda is dictated to the Supreme Court, together with the disputed norms, morals, and values at issue. The court's substantive holdings and rationales of course tell a lot about its beliefs and theoretical underpinnings.

Nevertheless, as explained in the Introduction, it is the legislative arena that should be examined when discussing the reflective and expressive functions of the law. My thesis here has been that the legislative evolution is not only an expression of substantive equality, it can also easily be interpreted as calling for a radically different conception of social structure. Adoption of substantive equality alone can be dismissed as still falling within the realm of liberal legal feminism. The process we are witnessing is more complex and far-reaching. Whether it is in what has traditionally been perceived as the "private sphere" of sexual relations, which the Prevention of Sexual Harassment Law unmasked as a form of gender discrimination that impairs women's personhood and dignity; in the realm of governmental responsibility for gender equality, which the Authority for the Advancement of Women Law boldly forced upon the government in unprecedented terms of commitment;[2] in relation to the overall status of women, which the proposed revision of the Women's Equal Rights Law constructs in the clearest terms of full personhood—I see all three legislative measures as signifying a totally different conception of gender. Moreover, besides envisioning a conceptually different gender regime, they depart from the former pattern of legislative reforms that focused more on particular subject matters and neglected the task of envisioning what might be.[3]

With all this said, the question remains whether these legislative measures will indeed stimulate the envisioned process of social change. In light of prior experience and the gap between the normative and social layers, are we not to expect the pattern to repeat itself? This is where, once again, the two themes of the thesis align: feminist legal theories, and law as a tool for social change. A well-known observation of the limits of law as an implement of social change is that of Yehezkel Dror, who contends that

> Law by itself is only one component of a large set of policy implements and usually cannot and is not used by itself. Therefore, focusing exclusive attention on law as a tool of directed social change is a case of tunnel vision, which lacks the minimum perspective necessary for making sense from the observed phenomena. (Dror 1970: 554)

Commenting on this, Roger Cotterrell further suggests that

> failure on the part of legislators in many Western societies in recent decades to recognize this may have contributed powerfully to current disillusionment with the proliferation in these societies of costly and seemingly ineffective bureaucracies, and more generally with the concept of "the directive state" and of social planning. The failure to see law as merely one aspect of a complex social whole affected by many social forces, and to see law as shaped by these forces probably to a far greater extent than it can shape them, leads to inevitable disillusionment when the legal instrument fails to achieve what the legal reformer intended. (Cotterrell 1992, 65)

Total reliance upon law alone, then, is almost a guarantee of failure. But isn't that an attribute of the first generation of feminist legal theories? Isn't that what characterizes liberal legal feminism, which, as I suggest, was the driving force and underlying ideology of Israeli "women's legislation" in its early stages, and until not so long ago? It seems that this could be a possible explanation for the apparent failure of the legal sphere, despite its comprehensive scope. By relying too much on legal change alone and failing to supply the practical infrastructure or to ensure the sociocultural infrastructure, the early stages of "women's legislation" in Israel could not "deliver the goods." Law and legislation are not independent social forces in themselves, but are connected to the interests that they represent, and their degree of efficacy reflects the power of their promoters to overcome resistance to change (Cotterrell 1992, 64). Law is only one factor, albeit a major one, in the overall structure of social life. Legal change is a prerequisite, it but is certainly not a sufficient condition to produce social change. Even on the pragmatic level, the Israeli case demonstrates these contentions: the very intensive legislation of the 1990s, described also as impulsive in nature, is in fact a central cause of the gaps between the normative and the social spheres in Israel, which reflect a certain degree of the law's failure to produce change. This is because the advanced legislative initiatives have by far preceded social progress, and their abundance simply increased the already existing gap between legal norms and their implementation.

Nevertheless, I would also suggest that perceiving the early stages only as a failure is too narrow a reading. Just like first-phase legal feminism was a prerequisite for the evolvement of the second and third phases, so, in a way, the early stages of "women's legislation" in Israel were necessary for the emergence of the current stage, which—even without the labels of "cultural" or "radical" feminism—certainly reflects a more sophisticated and mature feminist ideology, one that expresses more commitment and carries more potential for change and will eventually lead to smaller gaps between legal norms and social realities. Both cultural and radical feminist theories go beyond the boundaries of legal discourse. They both come from other discourses and offer comprehensive social visions of an overall reform of the gender regime. These visions both rely upon and are aimed at social fields and institutions other than the law, in addition to law itself. In this way they satisfy the need, as expressed above, to perceive law as "merely one aspect of a complex social whole affected by many social forces," which is a key for the law to be effective. Thus, the current stage of "women's legislation" in Israel, which corresponds to second generation feminist legal theories, carries with it substantial potential for social change, certainly more than the preceding stages.

This present stage also seems to come during a period of heightened feminist awareness in Israeli society in general. Let us recall several examples discussed broadly throughout the book. The first is the recruitment of women in the media to aid in the struggle of victims of sexual assault, something that could not have taken place ten years ago. The 1999 national elections serve as another example, with the increased public awareness of women's concerns during the campaigns. Most indicative of the heightened awareness was the public turmoil that accompanied the government formation, with only one token woman minister, in breach of concrete promises for greater women's representation that were made during the election campaign. Significantly, claims were even made by several women politicians of the connection between inadequate representation and the ever growing violence against women. While these claims were mostly met with animosity, the notable fact is that they were made in the first place, and not by feminist activists, but by mainstream female politicians. Another indication of change is the process that has been taking place within the IDF. This body, which used to be the most hostile to women, has emerged as the most progressive and willing to abide by the High Court of Justice rulings and respond to allegedly changing social norms. Notwithstanding the qualification made in Chapter 8, suspecting army officials of not fully undertaking commitment to gender equality, it does seem that the army is beginning a structural and ideological reform surpassing any other social institution in Israel.

All these are welcome developments that, together with the legal progress achieved, present an optimistic reading of women in Israel. However, maturation of feminist ideology as expressed in legislation and increased feminist awareness among the elite still fall short of true social reordering. These developments do not always represent societal and governmental espousal of these processes. If the pattern of budgetary cuts for women's needs and cessation of educational endeavors, seen again and again throughout this book, keeps repeating itself, then no matter how progressive the legislation is, it will not translate into real social change. The motto about the normative progress as a necessary but insufficient condition for social change holds true, regardless of the breadth and the nature of advancement in the normative sphere. Government commitment, which translates into allocation of resources, is an essential prerequisite for realization of the normative promise. Likewise, so long as politics of religion and state defeat feminist attempts to overturn the existing exclusive jurisdiction of religious law over marriage and divorce, no true change in gender power relations can be said to have taken place. Both these causes, the budgetary battle and religious politics, are fit causes to be embraced by second and third generation legal feminism.

It appears then, finally, that we are at a turning point where legal discourse and the accompanying legal feminism seem to facilitate a social change and the social arena is more open to change and development, at least in part. The next step then for the advancement of women in Israel should be a move from the "legislative turn" and toward promotion of implementation and fulfillment of its ideology, mainly through educational efforts and allocation of resources.

Notes

Chapter 1. Introduction

1. Convention on the Elimination of All Forms of Discrimination Against Women, adopted by GA Res 180, UN GAOR, 34th Sess., Supp. No. 46, at 193; UN Doc A/34/46 (1979).

2. "Mizrachi" refers to Jews and their descendants originating in Africa and the Middle East—historically underprivileged in Israeli society; "Ashkenazi" refers to generally European Jews and their descendants.

3. The last state to ratify was Mauritania, on May 10, 2001. See www.un.org/womenwatch/daw/cedaw/states.htm. Most of the nonratifying states are Islamic (see Cassel and Guzman 1999).

4. The CEDAW committee's concluding observations on Israel's Report can be found in Report of the Committee on the Elimination of Discrimination Against Women, 16th and 17th Sess., at pp. 87–92, paragraphs 132–83; UN Doc A/52/38/Rev.1(1997).

5. Ibid., paragraph 183.

6. For a discussion of this report see Chapter 6.

7. Statistics Ordinance (New Version), 1972, D.M.I. 500.

8. This is fully apparent when comparing the same type of data in the Statistical Abstracts from several years, such as table 22.21 in the 1999 Abstract with table 22.20 in the 2000 Abstract. Both tables address the issue of school dropouts, but only the latter gives, for the first time, a breakdown of the data along gender lines. See Central Bureau of Statistics (1999e), table 22.21; Central Bureau of Statistics (2000d), table 22.20.

9. Telephone conversation with Ms Nurit Yaffe of the Central Bureau of Statistics, September 27, 2000.

10. See also Chapter 11.

11. Central Bureau of Statistics (2001).

12. This is due to the Hebrew language, being gendered, having no neutral nouns; the rule is that male nouns are regarded as "neutral" and "include" the feminine. "Head of household" is a male noun.

13. UN Doc A/43/38.

14. See notes 27 and 29 below.

15. See, for example, Azmon and Izraeli (1993); Izraeli et al. (1999); B. Swirski and Safir (1993); Yishai (1997).

16. Other works on specific issues that employed an integrative methodology include Izraeli (1992), Herzog (1994), Amir (1996). While this book was in press, a volume reviewing a selection of legal and theoretical aspects of women's

life in Israel was commissioned by the Broadcast University from law professor Orit Kamir. This is the first accessible analysis in Hebrew of theoretical feminism, directed at general readership (Kamir 2002).

17. See http://hdr.undp.org/reports

18. See http://hdr.undp.org/aboutus/default.cfm

19. For more explanations, see "What Is Human Development" at http://hdr.undp.org/hd/default.cfm

20. A summary of HDR (1995) is found at http://hdr.undp.org/reports/global/1995/en/pdf/hdr_1995_foreword.pdf

21. For broader explanations of these measurements see HDR (1995), at http://hdr.undp.org/reports/global/1995/en/pdf/hdr_1995_overview.pdf

22. This is shown, for example, in the Annual Surveys of the National Insurance Institute, which regularly contain an introduction on trends and developments of the Israeli welfare system. See, for example, Yaniv (1998), E1–E47.

23. The Human Development Index (HDI), Gender-Related Development Index (GDI), and Gender Empowerment Measure (GEM).

24. These data are taken from the various Human Development Reports, all of which can be found at the HDR site at http://hdr.undp.org/reports

25. Prevention of Violence in the Family Law, 1991, S.H. 138; Equal Pay (Male and Female Employees) Law, 1996, S.H. 230; Single-Parent Families Law, 1992, S.H. 147; State Service (Appointments) Law (Amendment No. 7), 1995, S.H. 500. "State Service" is the official translation for what is termed "civil service" throughout this book.

26. The passage of the Equal Pay (Male and Female Employees) Law demonstrates this point. The law clearly adopts the pay-equity principle, but without creating any governmental enforcement mechanism it will probably remain useless. Indeed, no suit has been submitted on the basis of this law since its passage, and as the data prove, this cannot be explained by nonexistence of salary gaps between men and women.

27. See Chapter 8.

28. By "women's legislation" I mean any legislation whose purpose or effect is to promote women's status.

29. Women's Equal Rights Law, 1951, S.H. 248.

30. See also Chapter 2, where the amendment to the law is discussed.

31. Compulsory Education Law, 1949, S.H. 287; Equal Pay (Male and Female Employees) Law, 1964, S.H. 166.

32. Inasmuch as women's work legislation seems an exception to this generalization, this is discussed in Chapter 2, in the discussion of accommodation of parenthood.

33. The Namir Commission, discussed in detail in Chapter 2.

34. As discussed above, see text accompanying note 25 as well as later in this chapter. See also the section in Chapter 3 discussing the Knesset Committee on the Status of Women.

35. Note 25 above; affirmative action is discussed in detail in Chapter 8.

36. Under the Procedural Amendment Law (Amendment No. 2) (Questioning of Witnesses), 1995, S.H. 152, discussed in Chapter 9, and the Equal Retirement Age (Male and Female Employees) Law, 1987, 48, discussed in Chapter 11.

37. Note 25 above. This issue is elaborated below in Chapter 7.

38. For a broader view of this move, see Chapter 2, in the section on "Accommodation of Parenthood."

39. Women's Equal Rights Law (Amendment No. 2), 2000, S.H. 167.

40. The retraction in this sense is even graver, since the revision added a new qualification with specific reference to religious offices, such as judges in religious courts, as explained in Chapter 8 in the section on "Semi-Formal Expressions of Religion-State Integration."

41. Note 39 above, allowing a distinction not to be regarded as discrimination if it is "inevitable due to the fundamental differences between [men and women], or from the nature or substance of the matter." See Almog (2000).

42. Under the heading Authority for the Advancement of Women Law I include the Local Councils Law (Advisor on the Status of Women) (2000), which, while formally distinct from the Authority Law, similarly designates a special mechanism for specifically addressing the needs of women on the local level, as explained in the next chapter.

Chapter 2. Gender Equality in the Israeli Legal System

1. This is explained in the Introduction and more broadly discussed below in Chapter 11.

2. Basic Law: Human Dignity and Liberty, 1992, S.H. 150; Basic Law: Freedom of Occupation, 1994, S.H. 90.

3. Section 8 of Basic Law: Human Dignity and Liberty states: "Rights under this Basic Law must not be infringed, except by a law appropriate to the ethical values of the State of Israel, which has a valid purpose, and then to an extent that does not exceed necessity, or under an aforesaid Law by virtue of an explicit authorization in it." A similar clause appears in section 4 of Basic Law: Freedom of Occupation.

4. C.A. 6821/93, 1908/94, 3363/94, *United Mizrachi Bank v. Migdal Cooperative Village*, 49(4) P.D. 221; H.C. 1715/97 *Chambers of Investment Managers in Israel v. The Minister of the Treasury*, 51(4) P.D. 367; H.C. 6055/95, *Sagi Tzemach et al. v. Minister of Defense* (not yet published).

5. For example, Basic Law: Human Dignity and Liberty states in section 10: "This Basic Law shall not derogate from the effect of any enactment, which was in effect immediately before this Basic Law came into effect."

6. H.C. 453/94, 454/94, *Israel Women's Network v. The Government of Israel and Others*, 48(5) P.D. 501, at 521–22; H.C. 5394/92 *Hupert v. Yad Vashem*, 48(3) P.D. 353, at 362.

7. Women's Equal Rights Law (Amendment No. 2), 2000, S.H. 167.

8. Moreover, as noted in the Introduction, not only did this rule remain intact, but the amendment added further religious qualification with respect to religious offices. The effect of this qualification is explained in Chapter 8, under "Semi-Formal Expressions of Religion-State Integration."

9. H.C. 202/57 *Sidis v. The President and Members of the Great Rabbinical Court*, 12 P.D. 1528, at 1537, and see, for example, H.C. 1000/92 *Bavli v. The Rabbinical High Court*, 48(2) P.D. 221, at 240.

10. As further explained in Chapter 11.

11. H.C. 153/87, *Shakdiel v. The Minister of Religious Affairs and Others*, 42(2) P.D. 221; H.C. 104/87 *Nevo v. The National Labour Court and Others*, 44(4) P.D. 749.

12. The Lubinsky case, note 6 above; H.C. 335/76, *Lifshitz-Aviram v. Israel Lawyers' Association*, 31(1) P.D. 250.

13. Note 9 above. For further discussion see also Chapter 11.

14. H.C. 4541/94, *Alice Miller v. The Minister of Defense*, 49(4) P.D. 94. For further discussion see also Chapter 8.

15. Note 6 above. The case is broadly discussed below, see text following note 23. The Government Corporations Law (Amendment No. 6) (Appointments), 1993, S.H. 92.

16. H.C. 2671/98, *The Israel Women's Network v. The Minister of Labor and Welfare* 52(3) P.D. 630. See the discussion of this case below, text following note 24.

17. Equal Employment Opportunities Law, 1988, S.H. 38.

18. C.A. 89/85, *Beit Herut v. Glazman*, 41(3) P.D. 526.

19. Spouses (Property Relations) Law, 1973, S.H. 267; Prevention of Violence in the Family Law, 1991, S.H. 138.

20. Government Corporations Law (Amendment No. 6) (Appointments), 1993, S.H. 92.

21. Section 60A of the law applies the provisions of section 18A to government appointments to administrative councils of statutory corporations.

22. Draft bill amending the Government Corporations Law (No. 6) (Appointments), 1993 H.H. 72.

23. H.C. 453/94, 454/94, *Israel Women's Network v. The Government of Israel and Others*, 48(5) P.D. 501.

24. H.C. 2671/98 *Israel Women's Network v. The Minister of Labor and Welfare*, 52(3) P.D. 630.

25. Basic Law: Human Dignity and Liberty, 1992, S.H. 150.

26. See text accompanying note 24.

27. Letter from Noga Kadosh of the Public Committee for the Monitoring of Appointments, September12, 2000 (on file with the author).

28. State Service (Appointments) Law (Adequate Representation) (Amendment No. 7), 1995, S.H. 500.

29. See Chapter 8.

30. For the most recent legislation attempting to remedy these shortcomings, see text accompanyingnote 35 below.

31. Note 24 above.

32. Ruti Sinai, "The Ninth Man," *Ha'aretz*, May 25, 1999, B3.

33. Corporate Ordinance (Amendment No. 11) (Representation of both sexes in the board of directors of a public corporation), 1998, S.H. 245. Since then, the Corporate Ordinance was replaced by the Corporate Law, which has a similar provision in section 239(4), Corporate Law, 1999, S.H. 189.

34. Senior Citizens Law (Amendment No. 1), 1996 S.H. 76, section 4(b); National Health Insurance Law, 1994, S.H. 56, section 49(b); National Struggle Against Road Accidents Law, 1997, S.H. 196, sections 11(c) and 13(b); National Authority on Licensing Laboratories Law, 1997, S.H. 156, sections 8(b)(3) and 169c); Authority for the Advancement of Women Law, 1998, S.H. 171, section 9(e); perhaps most significant is the government decision to apply section 15A of the State Service (Appointments) Law to all municipal councils, published in 1997 Y.P. 4563 at 5392 (September 2, 1997).

35. State Service (Appointments) Law (Amendment No. 11), 2001, S.H. 78. See also the discussion of this amendment in Chapter 8, section on "Women in the Civil Service."

36. Employment of Women Law, 1954, S.H. 154.

37. Equal Employment Opportunities Law, 1988, S.H. 38.

38. Employment of Women Law (Amendment No. 7), 1986, S.H. 141.
39. Employment of Women Law (Amendment No. 15), 1998, S.H. 114.
40. Employment of Women Law (Amendment No. 14), 1997, S.H. 219.
41. Telephone interview with Tami Eliav of the National Insurance Institution, January 13, 2002.
42. Note, though, that this is not required of working mothers; they are eligible for these rights regardless of the working status of their spouses.
43. Civil Service Code, section 31.15.
44. Note 39 above.
45. For more details see Chapter 7.
46. Telephone interview with Judge Saviona Rotlevi, Tel Aviv District Court, May 13, 2001.
47. Report of the Committee on the Elimination of Discrimination Against Women, 16th and 17th Sess., pp. 87–92, paragraph 182; UN Doc A/52/38/Rev.1(1997).
48. Third Periodic Report of the State of Israel Concerning the Implementation of the United Nations Convention on the Elimination of all Forms of Discrimination Sgainst Women (CEDAW), submitted in 2001, at 175.

Chapter 3. The Promotion of Gender Equality

1. The term is taken from Riggs (1991), in order to distinguish between presidential systems such as in the United States and parliamentary systems where the head of the state is nevertheless termed "president."
2. Basic Law: The Government, S.H. 1396 (1992), 214. This law was replaced in March 2001 by a new Basic Law that would go into effect as of the elections for the 16th Knesset; see Basic Law: The Government, S.H. 1780 (2001), 158. Significantly, the new Basic Law does not require a minimum of ministers who are also member of the Knesset, but assumes the practice to continue.
3. See Chapter 9 and the discussion below on "Women in the Civil Service."
4. This fact was criticized in the CEDAW committee's concluding comments to the Israeli report. See Report of the Committee on the Elimination of Discrimination Against Women, 16th and 17th Sess., pp. 87–92, paragraphs 132–83, at paragraphs 159, 171; UN Doc A/52/38/Rev.1 (1997).
5. Authority for the Advancement of Women Law, 1998, S.H. 171.
6. Letters from Dina Berniker, Head of the National Council on the Status of Women, to Prime Minister Yitzhak Rabin, dated May 25 and June 23, 1993 (on file with the author).
7. Authority for the Advancement of Women Bill, 1996, section 16 (on file with the author).
8. Authority for the Promotion of Gender Equality Draft Bill, 1997, H.H., 120.
9. Authority for the Advancement of Women Law, 1998, S.H. 171, section 6.
10. As can be seen below, text following note 11, even this role has so far not been fulfilled by the authority.
11. *Networking for Women* 11, 3 (Summer 1998): 10.
12. Local Authorities Law (Advisor on the Status of Women), 2000, S.H. 278.
13. Prevention of Sexual Harassment Law, 1998, S.H. 166; Equal Pay (Male and Female Employees) Law, 1996, S.H. 230; State Service (Appointments) Law (Appropriate Representation) (Amendment no. 7), 1995, S.H. 500; Prevention

of Violence in the Family Law (Amendment no. 2), 1996, S.H. 243; Family Court Law, 1995, S.H. 393.

14. *Kol Ha-Nashim*, May 1999, 2: 10 (Hebrew).

15. The report is discussed in Chapter 8.

16. For example, women made up only 11 percent among the top six ranks in the Administrative Classification of the Civil Service in 1976 (Civil Service Commissioner 1976, 164).

17. See Chapter 7.

18. This provision is now included in section 12.360 of the Civil Service Code.

19. Civil Commissioner Announcement 32/97, July 14, 1997.

20. See Chapter 7.

21. Unpublished data submitted by the Ministry of Finance, Unit for Salary and Labor Agreements, dated November 24, 1996 and November 20, 2000 (on file with the author). For further details see Chapter 7.

22. For an extensive discussion of the tenders data, see Chapter 8.

23. This in fact had been the reason for the resignation in May 1997 of Professor Frances Raday, the head of the Steering Committee for the Implementation of the State Service (Appointments) Law (Adequate Representation); letter from Professor Raday to the Civil Commissioner, dated May 19, 1997 (on file with the author).

24. See Chapter 8, "Women in the Civil Service."

25. As reported by attorney Rivka Shaked, general supervisor on the advancement of women, in the 1998 Report of the Unit (on file with the author).

26. In a joint meeting of the Knesset Committee on the Status of Women and the Law Committee, November 16, 1999, protocol 34/15, p. 17.

27. This also seems to be a pattern that repeats itself, as we shall see later when discussing the commanding officer of the Women's Corps in the army, who is also not senior enough to participate in the highest decision-making meetings.

28. See Yael Yishai, "Why Are They Detached?" *Ha'aretz*, November 2, 1999, B2.

29. The parallel is not complete. Thus the lesbian women's organization CLAF is not discussed here but in Chapter 11 as part of the discussion of alternative forms of families and in Chapter 12 as part of the general discussion of lesbian women.

30. See Working Group on the Status of Palestinian Women in Israel (1997).

31. See, for example, Laurie Goodstein, "Women Taking Active Role to Study Orthodox Judaism", *New York Times*, December 21, 2000, A1, col. 5; Avi Machlis, "Orthodox Women in Israel Join Debate over Their Role in Community," *Jewish Telegraph Agency*, July 14, 1999; Ariele Mortkowitz, "Orthodox Women Demand Religious Equality," *Jerusalem Post*, July 15 1999; Calev Ben-David, "No More Yentls," *Jerusalem Post*, April 2, 1999; Gail Lichtman, "A Page in History," *Jerusalem Post Magazine*, May 20, 1999.

32. The information in this paragraph is based on the center's leaflet, and on a September 1999 conversation with Debbie Gross, who established and currently heads the center.

Chapter 4. Women and Health Care

1. National Health Ordinance, 1940, P.G., Sup. 1, 191 (Hebrew), 239 (English).

2. National Health Insurance Law, 1994, S.H. 156; Patient's Rights Law, 1996, S.H. 327.

3. National Health Insurance Law, section 1.

4. National Health Insurance Law, sections 3, 7.

5. National Health Insurance Law (Amendment No. 4), 1996, S.H. 253.

6. National Insurance Law (Consolidated Version), 1995, S.H. 210, section 238.

7. Invitation from Professor Yehoshua Shemer, general director, Ministry of Health (on file with the author).

8. Chaim Shadmi, "118 Services and Drugs Added to the Basic Basket," *Ha'aretz*, January 6, 2000, A6.

9. Combined Initial and Second Report of the State of Israel Concerning the Implementation of the United Nations Convention on the Elimination of All Forms of Discrimination Against Women (CEDAW), submitted in 1997, UN Doc CEDAW/C/ISR/1-2 (1997), at p. 154.

10. Chaim Shadmi, "More Premature Babies Are Born, While Care Is Insufficient," *Ha'aretz*, September 23, 1999, 1A, citing a Ministry of Health report dated September 21, 1999.

11. Ran Reznik, "How to Seat 2.5 Expectant Mothers in One Bed," *Ha'ir*, November 22, 1996, 30, citing National Council of Midwives and Gynecologists Report, March 1996.

12. Central Bureau of Statistics (2000d), Table 3.20.

13. World Health Organization (WHO) Regional Office for Europe, 1996, Highlights on Health in Israel, at p. 9.

14. National Insurance Institute (1999b), table C/2.

15. Central Bureau of Standards (2000d), table 24.15.

16. Penal Law, 1977, S.H. 322.

17. Penal Law (Amendment No. 8), 1979, S.H. 40.

18. Knesset Committee for the Advancement of the Status of Women, 15th Knesset, August 2000, p. 9.

19. Ibid., section 316(b).

20. Hospitalization Services Directive, Circular No. 64/90, dated June 15, 1990 (on file with the author); reiterated in Director-General Directive, Circular No. 23/93, dated November 14, 1993 (on file with the author).

21. Ibid.

22. Data supplied by the Ministry of Health, Information and Computer Service (undated, on file with the author).

23. Central Bureau of Statistics (2000d), table 3.17.

24. Central Bureau of Statistics (2000a), 10.

25. Central Bureau of Statistics (2000d).

26. Central Bureau of Statistics (2000a), 13.

27. Ruti Sinai, "Where's the Child," *Ha'aretz*, May 9, 2000, Independence Day Supplement, 16.

28. Central Bureau of Statistics (2000d), tables 3.14, 3.12.

29. Ibid., tables 3.12, 3.15.

30. Jewish women's fertility rate was lowest in 1995, at 2.53. By 1998 it was back to 2.67. Muslim women's fertility rate was lowest in 1996, at 4.65. By 1998, it was back to 4.76, higher than the rate in the late 1980s. See Central Bureau of Statistics (2000d), tables 3.14, 3.12.

31. Shachar Ilan, "When the Subsidies Increased, the Number of Children Doubled," *Ha'aretz*, July 24, 2000, B3.

32. National Insurance Law (Amendment No. 41), 2001, S.H. 2.

33. Central Bureau of Statistics (2000d), table 3.16.

34. Telephone interview with Dr. Yoram Lotan, deputy director of medical administration, Ministry of Health, May 20, 1999.

35. Ibid.

36. For an explanation of this point, see Chapter 11, under "Same-Sex Couples."

37. Surrogate Motherhood Agreements (Approval of Agreements and Status of Newborn) Law, 1996, S.H. 176. A detailed analysis of this law and its legal development is found in Chapter 11.

38. Letter from advocate Talia Edri of the Ministry of Health Legal Advisor Office, dated January 15, 2001 (on file with the author).

39. See a series of reports by Ran Reznik in *Ha'aretz*, February 9, 2000, A1; June 2, 2000, A7; August 23, 2000, A1.

40. Data supplied by Chava Klein of the Planning and Budgeting Committee, Council for Higher Education, letter dated November 11, 2000.

41. Knesset Committee for the Advancement of the Status of Women, 15th Knesset, 8.

42. Data supplied by Rena Bareket, senior coordinator (women's advancement) in the Civil Service, letter dated October 30, 2000 (on file with the author).

43. Calculated from unpublished data supplied by the Ministry of Finance, Unit for Salary and Labor Agreements, dated November 20, 2000 (on file with the author).

Chapter 5. Education

1. Central Bureau of Statistics (1999c), table 22.4.
2. Long School Day Law, 1997, S.H. 204.
3. Women's Equal Rights Law (Amendment No. 2), 2000, S.H.167.
4. Compulsory Education Law, 1949, S.H. 287.
5. Compulsory Education Law (Amendment No. 18), 1991, S.H.165.
6. State Education Law, 1953, S.H. 137.
7. School Inspection Law, 1969, S.H. 180.
8. Special Education Law, 1988, S.H. 114.
9. Council For Higher Education Law, 1958, S.H. 191.
10. Central Bureau of Statistics (1999c), table 22.1.
11. Central Bureau of Statistics (2000d), table 22.1.
12. Ministry of Education, Culture, and Sport (1997), 15 (Hebrew).
13. Ministry of Education, Culture, and Sport (1996), table 7.
14. Ministry of Education (1999), 12 (Hebrew).
15. Ibid., 15.
16. Ibid., 49.
17. Central Bureau of Statistics (1999c), table 22.23.
18. Ministry of Education (1999), 49.
19. Ibid., 45.
20. Ministry of Education, Culture, and Sport Director, General Directive, "Guiding Rules for Equal Attitude toward Man and Woman in Publications, Children's Books and School Textbooks," Circular no. 54/2m, dated October 1993 (on file with the author).

21. Letter from Chava Barnea, head of the Family Life and Sex Education Unit in the Ministry of Education, Culture and Sport, dated July 9, 1997 (on file with the author).

22. Reli Sa'ar, "Censorship Removed, Racism and Sexism Remained," *Ha'aretz*, May 12, 2000, A7.

23. Telephone interview with Miriam Schechter, supervisor on equality between the sexes in the Ministry of Education, December 15, 1999.

24. Letter from Miriam Schechter, supervisor on equality between the sexes in the Ministry of Education, dated November 14, 2000 (on file with the author).

25. Letter from Chava Barnea, head of the Family Life and Sex Education Unit in the Ministry of Education, Culture and Sport, dated May 5, 1999 (on file with the author), referring to "Sex Education and Sex Information for Youths," a telephone survey conducted by Guttman Institute for Applied Research, April 1994.

26. See Chapters 8 and 11.

27. See "The Emergence of Religious Women's Movement" in Chapter 3.

28. Central Bureau of Statistics (1999c), table 22.16.

29. Letter from Matityahu Dagan, head of the Administration for Religious Education, dated January 13, 1997 (on file with the author).

30. Ibid.

31. As this field is particularly dynamic and is constantly undergoing changes, it is impossible to quote exact numbers. For a taste of the interest and enthusiasm this process is generating, and the growing number of these institutes, see *Mirrors—National Magazine for the National Service Girl and the Young Religious Woman*, May 1997, issue 5; *Women in Judaism—Discussion Papers* 3–4, 2000, Fanya Gottesfeld Heller Center for the Study of Women in Judaism, Ramat Gan.

32. H.C. 744/95, *Nishmat v. The Minister of Religion* (not yet published).

33. This development is also discussed in Chapter 8, "Religion-State Integration and Its Effect on Women." See Larry Derfner, "A Step Up for Orthodox Women," *Jerusalem Post*, October 8, 1999; Gail Lichtman, "A Page in History," *Jerusalem Post Magazine*, May 20, 1999; Michele Chabin, "The New 'Poseks': Orthodox Women," *Jewish Week*, December 17, 1999.

34. Letter from Rivka Charka, supervisor on Family Life in the State Religious Education, January 1, 1997 (on file with the author).

35. Central Bureau of Statistics (1999c), table 22.16.

36. Ibid., table 22.28.

37. Central Bureau of Statistics, Ministry of Education, Culture and Sport (1993), 147.

38. Data submitted by the Ministry of the Treasury, Unit for Salary and Labor Agreements, 2000 (on file with the author).

39. Gideon Eshet, "Feminine Brain," *Yedioth Aharonot*, March 9, 1999.

40. Central Bureau of Statistics (2000), table 22.44.

41. Council for Higher Education (1995), 31.

42. Ibid., table 3.11, p. 98.

43. Central Bureau of Statistics (2000d), table 22.38.

44. Ibid., table 22.34.

45. Ibid., table 22.39.

46. Information given by the Israeli Academy of Science, e-mailed by Professor Marilyn Safir to the author, May 5, 1998 (on file with the author).

47. Based on information provided in Benmelech (2000).

48. *Israel Association for Feminist Studies*, November 1999, issue 1.

Chapter 6. The Welfare State

1. National Insurance Law (Consolidated Version), 1995, S.H. 210, section 225.
2. Obviously, women's share among those high-earners is very small, as seen in Chapter 7.
3. See "Obligatory Pension Plan Now," a pamphlet published by the Forum for the Advancement of Obligatory Pension Law, 1999 (Hebrew, on file with the author); Israel Women's Network (1999), 9.
4. National Insurance Institute (2001), tables 2.4, 3.3.
5. Letter from Brenda Morgenstern of the NII Research Department, dated November 1, 2000 (on file with the author).
6. National Insurance Law, 1953, S.H. 6; National Insurance Law, 1995.
7. For an explanation of the way the average wage is calculated, see Yaniv (1998), E1–E31, note 2.
8. The descriptions of NII programs are all based on National Insurance Institute (1996) and on a letter from attorney Ada Shamir-Orbito from the NII's Legal Department, dated January 8, 1997 (on file with the author).
9. Income Support Law, 1981, S.H. 30.
10. Law to Reduce the Scope of Poverty and Income Gaps (Legislative Reforms), 1994, S.H. 256.
11. For a detailed explanation of this law's effect, see Yaniv (1996), i–xxviii, at xiv.
12. See Chapter 8.
13. This point is critically developed in Chapter 7.
14. National Insurance Law, 1995, section 44.
15. National Insurance Law (Amendment No. 41), 2001, S.H. 2.
16. National Insurance Law, 1995, section 40.
17. An indirect amendment (No. 21) to the National Insurance Law, a part of the Employment of Women Law (Amendment No. 15), 1998, S.H. 114.
18. National Insurance Law, 1995, section 45.
19. Ibid., section 62.
20. Ibid., sections 238–69.
21. Letter from Carmit Naor of the NII legal Department, dated January 18, 2001 (on file with the author).
22. Ibid.
23. National Insurance Institute (2001), 27.
24. Letter from Brenda Morgenstern of the NII Research Department, dated January, 8 1997 (on file with the author).
25. National Insurance Law, 1995, sections 223–37.
26. Telephone interview with Irit Feldman, head of NII Disability Benefits Department, October 2000.
27. National Insurance Law, 1995, sections 195–222A.
28. National Insurance Law, 1995, sections 65–74.
29. National Insurance Law (Amendment 41), 2001.
30. See also Chapter 4, in the section "Fertility Rates, Treatments, and Services."
31. Alimony (Guarantee of Payment) Law, 1972, S.H. 87.
32. National Insurance Institute (2001), table 5.1.
33. Letter from Carmit Naor (note 21 above)
34. See text following note 52 below.

35. Single-Parent Family Law, 1992, S.H. 147.

36. Law to Reduce the Scope of Poverty and Income Gaps (Legislative Reforms), 1994, S.H. 256.

37. Single-Parent Family Law (Amendment), 1994, S.H. 92.

38. Meeting of the Knesset Committee for the Advancement of Women, October 19, 1999, protocol 10, at 24–25.

39. Ibid., 27.

40. Letter from Brenda Morgenstern of the NII Research Department, January 22, 1997 (on file with the author), and the letters mentioned in notes 5 and 21.

41. Telephone conversation with Brenda Morgenstern of the NII Research Department, January 22, 1997.

42. This conclusion was also reached by researchers from the Israel Women's Network who initiated a study of poverty of women in Israel (Steir and Lewin 1999).

43. Letter from Carmit Naor, note 21 above.

44. Letter from Brenda Morgenstern, note 40 above.

45. National Insurance Institute (2001), table 3.3.

46. Ibid., table 3.4.

47. Ibid., table 2.4.

48. Data in this paragraph are based on an unpublished NII Research Department report (Eliav 2000) and on the letters cited in notes 5 and 21.

49. Letter from Brenda Morgenstern, note 5.

50. These calculations are based on data in Eliav (2000).

51. See text accompanying note 31.

52. National Insurance Institute (1999b), table G/2.

53. Telephone conversation with Brenda Morgenstern, note 41. Interestingly, the opposite is true among employed non-Jewish men and women. The poverty rate among non-Jewish employed women was 20 percent, and among non-Jewish employed men was 23 percent. It should be noted that the pool of Arab employed women is extremely small to begin with, so these data cannot be taken simply at face value. These are the only official data in existence regarding the incidence of poverty among the specific population group of non-Jewish women. Poverty rates for the general non-Jewish population are available and are rather depressing: poverty among non-Jewish families increased from 28.3 percent in 1996 to 30.3 percent in 1997. NII researchers note that non-Jewish families tend to have relatively large numbers of children, which partially explains the high incidence of poverty, close to the rate of large families in general (36.8 percent in 1997); see Awad, Cohen, and Yaniv (1998), 68–70.

Chapter 7. The Work Women Do

1. See notes 69, 86, and 95 and accompanying text.

2. For a broader explanation of these measures and their analysis, see Chapter 8.

3. United Nations (1995).

4. Beneria (1992), quoted in Tomasevski (1998), 11.

5. UN Doc A/46/38.

6. A 2000 amendment to the 1996 Employment of Workers Through Manpower Contractors Law tries to deal with this phenomenon by requiring that

every worker employed through a personnel agency for more than nine months be in effect considered an employee of the work placement. In addition, the employment conditions in the workplace are to be applied to those employed through an agency. This amendment came into effect only in June 2001, and has generated much criticism, including from the pro-worker perspective, since, as argued, employers would now be tempted to discharge the agency employee after eight months of work.

7. A January 2000 amendment to the 1991 Foreign Employees (Unlawful Employment) Law sought to improve the status of foreign workers in Israel. In particular, it sought to prevent situations of exploitation and oppression common in the past. A detailed description of this amendment is beyond the scope of this chapter.

8. Michal Palti, "The Byte Generation," *Ha'aretz*, September 5, 2000, D1, quoting Professor Amira Galin of Tel Aviv University School of Management.

9. Michal Palti, "The Silicon Ceiling," *Ha'aretz*, July 24, 2000, D1, quoting research by Dalia Rachman-Mor and Nira Danziger of the College of Management.

10. Equal Pay (Male and Female Employees) Law, 1964, S.H. 166; Equal Pay (Male and Female Employees) Law, 1996, S.H. 230.

11. Women's Equal Rights Law, 1951, S.H. 248.

12. D.B.A. 3-25/73, *Union of Air Steward Staff v. Edna Hazin*, 4 P.D.A., 365.

13. Equal Retirement Age (Male and Female Employees) Law, 1987, S.H. 48.

14. H.C. 104/87, *Nevo v. The National Labor Court and others*, 44(4) P.D. 749.

15. Equal Employment Opportunities Law, 1988, S.H. 38.

16. Prevention of Sexual Harassment Law, 1998, S.H. 166.

17. Equal Employment Opportunities Law (Amendment No. 3), 1995, S.H. 95.

18. For a broader discussion of the sexual harassment provisions under this law, see Ben-Israel (1998), 889–913.

19. Civil Service Code, section 43.4.

20. The Civil Service Commission Supervisor on the Advancement of Women (1999), 8.

21. Equal Employment Opportunities Law, section 10(2).

22. D.B.A. 3-129/96, *Plotkin v. Izenberg Brothers Ltd*, Takdin-National 97(3), 2599.

23. Equal Employment Opportunities Law, 1988, section 18.

24. Equal Pay (Male and Female Employees) Law, 1996.

25. Ibid., section 3.

26. Equal Pay (Male and Female Employees) for Equal Value Work Draft Bill, 1995, H.H., 373.

27. Av. (Be'er Sheva) 001576/99, *Simi Nidam v. Rali Electrics and Electronics* (not published yet) (interim decision, final decision still pending).

28. This information is taken from a letter from Efraim Kahalon, Chief Supervisor of Labor Laws at the Ministry of Labor and Welfare, dated June 30, 1997 (on file with the author), and also from Ruti Sinai, "High Risk Pregnancy," *Ha'aretz*, March 7, 1999.

29. Employment of Women Law, 1954, S.H. 154, section 9.

30. Employment of Women Law (Amendment No. 15), 1998, S.H. 114.

31. Employment of Women Law (Amendment No. 20), 2000, S.H. 290.

32. Letter from Ruth Cahana-Avivi, Adv., Ministry of Labor and Welfare Legal Advisor to Michal Baron, Adv. and Gali Etzion, Adv. of Na'amat's Legal Division, dated October 29, 2000 (on file with the author).

33. Employment of Women Law (Amendment No. 21), 2001, S.H. 219.
34. Employment of Women Law (Amendment No. 15), 1998.
35. Ibid., section 7.
36. Sick Pay Law (Absence from Work due to Pregnancy and Childbirth of Spouse), 2000, S.H. 222.
37. Employment of Women Law (Amendment No. 15), 1954, section 6.
38. National Insurance Law (Amendment No. 83), 1994, S.H. 91.
39. Employment of Women Law (Amendment No. 14), 1997, S.H. 219.
40. Employment of Women Law (Amendment No. 15), 1998.
41. Employment of Women Law, 1954, section 7(c)(1).
42. National Insurance Law (Consolidated Version), 1995, S.H. 210, section 58.
43. National Insurance Law (Amendment No. 38), 2000, S.H. 66.
44. Employment of Women Law, 1954, section 7(c)(3).
45. Ibid., section 7(d).
46. Severance Pay Law, 1963, S.H. 136, section 7.
47. Sick Pay (Absence from Work Due to Child's Illness) (Amendment No. 5), 2001, S.H. 219.
48. See, for example, the cases cited in notes 60–61 and accompanying text.
49. Av. (Tel Aviv) 31993/96, *Menahem Yahav and Na'amat v. The State of Israel* (not published).
50. A.D.M. 300098/99, *Jacky Gross v. Tal Traveling and Tourism Inc.*, Takdin-National 2000(1), 470.
51. Employment of Women Law (Amendment No. 15), 1998.
52. Letter from Efraim Kahalon, chief supervisor of labor laws in the Ministry of Labor and Welfare, to Yvette Saadon, director of the Division for Women's Status, Daycare Centers, and Family Centers at the Ministry of Labor and Welfare, dated January 12, 1997 (on file with the author). See also letter from Ruth Cahana-Avivi, note 32.
53. Letter from Oren Karni of the Department of Supervision of Labor Laws to Yvette Saadon, director of the Division for Women's Status, Daycare Centers, and Family Centers at the Ministry of Labor and Welfare, dated January 7, 1997 (on file with the author).
54. Orit Soliciano, "A Sharp Rise in Calls to the Hotline During 1996," *Israel Women's Network Newsletter*, 97, 7 (January 1997): 4 (Hebrew).
55. Letter from the Legal Department of the Ministry of Labor and Welfare, addressed to Ephraim Cohen, Head of the Foreign Workers Administration, dated October 10, 2000 (on file with the author).
56. Minimum Wage Law, 1987, S.H. 68.
57. National Insurance Law (Consolidated Version), 1995.
58. For a further critique of this gender-specific concept of homemaker and disregard for her economic contribution see Chapter 6.
59. Letter from Brenda Morgenstern of the National Insurance Institute, dated January 20, 1997 (on file with the author).
60. T.B.A. (Be'er Sheva) 91-17/96, *Dvora Uzana v. The Employment Service*, Takdin-Avoda 96(4), 268; T.B.A. (Tel Aviv) 91-21/97 *Shefer Mariana v. The Employment Service*, Takdin-Avoda 97(1), 1500; T.B.A. (Tel Aviv) 91-1/97 *Jenny Berstein v. The Employment Service-Netanya and Others*, Takdin-Avoda 97(2), 16.
61. D.B.A. 3-91/96, *The Employment Service v. Gila Gaon*, Takdin-National 96(2), 162.
62. An indirect amendment (No. 34) to the National Insurance Law, a part of the of the State's Economy Regulations Law, 1999, S.H. 99, in section 20(4).

63. An indirect amendment (No. 37) to the National Insurance Law, a part of the State's Economy Regulations Law, 2000, S.H. 66, in sections 2(2) and 2(3).
64. Income Tax Ordinance, 1941, P.G., Sup. 1, 51.
65. Law amending the Income Tax Ordinance, 1952, S.H. 298.
66. C.A. 337/61, *Lubinsky v. Tel Aviv Assessing Officer*, 16 P.D. 403
67. Law amending the Income Tax Ordinance (No. 89), 1992, S.H. 177.
68. Central Bureau of Statistics (2000d), table 12.1.
69. See "Profile of People in Work" at http://hdr.undp.org/hdro/work.htm. For more statistics from the 1998 Human Development Report regarding industrial countries see http://hdr.undp.org/hdro/indicators.html.
70. See Central Bureau of Statistics (1995).
71. Ibid., 14–15, 18–21.
72. Ibid., 21–24.
73. See Central Bureau of Statistics (1996b), table 2, diagrams 1 and 2.
74. Central Bureau of Statistics (2000d), table 12.1.
75. Ibid., table 12.3.
76. Central Bureau of Statistics (1999a), tables 3 and 4.
77. Central Bureau of Statistics (2000d), table 12.5.
78. Central Bureau of Statistics (1999a), table 8.
79. Central Bureau of Statistics (2000d), table 12.5.
80. Central Bureau of Statistics (1996a), table 84.
81. Central Bureau of Statistics (2000d), table 12.1.
82. Ibid., table 12.16.
83. Ibid., table 12.14.
84. Central Bureau of Statistics (2000e), 10–11.
85. Ibid., 11.
86. See "Women's Participation in Economic and Political Life" at http://hdr.undp.org/hdro/iwompar.htm.
87. Zohar Blumenkrach, "Changes in Women's Image," *Ha'aretz*, March 13, 1995, D3.
88. See Forum of Women Managers in Industry, Manufacturers Association of Israel, "Summary of Activities June 1995–June 1996" (on file with the author) (Hebrew).
89. Data adapted from Shaked and Bareket (1999), 22 (on file with the author) (Hebrew).
90. Most of the data in this section are taken from Central Bureau of Statistics (1998a). This publication surveyed the gross monetary income of urban employees from wage and salary during 1997, of which approximately 54 percent were men and 46 percent were women. Unfortunately, this is the most recent CBS general income survey. Data relating to 1998 are from Central Bureau of Statistics (2000e). Current and regular CBS published data do not contain the gender breakdown of workers' income.
91. State Income Administration, Ministry of Finance (1999), 102.
92. Letter from Brenda Morgenstern of the National Insurance Institute Research Department, dated November 1, 2000 (on file with the author).
93. National Insurance Institute (1999a), table 51.
94. Letter from Brenda Morgenstern, note 92.
95. See "Gender-Related Development Index" at http://hdr.undp.org/hdro/98gdi.htm.
96. Data submitted by the Ministry of Finance, Unit for Salary and Labor Agreements, dated November 24, 1996 and November 20, 2000 (on file with the author).

97. Internal Intermediate Report on Women in the Civil Service, November 1997, prepared by Esther Breiman (on file with the author).
98. Most of the information in this section is based on S. Swirski and Hazan (1993).

Chapter 8. Political and Public Life

1. For a more detailed discussion of the Human Development Database see "The Situation of Women in Israel—An Overview" in Chapter 1.
2. See "Women as Agents of Change" in Chapter 3.
3. Basic Law: The Knesset, 1958, S.H. 69.
4. For a discussion of female representation and the role women's issues played in political campaigns in Israel see the next part of this chapter.
5. In fact, as of March 2001, the number of women MKs grew to 16, with the resignations of two male MKs and the appointment of women in their places.
6. The National Religious Party (Mafdal) had a woman on its list to the Knesset, but the place it secured for a woman candidate (8th) was unrealistic.
7. The quota system, which demands appointment of female candidates, varies between parties, from demanding a certain overall percentage of women to ensuring set places within the party's list.
8. The 14th Knesset Statistical Report can be found at the Knesset's official web site: http://www.knesset.gov.il/knesset/hebframe.htm.
9. See Hila Tov, "7.5 Percent of the Legislators, Double Share in Legislation," *Ha'aretz,* July 20, 1999, A6.
10. Ibid. In comparison, only 10 percent of the bills put forward by a male member of the Committee on the Status of Women involved women's status.
11. As mentioned in Chapter 2, Rachel Kagan played an instrumental role in the drafting of the Women's Equal Rights Law. The most recent attempts in the 1999 elections included Shin, the Women's Equality Party, led by manifestly feminist leaders, who withdrew from the race for lack of resources, and former model and successful businesswoman Pnina Rosenblum's party, which claimed it would dedicate itself to advance women's status. Indeed, her well publicized campaign almost did bring her and her party to the Knesset.
12. Interview with Esther Herzog, leader of Shin, in *Kol Ha-Nashim,* May 1999, 2: 7.
13. Haim Shibi, "Despite Female MK's Support," *Yedioth Aharonot,* October 14, 1999, A5.
14. Office Holders in the Authorities (President of the State and His Relatives) Pension Decision, 1981, K.T. 4266, 1433.
15. Information submitted to the Authority for the Advancement of Women by Nadia Hillu, counsel on women's advancement at the Local Authorities Center, October 14, 1999 (on file with the author).
16. Khouri (1993).
17. Information from Nadia Hillu, note 15.
18. This is the phrasing used by the authors of the Palestinian "Shadow Report" to CEDAW. See Working Group on the Status of Palestinian Women in Israel (1997).
19. Letter from Zehava Berlezon, head of IBA Welfare Department, dated December 13, 2000 (on file with the author).
20. Israel Women's Network press release, dated August 6, 1995.

21. Letter from Israel Meidad, head of Israel's Media Watch organization to Orit Soliciano, spokesperson of the IWN, dated February 19, 1996 (on file with the author).

22. IWN press release, note 20.

23. In fact, the official name (translated) is Women's Aid for Victims of Sexual Assaults.

24. See Knesset (1996), 9.

25. The data that follow are based on various annual reports of the Civil Service Commission, primarily an unpublished Internal Intermediate Report on Women in the Civil Service, November 1997, prepared by Esther Breiman (on file with the author), and on the 1999 report (see Shaked and Bareket 1999).

26. State Service (Appointments) Law (Appropriate Representation) (Amendment No. 7), 1995, S.H. 500.

27. This figure is calculated from data relating to the manner of placement of all workers placed in 1997, from the 1997 internal 1997 report, note 25.

28. Data concerning 1997–98 tenders are from Maor (2001).

29. In 1998, women's chances of success were slightly higher the men's in internal tenders (34 percent versus 33 percent) and slightly lower in public tenders (7 percent versus 7.5 percent).

30. See "State Feminism" in Chapter 3.

31. For an analysis of section 18A of the Government Corporations Law, see text accompanying note 42.

32. State Service (Appointments) Law (Amendment No. 11), 2001, S.H. 78; see "State Feminism" in Chapter 3.

33. Letter from advocate Ariel Giz of the Court Administration Research Division, dated January 11, 2001 (on file with the author).

34. Letter from Sara Cohen of the Court Administrator Office, dated October 30, 1996 (on file with the author).

35. Data submitted by the Ministry of the Treasury, Unit for Salary and Labor Agreements, dated November 24, 1996 (on file with the author).

36. See note 25.

37. No sociological work has been done on lawyers in Israel. For observations of this process in the U.S. legal field, see Seron and Fuchs Epstein (1998).

38. Basic Law: Judicature, 1984, S.H. 78, section 4(b).

39. Letter from Rina Ish-Shalom, a registrar in the National Labor Court, dated November 11, 1999 (on file with the author).

40. The compensation in 1999 stood at approximately $120 per district labor court meeting and $150 per national labor court meeting.

41. See the beginning of Chapter 9.

42. Government Corporations Law (Amendment No. 6) (Appointments), 1993, S.H. 92.

43. For a discussion of the amendment's effects, as well as the IWN case, see "Affirmative Action" in Chapter 2.

44. Letters from Noga Kadosh, secretary of the Committee for Scrutiny of Appointments, September 12, 2000, and from Ze'ev Oren, deputy director of the Government Corporations Authority, November 26, 1996 (on file with the author).

45. Letter from Ze'ev Oren, deputy director of the Government Corporations Authority, to Corporation Board Chairs and Directors, August 25, 1999 (on file with the author).

46. Defense Service Law (Amendment No. 11), 2000, S.H. 64. The broader legal framework is detailed below, in the text following note 57.

47. Women's Equal Rights Law (Amendment No. 2), 2000, S.H. 167, section 6D. The Defense Service Law also has the "substance and nature of the position" qualification.

48. Comments made by the head of the Women's Corps, Brigadier-General Orit Adato, and Lieutenant Colonel Tsiki Sela in Protocol No. 9, during the session of the Knesset Committee for the Advancement of Women (October 13, 1999).

49. Letter from Major Efrat Segev of the IDF Spokesman's Office, dated January 21, 2000 (on file with the author).

50. Letter from Major Efrat of the IDF Spokesman's Office, dated July 10, 2000 (on file with the author). See also Tsiki Sela's comments, note 48, p. 7.

51. See note 61 below, also the comments made by the army head of human resources Major General Yehuda Segev during an interview on the IDF radio station, dated November 2, 1999 (transcript on file with the author).

52. The head of the Women's Corps in her presentation to the Knesset Committee on the Advancement of Women clearly used this rhetoric, as did her predecessor in an interview with the author in September 1996. See letter from Major Segev, July 10, 2000, note 50.

53. From the Knesset debates, session 281, held January 26, 1999 (not published yet).

54. See note 48, Orit Adato's comments at p. 24 and Tsiki Sela's comments at p. 4.

55. See Amos Harel, "One by One," *Ha'aretz*, January 5, 2000, A8 (Hebrew); see also note 70.

56. Defense Service Law (Consolidated Version), 1986, S.H. 107.

57. In H.C. 3267/97, *Rubinstein v. the Minister of Defense*, 52(5) P.D. 481, the Supreme Court declared the blanket postponement or cancellation of army duty for ultra-Orthodox men studying in Talmudic institutions to be illegal and gave the Knesset one year to legislate a new arrangement for the potential drafting of these men.

58. National Service Law, 1953, S.H. 163.

59. See text accompanying 77 for data on this issue.

60. The 1952 Defense Service Regulations (Women's Roles in Service) were void as a result of a 1987 amendment to the Defense Service Law: Defense Service Law (Amendment No. 2), 1987, S.H. 137.

61. H.C. 4541/94, *Alice Miller v. the Minister of Defense*, 49(4), 94. Interestingly, until 1956 several women had served as air force pilots of carrier planes.

62. See the declaration by the commander of Israel's air force in the *Miller* case, note 61, p. 107.

63. Itsik Saban, "The First Female Combat Pilot," *Ma'ariv*, June 26, 2001 (Hebrew).

64. See note 61 and accompanying text.

65. Letter from Major Segev, January 21, 2000, note 48 above.

66. See the notes 48 and 51.

67. See note 48, Sela's comments, p. 8 and Adato's comments, p. 23.

68. Letter from Major Segev, January 21, 2000, note 49.

69. Palmach, acronym of Striking Force, was the armed unit of pre-state Haganah, the self-defense Jewish organization during the British rule of Palestine.

70. See Netty C. Gross, "Fighting the Wrong War?" *Jerusalem Report*, December 20, 1999. Although the effective exclusion of women from the general staff

forum is confirmed here, the writer also refers to Chief of Staff Mofaz's recent round of appointments, which included the advancement of women in two posts previously held by men, commander of the army's human resources training program and the top post in charge of retirees in the Personnel Division.

71. Letter from Captain Ayelet Harel, head of the Organization and Counseling Department for the Women's Corps, dated November 26, 1996 (on file with the author).

72. The analysis in this paragraph is based on the meeting referred to in note 48.

73. Amos Harel, "New Chief of Staff Instruction on Sexual Harassment Has Come into Effect," *Ha'aretz*, April 3, 2000, A10.

74. Letter from Major Segev, January 21, 2000, note 49.

75. Knesset Committee on the Status of Women, Protocol No. 14, June 6, 2001, pp. 7 and 3 respectively.

76. See Knesset (1999), p. 1.

77. Letter from Colonel Einat Ron, chief military prosecutor, July 10, 2000 (on file with the author).

78. In fact, even state officials who do have first-hand knowledge of the facts find it hard to supply concrete information. The state budget undergoes numerous changes from its original approved form to its final implementation. Actual expenditures might include surpluses from previous years, thus hindering direct comparison over time. Budget sections often bear obscure titles that similarly obstruct the grasp of the bottom line expenditure for particular purposes. This became clear to me during efforts to uncover the actual allocation of state resources to the prevention of violence against women and treatment of victims. Telephone interview with Meirav Shaviv of the Finance Ministry, Budgets Department, October 26, 2000.

79. See, e.g., deliberations of the Knesset Committee for the Advancement of Women, Protocol No. 2, July 26, 1999, debating with the Ministry of Finance representatives the amounts required for the implementation of the inter-ministerial committee recommendations for combating violence against women.

80. One may recall that a major initiative that the Authority for the Advancement of Women had sought to engage in was a comprehensive analysis of the state budget from the perspective of gender. Adva Center had been the commissioned institute, but the resulting document is regrettably not a comprehensive analysis but only a partial portrayal of several issues, reflecting the partial availability of information when no full disclosure of government information is available.

81. See Chapters 5 and 7.

82. See S. Swirski et al. (2001), 16. See also references to budgetary allocations in Chapter 9, toward the end of the section on "Sexual Violence Against Women: Some Facts and Figures."

83. Telephone interview with Meirav Shaviv, note 78.

84. See deliberations of the Knesset Committee for the Advancement of Women, Protocol No. 2, July 26, 1999, at 8, 12–13.

85. Ibid.

86. Telephone interview with Meirav Shaviv, note 78.

87. The following analysis is based on broader discussion in Halperin-Kaddari (2000b).

88. These countries include Afghanistan, Bangladesh, Egypt, Iran, Iraq, Jordan, Libya, Maldives, Mauritania, and Pakistan (Tomasevski 1998).

89. Convention on the Elimination of All Forms of Discrimination Against Women, K.A. 31, 180, at 195.

90. For a broader discussion of these points, see text following note 91.

91. Rabbinical Judges (Dayanim) Law, 1955, S.H. 68; Druze Courts Law, 1962, S.H. 20.

92. We are already witnessing the beginning of this process in the form of a special program in one of the Orthodox institutes for higher Torah learning for women in Israel, trains women to be "halachic advisors" on matters of family purity and reproduction. See Larry Derfner, "A Step Up for Orthodox Women," *Jerusalem Post,* October 8, 1999.

93. This issue is indeed unsettled in terms of halachic interpretation. Rabbi Uziel, the first Sephardi Chief Rabbi of Israel and one of the great Sephardi religious sages in the twentieth century, had in principle permitted women to serve as religious judges; see Uziel (1964). For an analysis of halachic opinions regarding women religious judges see Rosen-Zvi (1990), 246–47; Riskin (1999), 698–704.

94. Women's Equal Rights Law (Amendment No. 2), 2000, S.H. 167.

95. H.C 891/01, *Ubeid and others v. The Minister of Religious Affairs and others,* P.D. 55(3), 857.

96. Rabbinical Advocates Regulations, 1967, K.T. 2119, 16.

97. H.C. 6300/93, *The Institution for Rabbinical Advocates Training v. The Minister of Religion,* P.D. 48(4) 441.

98. H.C. 953/87, *Poraz v. Shlomo Lahat, Mayor of Tel Aviv,* 42(2) P.D. 309.

99. H.C. 153/87 *Shakdiel v. The Minister of Religious Affairs and others,* 42(2) P.D. 221.

100. In 1996, only 12 of 139 religious councils included a woman. This information was obtained by Ms Atara Kenigsberg, administrator of the Forum on Women's Status at Bar-Ilan University, after going through the records of all religious councils in the country.

101. Regulations on the Protection of Sacred Places for the Jewish People (Amendment), 1989, K.T. 5237, 190.

102. H.C. 257/89, *Anat Hofman v. The Commissioner of the West Wall,* 48(2) P.D. 309.

103. Recommendations of the Committee to Encourage the Use of Public Transportation Within the Ultra-Orthodox Sector, May 1997 (on file with the author); Israel Women's Network appeal to the High Court of Justice in H.C. 5079/97, *Israel Women's Network v. The Minister of Traffic* (on file with the author).

104. Appendix to the Israel Women's Network appeal, ibid.

105. *Brown v. Board of Education,* 347 US 483 (1954).

106. During the 1990s, the tension between the High Court of Justice and the religious community in Israel rose to an unprecedented peak (Hofnung 1996; Rosen-Zvi 1995).

Chapter 9. Violence Against Women

1. Radical feminism has not occupied center stage alone, of course. The 1980s also witnessed the advance in popularity of cultural feminism, among other theories of feminism that reject liberal feminism.

2. UN Doc A/44/38 and A/47/38.

3. To give an example, according to Yoram Shachar, during the twenty years

since the enactment of the 1977 Penal Law, 13 of the 20 amendments to the part that deals with specific offenses were in the area of sex, family, and children. See Shachar (1998).

4. See also the discussion in note 81 and accompanying text.

5. See Schulhoffer (1995); Scales (1986); Schneider (1986). For a similar discussion within the Israeli context, see Shachar (1993).

6. For a broader discussion of this system see text accompanying note 89.

7. For a broader look at the budgetary aspect see text accompanying notes 69–70, as well as the discussion in Chapter 8 in the section on "The Allocation of Resources: The Battle over the Budget."

8. This committee was mentioned in Chapter 8, in the section "The Allocation of Resources: The Battle over the Budget." See the discussion in the text accompanying note 88.

9. The other area is day care centers for children of working mothers.

10. Prevention of Sexual Harassment Law, 1998, S.H. 166.

11. Cr.C. (Jerusalem) 3185/00, *The State of Israel v. Mordechai* (not published).

12. Cr.A. (Jerusalem) 2206/01, *The State of Israel v. Mordechai* (not published).

13. Orna Coussin, "When Men Don't Get It," *Ha'aretz*, March 13, 2000, D4.

14. For a typical article see Atara Ofek, "Easy Pickings," *Ha'aretz* Supplement, March 17, 2000.

15. Letter from the state attorney, dated May 2, 1999 (on file with the author).

16. The survey was described in Chapter 4, and its findings on the issue of violence against women are discussed below.

17. Penal Law, 1977, S.H. 226; Penal Law (Amendment No. 22), 1988, S.H. 62; Penal Law (Amendment No. 26), 1990, S.H. 10; Penal Law (Amendment No. 30), 1990, S.H. 196.

18. See, for example, D.N. 37/80, *Cohen v. The State of Israel*, 35(1) P.D. 371.

19. It is probably relevant to mention a popular 1962 song: "When you say 'No,' what do you mean?" (which includes the line: "You say 'No' with such grace / It sounds much more inviting than a 'Yes'"). The song, by playwright and songwriter Dan Almagor, has been quoted regularly at Israeli rape cases by defense lawyers. In the wake of public outrage in response to the Shomrat case, see note 33 and accompanying text (where, once again, the defense lawyers had not failed to quote the song in their response to the state's appeal), Almagor added a verse to the song, repudiating everything implied by the question in the title. Some judges now use this final verse in answer to defense quotes of the first verse.

20. Penal Law (Amendment No. 61), 2001, S.H. 408.

21. For a discussion of marriage age, see Chapter 11.

22. Evidence Ordinance (New Version), 1971, D.M.I. 421.

23. Penal Law (Amendment No. 47), 1996, S.H. 42.

24. Procedural Amendment Law (Questioning of Witnesses), 1957, S.H. 16, as amended by Penal Law (Amendment No. 22), 1988, S.H. 62

25. Procedural Amendment Law (Amendment No. 2) (Questioning of Witnesses), 1995, S.H. 152.

26. Regulations for implementing these provisions, promulgated in 1997, provide for the use of closed circuit television systems in such cases: Procedural Amendment Regulations (Questioning of Witnesses) (A Sexual Offense Complainant's Testimony in the Accused's Absence), 1996, K.T. 5801, 275.

27. Prevention of Sexual Harassment Law, 1998, S.H. 166.

28. Equal Employment Opportunities Law, 1988, S.H. 38.

29. On the concept of the "reasonable person" in Israeli law, see Barak-Erez (1997).

30. Stalking Law, 2001, S.H. 2.

31. See the discussion following note 73.

32. Penal Law (Amendment No. 51), 1998, S.H. 270.

33. Cr.A. 5612/92, *The State of Israel v. Be'eri and Others*, 48(1) P.D. 302.

34. Recall the findings of the study of gender in the courts discussed in the last part of Chapter 2.

35. Cr.C. (Haifa) 290/90 *The State of Israel v. Biton and Others* (not published, sentence issued August 18, 1994).

36. Cr.A. 1156/96, *The State of Israel v. Biton and Others*, 50(2) P.D. 837.

37. Cr.A. 2800/93, *Kriksman v. The State of Israel* (not published); Cr.A. 993/93, *Abutbul v. The State of Israel*, 48(1) P.D. 485.

38. This phenomenon reached its height on International Women's Day 1999, an election year. That year, the president, the prime minister, and the leading opposition candidate for prime minister all visited shelters for battered women on Women's Day.

39. Prevention of Violence in the Family Law, 1991, S.H. 138.

40. C.A. 192/82, *Sadan v. Sadan*, 36(4) P.D. 169.

41. C.A. 4480/93, *Kirshner v. Kirshner*, 48(4) P.D. 461.

42. Prevention of Violence in the Family Law (Amendment No. 4), 1998, S.H. 308.

43. Interview with Ms Esther Sivan, legal advisor to the IWN, August 1999.

44. National Health Regulations (Notification of Suspected Violence), 1975, K.T. 3419, 275.

45. Prevention of Violence in the Family Law (Amendment No. 7), 2001, S.H. 10.

46. Such instructions are included in "Investigation Department Official Guidelines (Internal Instructions) on Police Handling of Violence Between Spouses" (on file with the author).

47. Criminal Procedural Law (Enforcement Authorities—Arrests), 1996, S.H. 338.

48. An indirect amendment (No. 2) to the Criminal Procedural Law (Enforcement Authorities—Arrests), a part of the Prevention of Violence in the Family Law (Amendment No. 3), 1998, S.H. 16.

49. Penal Law (Amendment No. 49), 1996, S.H. 241.

50. Penal Law (Amendment No. 55), 2000, S.H. 226.

51. Prevention of Violence in the Family Law (Amendment No. 2), 1996, S.H. 243.

52. See, for example, the findings of the parliamentary committee below, showing that in more than a third of the cases where women were murdered by their spouses between 1990 and 1995, a gun was used (see text following note 77). Likewise, in three out of the six murders during the first half of 1999, a licensed weapon was used. See Proceedings of the Committee for the Advancement of the Status of Women, Protocol 2, July 26 1999, 4–6.

53. An indirect amendment (No. 11) to the Weapon Law, a part of the Prevention of Violence in the Family Law (Amendment No. 3), 1998, S.H. 16.

54. Legal Aid Regulations (Amendment), 1995, K.T. 5700, 1754; Legal Aid Law, 1972, S.H. 95.

55. Letter from the Legal Aid Commissioner, dated July 9, 1997 (on file with the author).

56. Recompensation Law (Child Orphaned due to Domestic Violence), 1995, S.H. 376.

57. Victims of Offenses' Rights Law, 2001, S.H.183.

58. Internal directives of the State Prosecutor No. 2.5, 9.1 and 15.10, dated January 2, 1994.

59. Employment of Women Law (Amendment 19) (Limitations of Dismissals of Worker Who Stays in a Shelter for Battered Women), 2000, S.H. 246.

60. Single-Parent Families Law (Amendment No. 3), 2001, S.H. 218.

61. The committee had recommended the institution of regulations forbidding this procedure (Inter-Ministerial Committee 1998, 65)

62. Presentation at the conference on Family Courts' Handling of Violence Within the Family, Bar-Ilan University, March 9, 1999.

63. Cr.A. 6353/94, *Buhbut v. The State of Israel*, 49(3) P.D. 647.

64. On the syndrome in general, see Schneider (1986).

65. For more information on the public discourse of the Buhbut case, see Fletcher (1997).

66. Cr.A. 6353/94, *Azualus v. The State of Israel*, 50(2) P.D. 573.

67. The description of the help centers' background and activities that follows draws mainly on a letter and accompanying materials from Tami Shemesh, director for professional contacts at the Union of Help Centers (on file with the author).

68. Telephone interview with Meirav Shaviv of the Finance Ministry, Budgets Department, October 26, 2000; Swirski n.d., 16.

69. Telephone interview with Tal Kormann, chair of the Help Centers Union, October 26, 2000.

70. Investigation Department Official Guidelines (Internal Instructions) on Police Handling of Sex Offenses Against Women (on file with the author).

71. Letter from Malca Sofer, head of the Department of Offenses Casualties, to Oded Brook, legal counselor to the Ministry of Internal Defense, dated July 1, 1997 (on file with the author).

72. Unpublished data provided by chief superintendent Avi Davidovich, head of the Investigation Section of the Israeli police, dated November 10, 2000; letter from Oded Brook, legal counselor to the Ministry of Internal Defense, dated December 16, 1996 (on file with the author).

73. A more detailed description of the study appears in Chapter 3, in the section"Gender Bias in Israeli Courts."

74. The following data derive from the letters mentioned in note 72.

75. Unpublished data provided by chief superintendent David Sagiv, Department of Statistics, Israel Police, dated December 6, 2000 (on file with the author).

76. See Ruti Sinai, "Unseeing Doctors," *Ha'aretz*, January 29, 2001, 10.

77. For a comprehensive survey of government response to the raising of this problem see, for example, Swirski (1993b).

78. In 1962, MK Beba Edelson tried to raise the issue through a parliamentary question that was immediately put down. MK Marcia Freedman, in 1976, was the first to succeed in publicly raising the issue and demanding action. Her address to the house was repeatedly interrupted by laughter and scorn, but it prompted the establishment of the first committee to investigate the problem of battered women in Israel (see Swirski, 1993b; Freedman 1990).

79. See also text preceding note 39.

80. Internal guidelines of the Department of Investigations and Prosecutions

on Police Handling of Family Violence Offenses, Guideline No. 03.300.226, dated April 4, 1990 (on file with the author).

81. The study included quantitative analysis of 1,000 cases of domestic violence (including violence against children) and qualitative analysis of questionnaires and in-depth interviews of police personnel and welfare workers.

82. The cases analyzed were from 1995; the police interviews were conducted in 1997. The researchers note that some changes have occurred in police treatment of this problem in recent years, nevertheless the principal findings of both the actual treatment and outcome of cases, especially on police attitudes toward domestic violence, are still pertinent.

83. Israel police, unpublished data supplied by superintendent Esther Dominicini, head of personnel, letter dated December 18, 2000 (on file with the author).

84. This was the wording of the questions posed to the police personnel; see Eisikovits and Griffel (1998), 83.

85. The study consisted of analysis of 92 questionnaires filled out by police personnel in one police station in a central town in Israel, similar to the one where the previous study was conducted in 1997.

86. The study consisted of 30 investigators of a special domestic violence unit and 70 general investigators.

87. See also text accompanying note 8.

88. Letter from Advocate Nurit Ziv, head of Victims' Department, Ministry of Internal Security, February 3, 2000 (on file with the author).

89. See, for example, Shachar (1993) (discussing the Shomrat case, note 33); Kamir (1997) (discussing the Azualus case, note 66) and Bilski (1997) (discussing the Buhbut case, note 63). In addition to these, newspaper articles do sometimes focus on judges' expressions in holdings and in sentencing in order to raise attention to what they perceive as gender bias, but these are more anecdotal in nature.

90. Eisikovitz and Griffel (1998) found that 75 percent of police personnel think that sentencing levels should be more severe than their present levels.

91. For example, the number of court restraining orders issued through the Ministry of Justice Legal Aid Unit went up to 841 in 1999, from 483 in 1998 and 215 in 1995. See Ruti Sinai, "Family Violence," *Ha'aretz*, August 6, 2000, A1.

92. Letter form Orli Innes, national supervisor (Violence in the Family), Ministry of Labor and Welfare, to Dana Gordon of the Women's Status Committee, dated January 8, 1997 (on file with the author).

93. Ibid.

94. Letter from Tzipi Nachshon-Glick, Ministry of Welfare, dated October 30, 2000 (on file with the author).

95. Ministry of Health, Director General Directive, Circular 20/90 (August 28, 1990).

Chapter 10. The Exploitation of Women

1. Researchers estimate that 80 percent of women who have engaged in criminal activity had been victims of sexual exploitation in the past; see Committee for the Examination of Commercial Sexual Exploitation of Children in Israel (CECSECI) (1997), 24. Similarly, the women's prison deputy superintendent

estimates that 70 percent of the inmates were sexually abused during childhood; see Nina Pinto, "Second Rate Prisoners," *Ha'aretz*, July 28, 1999, B4.

2. Nisan Ben-Ami and Leah Gruenpeter-Gold, "Pornography is the PR of Violence against Women," unpublished manuscript dated November 21, 2000 (Hebrew, on file with the author).

3. Menachem Horovitz, "Prostitution Business," *Ha'aretz*, January 1, 1997, B2.

4. Anat Bashan, "White Slavery," 178 *Mar'ot* (Israel Police Bulletin) (July–August 2000): 6 (Hebrew), interviewing Superintendent Avi Davidovitch, head of the Investigation Department.

5. "Trafficking in Persons Report" released by the I.S. Department of State, July 2001. The report placed Israel in tier 3, countries who do not fully comply with the minimum standards of the Victims of Trafficking and Violence Protection Act, 2000 (U.S. acts, PL 106–386), including the vigorous investigation and prosecution of trafficking; protection of victims of trafficking; adoption of measures, including education, to prevent trafficking; and more.

6. A similar pattern is seen below with respect to the issue of minors' involvement in prostitution.

7. See text accompanying notes 22–25.

8. See *Ma'ariv*, August 16, 2000; August 27, 2000.

9. Dan Izenberg and Heidi Gleit, "Amnesty: Israel Failing to Deal with White-Slave Trade," *Jerusalem Post*, May 5, 2000.

10. Chen Nardi, Leah Gruenpeter-Gold, and Nisan Ben-Ami, "Prevention of Prostitution and Trafficking: A Social Challenge," September 2000, p. 28 (Hebrew, on file with the author).

11. Letter from Superintendent Avi Davidovitch, December 17, 2000 (on file with the author).

12. State of Israel, "Statement of Israeli Delegation to the World Congress Against Commercial Sexual Exploitation of Children," presented August 27–31, 1996, Stockholm, p.4.

13. "We Are Worthy" (Anahnu Shavot—also meaning "we are equal") is a support group for prostitutes established in 1991, aiming to "change the situation of women (and men) in the sex industry, create fair working conditions and to develop other options"; see *Anahnu Shavot* 2 (1993): 12 (Hebrew).

14. Penal Law, 1977, S.H. 226; see text accompanying note 32.

15. Leah Gruenpeter Gold, Nissan Ben Ami, Sigal Rosen, and Nomi Levenkron, 2001 National NGO report to the annual UN Commission on Human Rights: Evaluation of National Authorities Activities and Actual Facts on the Trafficking in Persons for the Purpose of Prostitution in Israel, March 2001.

16. Declaration according to Public Health Order (Medical Examinations and Instructions Regarding HIV), Y.P. 1988, 1154.

17. Public Health Order (Medical Examinations and Instructions Regarding HIV), 1987, 323.

18. Telephone interview with counselor of the Ministry of Health legal department, September 1999.

19. Law amending the Penal Code (Prostitution Offenses), 1962, S.H. 78.

20. These would include the following: when the woman is a minor under eighteen years of age; when the woman is the perpetrator's daughter or wife or when he is her custodian, teacher, or otherwise in charge of her; and when the perpetrator accused of solicitation was armed during the act.

21. Cr.A. 476/72, *Tertakovski and Others v. The State of Israel*, 27(1) P.D. 376.

22. This includes acting as a go-between for that purpose. See Penal Law

(1977), section 203A(a). Note also the gender-neutral language used here, as explained below following note 34.

23. These now include taking advantage of relations of dependency or any other form of distress on the part of the person prostituted, leading to ten years imprisonment; or the use of power or threatening such use, or abusing any situation that obstructs objection on the part of the person prostituted, or through manipulation or fraud, all leading to sixteen years imprisonment. See Penal Law (1977), section 203.

24. Penal Law (1977), section 203B.

25. Penal Law (1977), section 203A(b).

26. Woman's Equal Rights Law, 1951, S.H. 248, section 6B.

27. Significantly, the section also relates to abduction for purposes of severe battery or unlawful sexual relations.

28. Draft bill amending Penal Law (No. 58) (Prostitution, Sex, and Obscenity Offenses), 1997, H.C. 464.

29. See the Introduction to the explanatory notes of the draft bill.

30. Law amending the Criminal Code Ordinance (No. 37), 1975, S.H. 122.

31. As by the recently established interministerial committee mentioned above, see also text accompanying notes 39 and 55.

32. One of Ben Eato's committee's recommendations was to enforce this section against the clients of prostitutes.

33. Penal Law, 1977, old section 210, repealed by Penal Law (Amendment No. 56), 2000, S.H.226.

34. Penal Law, 1977, section 203C.

35. Note 43 below.

36. Interview with Betty Lahat, Neve-Tirza prison superintendent, January 1997 (transcript on file with the author).

37. The following data are taken from a letter from Superintendent Avi Davidovitch, August 15, 2001 (on file with the author).

38. Internal directives of the state prosecutor No. 2.2, dated January 2, 1994.

39. See text following note 6.

40. See, for example, Cr.A.135/69, *Meir v. The State Counselor,* 18(4) P.D. 516.

41. Cr.c. (T.A.) 367/89 *The State of Israel v. Prosper* (not published).

42. Cr.A. 135/64, *The State of Israel v. Alian,* 26(2) P.D. 732; C.A. 3763/92; *Anonymous v. Attorney General,* 47(1) P.D. 869.

43. Cr.A. 3520/91, *Turgemann v. The State of Israel,* 47(1) P.D. 441.

44. Cr.c. (Nazareth) 472/98, *The State of Israel v. Avitan* (not published).

45. Cr.A. 4511/93 *Pinchasov v. The State of Israel* (not published).

46. See note 43.

47. H.C. 1119/01, *Zaritzkia v. The Minister of Interior* (not yet published).

48. Data supplied by Superintendent Avi Davidovitch during *Ma'rot* interview, note 4, at 7.

49. Ibid., 9.

50. International Covenant on Civil and Political Rights, K.A. 1040, 269, Articles 8, 9, 10(2)(a).

51. UN document CCPR/C/79/Add.93, Concluding Observations, adopted July 28, 1998, para. 16.

52. State of Israel (2001), follow-up on first CEDAW report.

53. See, for example, the thorough report by the Committee for the Examination of Commercial Sexual Exploitation of Children in Israel, note 1, which was presented to the deputy attorney general in 1997.

54. Penal Law (Amendment no. 52), 1998, S.H. 316.
55. Text accompanying note 24.
56. Penal Law (1977), section 203C.
57. Penal Law (Amendment No. 52), 1998
58. These organizations include Avi, the international Association for Children's Rights; the Israel branch of this organization was opened in 1987 and is devoted to fighting against child commerce, child slavery, etc. Others include the National Council for the Well-Being of Children, a nonprofit organization founded in 1979, whose services include the identification of problems and the prevention of abuse and exploitation of minors, and MEITAL, an association for the treatment of sexually abused children and adults.
59. See note 53.
60. However, a prohibition against "obscene shows" was added to section 214 of the Penal Law (the 1991 reforms are analyzed in detail below).
61. Penal Law (Amendment No. 31), 1990, S.H. 34; Penal Law (Amendment No. 35), 1991, S.H. 208.
62. Draft bill amending the Penal Law (No. 58) (Prostitution, Sex and Obscenity Offences), 1997 H.H., 464. See discussion in note 66.
63. See text preceding note 67.
64. Penal Law (1977), section 214A.
65. See note 53 and accompanying text.
66. Draft bill amending the Penal Law (No. 58) (Prostitution, Sex and Obscenity Offences), 1997 H.H., 464. The bill also contained amendments to some provisions that deal with sexual assaults, which did not signify any change of policy with that respect, and are unrelated to our discussion here. See text accompanying and following note 28.
67. Penal Law (Amendment No. 52), 1998, S.H. 316.
68. See the explanation note for section 11 of the bill.
69. This is in line with the extraterritorial provision added to the Penal Law in 1998, regarding the use of minors for prostitution, as discussed above; see text accompanying note 57.
70. Unpublished data provided by chief superintendent David Sagiv, Department of Statistics, Israel police, dated December 6, 2000.
71. Nardi, Gruenpeter-Gold, and Ben-Ami, "Prevention of Prostitution and Trafficking," note 10, 33–34.
72. Letter from Oded Brook, legal counselor to the Ministry of Internal Defense, dated November 6, 2000 (on file with the author).

Chapter 11. The Halachic Trap: Marriage and Family Life

1. In its General Recommendation 21, the CEDAW committee noted with alarm the number of state parties that have entered reservations to Article 16, titled "Equality in Marriage and Family Law" and noted that many hold a belief in the patriarchal structure of the family, based on cultural or religious beliefs. This is indeed the case with Israel, as this article is one of the two that the State of Israel had ratified with reservations. The other one is Article 7 on Public Life, as explained in Chapter 8, where the mechanism of reservations is also detailed. The reservation to Article 16 reads, "The State of Israel hereby expresses its reservation with regard to Article 16 of the Convention, insofar as the laws of personal status binding on the several religious communities in Israel do not

conform with the provisions of that Article" (Convention on the Elimination of All Forms of Discrimination against Women, K.A. 31, 180 at 195).

2. In August 2000, then Prime Minister Ehud Barak attempted to initiate a comprehensive reform in religion and state relationships, under the title of a "Civil Revolution." Among other things, the reform would have introduced a new concept of "registered couples" similar to some forms of partners' registration in European countries, thus offering a venue for civil marriages without calling it such. See Shahar Ilan, "Beilin Proposes Partnership Law Instead of Civil Marriage," *Ha'aretz*, August 21, 2000. This attempt, though, was short-lived due to political circumstances.

3. For a comprehensive account in English of family law in Israel, see Einhorn (1997).

4. For example, in 1997 the percentage of never-married men aged 30–34 was only 18.8 percent, a sharp decrease from 48.1 percent among men aged 25–29. The decrease among the women was from 61.8 percent to 24.7 percent. The decreasing rate among Jewish women is even more impressive: from 30.6 percent among those aged 25–29 years to 12.4 percent among those aged 30–34. See Central Bureau of Statistics (2000d), table 2.19.

5. This conclusion is valid even when taking into consideration women's longer life span. Thus, for example, in 1998, of the total (30,765) Jewish men marrying in Israel, 9.4 percent were remarrying (compared to only 7 percent of marrying Jewish women). See Central Bureau of Statistics (2000d), table 3.5.

6. Ibid.

7. Ibid., table 3.12.

8. Ibid., tables 2.1 and 3.1.

9. Ibid., calculated from table 2.19.

10. Save for the possibility of consulate marriages where one or both of the parties involved are aliens, according to the consul's regulations, and save for cases of divorce between "mixed couples," that is, couples who do not belong to the same religion, according to the 1969 Jurisdiction of Dissolution of Marriage (Special Cases) Law, S.H. 573.

11. Official unpublished data supplied by Liora Binyamin of the Ministry of Interior Computer Department, letter dated November 28, 2000.

12. The calculation is simple: the number of all Israelis married during that time is the sum of those registered by the Ministry of Interior as married out of Israel and those included in the CBS statistics depicting official marriages in Israel. The former divided by the total makes close to 8 percent.

13. During 1997–98, of the 13,447 Israelis married outside Israel, 6,216 were married in Cyprus or Paraguay. Of these, 1,625 were Jewish couples, thus constituting a little more than half (3,250, or 52 percent) of the total marrying individuals there.

14. Palestine Order-in-Council, 1922–47, 3 L.S.I, 2738 (Hebrew), 2569 (English).

15. See, e.g., C.A. 15/64, *Moses v. Moses*, 18 (3) P.D. 141.

16. See, e.g., C.A. 238/53, *Cohen and Buslick v. Attorney General*, 8 P.D. 4.

17. Rabbinical Courts Jurisdiction (Marriage and Divorce) Law, 1953, S.H. 134.

18. H.C. 1000/92, *Bavli v. The Grand Rabbinical Court*, 48 (2) P.D. 6, discussed below, see notes 20 and 98 and accompanying texts.

19. This is where Women's Rights Law has had its most significant impact. Section 2 of the law, guaranteeing a married woman the same status and legal

capacity regarding her assets "as if she were single," was interpreted by the High Court of Justice in 1958 as contradicting the religious rule that grants a husband the rights to his wife's profits from her assets. Thus, this religious rule was found to be no longer applicable, and in fact no longer existing within the legal system in Israel. See C.A. 202/57, *Sidis v. The President and the Members of the Rabbinical High Court,* 12 P.D. 1528. This opened up the move to appropriate the whole subject of family assets and of property distribution as part of the civil-secular law and place it out of reach of the religious law (Rosen-Zvi 1990, 93). See H.C. 185/72, *Gur v. The Jerusalem Regional Rabbinical Court,* 26(2) P.D. 765, at 769; C.A. 384/88, *Ziserman v. Ziserman,* 43(3) P.D. 205, at 208.

20. *Bavli v. The Grand Rabbinical Court,* note 18.

21. Family Court Law, 1995, S.H. 393.

22. See Dvorah Shapira, "Liberal Divorce," Signon Supplement, *Ma'ariv,* May 27, 1998 (on file with the author).

23. Family Court Law, 1995, section 8(a).

24. Ibid., section 5.

25. Data supplied by Anat Inbar, national supervisor on family court service units, interview conducted on December 6, 2000.

26. According to the provisions of the Family Court Law, each family court was to be linked to a family court service unit, and the ratio of family court judges to service unit social workers should be 1 : 1. As of December 2000, only one court had yet to introduce such a service unit.

27. Conservative Judaism, which is also considered as adhering to Halacha, may differ on many of these issues. Examining this is obviously beyond the scope of this chapter, and is less relevant, since the predominant form of Judaism in Israel, certainly from the legal perspective, is Orthodoxy. On Conservative theories of Jewish law see Golinkin (1991).

28. The term "uncontested divorce" here describes a process based on petitions to ratify a divorce agreement reached by the parties out of court, usually through negotiation between the parties lawyers. Figures here are based on data supplied by Rabbi Eli Ben-Dahan, administrator of the rabbinical courts, letters, November 17, April 27, and June 22, 1999 and telephone interview, November 1996. The percentages in 1997 were quite similar to those for 1998: the rate of divorces promulgated in relation to the petitions was 49 percent, while 48 percent of the petitions were uncontested. Interestingly, these numbers of divorces vary somewhat from the CBS statistics, which should theoretically be identical. No explanation was supplied for the discrepancy.

29. This is more or less the average rate in the Rabbinical Courts, with the notable exception of the Rehovot and Ashdod courts (where 55 percent and 39 percent of the petitions were accepted respectively).

30. This power is guaranteed in the civil law as well, with the limitation that demands supervision of such decrees by the attorney general and the civil court, as provided in the Rabbinical Courts Jurisdiction (Marriage and Divorce) Law, section 6. See, e.g., H.C. 54/55, *Rosenzweig v. Chief Implementation Officer,* 9 P.D. 1542.

31. Unfortunately, these observations cannot be substantiated by empirical evidence, simply because no empirical study of rabbinical court files exists. Rabbinical court files are not computerized, and, like the general judicial system, rabbinical authorities are reluctant to let researchers in. Most rabbinical court decisions are unpublished, so a study of decisions alone is also impossible.

32. Letter from Rabbi Eli Ben-Dahan, administrator of the rabbinical courts, dated November 17, 1996 (on file with the author).

33. Women's organizations and the rabbinical establishment (rabbinical authorities, rabbinical courts, etc.) are in sharp disagreement as to the actual number of *agunot* cases in Israel. The disagreement is over which circumstances specifically constitute that state. For instance, while women's organizations classify the conditioning of a *get* upon surrender of the woman's property rights as a refusal to grant the *get*, rabbinical courts will not recognize that woman as an *aguna*. Consequently, women's organizations maintain that there are several thousand women who are being refused a *get*, while the rabbinical establishment claims there are only several dozen. The problem of the *agunot*, however, is inherent to the Orthodox Jewish law of marriage and divorce and is not unique to Israel. Since it is common to all Jewish communities, and it exists wherever Jewish people wish to follow both their religious laws and the laws of the state in which they live (Haut 1983; Shifman 1995b; Broyde 2001), an international coalition of Jewish women called ICAR (acronym of International Coalition for *Aguna* Rights, and a Hebrew word meaning "the most important thing") was formed in 1991 to advance solutions for the problem of the *agunot*. Despite their suggestions being all within the framework of Jewish law, they have mostly met with resistance and antagonistic reactions.

34. This is a common contention, clearly supported by the analyzed data above.

35. See, e.g., C.A. 162/72, *Amzelig v. Amzelig*, 27(1) P.D. 582; C.A. 5490/92, *Pagas v. Pagas* (not published).

36. For a broader explanation of property distribution see below, the section on "Distribution of Marital Property upon Divorce,"

37. Letter from Rabbi Eli Ben-Dahan, note 32.

38. Rabbinical Courts (Enforcement of Divorce Decrees) (Temporary Measures) Law, 1995, S.H. 139. The validity of the law was originally limited to a period of three years, but this limitation was lifted in a 1998 amendment: Rabbinical Courts (Enforcement of Divorce Decrees) (Temporary Measures) Law (Amendment no. 3), 1998, S.H. 118. These sanctions were further supplemented in 2000, with reference to where the recalcitrant husband was already serving a jail term for other reasons. In such cases, his rights as an inmate (including visitation, vacation, early release for good behavior) may be restricted: Rabbinical Courts (Enforcement of Divorce Decrees) (Temporary Measures) Law (Amendment No. 4), 2000, S.H. 133.

39. Unlike the previously available incarceration orders (see note 30), these orders do not have to pass the supervision of the civil system.

40. Data supplied by Rabbi Ben-Dahan, see notes 28 and 30.

41. These specific economic rules, unlike the rules that pertain to the actual marital relationship, can be altered by the couple by mutual consent.

42. To be more exact, rabbinical (oral) law did add a prohibition on married men's engagement in extramarital relations, but rabbinical law is inherently far less powerful than the Torah (written) law, hence the consequences of its breach—if it is enforced in the first place—are in no way comparable to the consequences of breaching the Torah law. For a more detailed explanation, see Halperin-Kaddari (2000a).

43. The Marriage Age Law, 1950, S.H. 286.

44. Marriage Age Law (Amendment no. 4), 1998, S.H. 318

45. For more information about the dichotomy between the state of Israel's commitment to freedom of religion and its concomitant intertwining of religion with state, see Treitel (1995).

46. C.A. 501/81, *Attorney General v. Anonymous*, 35(4) P.D. 430.
47. C.A. 4736/94, *Angel v. Attorney General* (not yet published).
48. Penal Law, 1977, S.H. 226.
49. Central Bureau of Statistics (2000d), tables 3.5 and 3.4.
50. Apparently, as part of advanced computerization of the entire judicial system, such separate data will be available in the foreseeable future, as mentioned in a letter from Judge Malka Aviv, head of research, report and evaluation, Court Administration Office, dated December 10, 2000 (on file with the author). This, however, only emphasizes the lack of specific awareness and commitment to these issues, and the denial of their view as deserving special attention and scrutiny.
51. Letter from Shirly Koren, manager of the Court Administration Office, dated January 8, 1997 (on file with the author); letter from Judge Malka Aviv, note 50.
52. The exact number of judicial permits is impossible to obtain, since, according to the Court Administration Office, the Tel Aviv District Court's records had already been archived.
53. Letter from Shirly Koren, note 51. While the figures supplied by the Court Administration Office do not depict the actual holding in each petition over the years, they do enable a general assessment of the approvals' rate throughout a period of time.
54. Letter from Rabbi Eli Ben Dahan, note 32.
55. D.N. 10/69, *Boronovsky v. Chief Rabbi*, 28(1) P.D. 7.
56. See note 10.
57. F.A. 1044/99, *Zinger-Brochovitch v. Brochovitch* (not yet published).
58. H.C. 143/62, *Funk-Schlezinger v. The Minister of Interior*, 17(1) P.D. 225.
59. C.A. 4590/92, *Cahana v. Cahana* (not published).
60. See note 64 and accompanying text.
61. C.A. 563/65, *Yeger v. Palevitch*, 20(3) P.D. 244.
62. Spouses (Property Relations) Law, 1973, S.H. 267; C.A. 52/80, *Shachar v. Friedman*, 38(1) P.D. 443.
63. Entry into Israel Law, 1952, S.H. 354.
64. C.A. 2000/97, *Lindorn v. Karnit* (not yet published).
65. H.C. 721/94, *El-Al Israel Airlines v. Danilovitch*, 48(5) P.D. 749.
66. Equal Employment Opportunity Law (Amendment), 1992, S.H. 37.
67. For judicial developments in areas other than family relations, see Harel (2000).
68. F.A. 8/94, *Shtyner v. Retribution Officer* (not published); M. A. 369/94, *Shtyner v. IDF* (not published)
69. Public Health (In Vitro Fertilization) Regulation, 1987, K.T. 5035, 978; Circular 34/92, Rules as to the Administration of Sperm Banks and Guidelines for Performing Artificial Inseminations, issued in 1992 (on file with the author).
70. H.C. 998/96, *Weitz et al. v. The Minister of Health* (not published). The subsequent directive appeared in a letter from the director general, Ministry of Health, dated February 23, 1997, to managers of general hospitals (on file with the author).
71. CLAF's Legal-Public Agenda, in a letter from attorney Ira Eden of Claf organization, dated December 12, 1999 (on file with the author).
72. H.C. 1779/99 *Kadish v. The Minister of Interior* 54(2) P.D. 368.
73. This distinction between the administrative level of the registration and the substantive legal level is a long-standing rule in Israeli law, as explained above in the context of civil marriage out of Israel.

74. DNGZ 4252/00, *The Minister of Interior v. Kadish* (not published).

75. F.C. 50A/97, *Anonymous v. The Ministry of Labor and Welfare* (not published). The guardian order was made upon the approval of the Ministry of Labor and Welfare's legal advisor, as the government organ in charge of the formal welfare and adoption services.

76. F.C. 49/97, *Anonymous v. The Ministry of Labor and Welfare* (not published).

77. F.A (T.A) 10/99, *Anonymous v. Attorney General* (not published).

78. F.C. 51601/98, *Anonymous v. Anonymous* (not published); P.A. 20209/99, *Anonymous v. Anonymous* (not published).

79. ACRI, Media Memo, March 30, 1998 (on file with the author).

80. Einat Fishbein, "Two Foreigners Recognized as Israeli Residents Based upon Same-Sex Cohabitation," *Ha'aretz*, February 14, 2000.

81. "Ima ve'Ima" ("Mom and Mom)," a documentary produced for the Israeli Second Channel, 1999 (on file with the author).

82. Legal Capacity and Guardianship Law, 1962, S.H. 120.

83. Women's Equal Rights Law, 1951, S.H. 248.

84. Dafna Hacker, "Parenthood, Divorce, and Law: A Sociological Analysis of the Legal Field," unpublished Ph.D. proposal, 2000 (Hebrew, on file with the author).

85. This figure does not include divorces in Christian and Muslim courts; see National Council for Children (2000), *Children in Israel* (2000), table 3.5.

86. See text following note 17.

87. H.C. 7/83, *Biares v. The Rabbinical Court*, 38(1) P.D. 673 ; C.A. 716/81, *Levi v. Levi*, 37(4) P.D. 132.

88. Family Law Amendment (Maintenance) Law, 1959, S.H. 72.

89. C.A. 591/81, *Portugez v. Portugez*, 36(3) P.D. 449.

90. C.A. 4480/93, *Anonymous v. Anonymous*, 48(3) P.D. 461.

91. Code of Maimonides, *Hilchot Ishut*, Chapter 2.

92. See note 17.

93. C.A. 2280/91, *Abulof v. Abulof*, 47(5) P.D. 596; C.A. 806/93, *Hadary v. Hadary*, 48(3) P.D. 685.

94. See note 62.

95. C.A. 964/92, *Oron v. Oron*, 47(3) P.D. 758.

96. See note 98 and accompanying text.

97. See note 36 and preceding text.

98. This of course explains why most divorces in Israel take place after the couple have negotiated and agreed on all aspects of the divorce, so that property distribution is mostly the result of private agreements and not of court rulings.

99. The most recent effort in reforming property distribution laws is in the form of a Ministry of Justice committee, headed by Justice Heshin of the Supreme Court, formed in 1997. By the beginning of the year 2000, the committee has still not handed its report, and it is to be expected that whatever its recommendations be, the chances for their enactment are null.

100. See above, "Marriage According to Jewish Law."

101. C.A. 1915/91, *Ya'acobi v. Ya'acobi*, 49(3) P.D. 529.

102. See text following note 17.

103. The Bavli case, note 18.

104. Names Law, 1956, S.H. 207.

105. H.C. 693/91, *Efrat v. The Population Registrar*, 47(1) P.D. 749.

106. Central Bureau of Statistics (2000d), table 3.16. No comparable data exist as to non-Jewish women.

107. Single-Parent Family Law, 1992, S.H. 147.

108. Motion (Nz.) 389/96, *Shlomi v. Kibbutz Tel Yosef* (not published).

109. All these observations are discussed in detail in Chapter 4.

110. Surrogate Motherhood Agreements (Approval of Agreements and Status of Newborn) Law, 1996, S.H. 176.

111. Public Health (In Vitro Fertilization) Regulation (IVF Regulations), 1987, K.T. 5035, 978.

112. See Ministry of Justice (1994), 59–61, 78–80.

113. The terms conventionally used in Israeli literature are "full" versus "partial" surrogacy, describing "gestational" versus "traditional" surrogacy respectively. In full gestational surrogacy, no genetic connection exists between the carrying mother and the child. The conception results from in vitro fertilization, and ideally (but not categorically) the fertilized egg is a combination of the intended parents' gametes. In partial traditional surrogacy, the carrying mother is genetically related to the child, as the conception results from her being artificially inseminated by the intended father's sperm. In this case, biological connection at all exists between the intended father's wife, who is usually the intended mother, and the child.

114. The law mandates equal gender representation on the committee, namely, three of the members must be either men or women. See Rabbi Dr. Mordechai Halperin's explanation at the Labor and Welfare Committee, 13th Knesset, Protocol 422 (unedited version, December 26, 1995) (on file with the author). These restrictions on family relationship clearly derive from the goal of preventing any possible labeling of the resulting child as a *mamzer.*

115. The uncertainty here stems from the law's use of the ambiguous term "spouse" without clarifying whether the term includes unmarried spouses.

116. Letter from Talia Edri, Adv., of the Ministry of Health Legal Advisor office, dated January 15, 2001 (on file with the author).

117. See notes 14 and 123.

118. See note 45.

119. See "'Muslim Shari'a Court Should Be Left to Its Own Creative Devices'—Conversation with Qadi Ahmad H. Natour," *Justice* 17 (1998): 16–22.

120. Note 83.

121. C.A. 3077/90, *Anonymous v. Anonymous,* 49(2) P.D. 578.

122. "'Muslim Shari'a Courts," note 119, 22.

123. Family Court Law (Amendment No. 5), 2001, S.H. 16.

124. Druze Courts Law, 1962, S.H. 20.

125. Conversation with Qadi Naim Henou, 1998; "Druze Religious Courts Do Not Intervene in Social Life But Modernization Has Its Repercussions," *Justice* 17 (1998): 23–26.

Chapter 12. Multiple Voices

1. Mizrachi refers to members or descendants of Jews who settled in Africa and the Middle East, while Ashkenazi refers to members or descendants of European Jews.

2. For a fascinating exchange reflecting the development of this awareness, see the several issues of *Mitsad Sheni* (*On the Other Hand*), a periodical issued by the Center for Alternative Information in Jerusalem, which included numerous articles, responses, and personal accounts of events and arguments surrounding

the emergence of Mizrachi feminism during the early to mid-1990s, by Tikva Honig-Parnas, Noga Dagan, Vicki Shiran, Ella Haviva Shochat, Simon Biton, Mira Elazar, and Shosh Madmoni. See *Mitsad Sheni* 2, 4, 5–6, 7 (1996–97) (Hebrew).

3. For an apt demonstration and analysis of this challenge, see the exchange between John Simons (1995) and Danny Rabinovitch (1995) in relation to a particularly horrifying "honor killing" in a northern Druze village.

4. The last component is less relevant to lesbian women as it is to the other groups described in this chapter.

5. For detailed accounts and analysis of these developments see *Mitsad Sheni*, note 2.

6. Central Bureau of Statistics (2000d), table 11.16.

7. Central Bureau of Statistics (2000b).

8. Central Bureau of Statistics (2000d), table 12.15.

9. S. Swirski and B. Swirski (1997), 17.

10. CLAF—Community of Lesbian Feminists, unpublished pamphlet, July 19, 1999 (on file with the author).

11. H.C. 273/97, *The Association for the Preservation of Privacy Rights v. The Minister of Education, Culture and Sport*, 51(5) P.D 822.

12. CLAF pamphlet, note 10.

13. This was the background for the legal battle mentioned in Chapter 11, in the section on same-sex couples, over the issue army recognition of the pension rights of the homosexual partner of a deceased officer.

14. Much of the information here is based upon research conducted by Betachin—Information & Counseling Center on Family Issues, *The Woman in Ethiopian Jewry in Israel* (Hebrew), unpublished monograph, provided by Yechiel Eran, Head of Absorption of Ethiopian Jewry, JDC-Israel, November 23, 2000 (on file with the author).

15. Ibid.

16. See, e.g., King (1997), Lifshitz and Wolfson (1997).

17. In this respect, I found the critical analysis offered by the authors of the Palestinian Women's Shadow Report submitted to the CEDAW Committee, similarly delineating a multilayered marginality and discrimination, to be very helpful. See Working Group on the Status of Palestinian Women in Israel (1997), pp. 5–6.

18. Central Bureau of Statistics (1999c), table 2.1.

19. National Insurance Institute (1998), p. 68.

20. National Health Insurance Law, 1994, S.H. 156.

21. Adva Center (1996).

22. Central Bureau of Statistics (2000d), table 3.20.

23. Swirski, Ka'naaneh, and Avgar (1999), 4.

24. Central Bureau of Statistics (2000d), table 3.10.

25. Ibid.

26. The survey used language parameters rather than asking participants to define their nationality. In effect, "Hebrew speaking" refers to Jewish and "Arabic speaking" to Israeli Palestinian (thus avoiding the politically laden definition "Palestinian" or "Arab Israeli").

27. Central Bureau of Statistics (2000d), table 12.1.

28. Central Bureau of Statistics (2000c), tables 3 and 4.

29. The results of this survey are quoted by the Arab Association for Human Rights, www.arabhra.org/article26/factsheet5.htm, referring to Arab Associa-

tion for Human Rights and A. Farris, 1998, *The Status of Arab Women Working in the Private Sector in Nazareth.*

30. Sikkuy (2001), p. 19.

31. Telephone interview with the secretary of the Council for Higher Education, September 2000.

32. Yosef Algazi, "More Arab Women Turn to Help," *Ha'aretz,* December 12, 1999, A12.

33. Help Centers Union, 2000, *Sexual Violence in Israel 2000: Annual Report of the Union of Help Centers for Victims of Sexual Violence* (Hebrew), p. 35.

34. The following is based on unpublished data provided by chief superintendent David Sagiv, Department of Statistics Israel police.

35. Nina Pinso, "Family Honor Takes a Hit," *Ha'aretz,* May 5, 1999.

36. Algazi, "More Arab Women Turn to Help," note 32.

37. Kathleen Frederick Abu-Saad, "From Birth to Death: A Look at the Health of Negev Bedouin," *Newsletter of the Center for Bedouin Studies and Development, Ben-Gurion University of the Negev* 1 (1998): 7.

38. Center for the Bedouin Studies and Development, Negev Center for Regional Development and Ben-Gurion University, *Statistical Yearbook of the Negev Bedouin,* no.1, 1999 (Hebrew), p. 49.

39. Compulsory Education Law, 1949, S.H. 287.

40. "A Call for Equality in Education," *Newsletter of the Center for Bedouin Studies and Development* 1 (1998): at 1.

41. *Statistical Yearbook of the Negev Bedouin,* note 38, p. 73.

42. "Students and Scholarships," *Newsletter of the Center for Bedouin Studies and Development, Ben-Gurion University of the Negev* 2 (1999): 6–7.

43. *Statistical Yearbook of the Negev Bedouin,* no. 1, note 38, table VI/30.

44. Aliza Arbeli, "Assessment: A Majority of Bedouin Women Are Battered," *Ha'aretz,* November 16, 1999.

45. Letter from the author to the attorney general requesting information and policy statement regarding this phenomenon for the purpose of preparing the Third Periodic Report to CEDAW remained unanswered.

46. Ibid.

47. See also the discussion of religion in Chapter 8.

48. www.who.int/frh-whd/FGM/infopack/English

49. As detailed in Chapters 4 and 11.

50. Ruti Sinai, "Rape in a Transitional Society," *Ha'aretz,* July 5, 1998.

51. Ibid.

Conclusion

1. On legal liberalism, see Barnett (1998), 121–34; Rhode (1990); Ross (1993).

2. I am not referring here to the actual manner in which this law is implemented, only to its ideology and potential.

3. This expression is borrowed from Villmoare, who described feminists as "constantly wondering what might be" (1999, 447). Compare Thomas Ross's (1993) reference to feminist *nomos* as vision and imagination of what might be.

Bibliography

Abdo, Nahla. 1997. "Muslim Family Law: Articulating Gender, Class, and the State." *International Review of Comparative Public Policy* 9: 169–93.

Abu-Saad, Ismael. 1994. "The Negev's Bedouin: Educational Profile of a Community in Transition." *Journal of Education Policy* 1, 2: 3–7.

———. 1996. "Provision of Public Educational Services and Access to Higher Education Among the Negev Bedouin Arabs in Israel." *Journal of Education Policy* 11, 5: 527–41.

Adler, Rachel. 1998. *Engendering Judaism: An Inclusive Theology and Ethics.* Philadelphia: Jewish Publication Society.

Adva Center. 1996. *National Health Insurance Law from the Perspective of Quality, Efficiency and Cost.* Tel Aviv: Adva Center. (Hebrew)

Al-Atawneh, Maged. 1993. "The Connection Between the Legal Status of the Bedouin Woman and Her Self Image and Psychological Welfare." M.A. thesis, Bar-Ilan University. (Hebrew)

Al-Krenawi, Alean and Rachel Wiesel-Lev. 1999. "Attitudes Toward and Perceived Psychosocial Impact of Female Circumcision as Practiced Among the Bedouin-Arabs of the Negev." *Family Process* 38: 431–43.

Almog, Shulamit. 1996. "Women, the Military and Equality: Following H.C. 4541/94 *Miller v. the Minister of Defense.*" *Mishpat u'Mimshal—Law and Government in Israel* 3: 631–47 (Hebrew)

Amir, Delila. 1996. "'Responsible,' 'Committed,' and 'Wise': The Construction of Israeli Femininity in Abortion Committees." *Theory and Critique* 4: 247–54. (Hebrew)

Amir, Delila and Orly Benjamin. 1992. "Abortion Approval as a Ritual of Symbolic Control." In *The Criminalization of a Woman's Body,* ed. Clarice Feinman. New York: Haworth Press. 5–25.

Amit, Miri and Nitza Movshovitz-Hadar. 1989. "Attribution of Performance in Mathematics to Gender Differences." *Megamot* 32, 3: 361–72.

Amnesty International. 2000. *Human Rights Abuses of Women Trafficked from Countries of the Former Soviet Union into Israel's Sex Industry.* AI Index: MDE 15/17/00. Tel Aviv: Amnesty International. (Hebrew)

Asali, Abed, Naif Khamaysi, Unis Aburabua, Simha Letzer, Buteina Halihal, Moshe Adovsky, Benjamin Maoz, and R. H. Belmaker. 1995. "Ritual Female Genital Surgery Among Bedouin in Israel." *Archives of Sexual Behavior* 24, 5: 573–78.

Avgar, Amy. 1997. "Women's Health in Israel: A Feminist Perspective." *Social Work in Health Care* 25: 45–61.

Avgar, Amy and Carol Gordon. 1996. *Your Health: Results of a Woman's Health Sur-*

vey. Jerusalem: Israel Association for the Advancement of Woman's Health. (Hebrew)

Avni, Nogah. 1990. "Battered Women and Policemen: Victims of the System." *Plilim—Israel Journal of Criminal Justice* 1: 171–84.

Avrahami-Ainat, Judith. 1989. *He and She in the Classroom*. Tel Aviv: Modan. (Hebrew)

Awad, Yaser, Rafaela Cohen, and Gideon Yaniv. 1998. "Trends of Development in Poverty and Income Inequality." In *Annual Survey 1997/98*. Jerusalem: NII. (Hebrew with an English supplement)

Awad, Yaser, Nirit Israeli, Yaakov Shaul, and Gideon Yaniv. 1996. "Poverty and Inequality in Distribution of Income in Israel." In *1995/96 Annual Survey*, ed. Gideon Yaniv. Jerusalem: National Insurance Institute. 143–206. (Hebrew)

Azaryahu, Sara. 1977. *Hebrew Women's Union for Equality of Right*. Haifa: Women's Aid Fund. (Hebrew)

Azmon, Yael. 1993. "Women and Politics: The Case of Israel." In *Women in Israel*, ed. Yael Azmon and Dafna Izraeli. Studies of Israeli Society 6. New Brunswick, N.J.: Transaction Publications. 253–57.

Azmon, Yael and Dafna Izraeli, eds. 1993. *Women in Israel*. Studies of Israeli Society 6. New Brunswick, N.J.: Transaction Publications.

Baker, Alan and Ady Schonmann. 1998. "Presenting Israel's Case Before International Human Rights Bodies." *Justice* 19: 23–30.

Barak, Aharon. 1994. *Interpretation in Law*. Vol. 3, *Constitutional Interpretation*. Jerusalem: Nevo. (Hebrew)

Barak-Erez, Dafna. 1997. "The Reasonable Woman." *Plilim—Israel Journal of Criminal Justice* 6: 115–35.

Barnett, Hilaire. 1998. *Introduction to Feminist Jurisprudence*. London: Cavendish.

Bartlett, Katherine T. 1991. "Feminist Legal Method." In *Feminist Legal Theory: Readings in Law and Gender*, ed. Katherine T. Bartlett and Rosanne Kennedy. Boulder, Colo.: Westview Press. 370–403.

Bar-Tzuri, Roni, Hana Fischer, and Shuki Hendeles. 1996. *Women in Israeli Politics—Perceptions Survey*. Tel Aviv: Israeli Institute for Economic and Social Research. (Hebrew)

Beiner, Theresa M. 1999. "What Will Diversity on the Bench Mean for Justice?" *Michigan Journal of Gender and the Law* 6: 113–52.

Belosh-Kleinman, Vered and Shlomo Sharlin. 1999. "Cohabitation Among Young Adults in Israel." *Hevra u Revaha* 19: 461–84. (Hebrew)

Ben Rephael, Eliezer. 1989. "Ethnicity and Society in Israel." In *Israeli Society: People and State*, ed. Shimel Stempler. Tel Aviv: Ministry of Defense Publications. 73–94. (Hebrew)

Beneria, L. 1992. "Accounting for Women's Work: The Progress of Two Decades." *World Development* 20: 1557.

Ben-Israel, Ruth. 1998. *Equality of Opportunities and Prohibition of Discrimination in Employment*. Tel Aviv: Open University Press. (Hebrew)

Benmelech, Avraham, ed. 2000. *Israel Awards 2000*. Jerusalem: Israel Publications. (Hebrew)

Ben-Moshe, Yosefa, Jenny Brodeski, and Arnold Rozin. 1999. "Women and Aging." *Livriut Nashim* 6, 1. (Hebrew)

Ben-Rabi, Dalia and Smadar Shmaia-Yadgar. 2000. *Family Court Services: An Evaluation of the First Two Years of Operation*. Jerusalem: JDC-Brookdale Institute. (Hebrew)

Berger, Morroe. 1952. *Equality by Status: Legal Controls over Group Discrimination*. New York: Columbia University Press.

Berkovitch, Nitza. 1997. "Motherhood as a National Mission: The Construction of Womanhood in the Legal Discourse in Israel." *Women's Studies International Forum* 20: 605–19.

Berkowitz, Eliezer. 1966. *Condition in Marriage and in Divorce.* Jerusalem: Mossad Harav Kook.. (Hebrew)

———. 1983. *Not in Heaven: The Nature and Function of Halakha.* New York: Ktav.

Berman, Eli. 1998. *Cult, Subsidy, and Sacrifice: An Economist's View of Ultra-Orthodox Jews.* Jerusalem: Jerusalem Institute for Israel Studies.

Berman, Shaul. 1976. "The Status of Women in Halachic Judaism." In *The Jewish Woman: New Perspectives,* ed. Elizabeth Koltun. New York: Ktav. 114–28.

Bernstein, Deborah. 1992. *Pioneers and Homemakers: Jewish Women in Pre-State Israel.* Albany: State University of New York Press.

Biale, Rachel. 1984. *Women and Jewish Law: An Exploration of Women's Issues in Halakhic Sources.* New York: Schocken Books.

Bilsky, Leora. 1997. "Battered Women: From 'Self Defense' to Defense of the Self." *Plilim—Israel Journal of Criminal Justice* 6: 5–64.

Birnhack, Michael Dan and David Gussarsky. 1999. "Designed Seats, Dissenting Opinions, and Judicial Pluralism." *Iunei Mishpat: Tel Aviv University Law Review* 22: 499–542. (Hebrew)

Bogoch, Bryna. 1997. "Gendered Lawyering: Difference and Dominance in Lawyer-Client Interaction." *Law and Society Review* 31, 4: 677–712.

———. 1999. "Courtroom Discourse and the Gendered Construction of Professional Identity." *Law and Social Inquiry* 24, 2: 329–75.

Bogoch, Bryna and Rochelle Don-Yechiya. 1999. *The Gender of Justice: Bias Against Women in Israeli Courts.* Jerusalem: Jerusalem Institute for Israel Studies. (Hebrew)

Bourdieu, Pierre. 1987. "The Force of Law: Toward a Sociology of the Juridical Field." *Hastings Law Journal* 38: 805–53.

Brownmiller, Susan. 1975. *Against Our Will: Men, Women, and Rape.* New York: Bantam.

Broyde, Michael J. 2001. *Marriage, Divorce, and the Abandoned Wife in Jewish Law.* New Jersey: Ktav.

Caspi, Dan and Yechiel Limor. 1995. *The Intermediaries: Media in Israel, 1948–1990.* Tel Aviv: Am Oved. (Hebrew)

Cassel, Douglas and Jill Guzman. 1999. "The Law and Reality of Discrimination Against Women." In *Women and International Human Rights Law,* vol. 1, ed. Kelly D. Askin and Dorean M. Koenig. New York: Transnational Publishers. 287–379.

Center for Jewish Pluralism. 1999. *Freedom of Choice in Marriage: A Guide to Legal Marriage out of Israel.* Jerusalem: Israel Movement for Progressive Judaism.

Central Bureau of Statistics. 1995. *Time Use in Israel, 1991–1992.* Jerusalem: Central Bureau of Statistics.

———. 1996a. *Labour Force Surveys: Current Briefings in Statistics No. 20.* Jerusalem: Central Bureau of Statistics.

———. 1996b. *Time Use in Israel: Additional Findings from the Time Budget Survey, 1991–1992.* Jerusalem: Central Bureau of Statistics.

———. 1998a. *Income of Employees 1997: Current Briefings in Statistics No. 34.* Jerusalem: Central Bureau of Statistics.

———. 1998b. *Statistical Abstract of Israel No. 49.* Jerusalem: Central Bureau of Statistics

———. 1999a. *Labor Force Surveys 1998.* Jerusalem: Central Bureau of Statistics.

———. 1999b. *New Statistical Projects and Publications in Israel: Quarterly No. 115.* Jerusalem: Central Bureau of Statistics.
———. 1999c. *Statistical Abstract of Israel No. 50.* Jerusalem: Central Bureau of Statistics.
———. 2000a. *Demographic and Social Characteristics of Applicants to Committees for Approvals of Pregnancy Termination in Israel 1996.* Jerusalem: Central Bureau of Statistics.
———. 2000b. *Income of Employees 1999.* Current Briefings in Statistics No. 34. Jerusalem: Central Bureau of Statistics.
———. 2000c. *Labor Force Surveys 1999.* Jerusalem: Central Bureau of Statistics.
———. 2000d. *Statistical Abstract of Israel No. 51.* Jerusalem: Central Bureau of Statistics.
———. 2000e. *Women and Men in Israel.* Jerusalem: Central Bureau of Statistics.
———. 2001. *Households in Israel 1997–1998.* Jerusalem: Central Bureau of Statistics.
Central Bureau of Statistics, Ministry of Education, Culture, and Sport. 1993. *Survey of Teaching Staff.* Series of Education and Culture Statistics 222. Jerusalem: Central Bureau of Statistics.
CESCR. 1997. "Combined Initial and Second Report of the State of Israel Concerning the Implementation of the United Nations Covenant on Economic, Social and Cultural Rights (CESCR)."
———. 1998. Pre-Session Working Group. "Issues Raised by the Pre-Session Working Group of the CESCR in Connection with Consideration of the Combined Initial and Second Report of the State of Israel." UN DOC.E/1990/S/Add.39, 19th Session of the Committee.
Charlesworth, Hilary. 1999. "General Introduction." In *Women and International Human Rights Law,* vol. 1, ed. Kelly D. Askin and Dorean M. Koenig. New York: Transnational Publishers. xix–xxiii.
Charney, Craig. 1998. *Empowerment of Women in Israel: Differences Between Men and Women, Significant Issues for Women, and Voting Patterns in Elections.* Jerusalem: Israel Women's Network Center for Policy Research. (Hebrew)
Chen, Martha A. 2000. "The Invisible Workforce: Women in the Informal Economy." *International Perspectives on Work and the Economy* 1: 2–8.
Chiang, Lois. 1999. "Trafficking in Women." In *Women and International Human Rights Law,* vol. 1, ed. Kelly D. Askin and Dorean M. Koenig. New York: Transnational Publishers. 321–64.
Churi, Amal. 1996. "The Arab Woman and the Legal and Legislative System in Israel." Paper presented at the Conference on the Status of Arab Women, November 17, Haifa University.
Civil Service Commissioner. 1976. *26th Report.* Jerusalem: Government Printer. (Hebrew)
———. 1998. *Report of the Committee for the Examination of Women's Wages in the Civil Service.* Jerusalem: Government Printer. (Hebrew)
Civil Service Commission Supervisor on the Advancement of Women. 1999. *Annual Activities Report of the Department for the Advancement of Women Within the Civil Service.* Jerusalem: Government Printer. (Hebrew)
Cohen, Yinon. 1998. "Socioeconomic Gaps Between *Mizrachim* and *Ashkenazim* 1975–1995." *Israeli Sociology* 1: 1–20.
Committee for the Advancement of Women. 2000. *The Fifteenth Knesset, First and Second Terms.* Jerusalem: Knesset. (Hebrew)
Committee for the Examination of Commercial Sexual Exploitation of Children

in Israel (CECSECI). 1997. *Destructive Exploitation: On Minors Who Are Sentenced to Physical and Mental Degradation as a Result of Sexual Abuse.* Jerusalem: Ministry of Justice. (Hebrew)

Cook, Rebecca J. 1993. "Women's International Human Rights Law: The Way Forward." *Human Rights Quarterly* 15: 230–61.

———. 1994. "State Responsibility for Violations of Women's Rights." *Harvard Human Rights Journal* 7: 125–75.

Cotterrell, Roger.1992. *The Sociology of Law.* 2nd ed. London: Butterworths.

Council for Higher Education. 1995. *The Higher Education System in Israel—Statistical Abstract and Analysis.* Jerusalem: Council for Higher Education.

Crenshaw, Kimberly. 1995. "Demarginalizing the Intersection of Race and Sex: Black Feminist Critique of Antidiscrimination Doctrine, Feminist Theory, and Antitrust Politics." In *Feminist Legal Theory*, vol. 1, *Foundations and Outlooks*, ed. Frances E. Olsen. New York: New York University Press. 423–44.

Curran, James and Michael Gurevitch, eds. 1991. *Mass Media and Society.* London: Edward Arnold.

Dagan, Noga. 1996. "The Identity Crisis of Feminism—Mizrachi Women's Conference as Part of a Global Procedure." *Mitzad Sheni* 4: 28–31. (Hebrew)

Dahan-Kalev, Henriette. 1997. "The Oppression of Women by Other Women: Relations and Struggle Between Mizrahi and Ashkenazi Women in Israel." *Israel Social Science Journal* 12, 1: 31–44.

———. 1999. "Feminism Between *Ashkenazi* and *Mizrachi* Women." In *Sex Gender Politics*, ed. Dafna N. Izraeli, Ariella Friedman, Henriette Dahan-Kalev, Sylvie Fogeil-Bijaoui, Hanna Herzog, Manar Hasan, and Hannah Naveh. Tel Aviv: Hakibbutz Hameuhad. 217–67. (Hebrew)

Dana, Nissim. 1998a. "Conclusion." In *The Druze.* Ramat Gan: Bar-Ilan University Press. 217–21. (Hebrew)

———. 1998b. "The Druze Religion—Law and Practice." In *The Druze.* Ramat Gan: Bar-Ilan University Press. 37–47. (Hebrew)

———. Forthcoming. "The Druze in the Middle East." Manuscript on file with author.

Donnerstein, Edward and Daniel Linz. 1996. "Mass Media, Sexual Violence, and Male Viewers: Current Theory and Research." In *Reconstructing Gender*, ed. Estelle Disch. Mountain View, Calif.: Mayfield. 498–513.

Dror, Y. 1959. "Law and Social Change." *Tulane Law Review* 33: 787–802.

Dworkin, Andrea. 1985. "Against the Male Flood: Censorship, Pornography, and Equality." *Harvard Women's Law Journal* 8: 1–70.

Efroni, Linda. 1990. "Salaries and Promotions of Women and Men in the Civil Service in Israel." Unpublished intermediate report, Jerusalem. (Hebrew)

———. 1994. "Minimum Wage Law—The Law and the Reality." *Labor Law Annual* 4: 121–43. (Hebrew)

———. 1997. "Changes in the Israeli Salary System." In *Women—The Rising Power: Promotion of Women at Work, Shattering the "Glass Ceiling"*, ed. Anat Maor. Tel Aviv: Sifriat Poalim. 45–54. (Hebrew)

Eilam, Esther. 1993. "Rape and Rape Survivors in Israel." In *Calling the Equality Bluff: Women in Israel*, ed. Barbara Swirski and Marilyn P. Safir. New York: Teachers College Press. 312–18.

———. 1994. "Multiculturalism and the Murder of Feminism." *Noga* 27: 28–33. (Hebrew)

Einhorn, Talia. 1997. "Equality in Israeli Family Law." In *Equality in Family Law: The Influence of Constitutions and International Conventions*, ed. Bea Verschragen. Bielefeld: Gieseking. 297–332.

Eisikovits, Zvi and Avi Griffel. 1998. *Police Intervention in Intimate Violence: An Evaluation Study*. Haifa: Haifa University Minerva Center for Youth Studies. (Hebrew)

Ekshtein, Zvi. 1999. *The Effect of Minimum Wage Law on the Market*. Jerusalem: Ministry of Labor and Welfare, Authority for Personnel Planning. (Hebrew)

Eliav, Tami. 1998. "Maternity Insurance." In *Annual Survey 1997/98*. Jerusalem: National Insurance Institute. 185–93. (Hebrew with English supplement)

———. 2000. "Single-Parent Families—Statistical Data." Report, National Insurance Institute Research Department. (Hebrew)

Elon, Menachem. 1978. *The Jewish Law: History, Origins, and Principles*. Jerusalem: Magnes. (Hebrew)

El-Or, Tamar. 1994. *Educated and Ignorant: Ultra-Orthodox Women and Their World*. Trans. Haim Watzman. Boulder, Colo.: Lynne Rienner.

———. 1998. *Next Pessach: Literacy and Identity of Young Religious Zionist Women*. Tel-Aviv: Am Oved. (Hebrew)

Emmett, Ayala. 1996. *Our Sisters' Promised Land: Women, Politics, and Israeli-Palestinian Coexistence*. Ann Arbor: University of Michigan Press.

Estrich, Susan. 1987. *Real Rape*. Cambridge, Mass.: Harvard University Press.

Evan, W. M. 1965. "Laws as an Instrument of Social Change." In *Applied Sociology*, ed. Alvin W. Gouldner and S. M. Miller. New York: Free Press. 285–93.

Falk, Ze'ev. 1973. *The Divorce Action by the Wife in Jewish Law*. Jerusalem: Institute for Legislative Research and Comparative Law. (Hebrew)

Farrior, Stephanie. 1997. "The International Law on Trafficking in Women and Children for Prostitution: Making It Live Up to Its Potential." *Harvard Human Rights Journal* 10: 215–55.

Felstiner, W. L. F., Richard Abel, and Austin Sarat. 1980. "The Emergence and Transformation of Disputes: Naming, Blaming, Claiming." *Law and Society Review* 15: 631–54.

Ferber, Marianne A. and Jane Waldfogel. 1996. "'Contingent' Work: Good, Bad, or Indifferent?" In *Changing Work in America Series: Perspectives on Employment Stability*. Cambridge, Mass.: Radcliffe Public Policy Institute. 15–32.

Finance Ministry. The Civil Service Commissioner. 1976. *26th Report*. Jerusalem: Government Printer. (Hebrew)

Fineman, Martha A. 1992. "Legal Stories, Change, and Incentives—Reinforcing the Law of the Father." *New York School Law Review* 37: 227–49.

Finley, Lucinda M. 1993. "Transcending Equality Theory: A Way Out of the Maternity and the Workplace Debate." In *Feminist Legal Theory: Foundations*, ed. D. Kelly Weisberg. Philadelphia: Temple University Press. 190–207.

Fletcher, George P. 1997. "Self Defense of Battered Women." *Plilim—Israel Journal of Criminal Justice* 6: 65–88.

Fletcher, Roger. 1981. *Sociology: The Study of Social Systems*. London: Batsford.

Fogeil-Bijaoui, Sylvie.1992. "Jewish Women's Struggle on the Right to Vote in Israel, 1917–1926." *Megamot* 34, 2: 284–62.

———. 1999. "Families in Israel: Between Familism and Post-Modernism." In *Sex Gender Politics*, ed. Dafna N. Izraeli, Ariella Friedman, Henriette Dahan-Kalev, Sylvie Fogeil-Bijaoui, Hanna Herzog, Manar Hasan, and Hannah Naveh. Tel Aviv: Hakibbutz Hameuhad. 107–67. (Hebrew)

Freedman, Marcia. 1990. *Exile in the Promised Land: A Memoir*. Ithaca, N.Y: Firebrand Books.

Freiman, Avraham Chaim. 1945. *Order of Betrothal and Marriage*. Jerusalem: Mossad Harav Kook. (Hebrew)

Frishtik, Mordechai. 1991. "Physical and Sexual Violence by Husbands as a Reason for Imposing a Divorce in Jewish Law." *Jewish Law Annual* 9: 145–70.
Gamason, W. A., D. Croteau, W. Haynes, and T. Sasson. 1992. "Media Images and Social Construction of Reality." *Annual Review of Sociology* 18: 373–93.
Gera, Remesis. 1998. "Developments in Select Insurance Branches: Long-Term Care." In *Annual Survey 1997/98*, ed. Gideon Yaniv. Jerusalem: National Insurance Institute. 195–203. (Hebrew with an English supplement)
Gillath, Nurit. 1993. "Women Against War: Parents Against Silence." In *Calling the Equality Bluff: Women in Israel*, ed. Barbara Swirski and Marilyn P. Safir. New York: Teachers College Press. 142–46.
Gilligan, Carol. 1982. *In a Different Voice.* Cambridge, Mass.: Harvard University Press.
Ginsburg, Ruth Bader. 1985. "Some Thoughts on Autonomy and Equality in Relation to Roe v. Wade." *North Carolina Law Review* 63: 375–86.
Glasser S., V. Barell, A. Shoham, A. Ziv, V. Boyko, A. Lusky, and S. Hart. 1998. "Prospective Study of Postpartum Depression in an Israeli Cohort: Prevalance, Incidence and Demographic Risk Factors." *Journal of Pshychosomatic Obstetetrics and Gynaecology* 19:155–64.
Glendon, Mary Ann. 1981. *The New Family and the New Property.* Toronto: Butterworths.
———. 1989. *The Transformation of Family Law.* Chicago: University of Chicago Press.
Golinkin, David. 1991. *Halakhah for Our Time: A Conservative Approach to Jewish Law.* New York: United Synagogue of America.
Greenberg, Blu. 1981. *On Women and Judaism: A View from Tradition.* Philadelphia: Jewish Publication Society.
———. 1990. "Female Sexuality and Bodily Functions in the Jewish Tradition." In *Women, Religion, and Sexuality: Studies on the Impact of Religious Teaching on Women*, ed. Jeanne Becher. Philadelphia: Trinity Press. 1–44.
Greenland, P., R. H. Reicher, U. Goldburt, and S. Behar. 1991. "In-Hospital and One Year Mortality in 1,524 Women After Myocardial Infarction: Comparison with 4,315 Men." *Circulation* 83, 2: 484–91.
Gross, Revital and Shuli Brammli-Greenberg. 2000. "Health and Welfare of Women in Israel: Findings of a National Survey." Unpublished manuscript, JDC-Brookdale Israel and the Commonwealth Fund. (Hebrew)
Haberfeld, Yitzhak and Yinon Cohen. 1995. *Schooling and Income Gaps Between Western and Eastern Jews in Israel 1975–1992.* Tel Aviv: Golda Meir Center for Labor and Social Research. (Hebrew)
———. 1996. *Earning Gaps Between Israel's Native-Born Men and Women: 1975–1993.* Tel Aviv: Pinhas Sapir Center for Development.
Hakimian, Rina. 2000. "Funding HERCEPTIN in Israel: Public Pressure and Public Health." Working paper, Gertner Institute for Health Policy Research.
Halperin, Ruth. 1989. "Husband's Adultery as a Ground for Divorce." *Bar-Ilan Law Studies* 7: 297–329. (Hebrew)
Halperin-Kaddari, Ruth. 1994. "Family Law and Jurisdiction in Israel and the Bavli Case." *Justice* 2: 37–41.
———. 1997a. "Rethinking Legal Pluralism in Israel: The Interaction Between the High Court of Justice and Rabbinical Courts." *Iunei Mishpat: Tel Aviv University Law Review* 20: 683–747. (Hebrew)
———. 1997b. "The Position of Women in Israel." *Justice* 13: 35–36.
———. 1999. "Redefining Parenthood." *California Western International Law Journal* 29: 313–37.

———. 2000a. "Gender Construction Under *Halachic* Marriage and Divorce Laws." *Talpiot* 22: 451–64. (Hebrew)

———. 2000b. "Women, Religion and Multiculturalism in Israel." *UCLA Journal of International Law and Foreign Affairs* 5: 339–66.

———. 2001. "Toward Completion of Civil Family Law in Israel." *Bar-Ilan Law Studies* 17, 1: 105–58. (Hebrew)

———. Forthcoming. "*Tav Lemeitav Tan Du Milmeitav Armalu*: Women's Perpetual Marital Preference and Their Construction as Other in Jewish Law." In *Jewish Legal Writings by Women*, vol. 2, ed. Micah D. Halpern and Chana Safrai.

Harel, Alon. 1996. "Gay Rights in Israel—A New Era?" *International Journal of Discrimination and the Law* 1: 261–90.

———. 2000. "Rise and Fall of the Israeli Gay Legal Revolution." *Columbia Human Rights Law Review* 31: 443–71.

Harel, Alon and Lilach Vagner. 1997. "The 'Contributory Fault' of Rape Victims: A Positive and Normative Analysis." *Plilim—Israel Journal of Criminal Justice* 6: 235–59. (Hebrew)

Harel, Yossi, Dafna Kanny, and Giora Rahav. 1997. *Health Behaviors in School-Aged Children (HBSC): A World Health Organization Cross-National Study*. Jerusalem: JDC—Brookdale Institute. (Hebrew)

Hasan, Manar. 1993. "Growing Up Female and Palestinian in Israel." pp In *Calling the Equality Bluff: Women in Israel*, ed. Barbara Swirski and Marilyn P. Safir. New York: Teachers College Press. 66–74.

———. 1999. "The Politics of Honor: Patriarchy, the State and the Murder of Women in the Name of Family Honor." In *Sex Gender Politics*, ed. Dafna N. Izraeli, Ariella Friedman, Henriette Dahan-Kalev, Sylvie Fogiel-Bijaoui, Hanna Herzog, Manar Hasan, and Hannah Naveh. Tel Aviv: Hakibbutz Hameuhad. 267–305. (Hebrew)

Hauptman, Judith. 1998. *Rereading the Rabbis: A Woman's Voice*. Boulder, Colo.: Westview Press.

Hauptman, Zipora. 1995. "Rape: The Consent Concept and the Law of Evidence." In *Women's Status in Israeli Law and Society*, ed. Frances Raday, Carmel Shalev, and Michal Liban-Kooby. Jerusalem: Schoken. 189–234. (Hebrew)

Haut, Irwin H. 1983. *Divorce in Jewish Law and Life*. New York: Sepher-Hermon Press.

Hazelton, Leslie. 1977. *Israeli Women: The Reality Behind the Myths*. New York: Simon and Schuster.

Helman, Sara and Tamar Rapoport. 1997. "Women in Black: Changing Israel's Gender and Socio-Political Order." *British Journal of Sociology* 48: 682–700.

Hernandez-Truyol, Berta E. 1999. "Human Rights Through a Gendered Lens: Emergence, Evolution, Revolution." In *Women and International Human Rights Law*, vol. 1, ed. Kelly D. Askin and Dorean M. Koenig. New York: Transnational Publishers. 3–39.

Hershkovitz, Shlomo. 2000. "Women Among University Senior Staff." *Academia* 7–8: 32–44. (Hebrew)

Hertz Lezrovitz, Rachel. 1995. "Creating an Egalitarian Educational Atmosphere in Class." In *A Gender Found Its Equality*, ed. Nava Segen and Orly Katzovitch. Jerusalem: Ministry of Education, Culture and Sports. 263–67.

Herzog, Ester. 1993. "Aspects of Gender Inequality in the Educational System." *Educational Times: The Educational Supplement of High School Teachers in Israel* (June): 6–24.

Herzog, Hanna. 1994. *Realistic Women: Women in Local Politics*. Jerusalem: Jerusalem Institute for Israel Studies. (Hebrew)

———.1999. "Women in Politics and Politics of Women." In *Sex Gender Politics*, ed. Dafna N. Izraeli, Ariella Friedman, Henriette Dahan-Kalev, Sylvie Fogeil-Bijaoui, Hanna Herzog, Manar Hasan, and Hannah Naveh. Tel-Aviv: Hakibbutz Hameuhad. 307–55. (Hebrew)

Hewlett, Sylvia A. 1986. *A Lesser Life*. New York: W. Morrow.

Hoffman, Anat. 1996. "Women and the Media." In *Women in Israel: Information and Analysis*. Jerusalem: Israel Women's Network.

Hofnung, Menachem. 1996. "The Unintended Consequences of Unplanned Constitutional Reform: Constitutional Politics in Israel." *American Journal of Comparative Law* 44: 585–604.

Holtzer, Gershon. 1970. "A Woman's Testimony in Jewish Law." *Sinai* 67: 94–112. (Hebrew)

Honig-Parnas, Tikva. 1996. "To Return the Respect of 'The Black Feminism,' 'The Mizrachi Feminism,' and 'The Socialistic Feminism.'" *Mitzad Sheni* 5–6: 34–39. (Hebrew)

Human Development Report. 1995. *Human Development Report 1995: Gender and Human Development*. http://hdr.undp.org/reports/global/1995/en.

Ifrah, Anekke, ed. 1999. *Women's Health in Israel: A Data Book*. Jerusalem: Hadassah and Israel Women's Network.

Interministerial Committee for Treatment of Violence in the Family. 1998. *A Report on Violence in the Family*. Jerusalem: State of Israel. (Hebrew)

International Women's Rights Action Watch (IWRAW) 1996. *Assessing the Status of Women: A Guide to Reporting Under the Convention on the Elimination of All Forms of Discrimination Against Women*. New York: United Nations.

———. 1999. *Equality for Women in Israel's Welfare State*. Jerusalem: Israel Women's Network. (Hebrew)

Israel Social Science Research. 1997. Special Issue, *Feminist Theory and Research* 12, 1–2.

Israel Women's Network. 1987. *The Status of Women in Israel*. Jerusalem: Israel Women's Network. (Hebrew)

———. 1994. *Reproduction, Health and Well-Being Among Women in Israel*. Jerusalem: Israel Women's Network. (Hebrew)

———. 1997. *Trafficking of Women to Israel and Forced Prostitution*. Jerusalem: Israel Women's Network. (Hebrew)

Ivancovsky, Michal, Bruce Rosen, and Dan Yuval. 1996. *Giving Birth in Israel: Summary of the Findings of a Survey of Obstetrics Patients in Ten Hospitals*. Jerusalem: JDC-Brookdale, (Hebrew)

Izraeli, Dafna N. 1990. "The Women Workers' Movement: First-Wave Feminism in Pre-State Israel." In *Women and Social Protest*, ed. Guida West and Rhoda Blumberg. Oxford: Oxford University Press. 134–55.

———. 1992. "Culture, Policy and Women in Dual Earner Families in Israel." In *The Dual Earner Family in Comparative Perspective*, ed. Susan Lewis, Dafna N. Izraeli, and Helen Hootsmans. London: Sage. 19–45.

———. 1994. "Outsiders in the Promised Land: Women Managers in Israel." In *Competitive Frontiers: Women Managers in a Global Economy*, ed. Nancy J. Adler and Dafna N. Izraeli. Boston, Mass.: Blackwell. 301–24.

———. 1996. *Report on the Representation of Women in Government Corporations' Board of Directors*. Ramat Gan: Bar-Ilan University. (Hebrew)

———. 1999a. "Gendering in the IDF Military Service." *Theory and Critique* 14: 85–108. (Hebrew)

———. 1999b. "Gendering in the Workplace." In *Sex Gender Politics*, ed. Izraeli,

Ariella Friedman, Henriette Dahan-Kalev, Sylvie Fogeil-Bijaoui, Hanna Herzog, Manar Hasan, and Hannah Naveh Tel Aviv: Hakibbutz Hameuhad. (Hebrew)

———. Forthcoming. "Gender Politics in Israel: The Case of Affirmative Action for Women Directors." Manuscript, on file with the author.

Izraeli, Dafna N., Ariella Friedman, Henriette Dahan-Kalev, Sylvie Fogeil-Bijaoui, Hanna Herzog, Manar Hasan, and Hannah Naveh, eds. 1999. *Sex Gender Politics.* Tel Aviv: Hakibbutz Hameuhad. (Hebrew)

Izraeli, Dafna N. and Ephraim Tabory. 1988. "The Political Context of Feminist Attitudes in Israel." *Gender and Society* 2: 463–81.

Izraeli, Dafna N. and Ilan Talmud. 1996. *Women and Men as Directors in Corporations Traded on the Stock Exchange.* Ramat Gan: Bar-Ilan University. (Hebrew)

Kahn, Susan. M. 2000. *Reproducing Jews.* Durham, N.C.: Duke University Press.

Kamir, Orit. 1996. "What's in a Woman's Name." *Mishpatim* 27: 327–82. (Hebrew)

———. 1997. "'Reason' Killed the Woman: Provocation, 'The Reasonable Israeli,' and 'The Average Israeli Woman' in *Azuelus.*" *Plilim—Israel Journal of Criminal Justice* 6: 137–85. (Hebrew)

———. 1998. "Is Sexual Harassment an Offense Against Equality, or Against Human Dignity?" *Mishpatim* 29: 317–88. (Hebrew)

———. 2002. *Feminism, Rights, and the Law.* Jerusalem: Ministry of Defense. (Hebrew)

Kannai, Ruth. 1999. "The Construction of the Discretion of the Judge in Sentencing." *Bar-Ilan Law Studies* 15: 147–96. (Hebrew)

———. 2000. "Criminal Law: Development and Directions." *Iunei Mishpat: Tel Aviv University Law Review* 23: 717–53 (Hebrew)

Karp Committee. 1989. *A Report Concerning the Investigation, Prosecution, and Legal Policy in Domestic and Spousal Violence Cases.* Jerusalem: Government Printer. (Hebrew)

Katz, Ruth and Yochanan Peres. 1996. "Divorce Tendencies in Israel and Their Implications for Family Therapy." *Society and Welfare* 16, 4: 483–502. (Hebrew)

Khouri, Violet. 1993. "Mayor of an Arab Village in Israel." In *Calling the Equality Bluff: Women in Israel,* ed. Barbara Swirski and Marilyn P. Safir. New York: Teachers College Press. 221–24.

Kimmerling, Baruch. 1993. "Militarism in the Israeli Society." *Theory and Critique* 4: 123–40. (Hebrew)

———. 1998. "The New Israelis: Many Cultures Without Multiculturalism." *Alpaim* 16: 264–308. (Hebrew)

King, Judith. 1997. *Evaluation of a Project for the Integration of Single-Parent Immigrant Women into the Business Sector.* Jerusalem: JDC-Brookdale Institute. (Hebrew)

Knesset. 1996. *Report and Conclusions of the Parliamentary Investigative Committee on Murder of Women by Their Spouses.* Jerusalem: Knesset. (Hebrew)

———. 1999. *Report of the Committee for the Advancement of Women—14th Knesset.* Jerusalem: Knesset. (Hebrew)

———. 2000. *Report of the Committee for the Advancement of the Status of Women—15th Knesset.* Jerusalem: Knesset. (Hebrew)

Konor, Etti. 2000. *Governmental Financing of Organizations Treating Victims of Violence Against Women, 1990–2000.* Tel Aviv: Adva Center.

Kormann, Tal. 1998. "Victims of Sexual Assault in Israel: Assault Characteristics and Ways of Coping." In *Sexual Assault Casualties in the Criminal Procedure—Anthology,* vol. 1. Jerusalem: Ministry of Justice. 2–10. (Hebrew)

Lahav, Pnina. 1993. "When the Palliative Simply Impairs: Debate in the Knesset on the Law for Women's Rights." *Zmanim* 46–47: 149–59. (Hebrew)

———. 2000. "Up Against the Wall: The Case of Women's Struggle to Pray at the Western Wall in Jerusalem." *Israel Studies Bulletin* 16: 19–22.

Lapidoth, Arye. 1992. "The Israeli 1992 Income Tax Amendment Relating to the Taxation of the Wife's Income." *Israel Law Review* 26, 3: 355–72. (Hebrew)

Lavie, Aliza. 2000. "News Is News: It Has No Gender." *Patuach* 4: 45–74. (Hebrew)

Layish, Aharon. 1982. *Marriage, Divorce, and Succession in the Druze Family.* Leiden: E.J. Brill.

———. 1985. "*Taquiyya* Among the Druzes." *Asian and African Studies* 19: 245–81.

———. 1995. "The Status of the Moslem Woman in the *Sharia* Courts in Israel." In *Women's Status in Israeli Law and Society,* ed. Frances Raday, Carmel Shalev, and Michal Liban-Kooby. Jerusalem: Schoken. 364–79. (Hebrew)

———. 1998. "The Druze Family in Israel—Continuity and Change." In *The Druze,* ed. Nissim Dana. Ramat Gan: Bar-Ilan University Press. 130–40. (Hebrew)

Lazarus-Yafeh, Hava. 1988. "Contemporary Fundamentalism—Judaism, Christianity, Islam." *Jerusalem Quarterly* 47: 27–39.

Lemish, Dafna. 1995. "Communicatively Equal: A Feminist Look at the Israeli Media." In *Communication and Democracy in Israel,* ed. Dan Caspi. Jerusalem: Van Leer Institute. 119–39.

Lemish, Dafna and Chava Tidhar. 1999. "Still Marginal: Women in Israel's 1996 Television Election Campaign." *Sex Roles* 41: 389–412.

Lester, A. and G. Bindman. 1972. *Race and Law.* Harmondsworth: Penguin.

Levi, Shlomit, Chana Levinson, and Elihu Katz. 1993. *Beliefs, Observance, and Social Relations in Israel.* Jerusalem: Gutman Institute for Applied Social Research. (Hebrew)

Levinson, Pnina N. 1990. "Women and Sexuality: Traditions and Progress." In *Women, Religion and Sexuality: Studies on the Impact of Religious Teaching on Women,* ed. Jeanne Becher. Philadelphia: Trinity Press. 45–63.

Liebman, Charles S. and Eliezer Don-Yehiya. 1984. "Religion and Politics in Israel." *Mulad* 5, 25–26: 89–71. (Hebrew)

Lifshitz, Chen and Michal Wolfson. 1997. *Follow-up Study of Ethiopian Immigrants Who Graduated from Vocational Training Courses—Summary Report.* Jerusalem: JDC-Brookdale Institute. (Hebrew)

Lifshitz, Shachar. 2001. "The Future of Secular Family Law in Israel: Classical Liberalism vs. Communitarian Liberalism." *Bar-Ilan Law Studies* 17: 159–262. (Hebrew)

———. 2002. "Married Against Their Will: A Liberal Analysis of Cohabitation Law in Israel." *Iunei Mishpat: Tel Aviv University Law Review* 25: 741–849. (Hebrew)

Limor, Yehiel and Dan Caspi. 1994. "The Feminization of the Israeli Press." *Qesher* 15: 37–45. (Hebrew)

Liran-Alper, Dalia. 2000. "The Future of Media in Women's Hands? The Committee for the Status of Women in the Israel Broadcasting Authority, 1993–1998." *Patuach* 4: 188–204. (Hebrew)

Littleton, Christine A. 1987. "Reconstructing Sexual Equality." In *Feminist Legal Theory—Readings in Law and Gender,* ed. Katherine T. Bartlett and Rosanne Kennedy. Boulder, Colo.: Westview Press. 35–56.

Livnat, Yuval. 2000. "What Kind of Feminism? Reflections on the *Galili* Affair." *Bar-Ilan Law Studies* 16: 486–71. (Hebrew)

Lorber, J. 1998. *Gender in Equality*. Los Angeles: Roxbury .

MacKinnon, Catherine A. 1987. *Feminism Unmodified: Discourses in Life and Law.* Cambridge, Mass.: Harvard University Press.

———. 1989. *Toward a Feminist Theory of the State.* Cambridge, Mass.: Harvard University Press.

Maor, Moshe. 2001 "The Advancement of Women in the Israeli Civil Service: The Gender Equality Policy Approach." *Bitachon Sotziali* 61: 127–53. (Hebrew)

Maoz, Asher.1985. "Civil Court's Intervention Policy in Rabbinical Court's Jurisdiction and its Effects on Family Law in Israel. Ph.D. Dissertation, Tel Aviv University." (Hebrew)

Mar'i, Mariam M. and Sami Kh. Mar'i. 1993. "The Role of Women as Change Agents in Arab Society in Israel." In *Calling the Equality Bluff: Women in Israel,* ed. Barbara Swirski and Marilyn P. Safir. New York: Teachers College Press. 213–21.

Matsuda, Mari. 1989. "When the First Quail Calls: Multiple Consciousness as Jurisprudential Method." *Women's Rights Law Reporter* 11: 7–10.

Mautner, Menachem. 1993. *The Decline of Formalism and the Rise of Values in Israeli Law.* Tel Aviv: Maagalay Daat.

———. 1999. "The Hidden Law." In *Mincha Le'yitzhak: Essays in Honor of Judge Itzhak Shilo on his 80th Year,* ed. Aharon Barak and Menashe Shava. Tel Aviv: Bar Association. 59–89. (Hebrew)

Mautner, Menachem, Avi Sagi, and Ronen Shamir, eds. 1998. *Multiculturalism in a Democratic and Jewish State.* Tel Aviv: Ramot Publications.

Mazur, Amy G. 2001. "State Feminism, Women's Movements, and Job Training: Comparative Findings." Paper presented at the law and Society Annual Meeting, Budapest, May 2001.

McLindon, James B. 1987. "Separate But Unequal: The Economic Disaster of Divorce for Women and Children." *Family Law Quarterly* 21, 3: 351–409.

Meiselman, Moshe. 1978. *Jewish Woman in Jewish Law.* New York: Ktav.

Meler, Zofia. 1995. "Reflection of Sexist Stereotypes in School Books in the Formal Education in Israel." *Hacheenooch U'sveevo* [*Education and Its Context*] 13: 86–100. (Hebrew)

Mendelson, Yoseph. 1995. "Property Relations Between Spouses." In *Women's Status in Israeli Law and Society,* ed. Frances Raday, Carmel Shalev, and Michal Liban-Kooby. Jerusalem: Schoken. 437–58. (Hebrew)

Ministry of Education. 1999. *Matriculation Exams Data.* Jerusalem: Ministry of Education. (Hebrew)

Ministry of Education, Culture, and Sport. 1996. *Educational Institutions 1994/1995.* Current Briefings in Statistics 16. Jerusalem: Ministry of Education, Culture, and Sport. (Hebrew)

———. 1997. *Matriculation Exams Data.* Jerusalem: Ministry of Education, Culture, and Sport. (Hebrew)

Ministry of Health. 1996. *Health in Israel.* Jerusalem: Ministry of Health Information and Computer Services. (Hebrew)

Ministry of Justice 1977. *Report of the Committee to Investigate the Problems of Prostitution.* Jerusalem: Government Printer. (Hebrew)

———. 1994. *Report of the Public-Professional Commission in the Matter of* In Vitro *Fertilization.* Jerusalem: Ministry of Justice. (Hebrew)

Ministry of Labor and Welfare. 1991. *Main Tendencies of Women's Development in the Israeli Labor Force in the Last Decade, 1980–1990.* Jerusalem: Ministry of Labor and Welfare. (Hebrew)

Minow, Martha. 1989. "Pluralisms." *Connecticut Law Review* 21: 965–85.

Mishelov, David Y. 1986–88. "The Jewish Woman in Jewish Law." *Dinei Israel* 13–14: 263–312. (Hebrew)

Moore, Tracy, ed. 1995. *Lesbiot: Israeli Lesbians Talk About Sexuality, Feminism, Judaism and Their Lives.* London: Cassell.

Morcos, Nabihah. 1999. *Double Discrimination: Women in the Mirror of Fifty (Years to the State of Israel).* Jerusalem: Israel Women's Network. (Hebrew)

Natanzon, Rubi. 1997. *Women in the New Employment World in Israel,* Tel Aviv: Israeli Center for Social and Economic Research. (Hebrew).

Natanzon, Rubi.1999. *The New Workers.* Tel Aviv: Hakibbutz Hameuhad. (Hebrew)

National Council for Children. 2000. *Children in Israel.* Jerusalem: National Council for Children. (Hebrew)

National Insurance Institute. 1996. *National Insurance Programs in Israel.* Jerusalem: National Insurance Institute. (Hebrew with an English supplement)

———. 1998. *Annual Survey 1997/98.* Jerusalem: National Insurance Institute. (Hebrew with an English supplement)

———. 1999. *Average Wage and Income by Settlement and by Various Economic Variables, 1995–1996.* Jerusalem: National Insurance Institute. (Hebrew)

———. 1999. *Quarterly Statistics* 29, 2. Jerusalem: National Insurance Institute. (Hebrew)

Notzer Neta and Susan Brown. 1995. Women Doctors' Status in Israel." *Harefua—Journal of the Israel Medical Association* 129, 11: 449–51. (Hebrew)

O'Connell Davidson, Julia. 1998. *Prostitution, Power, and Freedom.* Ann Arbor: University of Michigan Press.

Office of the Prime Minister. 1978. *Recommendations of the Commission on the Status of Women.* Jerusalem: Government Printer. (Hebrew)

Okin, Susan M. 1989. *Justice, Gender, and the Family.* New York: Basic Books.

———. 1999. "Is Multiculturalism Bad for Women?" In *Is Multiculturalism Bad for Women?,* ed. Joshua Cohen, Matthew Howard, and Martha C. Nussbaum. Princeton, N.J.: Princeton University Press. 7–24.

Olsen, Frances. 1984. "The Politics of Family Law." *Law and Inequality Journal* 2: 1–19.

———. 1985. "The Myth of State Intervention in the Family." *University of Michigan Journal of Law Reform* 18: 835–64.

———. 1990. "The Sex of Law." In *The Politics of Law: A Progressive Crytique,* ed. David Kairys. 2nd ed. New York: Pantheon. 453–67.

Oppenheimer, Jo. 1993. "The Pressure to Be Heterosexual."In *Calling the Equality Bluff: Women in Israel,* ed. Barbara Swirski and Marilyn P. Safir. New York: Teachers College Press. 108–14.

Palu, Karnit and Nitza Kassir. 1994. "Obedience to the Minimum Wage Law in the Business Sector." Discussion Paper Series 94.12. Jerusalem: Bank of Israel Research Department. (Hebrew)

Peres, Yochanan. 1977. *Ethnic Relations in Israel.* Tel Aviv: Sifriat Poalim. (Hebrew)

Peres, Yochanan and Ruth Katz. 1980. "Family and Familism in Israel." *Megamot* 26: 37–56. (Hebrew)

———. 1991. "Family in Israel: Change and Continuity." In *Families in Israel,* ed.

Leah Shamgar-Hendelman and Rivka Bar-Yosef. Jerusalem: Akdamon. 9–32. (Hebrew)

Plaskow, Judith. 1990. *Standing Again at Sinai: Judaism from a Feminist Perspective.* New York: HarperCollins.

Polan, Diane. 1993. "Toward a Theory of Law and Patriarchy." In *Feminist Legal Theory: Foundations,* ed. D. Kelly Weisberg. Philadelphia: Temple University Press. 419–26.

Police Comptroller. 1993. *Final Report on Police Treatment of Spousal Violence.* Jerusalem: Police Ministry.

Polikoff, Nancy. 1990. "This Child Does Have Two Mothers: Redefining Parenthood to Meet the Needs of Children in Lesbian-Mother and Other Nontraditional Families." *Georgetown Law Journal* 78: 459–575.

Polivka, Anne E. and Thomas Nardone. 1989. "On the Definition of 'Contingent Work'." *Monthly Labor Review* 112, 12: 9–16.

Pope, Juliet J. 1993. "Conflict of Interest: A Case Study of Na'amat." In *Calling the Equality Bluff: Women in Israel,* ed. Barbara Swirski and Marilyn P. Safir. New York: Teachers College Press. 225–33.

Pound, R. 1917. "The Limits of Effective Legal Action." *International Journal of Ethics* 27: 150–67.

Public Complaints Commissioner. 1999. *26th Annual Report.* Jerusalem: Government Printer. (Hebrew)

Public Professional Committee. 1989. *The Professional Public Committee for General Examination of the Civil Service and State Supported Institutions (Koberski Report).* Jerusalem: Government Printer. (Hebrew)

Ra'anan, Ofra. 1998. "Mortality Differences Between Women and Men After By-Pass Surgery: The Role of Social Factors." M.A. thesis, Bar-Ilan University.

Rabinovich, Danny. 1995. "Saving Brown Women." *Theory and Criticism* 7: 5–19. (Hebrew)

Raday, Frances. 1993. "The Concept of Gender Equality in a Jewish State." In *Calling the Equality Bluff: Women in Israel,* ed. Barbara Swirski and Marilyn P. Safir. New York: Teachers College Press. 18–28.

———. 1994. "On Equality." *Mishpatim* 24, 2: 241–81. (Hebrew)

———. 1995. "Women in the Labor Market." In *Women's Status in Israeli Law and Society,* ed. Frances Raday, Carmel Shalev, and Michal Liban-Kooby. Jerusalem: Schoken. 64–116. (Hebrew)

———. 1996a. "Religion, Multiculturalism and Equality: The Israeli Case." *Yearbook on Human Rights* 25: 193–241.

———. 1996b. "Women in Law in Israel: A Study of the Relationship Between Professional Integration and Feminism." *Georgia State University Law Review* 12: 525–52.

———. 2000. "The Army: Feminism and Citizenship?" *Plilim—Israel Journal of Criminal Justice* 9: 185–216. (Hebrew)

Raday, Frances, Carmel Shalev, and Michal Liban-Kooby, eds. 1995. *Women's Status in Israeli Law and Society.* Jerusalem: Schoken. (Hebrew)

Resnik, Judith. 1996. "Asking About Gender in Courts." *Signs: Journal of Women in Culture and Society* 21, 4: 952–90.

Rhode, Deborah L. 1989. *Justice and Gender: Sex Discrimination and the Law.* Cambridge, Mass.: Harvard University Press.

———. 1991. "The 'No Problem' Problem: Feminist Challenges and Cultural Change." *Yale Law Journal* 100: 1731–93.

———. 1992. "Sexual Harassment." *Southern California Law Review* 65: 1459–66.

Riggs, Fred W. 1991. "Public Administration: A Comparative Framework." *Public Administration Review* 51, 6: 473–77.

Riskin, Shlomo. 1999. "Women as Canon Teachers." In *A Good Eye: Dialogue and Polemic in Jewish Culture,* ed. Ilan Nahem. Tel Aviv: Hakibbutz Hameuhad. 698–704. (Hebrew)

Rom, Yael. 1995a. "NAALEH Program: Girls Studying Engineering and Science." In *A Gender Found Its Equality,* ed. Nava Segen and Orly Katzovitch. Jerusalem: Ministry of Education, Culture, and Sport. 273–74. (Hebrew)

———. 1995b. "Subject Selection in High Schools." In *A Gender Found Its Equality,* ed. Nava Segen and Orly Katzovitch. Jerusalem: Ministry of Education, Culture, and Sport. 223–35. (Hebrew)

Rosen-Zvi, Ariel. 1989. "The Jurisdictional Race in Matters Connected with Divorce Suits and its Impact on Family Law." *Tel Aviv University Law Review* 14: 67–99. (Hebrew)

———. 1990. *Israeli Family Law: The Sacred and the Secular.* Tel Aviv: Tel Aviv University Press. (Hebrew)

———. 1995. "'A Jewish and Democratic State'": Spiritual Parenthood, Alienation, and Symbiosis—Can We Square the Circle?" *Tel Aviv University Law Review* 19: 479–520. (Hebrew)

Ross, Thomas. 1993. "Despair and Redemption in the Feminist Nomos." *Indiana Law Journal* 69: 101–36.

Roth, Joel. 1986. *The Halakhic Process: A Systemic Analysis.* New York: Ktav.

Rubinstein, Amnon. 1996. *The Constitutional Law of the State of Israel.* 5th ed. Tel Aviv: Schoken. (Hebrew)

Rubinstein, Dorit. 2000. "What's the Matter, Part Time?" *Noga* 38: 13–17.

Ruether, Rosemary Radford. 1983. *Sexism and God-Talk: Toward a Feminist Theology.* Boston: Beacon Press.

Sa'b, Afifa. 1998. "The Need to Change the Present Status of the Druze Woman." In *The Druze,* ed. Nissim Dana. Ramat Gan: Bar-Ilan University Press. 119–22. (Hebrew)

Sabatello, Eytan F., Yisrael Adler, Ronny A. Shtarkshall, and Eric Peritz. 1996. "The Development of Fertility Among Moslem Women in Israel in the Last Decade: A Longitudinal Study." *Social Security* 46: 64–86.

Safir, Marilyn P. 1986. "The Effects of Nature or Nurture on Sex Differences in Intellectual Functioning: Israeli Findings." *Sex Roles* 14, 11/12: 581–90.

———. 1993. "Religion, Tradition, and Public Policy Give Family First Priority." In *Calling the Equality Bluff: Women in Israel,* ed. Barbara Swirski and Marilyn P. Safir. New York: Teachers College Press. 57–66.

Sagi, Avi. 1996. *'Elu ve'Elu: The Meaning of the Halakhic Discourse.* Tel Aviv: Hakibbutz Hameuhad. (Hebrew)

Saleh, Shakib. 1998. "The Precepts of the Druze Faith." In *The Druze,* ed. Nissim Dana. Ramat Gan: Bar-Ilan University Press. 29–36. (Hebrew)

Scales, Ann C. 1986. "The Emergence of Feminist Jurisprudence: An Essay." *Yale Law Journal* 95: 1373–1403.

Schiffer, Varda. 1998. *The Haredi Education System, Allocation, Regulation, and Control.* Jerusalem: Floersheimer Institute for Policy. (Hebrew)

Schneider, Elizabeth M. 1986. "Describing and Changing: Women's Self-Defense Work and the Problem of Expert Testimony on Battering." *Women's Rights Law Reporter* 9: 195–222.

Schulhoffer, Stephen J. 1995. "The Feminist Challenge." *University of Pennsylvania Law Review* 143: 2151–52.

Schultz, Vicki. 1998. "Re-conceptualizing Sexual Harassment." *Yale Law Journal* 107: 1683–1805.

Segen, Nava and Orly Katzovitch, eds. 1995. *A Gender Found Its Equality.* Jerusalem: Ministry of Education, Culture and Sports. (Hebrew)

Semyonov, Moshe. 1990. *Trends in Gender Linked Earning Inequality in Israel.* Tel Aviv: Golda Meir Institute for Social and Labor Research. (Hebrew, with English abstract)

Seron, Carroll and Cynthia Fuchs Epstein. 1998. *The Part-Time Paradox: Time Norms, Professional Life, Family, and Gender.* New York: Routledge.

Sered, Susan. 1997. "Women and Religious Change in Israel: Rebellion or Revolution." *Sociology of Religion* 58: 1–24.

Shachar, Ayelet. 1993. "The Sexuality of Law: The Legal Discourse About Rape." *Iunei Mishpat: Tel Aviv University Law Review* 18, 1: 159–99.

Shachar, Rina and Judith Avrahami-Ainat, eds. 1993. *Equal Opportunities for Boys and Girls in the Education System.* Jerusalem: Israel Women's Network. (Hebrew)

Shachar, Yoram. 1998. "Criminal Law and Culture in Israel." *Plilim—Israel Journal of Criminal Justice* 7: 77–120.

Shadmi, Erela. 1997. "Police Handling of Wife Beating in Israel: Radical Feminist Critique and Public Policy." *Israel Social Sciences Research* 12, 2: 55–74.

Shaked, Rivka. 1997. "Application of the Law Concerning the Proper Representation of Women in the Civil Service—Report." In *Women—The Rising Power: Promotion of Women at Work, Shattering the "Glass Ceiling"*, ed. Anat Maor. Tel Aviv: Sifriat Poalim. 273–76. (Hebrew)

Shaked, Rivka and Rena Bareket. 1999. *Report of the Unit for the Advancement of Women in the Civil Service Commission 1999.* Jerusalem: Civil Service Commission Supervisor on the Advancement of Women. (Hebrew)

Shalev, Carmel. 1995a. "Freedom to Marry and to Joint Life." In *Women's Status in Israeli Law and Society*, ed. Frances Raday, Carmel Shalev, and Michal Liban-Kooby. Jerusalem: Schoken. 459–502. (Hebrew)

———. 1995b. "On Equality, Difference and Sex Discrimination." In *Landoi Book: Essays*, vol. 2, ed. Aharon Barak and Elinoar Mazuz. Tel Aviv: Bursi. 893–930.

———. 1995c. "Reproductive Law and the Right to Parenthood." In *Women's Status in Israeli Law and Society*, ed. Frances Raday, Carmel Shalev, and Michal Liban-Kooby. Jerusalem: Schoken. 503–33. (Hebrew)

Shalhoub-Kevorkian, Nadera. 1997. "Wife Abuse: A Method of Social Control." *Israel Social Science Research* 12, 1: 59–82.

Shamgar-Hendelman, Leah and Rivka Bar-Yosef, eds. 1991. *Families in Israel.* Jerusalem: Akademon. (Hebrew)

Shamir, Ronen. 1999. "Dislocated in the Wilderness: Bedouin and the Legal Regime in Israel." In *Law and History*, ed. Daniel Guttvein and Menachem Mautner. Jerusalem: Zalman Shazar Center. 473–96. (Hebrew)

Shamir, Ronen, Michal Shitrai, and Nelli Elias. 1997. "Mission, Feminism, and Professionalism: Women Rabbinic Advocates Within the Orthodox-Religious Community." *Megamot* 38: 313–48. (Hebrew)

Shava, Menashe. 1972. "Coupling of Causes of Action and Genuineness. Will the Race for Attracting the Jurisdiction in Maintenance Matters to the District of Rabbinical Courts Ever Cease?" *Iunei Mishpat: Tel Aviv University Law Review* 2: 719–40.

———. 1991. *The Personal Law in Israel.* 3rd ed. Vols. 1, 2. Givataim: Massada. (Hebrew)

Sheffer, Naomi. 1997. *Women in Israel: Employment and Training. Report of the Unit for the Advancement of Women and Girls, the Division for Training and Development.* Jerusalem: Ministry of Labor and Welfare. (Hebrew)

———. 1999. "Day-Care Centers in Israel and Women's Equality." In *Equality for Women in Israel's Welfare State.* Jerusalem: Israel Women's Network. 47–49. (Hebrew)

Shershevsky, Benzion. 1993. *Family Law.* Jerusalem: Mass Publishers. (Hebrew)

Shifman, Pinhas. 1989. *Family Law in Israel.* Vol. 2. Jerusalem: Hebrew University Press. (Hebrew)

———. 1995a. "Child Custody and Maintenance." In *Women's Status in Israeli Law and Society,* ed. Frances Raday, Carmel Shalev and Michal Liban-Kooby. Jerusalem: Schoken. 534–45. (Hebrew)

———. 1995b. *Civil Marriage in Israel: The Case for Reform.* Jerusalem: Jerusalem Institute for Israel Studies. (Hebrew)

———. 1995c. *Family Law in Israel.* 2nd ed. Vol. 1. Jerusalem: Hebrew University Press. (Hebrew)

———. 1996. "Community Property After All." *Mishpatim* 26, 2: 399–408.

———. 1999. "State's Recognition of Jewish Marriage: An Empty Symbol?" In *Judaism: A Dialogue Between Cultures,* ed. Avi Sagi, Dudi Schwartz and Yedidia Z. Stern. Jerusalem: Hebrew University Press. 270–78. (Hebrew)

Shilo, Margalit, ed. 2001. *To Be a Jewish Woman.* Jerusalem: Urim Publications. (Hebrew)

Shiran, Vicki. 1993. "Feminist Identity vs. Oriental Identity." In *Calling the Equality Bluff: Women in Israel,* ed. Barbara Swirski and Marilyn P. Safir. New York: Teachers College Press. 303–11.

Shochat, Ella. 1995. "The Conflict as a Starting Point: Towards Multicultural Feminism." *Noga* 28: 20–21. (Hebrew)

———. 1996. "Mizrachi Feminism: Politics of Gender, Race and Multiculturulism." *Mitzad Sheni* 5–6: 29–33. (Hebrew)

———. 1999. "Attitudes of Policemen Toward Spousal Violence." *Hevra uRevaha* 19: 283–302. (Hebrew)

———. 2000. "The Battered Wife's Perception of the Characteristics of Her Encounter With the Police." *International Journal of Offender Therapy and Comparative Criminology* 44, 2: 242–57.

———. Forthcoming. "Policing Domestic Violence in Israel in the 21st Century." *Police and Society.*

Shoham, Efrat and Yair Regev. 2000. "The Attitudes of Police Officers Toward Complaints of Battered Women." *Police and Society* 4: 135–53. (Hebrew)

Shreibmen, Elana. 2000. "Benefits for Single Mothers: Supporting Rehabilitation and Employment or Negative Work Incentive?" Paper presented at the Women in the Israeli Welfare State Conference, Hebrew University, Jerusalem.

Sikkuy. 2001. *Quality and Integration of Arab Citizens: Governmental Development Plan; Fair Representation in Governmental Institutions; The Five Year Plan for Arab Education.* Jerusalem: Association for the Advancement of Civic Equality.

Simons, John. 1995. "Feminism at the Border Zones." *Theory and Critique* 7: 20–30. (Hebrew)

Solimine, Michael E. and Susan E. Wheatley. 1995. "Rethinking Feminist Judging." *Indiana Law Journal* 70: 891–920.

Solomon, Alison. 1993. "Anything for a Baby: Reproductive Technology in Israel." In *Calling the Equality Bluff: Women in Israel,* ed. Barbara Swirski and Marilyn P. Safir. New York: Teachers College Press. 102–7.

Sommer, Hillel. 1997. "Non-Enumerated Rights: The Scope of the Constitutional Revolution." *Mishpatim* 28, 1–2: 257–340. (Hebrew)

State Comptroller. 1992. *42nd Annual Report.* Jerusalem: State of Israel. (Hebrew)

———. 1998. *Report on the Appointment of Directors in Government Corporations on Behalf of the State.* Jerusalem: State of Israel. (Hebrew)

State Income Administration, Ministry of Finance. 1999. *1999 Annual Report No. 49.* Jerusalem: State Income Administration. (Hebrew)

State of Israel. 1995. *A Decade of Progress: The Israeli National Report to the Fourth World Conference on Women, Beijing 1995.* Jerusalem: Prime Minister's Office. (Hebrew)

———. 1997. *Continued Progress: National Report on the Status of Women in Israel.* Jerusalem: Government Printer. (Hebrew)

———. 1998. *The Inter-Ministerial Committee for Treatment of Violence in the Family.* Report No. 1: *Violence Against Women in the Family.* Jerusalem: Government Printer. (Hebrew)

———. 2001. *Third Periodic Report of the State of Israel Concerning the Implementation of the United Nations Convention on the Elimination of All Forms of Discrimination Against Women.* Jerusalem: Ministry of Justice and Ministry of Foreign Affairs.

Steir, Haya. 1995. *Women in Part-time Employment in Israel.* Tel Aviv: Golda Meir Institute for Social and Labor Research. (Hebrew with an English abstract).

Steir, Haya and Alisa Lewin. 1999. *Poor Women in Israel.* Jerusalem: Israel Women's Network. (Hebrew)

Stetson, Dorothy M. 2001. "Movements, Policy Agencies, and Abortion Policy: Does State Feminism Exist?" Paper presented at the Law and Society Annual Meeting, Budapest, May.

Strum, Philippa. 1989. "Women and the Politics of Religion in Israel." *Human Rights Quarterly* 11: 483–503.

Swirski, Barbara. 1989. "Not Feminism from Above." *Politics* 27: 48–51. (Hebrew)

———. 1993a. "Israel Feminism New and Old." In *Calling the Equality Bluff: Women in Israel,* ed. Barbara Swirski and Marilyn P. Safir. New York: Teachers College Press. 57–65.

———. 1993b. "Jews Don't Batter Their Wives: Another Myth Bites the Dust." In *Calling the Equality Bluff: Women in Israel,* ed. Barbara Swirski and Marilyn P. Safir. New York: Teachers College Press. 319–27.

———. 1999. "Women's Equality Within Israel's Welfare State." In *Equality for Women in Israel's Welfare State.* Jerusalem: Israel Women's Network. 20–22. (Hebrew)

Swirski, Barbara, Hatam Ka'naaneh, and Amy Avgar. 1999. *Health Services in Israel.* Israel Equality Monitor, Issue 9. Tel Aviv: Adva Center. (Hebrew)

Swirski, Barbara and Marilyn P. Safir, eds. 1993. *Calling the Equality Bluff: Women in Israel.* New York: Teachers College Press.

Swirski, Shlomo. 1999a. *Adva Center's Comments on the State Budget for the Year 2000.* Tel Aviv: Adva Center. (Hebrew)

———. 1999b. *Goals for Social Policy.* Tel Aviv: Adva Center. (Hebrew)

———. 1999c. *The Impact of Budget 2000 on Women in Israel.* Tel Aviv: Adva Center. (Hebrew)

———. 1999d. *Update: The Ministry of Education Budget, 1999.* Tel Aviv: Adva Center. (Hebrew)

———. 2000. *Residency and Salary Levels in Israel, 1997.* Tel Aviv: Adva Center.

Swirski, Shlomo and Hale Hazan. 1993. *Pre-School Education in Israel.* Israel Equality Monitor, Issue 3. Tel Aviv: Adva Center. (Hebrew)

Swirski, Shlomo, Etty Konor, and Yaron Yechezkel. 1999a. *A Social Portrait of Israel, 1999.* Tel Aviv: Adva Center. (Hebrew)

Swirski, Shlomo, Etty Konor, Yaron Yechezkel, and Barbara Swirski. 1999b. *A View of the State Budget for 2000.* Tel Aviv: Adva Center. (Hebrew)

Swirski, Shlomo, Merav San-Zangi, and Barbara Swirski. 1996. *A View of the 1997–1999 Health Budget.* Tel Aviv: Adva Center. (Hebrew)

Swirski, Shlomo and Barbara Swirski. 1997. *Higher Education in Israel.* Israel Equality Monitor, Issue 8. Tel Aviv: Adva Center. (Hebrew)

Swirski, Shlomo and Yaron Yechezkel. 1999a. *Eligibility to High School Diploma by Settlement 1998–1996.* Tel Aviv: Adva Center. (Hebrew)

———. 1999b. *Women's Representation in Parliament and Government in Israel and throughout the World.* Tel Aviv: Adva Center. (Hebrew)

Swirski, Shlomo, Yaron Yechezkel, Etty Konor, and Barbara Swirski. 2000. *State Budget for 2000: An Update.* Tel Aviv: Adva Center. (Hebrew)

Tal, Sigal. 1995. *The Bedouin Woman in the Negev in an Era of Changes.* Lahav: Jo Allon Study Center.

Tamir, Yael. 1998. "Two Concepts of Multiculturalism." In *Multiculturalism in a Democratic and Jewish State,* ed. Menachem Mautner, Avi Sagi and Ronen Shamir. Tel Aviv: Ramot Publications. 79–92.

Thomas, Cheryl. 1990. "Domestic Violence." In *Women and International Human Rights Law,* vol. 1, ed. Kelly D. Askin and Dorean M. Koenig. New York: Transnational Publishers. 219–56.

Tirosh, Yofi. 1999. "Guidelines for Implementing Due Gender Representation in Israel's Civil Service." *Mishpatim* 30: 183–245.

———. 2001. "On the Politics of Textual Representation in Cr. A. 3031/98 The State of Israel v. Shabtai." *Mishpatim—Hebrew University Student Law Journal* 31: 579–622. (Hebrew)

Toledano, Esther. 1999. *Women Receiving Alimony Payments by Means of the National Insurance Institute in 1998.* Jerusalem: National Insurance Institute Research and Planning Administration. (Hebrew)

Tomasevski, Katarina. 1998. *A Primer on CEDAW for International Development Cooperation Personnel.* Stockholm: Sida.

Toren, Nina. 2000. *Hurdles in the Halls of Science: The Israeli Case.* Lanham, N.Y.: Lexington Books.

Treitel, Andrew. 1995. "Conflicting Traditions: Muslim Shari'a Courts and Marriage Age Regulation in Israel." *Columbia Human Rights Law Review* 26: 357–438.

Tzameret, Hagar. 1999. *A Profile of the Israeli Woman at the Dawn of the 3rd Millennium.* Tel Aviv: The Israeli Institute for Economic & Social Research.

Tzivoni, D. 1991, "Women and Heart Disease." In *Women's Health in Israel,* ed. Amy Avgar. Jerusalem: US/Israel Women to Women.

United Nations. 1995. *Women in a Changing Global Economy: 1994 Survey on the Role of Women in Development.* New York: United Nations.

———. 1997. *Combined Initial and Second Report of the State of Israel Concerning the Implementation of the United Nations Convention on the Elimination of all Forms of Discrimination against Women.* UN Doc CEDAW/C/ISR/1–2 (1997).

Vago, Steven. 2000. *Law and Society.* 6th ed. Upper Saddle River, N.J.: Prentice Hall.

Villmoare, Adelaide H. 1999. "Feminist Jurisprudence and Political Vision." *Law and Social Inquiry* 24: 443–75.

Wegner, Judith Romney. 1988. *Chattel or Person? The Status of Women in the Mishnah.* New York: Oxford University Press.

Weimann, Gabriel, Arie Rathner, and Gideon Fishman. 1988. "Who Is Visually Perceived as a Criminal?" *Megamot* 31: 208–20. (Hebrew)

Weisberg, D. Kelly, ed. 1993. *Feminist Legal Theory: Foundations.* Philadelphia: Temple University Press.

———, ed. 1996. *Applications of Feminist Legal Theory to Women's Lives: Sex, Violence, Work, and Reproduction.* Philadelphia: Temple University Press.

Weitzman, Lenore J. and Mavis MacLean. 1991. *Economic Consequences of Divorce: The International Perspective.* Oxford: Clarendon Press.

Wenzel, Mirjam. 1996. *Women's Movements in Israel.* Jerusalem: Hans Ebert Foundation .

West, Robin. 1988. "Jurisprudence and Gender." *University of Chicago Law Review* 55: 1–72.

Williams, Wendy M. 1982. "The Equality Crisis: Some Reflections on Culture, Courts, and Feminism." *Women's Rights Law Reporter* 7:175.

Working Group on the Status of Palestinian Women in Israel. 1997. *NGO Report: The Status of Palestinian Women in Israel.*

Yaniv, Gideon. 1996. "Trends of Development in National Insurance." In *Annual Survey 1995/1996.* Jerusalem: National Insurance Institute. i–xxviii. (Hebrew with an English supplement)

———. 1998. "Trends of Development in National Insurance." In *Annual Survey 1997/1998.* Jerusalem: National Insurance Institute. E1-E31. (Hebrew, with an English supplement)

Yaniv, Gideon and Tamar Haron. 1999. "Income Support to the Less-Abled." In *Annual Survey 1997/1998.* Jerusalem: National Insurance Institute. 103–21. (Hebrew with an English supplement)

Yishai, Yael. 1997. *Between the Flag and the Banner: Women in Israeli Politics.* Albany: State University of New York Press.

Yonay, Yuval. 1998. "The Law Regarding Homosexuality: Between History and Sociology." *Mishpat u'mimshal—Law and Government in Israel* 4: 531–86. (Hebrew)

Yuval-Davis, Nira. 1980. "The Bearers of the Collective: Women and Religious Legislation in Israel." *Feminist Review* 11: 15–27.

Zilberg, Moshe. 1957. *Personal Status in Israel.* Jerusalem: Hebrew University Press. (Hebrew)

Zilbershatz, Yaffa. 1996. "Adoption of International Law into Israeli Law: The Real Is Ideal." *Israel Yearbook of Human Rights* 25: 243–79.

Zohar, Hanna. 1999. "The Most Vulnerable Women Workers: Personnel Companies Employees and Foreign Workers." In *Equality for Women in Israel's Welfare State.* Jerusalem: Israel Women's Network. 30–32. (Hebrew)

Index

Acknowledgments

As I thought about and wrote this book, I was aided by a number of people. I am indebted to all of them.

As the book originated from the official reports that I wrote on behalf of the State of Israel to the UN Committee on Elimination of all forms of Discrimination Against Women, I had the privilege of working together with Judge Nili Arad, then director general of the Ministry of Justice, as well as with Sue Kahn, who edited the first report. Throughout the process I benefited from the skillful work of several research assistants, all of whom were law students at Bar-Ilan University, including Leila Margalit, Irit Harmel, and, above all, Eric Lifschitz. Attorney Atara Kenigsberg wisely managed and coordinated the various stages of material collection and organization. Dr. Bryna Bogoch offered most helpful comments on parts of the manuscript. Tamar Fox, my editor, provided impeccable work and attention to every detail, patiently enduring the endless revisions and alterations.

The late Professor Dafna Izraeli contributed invaluable advice in the early stages of this work. How I wish I could present her with the final result.

I received generous support from the Bar-Ilan University Faculty of Law, as well as from the Ruth and Emanuel Rackman Center for the Advancement of the Status of Women and from the Pogatch Foundation.

Most of all, I am indebted to my family, my husband Haim Halperin and our children, for their patience and encouragement throughout this long journey.

www.ingramcontent.com/pod-product-compliance
Lightning Source LLC
LaVergne TN
LVHW091515200926
848483LV00005B/423/J